FREE TRADE AREAS
AND U.S. TRADE POLICY

JEFFREY J. SCHOTT, EDITOR

Free Trade Areas and U.S. Trade Policy

INSTITUTE FOR INTERNATIONAL ECONOMICS
WASHINGTON, DC 1989

Jeffrey J. Schott, Research Fellow at the Institute, was a Senior Associate at the Carnegie Endowment for International Peace (1982–83) and an International Economist at the US Treasury (1974–82). He is the co-author of The Canada–United States Free Trade Agreement: The Global Impact *(1988),* Auction Quotas and United States Trade Policy *(1987),* Trading for Growth: The Next Round of Trade Negotiations *(1985), and* Economic Sanctions Reconsidered: History and Current Policy *(1985).*

Many colleagues at the Institute contributed significantly to the planning and preparation of this volume. Special thanks are due to Capathia Adams, Angela L. Barnes, Terry Kannofsky, Cynthia L. McKaughan, and Michael Treadway for their assistance in preparing the manuscript for publication.

INSTITUTE FOR INTERNATIONAL
ECONOMICS
11 Dupont Circle, NW
Washington, DC 20036
(202) 328-9000 Telex: 261271 IIE UR
Fax: (202) 328-5432

C. Fred Bergsten, *Director*

The Institute for International
Economics was created by, and receives
substantial support from, the German
Marshall Fund of the United States.

Printed in the United States of America
93 92 91 90 89   5 4 3 2 1

Library of Congress Cataloging-in-Publication Data

Free trade areas and U.S. trade policy

Papers presented at a conference held
31 October–1 November 1988

Includes References
1. United States—Commercial policy. 2. Customs unions. 3. Free trade. 4. Commercial treaties—United States.
I. Schott, Jeffrey J., 1949–
HF1455. F74 1989
382'.71'0973 89–7633

ISBN 0–88132–094–3

Contents

FIGURES

Preface

Fundamental questions are being raised in a number of quarters about the proper course for US trade policy and the nature of the world trading system. One such question is whether the United States should seek to negotiate additional bilateral trade pacts, along the lines of the agreements reached in recent years with Canada and Israel.

The Institute for International Economics held a two-day conference to address this question on October 31 and November 1, 1988. The session brought together trade experts from all of the major trading countries. Papers were presented on the desirability and feasibility of "more free trade areas" (FTAs) with a series of candidate countries, taking into consideration the effects of such arrangements on third countries and the world trading system as well as on potential participants. The experience of previous FTAs was reviewed in an effort to derive lessons for the future.

As with several earlier Institute studies, we are releasing our findings in two different formats in an effort to meet the needs of different groups of readers. This book includes the full proceedings of the conference, including the individual papers and comments on them. Chapter 1 of the book, which summarizes the main analytical conclusions and policy recommendations that emerged from the process and the author's own research, is being released simultaneously as a separate volume entitled *More Free Trade Areas?*

The Institute for International Economics is a private nonprofit institution for the study and discussion of international economic policy. Its purpose is to analyze important issues in that area, and to develop and communicate practical new approaches for dealing with them. The Institute is completely nonpartisan.

The Institute was created by a generous commitment of funds from the German Marshall Fund of the United States in 1981 and now receives about 20 percent of its support from that source. In addition, major institutional grants are being received from the Ford Foundation, the William and Flora Hewlett Foundation, and the Alfred P. Sloan Foundation. A number of other foundations and private corporations are contributing to the increasing diversification of the Institute's resources. The Dayton Hudson Foundation provides partial support for the Institute's program of studies on trade policy.

The Board of Directors bears overall responsibility for the Institute and gives general guidance and approval to its research program, including identification of topics that are likely to become important to international economic policymakers over the medium run (generally one to three years), and which thus should be addressed by the Institute. The Director, working closely with the staff and outside Advisory Committee, is responsible for the development of particular projects and makes the final decision to publish an individual study.

The Institute hopes that its studies and other activities will contribute to building a strong foundation for international economic policy around the world. We invite readers of these publications to let us know how they think we can best accomplish this objective.

C. FRED BERGSTEN
Director
March 1989

More Free Trade Areas?

Jeffrey J. Schott

Overview

At the midpoint of the Uruguay Round of multilateral trade negotiations, prospects for comprehensive trade liberalization seem uncertain. Longstanding merchandise trade barriers remain intractable, and new barriers are being erected in pursuit of neomercantilist trade strategies. Trade, finance, and debt problems have become increasingly interlinked and are fueling protectionist pressures in developed and developing countries alike. In turn, these pressures have generated a myriad of trade disputes, which seem immune to resolution through the procedures set out in the General Agreement on Tariffs and Trade (GATT).

Moreover, the major trading nations seem distracted from the task at hand in the GATT talks in Geneva. Many countries have sought to complement the multilateral GATT process with a variety of bilateral and regional trade initiatives. Concern about the efficacy of the GATT process has led some countries to focus more on such arrangements than on their participation in the multilateral negotiations.

For example, the 12 members of the European Community (EC) are focusing on internal market reforms that aim to establish a single European market by 1992. For these countries, the elimination of barriers within the EC seems to overshadow in importance the gains likely to be achieved in the GATT, although there are important linkages in specific areas between the 1992 process and the Uruguay Round negotiations. Meanwhile Japan focuses on ways to better manage its bilateral trading relationships with the United States and with other countries in the Pacific Basin. The United States, the *demandeur* of the Uruguay Round, threatens to pursue bilateral or plurilateral trade pacts with "like-minded countries" if its objectives for the GATT talks are not met (Baker 1988).

Indeed, the United States has already adopted a bifurcated approach to trade negotiations. Parallel to the preparations for, and early stages of, the Uruguay Round, bilateral free trade agreements have been concluded with Israel in 1985 and Canada in 1988. Because of the strong political ties between those countries and the United States, the negotiations proceeded expeditiously and relatively harmoniously, although ratification in Canada was marred by a rancorous debate over national sovereignty. Tariff barriers are being phased out, numerous nontariff restrictions are being removed, and new consultative and dispute settlement mechanisms have been established. Bilateral trade and investment should soon respond to the increased opportunities created by these free trade areas (FTAs), although it is too early to distill clear evidence of such movement in either case (see Rosen, this volume, and Schott 1988).

At the same time, informal overtures by US officials during the Reagan administration have been made to a number of other countries to explore new bilateral trade arrangements. Studies are under way in Japan, Korea, Taiwan, and the Association of Southeast Asian Nations (ASEAN) to examine prospects for FTAs with the United States.[1] Australia previously studied and rejected the idea of a bilateral FTA with the United States, although it would likely reevaluate its opposition if negotiations began with other countries in the region (Snape 1986 and this volume). In addition, regional trade initiatives involving a number of Pacific Rim nations have been advocated by former Japanese Prime Minister Yasuhiro Nakasone and by Secretary of State George Shultz and others during the Reagan administration.[2]

In essence, the United States has been using bilateralism as both a carrot and a stick to further the process of trade liberalization. Bilateralism has been used to close the leaks in the multilateral system until solutions could be negotiated in the GATT, and to establish building blocks for broader multilateral accords that could be negotiated in the new round of GATT negotiations. If the GATT talks falter, however, the United States has threatened to resort to bilateral agreements as a substitute rather than a complement to the GATT.

However, the successful conclusion of the Israel and Canada pacts has raised the question of whether the United States should concentrate on more bilateral FTAs rather than on protracted GATT talks. Moreover, some critics of the GATT argue that trade balancing or managed trade objectives

---

1. These countries would have to initiate such negotiations with the United States because provisions of US trade law limit recourse to "fast-track" implementing procedures to bilateral FTAs that are requested by other countries.

2. See, for example, Nakasone (1988) and Elaine Sciolino, "Shultz Calls for Free Trade in Asia," *New York Times*, 12 July 1986, D6.

should supersede trade liberalization goals in bilateral negotiations. The ensuing debate has created uncertainty as to whether the United States is interested in more FTAs for tactical purposes (i.e., to goad other countries to move the GATT talks forward) or whether it actually plans to negotiate bilaterally with other countries as an alternative. Concerns have been expressed that the pursuit of other bilateral agreements would weaken US interest in, and political support for, the Geneva talks, and lead to a devolution of the GATT system into regional trading blocs.[3]

Clearly, the debate has raised important questions—both at home and abroad—regarding the future direction of US trade policy. Will the United States pursue FTAs with other countries, or will it devote its efforts to the negotiation of new multilateral agreements in the Uruguay Round? Should—and can—it do both?

The following sections analyze the feasibility and desirability of negotiating additional FTAs between the United States and many of its key trading partners. The first section examines the reasons for the recent growth in bilateralism, the US interest in FTAs (compared to other types of trade agreements), the objectives being sought, and the challenges to US policy of continuing to pursue the bilateral approach.

The second section reviews the arguments—pro and con—for pursuing FTAs, and the complications that can arise when a series of separate agreements are negotiated. It also examines the compatibility of FTAs with the GATT, both in theory and in practice.

The third section analyzes the prospects for FTAs with "candidate" countries that have already received formal or informal overtures from the United States. It then summarizes the interests of those countries in an FTA with the United States, and the pros and cons of a prospective deal for each country as well as for the world trading system as a whole.

The final section sets out conclusions and policy recommendations for the United States. It contrasts the expected gains from additional FTAs and the GATT process, and the implications for US trade policy.

The Growth of Bilateralism

Since the inception of the GATT in 1948, the United States has been both its leader and the *demandeur* of all eight rounds of GATT negotiations. In many respects, however, the GATT has been a victim of its own success. The past seven rounds of negotiations have achieved sharp reductions in

---

3. Interestingly, these concerns mirror US apprehension about the impact of the 1992 process on EC participation in the Uruguay Round.

tariff barriers. Yet even though tariffs have fallen to levels that average below 5 percent in the United States, the EC, and Japan, traded goods remain vulnerable to a broad range of nontariff restrictions imposed by governments both at the border (e.g., import licensing and customs regulations) and within their domestic markets (e.g., subsidies, and health and safety standards). Attempts to extend multilateral discipline to such practices have met strong resistance in developed and developing countries alike, and have contributed to dissatisfaction with the operation of the GATT.

Furthermore, the GATT system has been slow to adjust to the changing pattern of international commerce. In some areas, new GATT rules need to be elaborated. For example, the liberalization of capital markets and advances in information technologies have facilitated trade in banking, insurance, and telecommunications services, which are not yet subject to GATT discipline. In other areas, existing GATT rules need to be revised. Antidumping rules, for example, seem inadequate to address the pricing practices of firms in high-technology sectors.

US concerns about the GATT system have been growing since the failure of the 1982 GATT Ministerial to initiate preparations for a new round of trade negotiations.[4] Opposition by some countries to a new GATT round was equated with unwillingness to liberalize trade barriers and to open their markets to foreign goods *and* services. Strong foreign resistance to new negotiations for almost four years, from 1982 to 1986, on top of already strong concerns about job losses due to the trade deficit, reinforced US doubts about the GATT process.

Congressional representatives at the 1982 Ministerial came away skeptical about the efficacy of GATT rules and procedures, and more convinced of the need to pursue alternative approaches to defend US trading interests. Other means were sought in parallel with the GATT process to promote trade liberalization through both unilateral pressure (for example, using the threat of retaliatory actions under section 301 of the Trade Act of 1974 to open foreign markets to US exports) and bilateral negotiation (the Israel and Canada pacts).

As a result of the 1982 meeting, US Trade Representative William E. Brock also left Geneva with a bad taste for GATT negotiations, and soon after began to pursue bilateral talks with Israel and Canada. FTAs became

---

4. In 1982, the United States called for an extraordinary meeting of GATT trade ministers to prepare for a new round of trade negotiations. The United States sought a highly ambitious agenda for reforming agriculture and extending GATT discipline to services, investment, and new technologies. The failure of that meeting did little to restore confidence in GATT processes. For an analysis of the results of the 1982 GATT Ministerial, see Schott (1983). For the congressional reaction, see Destler (1986, 77ff.).

part of a two-track US strategy to provide a complement to, and potentially a substitute for, multilateral efforts to liberalize trade.

FTAs with Israel and Canada

The FTA negotiation with Israel was the first US attempt to negotiate comprehensive trade liberalization on a bilateral basis. Israel was a perfect test case for Brock's two-track strategy, since US trade with Israel does not account for a significant share of overall US trade. Moreover, since a key objective of the negotiations was the strengthening of the political relationship, there was little risk that US concessions would provoke political opposition.

The US–Israel FTA was concluded in 1985 and will result in the elimination of all tariffs on bilateral trade within 10 years.[5] The effect of these tariff cuts should not be exaggerated, however. Israel already benefited from zero tariffs in many areas under the US Generalized System of Preferences (GSP). The FTA provisions effectively secured the continuation of those preferences, which Israel perceived to be at risk because of congressional pressures to reform the GSP program.

Overall, the Israeli tariff concessions will eliminate the discrimination against US exports caused by the preferences accorded EC suppliers under the 1975 EC–Israel FTA. However, the initial Israeli tariff concessions mainly duplicate commitments made to cut tariffs in the Tokyo Round, with "new" cuts to be implemented only in the 1990s.

The FTA accord also contains a framework agreement on trade in services, which commits each country to make "best efforts" to negotiate substantive rules on services. This framework on services established a building block from which US and Canadian negotiators later elaborated specific rights and obligations in this "new" area.

Building on the success of the US–Israel talks and the failure of bilateral sectoral negotiations, the United States and Canada entered FTA negotiations in May 1986.[6] In essence, Canada sought more secure access to the US market through both trade liberalization and greater certainty about how US trade remedy laws would be administered. In contrast, US objectives focused primarily on improved rulemaking. The United States put great stock in the conclusion of agreements on services and investment both to

---

5. For a detailed review of the background to and contents of the US–Israel FTA, see Rosen (this volume).

6. For an analysis of the major provisions of the Canada–US FTA and its impact on the United States, see Schott (1988).

establish building blocks for GATT accords and to facilitate cross-border trade and investment. Trade liberalization was also important for US industries, especially cuts in high Canadian tariffs on furniture and other products and the elimination of nontariff barriers (NTBs) such as the duty remission subsidies for autos.

The Canada–US FTA entered into force in January 1989. The agreement eliminates all tariffs on bilateral trade within 10 years, opens up more government contracts to competitive bidding, and bars most border restraints on bilateral energy trade. It also establishes innovative approaches to dispute settlement as well as contractual obligations regarding public policies toward investment and the regulation of service industries—including those of state, local, and provincial governments.

The conclusion of FTAs with Israel and Canada further stimulated interest in the bilateral approach and criticism of the multilateral process. The success of these bilateral negotiations posed a sharp contrast to ongoing US efforts in the GATT. Doubts have grown about the efficacy of the GATT for governing trade in the 1990s and beyond. Some argue that FTA negotiations should supplement the GATT process; others counter that FTAs should substitute for GATT talks because GATT rules do not cover a substantial portion of world trade. The latter note that US efforts to extend the coverage of GATT discipline to areas such as services, investment, and intellectual property rights (IPRs) have met strong opposition—mostly from developing countries—so far in the Uruguay Round.

In addition, there are doubts as to whether the results of previous trade rounds really have benefited US trading interests. Criticism that US negotiators always get snookered by their wily foreign counterparts resonates well in public debate.[7] As a result, questions have been raised whether the United States could make better use of its economic and political leverage in a bilateral or regional context.

Why FTAs?

The growth in interest in FTAs can be traced directly to two related concerns about US trade policy. First, critics charge that the weaknesses in the multilateral system have rendered the GATT system ill-equipped to meet, and unable to adapt to, the new challenges of postwar merchandise trade,

---

7. This perception may be due in part to the tendency of politicians to oversell the results of GATT negotiations to the Congress. Nonetheless, analysis of the results of the Kennedy and Tokyo Rounds indicates that the United States has not fared badly in either negotiation (Preeg 1970; Winham 1986).

much less "postindustrial" trade in services and intellectual property. Questions thus have been raised whether the GATT negotiations can achieve substantial trade reforms that promote the economic welfare of the member countries.

The second concern is that the current US policy, based on the open trade principles of the GATT, has failed because US firms have faced stronger and stronger foreign competition at home and abroad, as evidenced by the string of record US trade deficits in the 1980s. These concerns have led to increasing calls—particularly in the Congress, the US labor movement, and the US business community—for a more aggressive trade policy involving both unilateral actions and bilateral negotiations, to try to "level the playing field" and remedy the persistent trade deficits.

Concern About the GATT—What is wrong with the GATT? Critics charge that the GATT process is too slow, that the negotiations are too complex, and that GATT rules are inadequate and inadequately enforced. By contrast, they see bilateral negotiations as providing the United States greater leverage to achieve its objectives with its major trading partners.

The first criticism of GATT concerns the pace of negotiations. The Tokyo Round lasted from 1973 to 1979, and many observers believe that the Uruguay Round will extend well past its scheduled 1990 deadline (Bergsten 1988; Aho and Aronson 1985). By contrast, the negotiation of the Canada–US FTA took 18 months. The political system, responding to pressures from trade-impacted industries, demands more immediate results than the GATT process seems able to provide.

Second, the GATT talks involve varied interests among a large number of participants. To accommodate the interests of the 96 member countries, the agenda of GATT talks is complicated, involving 15 different negotiating groups in the case of the Uruguay Round. The increasing complexity of the talks contributes to the lengthening of the negotiating process (compared with earlier rounds that concentrated on tariff cuts). Another factor is the GATT's de facto consensus rule, which has been used by countries to block progress in negotiations until their demands have been met. For example, India and a few other developing countries blocked the adoption of recommendations on IPRs in the Ministerial declaration at the Montreal midterm review in December 1988. The problem of such "foot draggers" has become even worse as GATT talks focus more on the negotiation of trading rules than on reciprocal trade liberalization (see Hufbauer and Schott 1985b). In principle, such problems do not arise in bilateral or plurilateral negotiations among "like-minded" countries.

The third set of criticisms of the GATT involve the scope and coverage of its rules and the efficacy of its enforcement mechanisms. These criticisms reflect concern more about the GATT agreement itself than about the GATT as a negotiating forum. GATT rules suffer from numerous exceptions (most notably in textiles and apparel), the proliferation of so-called "gray area" measures[8] that fall outside the spirit if not the letter of the rules, and inadequate discipline on agriculture and subsidies in general. Furthermore, legal GATT loopholes such as the balance of payments exceptions in Article XVIII enable many countries to avoid GATT obligations to liberalize trade, even though they continue to benefit from reforms made by other countries (that is, to "free ride") under the most-favored-nation (MFN) principle. In addition, trade-related services, investment, and intellectual property issues are hardly addressed at all. If one deducts all textiles trade, nonfactor services, and the trade of nonmembers of the GATT, as well as trade subject to gray area restraints, only about 60 percent of world trade in goods and services is subject to GATT disciplines.[9]

Finally, the record of enforcement of GATT rules has been mixed. The dispute settlement process is prone to delaying tactics; indeed, decisions can be blocked outright by the disputing parties—another unfavorable side effect of the consensus rule. The United States and the EC have been the foremost practitioners of such tactics. For example, the United States spent years evading action to conform its export subsidies provided under the Domestic International Sales Corporation (DISC) program to GATT rules; more recently, the EC has also obfuscated with regard to disputes over citrus, pasta, and its sugar program. However, perhaps the biggest problem with GATT dispute settlement is not the procedural delays but the vagueness of GATT obligations, particularly with regard to agriculture; both, however, need improvement.

By contrast, FTAs often are regarded as a more effective and expeditious means to achieve trade liberalization among "like-minded" trading partners. Proponents cite the benefits of negotiating with only one or a few countries that are willing to pursue reciprocal trade bargains. The agenda can be targeted to the specific interests of the FTA partners, and special administrative bodies can be established, as in the Israel and Canada pacts, to

---

8. Gray area measures include, *inter alia*, voluntary export restraints, orderly marketing arrangements, and intraindustry agreements. The GATT Secretariat has documented more than 200 such measures currently imposed by member countries (GATT 1988).

9. Choate and Linger (1988) argue that only 5 percent of global transactions (trade and capital flows) is covered by the GATT. Such aggregation includes daily capital-balancing transactions of central banks and other short-run capital flows. In dollar terms, they far exceed the value of traded goods and services. Because such capital flows have limited relevance to trade and investment decisions, however, using such a statistic yields a gross misrepresentation of GATT coverage of international current account transactions.

provide a forum "for members only" for consultation and settlement of disputes. Moreover, the absence of third-country participation should streamline the process and provide for expeditious review of disputes. In sum, FTAs can be tailored to the specific circumstances of the bilateral trade.[10]

Concern About the US Trade Deficit—The main objective of US trade policy in recent years has been to manage the political fallout, and to deflect protectionist pressures, generated by the trade deficit. To counter these pressures and sustain domestic support for an open trade policy, the United States has resorted to a mixture of unilateral, bilateral, and multilateral actions to reduce foreign barriers to US exports and to counter unfair trade practices benefiting foreign competitors to US firms. Major trade bills were enacted in 1984 and 1988 to bolster the arsenal of US trade laws, which have been used more aggressively since September 1985 to these ends. Proponents of such measures recognize that trade policy measures alone cannot contribute much to solving the trade deficit problem, but that open markets for US exports are a necessary condition for an orderly adjustment of the US current account imbalance (Bergsten 1988). Indeed, Rep. Richard Gephardt (D-MO; 1988) has acknowledged that trade barriers explain only 10 to 15 percent of the US trade deficit.

The main focus of US efforts to correct its large trade deficit has been exchange rate policy and macroeconomic policy coordination with its major industrial trading partners. The Plaza Agreement of September 1985 provided an impetus for the dollar depreciation needed to strengthen US international competitiveness. The dollar fell by about 40 percent in trade-weighted terms over the following three years, and the United States cut its trade deficit to $137 billion in 1988 from its peak of $170 billion in 1987.

The dollar depreciation contributed significantly to reversing the trend of rapidly increasing deficits, which could have reached $300 billion by 1990 without the policy changes. However, the impact of the dollar depreciation will likely be fully reflected in the US trade balance by late 1989 or early 1990; if current exchange rates and macroeconomic policies are maintained, the US trade deficit will remain above $100 billion (Bergsten 1988; Cline 1989). An impasse on new US budget cuts would make matters worse.

The small absolute improvement in the trade account and the prospect of

---

10. Some proponents of this strategy argue that a tailored trade approach "would enable American representatives to match the negotiations to the economic system with which we were negotiating. For example, talks would draw free-trade arrangements with free-trade economies, managed-trade agreements with managed-trade economies, and appropriately tailored, mixed agreements with those economic systems in between" (Choate and Linger 1988, 91).

renewed deterioration next year have raised the question whether US policymakers should search for alternative solutions to the US trade deficit. The persistence of high US deficits risks discrediting the macroeconomic approach to redressing the US imbalances. Some critics of current policy argue that such adjustments cannot work because of the weaknesses in the multilateral trading system noted above; others argue that countries manage their exchange rates for competitive advantage; and still others cite the political unwillingness of some countries to abide by the spirit and the letter of multilateral compacts. There is some evidence that the adjustments of trade to exchange rate changes have been limited by the growth of trade barriers (Bhagwati 1988). For these reasons, some critics argue that a bilateral approach is needed—one fully invoking US economic leverage—to "tailor trade" to meet US economic objectives (Choate and Linger 1988).

US Objectives

In light of concerns about the erosion of GATT discipline and the more general concern about the US trade deficit, several policy objectives have been put forward for exploring the FTA option. Most of them seek traditional trade policy goals: reduction in foreign trade barriers, the promotion of new multilateral accords via the building block approach, and the better management of bilateral trade relations. In addition, FTAs have been proposed as a means to balance bilateral trade flows.

Reducing Foreign Trade Barriers—FTAs are seen as a means to promote trade liberalization, since FTA negotiations are likely to involve countries that share similar or complementary objectives, and may be more likely to lower trade barriers because such reforms would be extended only to the partner countries, thus eliminating the free-rider problem. The reduction of foreign barriers is a constructive way to deflect protectionist pressures at home, and to encourage increased US exports as a means to contribute to a reduction of the US trade deficit. Moreover, since FTAs involve by definition reduction in barriers on "substantially all" the trade between the partner countries,[11] FTA objectives are regarded as consistent with the GATT. As such, they are also seen as keeping the "bicycle" of trade liberalization upright to spur further multilateral reforms.

---

11. More precisely, that is one of the requirements set out in GATT Article XXIV for FTAs to be compatible with the partner country's GATT obligations. See the discussion in the following section.

Promoting Multilateral Accords—Part of the rationale for liberalization is to use FTAs as building blocks for multilateral agreements. In this sense, FTAs are seen as an offensive strategy to set precedents for the GATT. This was one of the primary US objectives in the Canada–US FTA, where the development of rules on trade in services and trade-related investment were regarded as useful precedents for current GATT negotiations in these areas.

Alternatively, some believe that FTA accords can go further than multilateral pacts particularly with regard to rulemaking because of the absence of "foot draggers" in the negotiations. Because of this, they regard FTA disciplines in areas such as services and investment to be potentially more comprehensive than what could be achieved in a GATT round.

The negotiation of FTAs can also serve as a strategy to promote multilateral accords. FTAs are seen as a way to goad other countries to the negotiating table in Geneva, and then to "keep their feet to the fire" during GATT negotiations. In this sense, FTAs are a threat that the United States has as an alternative if the GATT talks falter. Such a strategy was expounded in the runup to the launching of the Uruguay Round, and is evident today in US warnings that the EC 1992 initiative avoid creating a "fortress Europe" lest the United States respond by establishing its own trading bloc.

Improving Management of Bilateral Trade Relations—FTAs also are seen as a way to establish a special bilateral relationship between the partner countries. For example, administrative and dispute settlement provisions in FTAs, such as the binational commission and panels established by the Canada–US FTA, provide a strong foundation for bilateral trade relations, and help improve consultation and cooperation on trade issues. By entering into FTA negotiations, each country establishes a stake in its success, since once the negotiating process begins, it is hard to go back to the status quo ante. Expectations get built into the process, and if results are not achieved, there is a risk that a backlash could worsen relations. Thus, by focusing attention on the overall bilateral relationship, the successful conclusion of an FTA takes on importance for many reasons beyond the economic ones. This was clearly evident in the Canada–US case, especially in October 1988 when it looked as if Canada might not ratify the pact.

The FTA option can also be used to direct attention toward new and important trading partners. For the United States, FTAs are seen as a means to implement a Pacific Rim-oriented trade policy.

Balancing Bilateral Trade Flows—More unusual and more controversial is the goal of redressing bilateral trade imbalances through FTAs. Bluntly put, the purpose is to set bilateral quotas or otherwise divert trade from third countries so that the trade flows of the partner countries are more evenly matched. Such an approach has been advocated by some US critics of the GATT to manage trade with countries that run persistent trade surpluses, and by officials of some foreign governments such as Taiwan in order to reduce US protectionist pressures, to justify their own import liberalization, and thus to remove strains on the overall bilateral relationship.

Challenges to US Trade Policy

The negotiation of additional FTAs between the United States and its major trading partners could pose major challenges to US trade policy. As in multilateral negotiations, long-entrenched trade barriers would have to be liberalized, and trade policies toward third countries as well as the impact on the GATT and the world trading system as a whole would have to be reassessed. Each poses some challenges to US trade policy, in either political or economic terms, which have to be factored into the cost-benefit analysis of more FTAs.

Trade Liberalization—In the negotiation of FTAs with Israel and Canada, US objectives focused more on the elaboration of trading rules for areas such as services and investment than on the liberalization of NTBs. Although both pacts make significant progress toward freer trade by eliminating tariffs, many of the major NTBs to the US market have been left intact, either because they did not impede bilateral trade significantly or because they were part of a broader network of protection (for example, agricultural subsidies) that was not amenable to change through a bilateral pact: This has simplified the ratification of both pacts by the US Congress, but it may have provided a false impression of what the United States may have to do in future FTAs regarding the liberalization of its trade barriers.

Proponents of FTAs seem to believe that the United States can negotiate reductions in foreign trade barriers in return for tariff cuts and a promise not to raise US NTBs. In this regard, FTAs would build on the precedents of trade agreements negotiated under the pressure of US retaliation under section 301 of the Trade Act of 1974 to "level the playing field" for US trading interests. In return, the United States would establish a special bilateral relationship with its FTA partner and provide it tariff preferences; however, the value of such concessions could well erode if the United States entered other FTAs or reduced tariffs during the Uruguay Round and subsequently.

Such an approach may work with countries where US leverage is great because of the trade dependence of the partner countries (and in some cases because of political interests as well). In such cases, a credible US standstill commitment has real value for partner countries. However, the stakes rise sharply when negotiations involve major trading partners and trade in politically sensitive products. When US negotiators seek liberalization of rice quotas and other farm barriers, Japan, the EC, and others are likely to demand more traditional reciprocity in terms of *greater* access to the US market. Such considerations also need to be kept in mind when negotiating with Pacific Rim countries, whose exports of steel, textiles and apparel, machine tools, and agricultural products are impeded by US tariffs and NTBs.

Third-Country and Systemic Effects—The negotiation of more FTAs would also have important implications for nonparticipating "third countries." Many third countries are likely to be debt-ridden and/or developing countries that would be less able to take advantage of the trade-creating effects of the FTA. As the weakest members of the GATT system, they would stand to lose the most from an erosion in the discipline of the multilateral system. In principle, these countries would continue to receive benefits under the GATT, but the value of the MFN concession, as well as applicable preferences under the GSP, would diminish as more countries receive discriminatory preferences under FTAs.

Alternative Types of Trade Agreements

Much of the focus of the trade policy debate has been on the negotiation of free trade areas because of the precedents set by the US–Israel and Canada–US pacts. In fact, however, FTAs have been used as a code word for a wide range of bilateral arrangements, involving different levels of coverage and policy instruments. Most involve very selective trade liberalization, along with consultative and dispute settlement mechanisms to minimize the impact of the application of US trade laws. Some are consistent with MFN obligations; others entail discriminatory preferences. Some envisage broad-based agreements that cover tariffs and NTBs on investment *and* trade in goods *and* services; others limit the scope of a prospective pact only to tariffs and to merchandise trade; and still others argue that trade agreements alone are insufficient and require complementary commitments on exchange rates and debt.[12] The scorecard of players and proposals is complex indeed, and each approach has its pros and cons.

---

12. In that regard, sections 1124 and 3004 of the Omnibus Trade and Competitiveness Act of 1988 recognize that "the benefits of trade concessions can be adversely affected by misalignments in currency" and thus direct the President to negotiate with other countries to achieve "better coordination of macroeconomic policies" and reforms of the exchange rate system "to provide for long-term exchange rate stability." Senator Max Baucus (D-MT; 1988) incorporates this approach in his proposals for a US–Japan economic agreement.

Consultative Framework—A consultative framework agreement sets out guidelines for the conduct of bilateral consultations and prospective negotiations. It provides some impetus for talks but usually entails few substantive obligations or formal dispute settlement procedures. As such, it should not impair GATT commitments or obligations. Illustrative of such pacts is the US–Mexico framework agreement signed in November 1987, which establishes an annotated agenda for prospective bilateral trade and investment talks (see "A US–Mexico FTA?" below).

In many respects, US friendship, commerce, and navigation (FCN) treaties are close relatives of these consultative arrangements. The United States currently has FCN treaties with 47 countries. However, unlike consultative arrangements, FCN treaties set out substantive rules to govern bilateral trade and investment that cover many of the same principles (for example, MFN and national treatment) embodied in the GATT.[13] In addition, they typically contain administrative provisions, although not dispute settlement provisions, to ensure the transparency of national trade and investment regulations. Interestingly, the lack of an FCN treaty between Canada and the United States was a factor in the pursuit of FTA negotiations.

Product- or Sector-Specific Agreements—Bilateral agreements can be limited to one or involve a specified number of products or sectors. Product-specific agreements are most commonly concluded to resolve disputes involving unfair trade practices (such as the US–Japan pact on semiconductors) or to gain preferential access to a restricted foreign market (such as the US–Japan accord on beef and citrus or the US–Korea agreement on insurance).

Sectoral agreements are often promoted as a means to pursue trade liberalization in a discrete segment of the economy without committing to a more comprehensive agenda of reforms, and as building blocks to multilateral accords. In most cases, liberalization is accorded only to the partner countries and not on an MFN basis as required by the GATT for merchandise trade. To comply with GATT obligations, a waiver would need to be obtained under Article XXV:5, as the United States did in the case of the US–Canada Auto Pact. This requirement would not hold for service sector pacts, because services are not currently subject to GATT discipline.

Limiting coverage to a particular sector means that trade-offs have to be made within a sector instead of between sectors of an economy. In other words, the sector that benefits from new trade reforms has to "pay" for them by reducing its own trade protection. Political support for the agreement

---

13. The MFN obligation in some FCN treaties can complicate the granting of preferences in bilateral accords or in GATT codes, as it did in the Tokyo Round when the injury test in US countervailing duty cases had to be accorded to seven countries despite their lack of accession to the GATT Subsidies Code.

thus will be split between the winners and losers in each sector. Such pacts thus highlight both the trade gains and the adjustment pressures in each country.

The above discussion seems to imply that the limited nature of sectoral pacts should facilitate their negotiation. However, as the attempt to negotiate a sectoral pact on transportation services in the Canada–US FTA clearly demonstrated, achieving liberalization that is acceptable to both countries can also be complicated by the sectoral limitations. Indeed, the failure to achieve trade-offs in sectoral negotiations between the United States and Canada from 1983 to 1985 led the Canadian government to propose the more comprehensive FTA approach (see Schott and Smith 1988, chapters 1 and 2).

Free Trade Areas—In principle, FTAs eliminate barriers to trade at the border between the partner countries. Unlike customs unions, however, each country maintains its own restrictions against trade from third countries. As a result, FTA partner countries receive preferential access to each other's market at the expense of nonmembers. To protect those preferences, such agreements usually set out rules of origin to prevent goods from nonmembers being transshipped through a partner FTA country with low external trade barriers to another with higher barriers. Such agreements are more complicated to negotiate than a product- or sector-specific pact, but they can accommodate cross-sectoral linkages and thus expand the breadth and depth of potential liberalization.

FTAs can be consistent with the GATT, if they meet the three-part test of Article XXIV relating to notification, trade coverage, and level of barriers to third-country trade (see discussion in "FTAs and the GATT" below). These provisions require that FTA obligations affect "substantially all" the merchandise trade between the partner countries. For sectors such as services that are not currently subject to GATT disciplines, the GATT tests do not apply, and FTA coverage need not be comprehensive.

FTAs can be self-contained or open to additional signatories. New members can be added either under the same terms of entry as the original partners or subject to negotiated protocols of accession. Because the introduction of new members can dilute the value of preferences received by existing FTA members, there are few examples of open-ended FTAs; most require new entrants to make additional concessions to compensate for such potential effects. Indeed, to guard against such "dilution" of benefits, the 1988 Trade Act forbids the extension of FTA benefits to additional countries without new congressional approval.[14]

---

14. However, the United States could negotiate similar pacts with different countries,

GATT-Plus—The negotiation of an open-ended FTA is similar in form to the concept of a "GATT-Plus," which was originally proposed in a report of the Atlantic Council during a lull in the Tokyo Round. This option involves the negotiation of multilateral agreements that supplement the GATT obligations of participating countries by committing to additional disciplines in areas covered by GATT provisions and in new areas such as services that are not yet subject to GATT rules. The benefits are to be accorded to all GATT members in a manner consistent with the MFN principle, thus providing nonsignatories a "free ride" (Atlantic Council 1976). However, such pacts could instead be negotiated on a conditional-MFN basis so that the free-rider problem would not discourage participation in the agreement (as was done, for example, in the GATT Subsidies and Government Procurement codes).

GATT Negotiations—Because of the large number of countries involved, and the broad range of issues on the negotiating agenda, multilateral trade negotiations have the potential to yield substantial trade liberalization. Multilateral negotiations allow countries to negotiate on a package of agreements that enables trade-offs to be made between sectors, products, or even rules on trading practices. In principle, they can generate a "pot" that is big enough to induce countries to offer concessions that are desirable in economic terms, but difficult to make for political reasons, in return for substantive reforms by their trading partners. The basic policy question addressed by this study is whether these potential gains can actually be realized.

Furthermore, there are a number of systemic reasons for pursuing multilateral agreements in the GATT. GATT agreements are bound in a framework of rights and obligations supported by common procedures for consultation and dispute settlement. GATT procedures facilitate the monitoring of concessions gained during trade negotiations, and the enforcement of those concessions if countries derogate from their commitments. GATT members have a lot at stake in the maintenance of trading rights and concessions "paid for" in reciprocal trade negotiations; this provides some moral suasion for countries to live up to their GATT obligations lest they risk unraveling concessions they have already achieved. In essence, the greater stakes of the multilateral process enhance conformity with GATT rules because there is more at risk if one goes astray.

---

effectively creating a star-shaped FTA with the United States at the center (Park and Yoo, this volume). Each would require separate congressional approval. Such an approach, using a "model" FTA, would be analogous to the hub-and-spoke nature of the US FCN treaty system.

FTAs and the GATT: Complements or Substitutes?

This section explores the benefits that can be derived from an FTA, and the problems that can arise from the negotiation of a series of bilateral FTAs. The efficacy of the FTA option is contrasted with the traditional multilateral process of the GATT, and the compatibility of FTAs with the GATT is critically assessed.

Bilateralism and the GATT

At the outset, it is important to emphasize that bilateral negotiations are not antithetical to the multilateral process. In many respects, the GATT itself is a multilateral extension of the bilateral trade agreements negotiated by the United States in the decade following the passage of the Reciprocal Trade Agreements Act of 1934.[15] Bilateral accords have played a dominant role in shaping the trade liberalization achieved in the past seven rounds of GATT negotiations.

In the early decades, GATT negotiations primarily involved tariffs. Countries negotiated with the principal suppliers of goods of interest to them and then extended the concessions to all other GATT members pursuant to the MFN obligation of GATT Article I. Bilateral negotiations were thus translated into multilateral commitments. Free riders, or countries benefiting from the MFN tariff cuts without making reciprocal cuts in their own duties, were plentiful, since concessions were asked mainly from countries whose firms were competitive enough to be principal suppliers.

The MFN obligation was designed to yield deep and broad-based trade liberalization, as was noted in the first section. With the development of competitive industries in Japan and the developing countries, particularly the Asian newly industrializing countries, traditional free riders became powerful competitors. Not surprisingly, countries began to question the wisdom of the MFN policy.

Because of political pressures to avoid the free-rider problem, the MFN rule began to impart a perverse cast to the GATT negotiations. Countries began to withhold concessions until reciprocal measures were taken by others. This created what Wonnacott and Lutz have called the "convoy" problem, in which "the least willing participant determines the pace of negotiations; the speed of the convoy moving toward freer trade is limited by the speed of the slowest ship" (Wonnacott and Lutz, this volume). It

---

15. For a review of the bilateral precursors of the GATT, see Diebold (1952 and 1988, chapter 1) and Destler (1986).

also led to renewed interest in the conditional-MFN principle, whereby trade concessions and the rights and benefits of new codes of trade conduct apply only to the signatories. In the Tokyo Round, the United States insisted on the conditional-MFN application of the government procurement and subsidies codes.[16]

The other option for dealing with the free-rider problem was to negotiate FTAs among "like-minded" countries, that is, those interested in advancing trade liberalization. This was seen as a way to avoid the convoy problem in the GATT, yet still be consistent with GATT provisions, since FTAs are sanctioned if they meet the test of Article XXIV (see below). At the same time, it would give a boost to GATT efforts by demonstrating that further liberalization could be achieved. As the Canada–US FTA demonstrated, such a strategy was clearly a "win-win" proposition (Schott and Smith 1988, chapter 7).

FTAs in Theory and Practice

The economic benefits of FTAs have been the subject of rigorous debate among economists; all rely heavily, however, on the arguments pro and con put forward in Jacob Viner's classic analysis, *The Customs Union Issue* (Viner 1950). In a nutshell, Viner argued that FTAs can create new trading opportunities by reducing barriers to bilateral flows between the partner countries. Trade creation allows producers and consumers in the partner countries to shift from high-cost protected suppliers to low-cost foreign suppliers, thus promoting economic efficiency and growth.

However, FTAs also can divert trade by according preferences to the FTA partners that allow them to replace lower-cost suppliers from third countries. Such trade diversion imposes global welfare losses. A simple test of the economic value of an FTA thus could be whether its impact was more trade creating or trade diverting. Of course, such welfare calculations do not determine whether FTAs could be useful in achieving other, noneconomic goals.

As with everything in economics, the issue obviously is not that simple. Trade diversion can also promote growth, and thus trade, by lowering input costs for producers and thereby increasing consumer welfare. In addition, Viner's test does not consider the dynamic effects of trade diversion,

---

16. The legality of this approach was questioned in 1979 immediately after the round with regard to the subsidies code, which interpreted and elaborated the rights and obligations of code signatories under GATT provisions. The government procurement code was less controversial in this regard because of the exception of such transactions from GATT rules pursuant to GATT Article III:8(a). See Hufbauer et al. (1980).

including the gains that can result over time from the introduction of scale economies.[17]

The postwar period has been marked by numerous attempts to construct FTAs. Some have been notable successes, such as the European Free Trade Association (EFTA); many others have not worked. The record of FTAs among developed countries has been far better than among developing countries, with the early years of the Central American Common Market and the Andean Pact being the sole examples of qualified successes (and even these FTAs later failed).

What factors seem to contribute to the success of FTAs? Successful partnerships usually are between countries at comparable levels of development and in close geographical proximity. In theory, the latter is not crucial to economic integration, but closeness may explain complementarities in the structures of the countries' economies that increase the potential benefits from an FTA. However, several FTAs between neighbors have failed (e.g., the East African Community). Geographical proximity therefore is not a ticket to success. Interestingly, there have been few examples of FTAs between developed and developing economies; such arrangements usually take the form of one-way preference schemes like the EC agreement with African, Caribbean, and Pacific developing countries, and the US Caribbean Basin Initiative.

Are FTAs Superior to GATT Negotiations?

Because of the GATT's MFN rule, multilateral negotiations can yield the welfare benefits of trade creation without the drawbacks of trade diversion. However, as noted in the previous section, there are serious concerns regarding the efficacy of the GATT process. Proponents regard FTAs as more effective than the GATT in promoting substantial trade reforms and achieving results in a timely manner. But are the criticisms of the GATT justified, and is the FTA approach a superior route to trade liberalization?

Under close examination, both the benefits of FTAs and the drawbacks of the GATT process seem exaggerated. A brief review of each of the main criticisms of the GATT process explains why.

The Pace of Negotiations—Although GATT rounds have taken longer than recent FTA negotiations, the actual negotiating phase of GATT talks, which can begin only after the entry of the key players who will be around at the completion of the talks, is much shorter. The hard bargaining stage of a

---

17. For a more detailed review of the theory and historical experience with FTAs, see Wonnacott and Lutz (this volume).

GATT round only begins after the installation of new administrations in Washington and Brussels whose mandate extends past the deadline for the GATT talks. In the Tokyo and Uruguay Rounds, the Ford and Reagan administrations, respectively, were only able to launch the negotiations and set out initial negotiating positions. Little was done on the hard issues such as subsidies or textiles. In the Tokyo Round, the "real" negotiations lasted only 18 months (September 1977 to March 1979), about the same as the Canada–US talks. The Uruguay Round is on the same timetable as the Tokyo Round; the "real" negotiations could be completed within a comparable time period and still conclude by the scheduled deadline of 1990 or by the first half of 1991.

The Complexity of Negotiations—Complexity derives from the number of countries and the number of issues involved in a negotiation. The numbers are deceiving. In the GATT talks, it is impossible for all 96 members to engage in the drafting of any agreement. In fact, the negotiating process evolves through concentric circles of countries that are increasingly more engaged in the actual negotiation. At the core is a critical mass of countries—including the United States, the EC, Japan, and a few other developed and developing countries, depending on the subject matter—without whose participation the "pot" of potential trade concessions is too small to induce a multilateral bargain. Most GATT members cannot keep up with the detail of the numerous negotiating groups and thus simply "go with the flow." For this reason, GATT negotiations are not nearly as complicated as is asserted by the proponents of bilateral talks.

Furthermore, a new wrinkle has been added in the Uruguay Round. Coalitions of countries such as the Cairns Group of agricultural exporters and the "de la Paix" group of middle-sized developed and developing countries have formed to serve as catalysts by presenting compromise proposals to spur reactions by the major trading powers (Hamilton and Whalley 1988). Such groups have already sponsored compromise proposals, which contributed to the passage of the Punta del Este declaration that launched the Uruguay Round, and which could bridge the gap between US and EC positions on agriculture.

It should also be noted that the proposed alternative to GATT talks is not a single bilateral agreement but a series of them. US negotiators would have to calculate how each particular agreement affected both the provisions of each previous one and of those that might be concluded in the future. GATT negotiations seem simple and straightforward compared with the maze of problems that would result if the United States negotiated a series of bilateral FTAs (see below).

The complexity of the negotiating *agenda* cannot be denied. GATT trade negotiators can no longer merely be experts in tariff schedules but must understand the intricacies of antitrust and competition law, trade–finance–debt linkages, and innovation policies in high-technology industries. However, the same holds true for FTA negotiators. The agenda for the Canada–US talks, for example, mirrored almost precisely the items under negotiation in the Uruguay Round. Even so, one can argue that FTAs are less complicated because the talks involve only one or a few interests on each issue. However, fewer participants can also make it harder to resolve differences through concessions that cut across various issues or sectors. Indeed, the resolution of some issues requires a multilateral approach, as was demonstrated by the lack of agreement on subsidies in the Canada–US FTA.

Coverage and Enforcement—The loopholes in the coverage of GATT discipline have been well documented; indeed, their removal is one of the principal objectives of the Uruguay Round. However, it has not been demonstrated that FTAs can extend disciplines to areas not covered by GATT rules, with the notable exceptions of trade-related services and investment, where FTA agreements have been developed that can serve as building blocks for GATT accords. Many key NTBs have survived unscathed from the US–Israel and Canada–US pacts, either because they did not play a big role in bilateral trade or because they were too sensitive to change given the limited concessions available in the bilateral talks. As demonstrated in the Canada–US negotiations, the extension of disciplines to subsidies, particularly in the agricultural sector, is too broad a problem to be amenable to bilateral solutions.[18] Similarly, liberalization of NTBs on textiles and steel may be even less likely in FTAs than in the GATT talks.

The record of enforcement of GATT rules has been unduly criticized. Of the 75 disputes brought before the GATT up to September 1985, 88 percent were settled or dropped by the complaining country (US International Trade Commission 1985). Only a few cases, mainly in the agricultural sector, have caused problems, in large part due to the vagueness of substantive rules and obligations in certain areas and the political reluctance in the United States and the EC to reform domestic policies in response to GATT rulings. Both have delayed the formation of GATT panels and blocked consideration of the subsequent panel reports in cases involving major domestic programs. Procedural remedies are under negotiation in the Uruguay Round, but improvement in GATT enforcement will also require agreement on more clearly defined rights and obligations.

---

18. Nonetheless, the Canada–US FTA provides for continuing negotiations on subsidies over the next five to seven years. These bilateral talks will overlap with the Uruguay Round negotiations on subsidies, and may lead to increased bilateral cooperation toward the achievement of multilateral discipline on subsidy practices.

The problem of enforcement goes beyond the coverage and dispute settlement issues. The GATT provisions themselves provide several safeguards for countries suffering balance of payments problems or requiring temporary import relief for domestic industries or protection for national security and health and safety reasons. Such safeguards are legitimate, but have been prone to abuse. Here again, an important objective of the Uruguay Round is to close loopholes so that these exceptions are limited to tightly circumscribed situations.

One additional area of concern about GATT coverage and enforcement relates to the free-rider problem. FTAs deal with it explicitly in that they involve preferences solely among the partner countries, unless concessions are accorded on an MFN basis. The GATT also has at least a partial remedy: both the GATT subsidies and government procurement codes can be applied on a conditional-MFN basis. Provisions in both agreements were added expressly to meet the free-rider problem.

One, Two, . . . Many FTAs?

One of the advantages of a multilateral trade negotiation is that it results in a single, self-balancing package of concessions among all the participating countries. Critics have charged, however, that such a package devolves into the least common denominator of the interests of those countries. By contrast, FTAs negotiated among "like-minded" countries can extend the reach of trade liberalization.

Nonetheless, there are several problems with the FTA approach that raise serious doubts as to whether the pursuit of more FTAs by the United States could achieve such results. In particular, the negotiation of a series of FTAs would create problems with regard to the sequencing of trade concessions and the elaboration of rules of origin. In other words, how would the rights and obligations of subsequent FTAs affect the provisions of existing agreements? And how would one deal with the transshipment of goods through FTA partners to determine which goods are eligible for FTA preferences, especially when these preferences differ among the various FTA partners?

Sequencing—Each new US agreement would undercut the value of concessions obtained by partner countries in previous FTAs, because the preferences in the US market would be shared, and thus diluted, by the new FTA partners. For example, Canadians clearly would be concerned if the United States negotiated an FTA with Mexico. Canada does have the right under the Canada–US FTA to consult with the United States if such a pact adversely affected Canadian trade interests, but Canada's recourse is unclear except to initiate a bilateral dispute procedure. Alternatively, or concurrently, Canada could negotiate new pacts with third countries that trade in both markets, as is now being considered between Canada and Australia–New Zealand (Holmes et al. 1988).

Such pacts also could generate trade frictions if it is perceived that the new partner got a better deal than another with the United States. Such a problem has already occurred with Israel, which deems the provisions on trade in services and on dispute settlement in the Canada–US FTA to be much more desirable than the benefits accorded in its FTA with the United States. One solution to this problem would be to negotiate an open-ended FTA, that is, an FTA whose rights and obligations could be extended to any country willing to pay a common entry price. The US Congress has not favored such an approach, because of the uncertainty about which countries would join and thus what the anticipated adjustment pressures and trade effects would be. In fact, under US law only self-contained FTAs may qualify for "fast-track" implementing provisions.

Rules of Origin—Rules of origin exist to preserve the value of preferences granted in a trade agreement, when the partner countries maintain different external tariffs, by establishing a set percentage of value-added in the traded good that must originate in the partner country. The rules prevent goods originating in third countries from entering the partner country with the lower external tariff for transshipment to a partner that maintains higher tariffs against the third country's goods.[19]

The determination of origin gets more complicated as more FTAs are negotiated, each with its own rules of origin. The different schedule for tariff cuts in each FTA would create a mass of paperwork for customs officials as they tried to certify which shipment could benefit from which set of preferences. Such a system would also create additional red tape and uncertainty for traders and businessmen, especially those with global operations. The United States could establish common rules of origin for all its FTAs, but this would still leave untouched the problem of how to deal with transshipments between the different FTA partners. Such a procedure would also constrain US negotiating leverage in these bilateral agreements, since rules of origin are often used as implicit devices to protect manufacturing industries.[20]

---

19. For a discussion of this issue in the US–Canada context, see Wonnacott (1987, 135 ff.).

20. This point arose with regard to auto parts in the Canada–US FTA.

Compatibility of FTAs With the GATT

The prospect of more free trade areas poses important policy questions for the world trading system: would the negotiation of FTAs between the United States and other countries be compatible with GATT principles and obligations? More specifically, would such agreements reinforce GATT discipline and objectives, or would they contribute to its further decline?

The cornerstone of the GATT is the commitment to nondiscrimination and to the MFN principle of GATT Article I. Trade concessions granted to one GATT member are to be applied as well to the trade of all other signatories. By definition, FTAs run counter to the nondiscrimination and MFN principles. Concessions are extended only to the partner countries, whose traders receive preferential market access that often enables them to displace third-country suppliers in the partner's market. The MFN principle does not apply, and prior concessions made to third countries may be impaired by the preferences granted to the FTA partners.

However, the GATT recognizes the desirability of promoting trade liberalization through the "closer integration between the economies of the countries parties to such agreements." For that reason, GATT Article XXIV allows derogations from the MFN obligation of Article I, provided the FTA meets a three-part test: detailed notification of the agreement is given to the GATT signatories (Article XXIV:7a); the agreement applies to "substantially all" trade between the partner countries (Article XXIV:8b); and the agreement does not raise barriers to third-country trade (Article XXIV:4).

The provisions of Article XXIV are vague, however, as to whether an FTA must be *on balance* trade creating. The GATT merely implies that "the desirability of increasing freedom of trade" (XXIV:4) through FTAs or customs unions is the rationale for the derogation from the MFN obligation. However, the presumption that an FTA must be more trade creating than trade diverting has been incorporated into GATT working party reviews of FTA notifications,[21] and is now generally considered the key standard by which to judge the value of FTAs to third countries.

GATT reviews of Article XXIV notifications have been held quite frequently, but have yielded inconclusive results as to the compatibility of FTAs with GATT rules. Since 1948, a total of 69 FTAs and preferential trade agreements, and subsequent amendments, have been examined by the GATT under the provisions of Article XXIV (see Annex A). GATT working parties have reported on each of these arrangements. Only four agreements were

---

21. See, for example, the report of the working party on the EC association agreements with African and Malagasy States and Overseas Countries and Territories in GATT, *Basic Instruments and Selected Documents*, 14th Supplement, July 1966, 106.

deemed to be compatible with Article XXIV requirements;[22] on the other hand, no agreement has been censured as incompatible with GATT rules.

In most cases, there were disagreements among members of the working party on the conformity of the agreement with Article XXIV provisions relating to third-country effects, trade coverage, and timing and implementation of the agreement. For example, ambiguities in the language of Article XXIV have allowed exceptions in the coverage of agriculture and other sectors in many agreements of which the GATT has been notified. In those cases no decision was taken, although countries reserved their rights under Article XXIII regarding nullification and impairment of trade concessions. Such action implicitly threatens retaliation if national trade interests are impaired; however, such threats have rarely been exercised.

As a result, countries have derogated from their MFN obligations with little risk of response from affected third countries. The lack of ongoing surveillance of Article XXIV agreements virtually ensures that GATT discipline will not be brought to bear on such pacts. One could thus envisage that prospective US FTAs could also be crafted to meet the lax discipline of Article XXIV.

Why has the discipline of GATT Article XXIV fallen into disuse? Besides the ambiguity of its provisions, political considerations have often outweighed other factors in decisions to accede to the terms of the agreements.[23] In addition, affected third countries have been reticent to criticize preferential deals because the majority of GATT members participate in such arrangements.

The question remains, however, as to the impact a proliferation of Article XXIV notifications by the United States would have on the GATT system. To date, most of the arrangements notified under Article XXIV have been FTAs among contiguous European nations or preferential pacts between the EC and countries in the Mediterranean Basin and Africa.[24] Almost all of those agreements were concluded by the late 1970s. During the past

---

22. The South Africa–Rhodesia customs union (1948); the Nicaragua–El Salvador FTA (1951); Nicaraguan participation in the Central American Free Trade Area (1958); and the Caribbean Community and Common Market (1973).

23. The watershed for Article XXIV was the review of the formation of the European Community. The EC notification was not contested in part because of US hopes that the formation of the EC "would enhance the area's political cohesion, sense of responsibility, and military strength" (Patterson 1966, 156). In acceding to the EC notification, the United States placed political considerations over concerns about conformity with the legal tests of Article XXIV, and set a precedent for GATT inaction that has been difficult to reverse.

24. The latter did spark disputes about conformity with GATT provisions, and led to the Casey–Soames agreement, which limited the geographic scope of new EC preference schemes.

decade, Article XXIV has been used much less frequently, and only recently has the United States invoked Article XXIV—to justify the pacts with Israel and Canada.

Recently, however, the lax enforcement of Article XXIV obligations has been sharply criticized by a wisemen's report commissioned by the GATT and issued in 1985.[25] The report warned that "exceptions and ambiguities have thus been permitted ... [and] have set a dangerous precedent for further special deals, fragmentation of the trading system, and damage to the trade interests of non-participants" (Leutwiler et al. 1985, 41).

The warning of the GATT wisemen is not unfounded, and raises the prospect that the more extensive use of Article XXIV by the United States for FTAs, notably in the Pacific Basin, could have a significant impact on the GATT system. Talk of blocs and bilateral agreements has become so pervasive that it threatens to become a self-fulfilling prophecy. An increasing number of countries are devoting scarce time and resources to developing and pursuing bilateral or regional approaches, largely as a defensive reaction to perceived movement toward blocs elsewhere, at the expense of the Uruguay Round. The following section examines in more detail the reactions of potential FTA partners with the United States.

Are More FTAs Feasible and Desirable?

With the successful conclusion of FTAs with Israel and Canada, consideration has been given to the negotiation of additional pacts among "like-minded" countries. During the Reagan administration, US officials made informal overtures to a number of countries to explore the possibility of a free trade agreement. These overtures had the interrelated objectives of establishing building blocks for broader GATT reforms in areas such as services and staking out a credible alternative to multilateral trade negotiations in the event the GATT process should falter.[26]

This section examines the potential candidates for FTAs with the United States and why both they and the United States may be interested in negotiations. The pros and cons of each prospective bilateral FTA are analyzed, along with its implications for the GATT system, to determine

---

25. The wisemen's group was chaired by Fritz Leutwiler of Switzerland. The US participant was Senator Bill Bradley (D-NJ).

26. Although senior officials in the Reagan administration strongly promoted the bilateral option, they avoided openly pushing for additional FTAs beyond Canada in deference to ongoing GATT talks. Secretary Baker expressed the hope that "follow-up liberalization [to the Canada–US FTA] will occur in the Uruguay Round" (Baker 1988, 41).

whether such agreements are feasible and desirable or whether other types
of trade arrangements might be forthcoming instead.

Candidate Countries

Not surprisingly, the list of candidates for FTAs with the United States
looks like a "who's who" of the leading US trading partners, with the
notable exception of the EC.[27] Indeed, the FTA option has put the EC on
notice that a continuation of its hardline position on agricultural reform,
and an inward turn in the context of the 1992 initiative, could lead the
United States to develop counterweights. US overtures have been directed
primarily toward countries in the Pacific Basin, reflecting a clear shift in
focus of US trade policy from the Atlantic to the Pacific.

The countries most frequently cited as potential FTA partners are Japan,
Korea, Taiwan, Mexico, the ASEAN, and, less often, Australia (US International Trade Commission 1988 and 1989). The Asian countries in this
group are among the fastest-growing and most vibrant economies in the
world, and account for the largest share of growth in US trade in recent
years. Most of them run substantial trade surpluses with the United States
(see table 1.1).

A number of these countries already have expressed an interest in exploring
new trade arrangements with the United States. The reason for their interest
in the US trade relationship is clearly demonstrated in table 1.2. In most
cases, exports to the United States account for a substantial share of the
country's total exports, ranging from almost 70 percent for Mexico; to 37 to
44 percent for Taiwan, Korea, and Japan; to 21 percent for the ASEAN
countries (with Australia the outlier at 11 percent).[28] Moreover, such exports
contribute substantially to overall GNP in the cases of Taiwan (24 percent),
Korea (15.5 percent), and Mexico (13 percent). On the import side, the
trade linkage with the United States is not as dominant except for Mexico,
although most of the countries take about one-fifth of their imports from
the United States.

The candidate countries share one other common characteristic. Except

---

27. The EC has been omitted because a US–EC FTA would parallel closely the
multilateral talks and because of the EC's preoccupation with its 1992 internal market
initiatives. For that very reason, however, Rep. Richard Gephardt (d-mo; 1988) has
proposed a US–EC trade agreement to create an "economic NATO."

28. Even within ASEAN, there is substantial variation in trade dependence on the
United States. The Philippines relies on the US market for 36 percent of its exports,
Malaysia for only 16.6 percent, and Brunei for less than 1 percent. In addition, exports
to the United States account for 34 percent of Singapore's GNP.

Table 1.1 Trade balances of FTA candidate countries[a]

Country/region	Trade balance with US (millions of dollars)	Trade balance with world (millions of dollars)
Japan	48,720	70,385
Korea	7,076	2,886
Taiwan	13,204	15,084
Australia	−2,848	−920
Mexico	3,783	6,628
ASEAN	4,511	4,541
Israel	538	−4,444
Canada	12,525	8,723

a. Average trade balance for the years 1985–87. Export data are reported f.o.b. and import data c.i.f. except Australia, Mexico, and Canada, which are reported f.o.b.

Sources: International Monetary Fund, *Direction of Trade Statistics Yearbook* 1981–87. Ministry of Economic Affairs, Taiwan, *Foreign Trade Development of the Republic of China 1988.*

Table 1.2 GNP and trade linkages with FTA candidate countries, 1987[a]

Country/ region	GNP (billions of dollars)[b]	GNP as % of US GNP	Exports to US — as % of total exports	Exports to US — as % of GNP	Imports from US — as % of total imports	Imports from US — as % of GNP
Japan	2,384.5	52.8	36.8	3.6	21.2	1.3
Korea	118.6	2.6	38.9	15.5	21.4	7.4
Taiwan	99.4	2.2	44.2	23.8	22.1	7.7
Australia	186.8	4.1	11.3	1.6	21.4	3.1
Mexico	140.0	3.1	69.6	13.3	73.5	10.4
ASEAN	202.0	4.5	21.4	8.7	14.8	5.6
Israel	31.5	0.7	30.7	8.1	13.4	6.1
Canada	402.0	8.9	72.8	17.8	65.9	14.8

a. Export data are reported f.o.b., and import data c.i.f. except Australia, Mexico, and Canada, which are f.o.b.
b. 1986 GDP used as GNP approximation for Brunei; 1987 GDP used as GNP approximation for Mexico.

Sources: International Monetary Fund, *International Financial Statistics,* December 1988; *Direction of Trade Statistics Yearbook 1988.* The Central Bank of China, Taiwan, *Financial Statistics,* September 1988. Ministry of Economic Affairs, Taiwan, *Foreign Trade Development of the Republic of China 1988*; National Institute of Statistics, Secretariat of Programming and Budget, Mexico; Economic Planning Unit, Ministry of Finance, Brunei.

for Japan, all current and potential FTA partners are small countries or regional groupings with GNPs less than one-twentieth that of the United States.

Candidate Country Objectives

Why have the candidate countries generally been receptive to the FTA overtures by the United States? Although each country has particular interests at stake in its trade relations with the United States, four common and interrelated objectives seem to arise in each case. These goals indicate that the candidate countries generally do not regard FTAs as a complement to GATT negotiations, but rather as a defensive reaction to the threat of protectionism and bilateralism by the United States. As such, they pose a sharp contrast to the building-block approach to trade liberalization sought by many in the United States. Each objective is summarized below.

Maintaining Market Access—The most prevalent concern among the candidate countries is the preservation of access to the US market. This is clearly a response to the perceived growth in "process protectionism" in the United States, abetted by their strong trade dependence.[29] This was also the primary Canadian concern in negotiating its FTA, given its sensitivity to countervailing and antidumping duty investigations against its exports to the United States. Liberalization of US trade barriers seem to be of secondary concern, since US tariffs overall are quite low, and these countries recognize that they have little leverage in bilateral negotiations to reduce US NTBs affecting their exports.

Achieving more secure access to the US market requires the avoidance of future trade controls. To that end, the interests of candidate countries lie in attaining an exemption from, or discriminatory preferences pursuant to, the application of US trade laws (Snape 1988, 12). Whereas for Canada the primary concern was the rash of countervailing duty cases, for countries in the Pacific Rim the greater threat is the imposition of new US restrictions pursuant to section 301 cases.[30] Since the adoption of a more aggressive US

---

29. For a discussion of the evolution of US process protectionism, see Destler (1986) and Schott (1989a). The latter paper also examines the implications for Korea of this trend.

30. Under section 301 of the Trade Act of 1974, almost any foreign practice could be subject to US retaliation if it were construed as "unreasonable, unjustifiable, or discriminatory"—a very open-ended standard. In practice, however, presidents have been quite cautious in applying this statute for fear of disrupting world trade and impairing US obligations under the GATT. President Reagan began to move away from this position after adopting a more aggressive trade policy, including self-initiation of section 301 cases, in mid-1985.

trade policy in 1985, more than a dozen complaints have been investigated under section 301, most against practices by Japan, Korea, and Taiwan. The negotiation of FTAs could be seen as a way to cast potential disputes in a less contentious light and perhaps avoid selection under the super 301 process.

Of course, the threat of retaliation using section 301 authority can have beneficial effects for US trading partners. For example, section 301 cases often are brought in areas where GATT rules are vague or incomplete—such as in services and IPR issues—where failure to accept the US interpretation of "fair trade" carries a real risk of retaliation. Such pressure can be used by foreign governments to justify the liberalization of their import barriers, and thus to overcome domestic political opposition to actions deemed economically desirable but politically difficult to implement.

The market access objective can be achieved at least in part through the negotiation of a "standstill" commitment, which would provide a firebreak against new protectionist pressures (which are likely to strengthen if the US trade deficit is not reduced substantially in the coming years). In essence, a standstill commitment provides an insurance policy against new trade barriers and against the promulgation of discriminatory regulations that could impede market access.[31] It provides greater certainty to firms in the partner countries that the rules of the game will not be altered to their disadvantage in the future, and thus allows them to better plan their trade and investment strategies. I have argued elsewhere that the standstill was one of the most important US concessions granted in the FTA with Canada (Schott 1988).

Improving Bilateral Relations—FTAs are also sought to better manage the bilateral trade relationship with the United States. First, the agreement itself focuses increased attention on the bilateral relationship. Second, the monitoring and enforcement of FTA provisions perforce give the relationship higher priority among US trading partners. In addition, FTAs are sought as a vehicle to enhance political recognition of the candidate country by the United States (e.g., in the case of Taiwan), or to strengthen the political ties between the two countries (e.g., in the case of Israel).

These factors cut two ways, however. They create an incentive to settle problems amicably, but they also place existing trade problems under a

---

31. The value to prospective FTA partners of such an insurance policy depends on whether the "price" of the insurance premiums is worth the forgone risk. The price includes their concessions and the possible diminution of multilateral discipline against new US protectionism; the risk is potential US trade actions resulting from the trade estimates report and other provisions of the Omnibus Trade and Competitiveness Act of 1988.

microscope. This may explain why candidate countries regard administrative, consultative, and dispute settlement provisions as so important, and the Canada–US pact as a useful model in this regard.

Promoting Trade Diversion—One of the ways in which countries seek to improve bilateral relations is by reducing the tensions created by large trade imbalances. In this respect, FTAs are seen by some countries as a way of instituting discriminatory preferences favoring the deficit country (i.e., the United States) and against the surplus country (i.e., Japan), in this case so that the United States could compete better against suppliers from Japan and other East Asian countries. Such a policy is likely to result in welfare losses in the candidate country due to the effects of trade diversion (Tsiang, this volume). However, officials in some countries, such as Taiwan, have argued explicitly that the political benefits to be derived from a lessening of bilateral trade tensions more than justify the economic costs in terms of reduced welfare.

Avoiding Discrimination—The flip side of the previous objective is the avoidance of discrimination should other countries negotiate FTAs with the United States. In this regard, FTAs are a defensive strategy to get to the front of the negotiating queue to preclude the negative impact of trade diversion from one's own suppliers as a consequence of other FTAs. Of course, the preferences received in the FTA are quickly dissipated if other countries also negotiate bilateral deals with the United States, but at least the threat of discrimination in the US market is avoided.

Prospective FTAs: Pros and Cons

Although one can generalize the objectives of the candidate countries, in fact each case has specific problems and elements unique to the country's bilateral relationship with the United States. The following subsections explore the pros and cons of negotiating a bilateral FTA in order to evaluate the feasibility and desirability of going down that road.

A US–Japan FTA?

Undoubtedly the most attention has been focused on the prospects for an FTA between the world's two economic superpowers. The size of the two economies, their relative parity in terms of per capita GNP, and the large bilateral trade imbalance differentiate this pact from any other under consideration. The two countries' economic power also means that an FTA would have a far-ranging impact both on third countries and on the world trading system as a whole. Even the potential for a US–Japan agreement requires other countries in East Asia and beyond to plan (and possibly act on) defensive strategies to deal with the trade diversion that might result from such an arrangement.

Consideration of a US–Japan FTA has been promoted for several years by former US Ambassador to Japan Mike Mansfield. Although he has not been sanguine about the prospects that an FTA could be easily or quickly negotiated, he has argued that such an exercise "could be helpful in defining the economic goals of our relationship. It is better to face up to the whole of a policy rather than submit to nickle and diming on every single issue" (Mansfield 1987). This view was echoed by former Commerce Secretary C. William Verity, who, while not endorsing an FTA, noted that "an honest and two-way examination of the issues of free trade would underline both for us and for Japan the responsibilities we bear to each other and particularly to other nations . . ." (Verity 1988).

A much more broad-based approach than an FTA has since been advocated by Senators Robert Byrd (D-WV), Max Baucus (D-MT), and Bill Bradley (D-NJ). Their proposals differ widely with regard to both scope (a G-2 for Baucus versus a PAC-8 for Bradley, and bilateral versus "open-ended") and coverage (a mixture of trade, debt, exchange rate, and "burden-sharing" issues).[32] All three, however, seek significant trade reforms *by Japan*.

There are, of course, several notable precedents for a US–Japan trade pact. The most important, and perhaps least recognized, may be the Treaty of Friendship, Commerce, and Navigation concluded in 1953. During the past decade there have been a series of agreements relating to specific products or sectors, from the Strauss–Ushiba accord[33] in the late 1970s, to the formation of the Trade Facilitation Committee, to the market-oriented sector-specific (MOSS) talks, to the 1986 semiconductor pact, to recent accommodations on beef and citrus and 12 other agricultural commodities. These have made a patchwork quilt of the bilateral trade relationship.

Despite these agreements, trade continues to be a flashpoint in bilateral relations. In the United States, the continued large bilateral trade deficit

---

32. For details, see the letter of 30 September 1988 to Prime Minister Noboru Takeshita from Senator Byrd reprinted in *Inside US Trade*, 7 October 1988, 5; see also Bradley (1988) and Baucus (1988).

33. After several months of fractious bargaining in late 1977, Japan committed on 13 January 1978 *inter alia* to tariff cuts on $2.6 billion in trade, increasing its hotel beef import quota, doubling its foreign aid, and increasing its imports of manufactures. The United States offered general commitments regarding its macroeconomic policies and efforts to secure enactment of a new energy program. See Destler (1979, 213–15).

with Japan, which averaged almost $50 billion annually from 1985 to 1988, has raised doubts, particularly in Congress, as to the efficacy of the piecemeal approach to trade policy. In Japan, frustration is also high because of the seemingly endless round of product-specific disputes—what Mansfield called "nickle and diming"—that has not improved, and indeed may have worsened, trade relations with the country that accounts for about 70 percent of its global trade surplus.

It is therefore not surprising that proposals for more comprehensive negotiations have been put forward on both sides of the Pacific. The Japanese seem to have three main objectives. The first involves market access and is prompted by the fear that new trade and investment controls will result from the Omnibus Trade and Competitiveness Act of 1988. Second, Japan hopes that a bilateral pact will reduce the risk that trade and investment disputes will spill over to involve security issues. Third, the negotiation of new rules in areas such as services, investment, and IPRs, as well as the establishment of formal administrative mechanisms for bilateral consultation and dispute settlement, is seen as essential to the better management of the bilateral economic relationship.[34] Clearly, the focus of Japanese interest is less on liberalization than on maintaining US market access, a defensive approach to the threat of new US protectionism.

By contrast, the major thrust of the various US proposals involves much broader objectives. Given the failure of the piecemeal approach, these proposals seek to coordinate and integrate US policy initiatives on trade and other related issues, including in some cases defense, because of the budgetary implications of military spending and the imbalance in such expenditures between the two countries. In essence, they would force the United States to set priorities, and then try to use the leverage of the overall economic relationship to promote Japanese trade liberalization. Such prioritization would require a bureaucratic reorganization to centralize decision making on all economic issues with Japan, probably in the White House.[35] What is unclear is whether such centralization would lead to a greater or a lesser emphasis on trade policy concerns, which involve only a small part of the economic relationship and account, according to most analyses, for only a minor share of the bilateral trade imbalance (Bergsten and Cline 1987).

In addition, a US–Japan FTA is seen as a means to redirect US trade

---

34. For an elaboration of these points, see Kuroda (this volume) and the interim report of the Asia–Pacific Trade and Development Study Group of the Japanese Ministry International of Trade and Industry, June 1988.

35. Some proposals advocate linking trade and debt issues, suggesting Japanese "burden-sharing" with regard to the developing country debt crisis (Bergsten 1988; Kissinger and Vance 1988; Baucus 1988; and Brzezinski 1988).

policy toward the Pacific Rim. In part such proposals are a response to the EC 1992 initiative, threatening to establish a counterweight if EC policies create a "fortress Europe." At the same time, an FTA is a means to refocus the agenda of US trade policy toward high-technology issues (for example, supercomputers, semiconductors, and biotechnology), with less emphasis on "traditional" merchandise such as autos, textiles, and steel.

Finally, the US proposals share a common objective with Japan in rulemaking and more effective dispute settlement procedures. The Canada–US FTA serves as a useful model in these areas; indeed, in several areas that pact could be "trilateralized," particularly with regard to services, financial services, and investment, with relatively minor alterations. However, no official in any of the three countries has yet proposed such a step.

None of the proposals are very specific about how and how much trade liberalization could and should be achieved in an FTA. Indeed, discussion to date of a US–Japan FTA has served only to promote a comprehensive reevaluation of the US–Japan economic relationship—which is all to the good. Less attention has been focused on the specifics of trade policy and the negotiation of an FTA because of several major problems, which are well recognized on both sides.

First and foremost, there is the daunting political problem: a US–Japan FTA is regarded in many quarters as a "nonstarter" because of the political difficulties that would arise in both countries with regard to the coverage of such traditionally sensitive items as rice, textiles and apparel, and steel as well as such high-technology sectors as computers and biotechnology. The political problem is aggravated by growing mistrust in Japan of US efforts to redirect its macroeconomic policies and to promote open trade, the latter reflecting in part a backlash from the series of bilateral product-specific disputes. In the United States, there is substantial skepticism that the removal of overt Japanese trade barriers would affect bilateral trade flows significantly, and that an FTA would achieve trade liberalization or enhance market access. This is fed by concern that the "real" Japanese trade barriers are not amenable to trade negotiations, but arise from biases inherent in the distribution system, in technical and health and safety requirements, in industrial targeting practices, in antitrust policies, and even in the legal system as a whole, and that structural reforms are needed in the Japanese economy (for example, regarding land use policies) to promote import expansion and sustained growth in domestic demand (Balassa and Noland 1988).

Second, even if Japanese trade liberalization were to be achieved in the context of the FTA, there remains the problem of what the United States would pay for the Japanese concessions. Given the skepticism over the value of reforms of overt trade barriers already noted, it is unlikely that US concessions would go very far. Moreover, the removal of voluntary Japanese export restraints could worsen the bilateral trade imbalance, and thus further inflame US protectionist pressures. In light of the existing trade imbalance, a standstill commitment on new US barriers may be all that could be justified politically in return for Japanese trade reforms—and even that could be difficult in the high-technology sectors.

The problem of reciprocity in concessions is less significant with regard to rulemaking. For that reason, if an agreement were negotiated, it could very possibly follow the precedent of the Canada–US pact and emphasize the establishment of trading rules in services, investment, and IPRs more than liberalization of NTBs.

Indeed, both countries seem to be more interested in a "modern" FCN treaty than in a free trade agreement. The focus of such a pact would be on a consultative mechanism, supporting new contractual obligations in non-GATT areas as well as on new dispute settlement provisions perhaps similar to those in the Canada–US FTA. Such an arrangement would not necessarily violate the GATT, and indeed could serve as a heralded building block for multilateral accords in these areas.

Third, a US–Japan FTA would trigger attempts by other Asian countries to "regionalize" the agreement; indeed, such efforts are already under way merely in response to the unofficial discussion of such a negotiation. In addition, an FTA would provoke a strong reaction by the EC, creating a backlash that could bolster supporters of a fortress Europe as a defense against the newly emerging Pacific trading bloc.

Whatever the motivation, a US–Japan FTA would be seen as a move away from the Uruguay Round and thus would contribute to the erosion of GATT discipline over world trade. Such a pact would require an army of trade negotiators and thus would divert resources from the Geneva effort. More importantly, a US–Japan FTA would contribute to the self-fulfilling prophecy noted at the end of the preceding section. It would strengthen the presumption that the world was heading toward a system of regional blocs, and could result in other countries scrambling to join a bloc (e.g., several East Asian countries) or to strengthen their own counterweights (e.g., the EC with its 1992 process). As Michael B. Smith, the former Deputy US Trade Representative, has pointed out, if two of the powers in world trade go off by themselves to negotiate, the multilateral process will soon deteriorate.[36]

Finally, it is well recognized that an FTA alone will not reduce the bilateral

---

36. The comments of Ambassador Smith were made at a luncheon speech to the Institute for International Economics on 1 November 1988 and are cited in the *National Journal*, 3 December 1988, 3055.

trade imbalance significantly. Indeed, the failure of the US deficit to go down sharply could raise new tensions, discrediting trade as well as macroeconomic remedies to the deficit problem that have been pursued since 1985. For this reason, most proposals to date have sought a broader agreement than an FTA, one that would accommodate a wide range of trade–debt–finance linkages. The concept of a "G-2," originally proposed by C. Fred Bergsten (1987) and recently adapted by Senator Baucus in S.292, has resurfaced with its focus on cooperative macroeconomic policies and the establishment of a yen–dollar target zone. By placing trade in its broader economic context, such an approach inevitably places less emphasis on trade policy concerns. Negotiations are thus more likely to move away from the concept of an FTA and revert to the elaboration of more traditional macroeconomic mechanisms, with trade concerns perhaps being handled in a modernized FCN treaty as suggested above.

A US–Taiwan FTA?

Consideration of a US–Taiwan FTA has been driven by the concern in Taiwan that the large bilateral trade imbalance with the United States could color the political relationship as well as lead to increased US protectionism. In this regard, Taiwan is different from the other candidate countries in that, like Israel earlier, political considerations dominate the economic agenda.

Since early 1986, when protectionist pressures began to mount rapidly in the US Congress, an FTA has been seen in Taiwan as a way to separate Taiwan from measures being aimed at other East Asian countries, particularly Japan. The removal of Taiwan from eligibility under the US GSP as of January 1989 is cited as evidence of this problem. Taiwan had been the largest beneficiary under the US GSP program, shipping $3.7 billion annually to the United States in recent years; an FTA could effectively restore those preferences.[37]

In this context, the negotiation of an FTA with the United States is part of a strategy to use trade to strengthen political ties and reduce trade tensions, which are seen as a threat to good relations. In addition, there have been extensive Taiwanese efforts to manage the trade problem by encouraging buying missions in the United States and by substantial gold imports. Most recently, Taiwan adopted in March 1989 a "detailed action plan," *inter alia*, to stimulate imports from the United States. The plan

---

37. See comments by Dr. Chang King-yuh, director of the Institute for International Relations in Taipei, in Brooks (1988, 86).

includes additional trade liberalization in both goods and services sectors, export credit subsidies for US exporters, an intensified "Buy American" policy, enhanced protection of IPRs, and a commitment to reduce Taiwan's export dependence on the US market. The plan was explicitly promulgated "in view of the new directions and emphasis in the formulation of United States trade policy as articulated in the Omnibus Trade and Competitiveness Act" (Republic of China 1989, 1).

Taiwan also sees an FTA as a way to enhance the importance of the bilateral trade relationship through the establishment of a binational commission and dispute settlement procedures following the precedent of the Canada–US FTA. Such steps would supplement the procedures set out in the Taiwan Relations Act of 1978, and compensate in part for Taiwan's absence from the GATT forum.

Taiwan has sought an FTA with the United States for several economic reasons as well. Although Taiwan is not a member of the GATT, it is one of the world's 13 largest traders. Like the other candidate countries, Taiwan has a strong export dependence on the US market and sees an FTA as a way to avoid US protectionism. About 44 percent of Taiwanese exports go to the US market, and 88 percent of Taiwan's global trade surplus is accounted for by trade with the United States. As noted above, these exports account for about 24 percent of Taiwan's GNP. Taiwan thus has a strong interest in secure market access, particularly in light of the growing use of voluntary export restraints (VERs) and section 301 actions by the United States.[38] More secure market access in turn "will allow the development of high technology exports, and will also encourage US and third country investment in the ROC's hi-tech industries."[39]

For the United States, the main trade objective is improved market access, primarily through tariff reductions by Taiwan and improvement in Taiwanese protection of IPRs. However, like Mexico and South Korea, Taiwan has undertaken significant unilateral tariff cuts (for example, cutting tariffs on 3,570 items in February 1988), but the main beneficiaries have turned out to be Japanese and South Korean firms. Indeed, Taiwan fears that continued MFN tariff liberalization could exacerbate bilateral imbalances with the United States.

Instead, Taiwan has sought to extend bilateral preferences to the United

---

38. Taiwan is particularly concerned about potential US complaints about abuses of workers' rights (an unfair-trade practice explicitly cited in the 1988 US Trade Act as actionable under section 301), given the large wage disparity between the two countries and Taiwan's relatively weak labor protection laws compared to those in the United States.

39. Comments by Vincent C. Siew, director general of the Board of Foreign Trade of Taiwan, as quoted in Chen (1986, 57).

States through an FTA, in the view that an FTA "would definitely help to ensure that U.S. firms will not only secure the lion's share of our market, but will also find the ROC useful as a springboard for further expanding their markets in other Asian-Pacific countries."[40] In essence, Taiwanese representatives argue that the United States will gain by displacing trade from Japan and other countries. In most cases, such trade diversion would be detrimental to Taiwanese economic welfare because of both the substitution of a higher-cost US supplier and the lost tariff revenues (see Tsiang, this volume), but this seems to be a price Taiwan is willing to pay for the political gains that could accrue from an FTA.[41]

At the same time, however, the discriminatory preferences could serve a broader purpose if the United States used an FTA with Taiwan as a wedge to induce FTAs with Japan and other countries in East Asia (Tsiang 1989). However, the intense competition between Taiwan and Korea in certain product sectors would make such broader arrangements quite difficult to achieve (see discussion below on regional FTAs).

One area where an FTA is unlikely to yield new market access opportunities is agriculture. As with Japan and Korea, the main problem is rice. The agricultural constituencies in all these countries are particularly vocal and politically powerful; any progress toward import liberalization is likely to be made grudgingly and implemented over an extended period of time. In Taiwan, a major rationale for protection is a concern about security of supply. Given Taiwan's strong political interest in a pact with the United States, an FTA may be a possible vehicle to reduce rice controls. One way to deal with this problem would be to resort to increased storage of rice in Taiwan, which could enhance food security and perhaps facilitate at least partial liberalization of rice controls. However, the United States may need to provide greater overall security guarantees to induce farm reforms in Taiwan (Tsiang, this volume).

The security question raises the sensitive issue of the impact of a US–Taiwan FTA on the People's Republic of China (PRC). Although Taiwan officially maintains a policy of no contact with Beijing, there has been a significant increase in trade in recent years via transshipments through

---

40. P. K. Chiang, director general of the Board of Foreign Trade of Taiwan, "Toward Balanced Trade with the USA: ROC Efforts and Progress," presented to the Institute for International Economics, 15 March 1989.

41. In 1986, about 95 percent of the $5.4 billion of US exports to Taiwan were dutiable at an average rate of 7.93 percent. Therefore, tariff elimination would have led to about $408 million in forgone tariff revenue for Taiwan (see Chen 1986, 57). Subsequent unilateral tariff cuts should reduce the expected revenue losses from an FTA, which in any event would have little adverse impact on Taiwan's strong budget position.

Hong Kong.[42] An FTA could be seen as a means to shore up the political support of those concerned about Taiwan's small economic opening with Beijing, or it could be seen as a way to isolate and limit PRC trade contacts because of the preferences accorded US trading interests.

An FTA with Taiwan would also have important implications for US–PRC relations. A US–Taiwan FTA could increase trade tensions between the United States and the PRC and threaten to undercut the political and economic relations built up over the past decade. The Chinese ambassador to the United States already has warned that such a pact with Taiwan would violate existing US–China agreements.[43] However, an FTA also could be seen by the PRC as a future precedent for bilateral trade, with nearer-term benefits if it establishes a trading "foot in the door" in Taiwan.

A US–Korea FTA?

In many respects, Korean interest in an FTA with the United States parallels that of Taiwan, although the political motivation is more muted. Both countries have strong trade linkages with the United States, and both have been vulnerable to US economic pressures because of their reliance on the US security relationship (see Hufbauer and Schott 1985a; Bayard and Young 1989).

Korean objectives focus on security of access to the US market and on the establishment of a more stable bilateral relationship, which in turn will encourage inflows of foreign capital and technology. Korea is strongly dependent on trade with the United States. Exports to the United States accounted for 39 percent of total exports and 15.5 percent of GNP in 1987. Moreover, Korea's trade surplus with the United States averaged about two and a half times greater than its overall surplus from 1985 to 1987—another gauge of Korea's vulnerability to new US protectionism.[44]

In response to these developments, Korea has sought to diversify its export markets. An FTA with the United States could impede that effort and even lead to increased dependence on the US market. Such a development would likely exacerbate national sovereignty concerns that have already

---

42. For data on this "bilateral" trade, see P.T. Bangsberg, "Taiwan, China Plan Conference on Trade," *Journal of Commerce,* 13 September 1988, 3A.

43. Excerpts from a letter from Chinese Ambassador Han Xu are quoted in Cristina Lee, "Taiwan Free Trade Pact Could Help US Firms," *Journal of Commerce,* 9 March 1989, 5A.

44. In 1988, however, Korea's global trade surplus exceeded its $8.9 billion bilateral trade surplus with the United States.

surfaced in current bilateral trade disputes on agriculture and telecommunications.

Korea recognizes that its negotiating position is constrained in bilateral trade talks with the United States, and thus prefers to work in the multilateral forum of the GATT. However, there are two problems with that approach. First, like Taiwan, Korea is concerned that trade tensions with the United States will not be resolved by MFN tariff cuts, which would tend to benefit Japan more than the United States. Second, as a defensive measure, Korea would have to follow suit if the United States entered FTA negotiations with other Pacific Rim countries.[45] Indeed, the concern that other bilateral agreements could discriminate against Korean trade is perhaps the strongest motivation to pursue an FTA with the United States.

Furthermore, an FTA is seen as a better approach for easing bilateral trade problems than product-specific talks (such as the recent acrimonious disputes over agriculture, insurance, cigarettes, and IPRs). Such problems are likely to continue in coming years as US firms seek to remove barriers to the Korean market by invoking the new authorities of the 1988 Trade Act. A dispute over telecommunications has already emerged, and Korea is vulnerable to additional complaints that could be filed under the enhanced provisions of section 301.[46] An FTA would establish a special framework for negotiations on a comprehensive set of items, and procedures for future consultation and dispute settlement, and thus could diffuse the tensions generated by a continuous stream of product- or sector-specific disputes.

For the United States, the objectives of an FTA with Korea would resemble somewhat those set for the US–Israel pact, although "it is unlikely that the United States would agree to anything less comprehensive than it negotiated with Israel" (Allgeier 1988, 95). Besides the comprehensive tariff cuts that would be required *inter alia* to make the FTA consistent with GATT Article XXIV, such an agreement could also provide for Korean accession to the GATT codes on government procurement and licensing, the forswearance of VERs by both countries, and the development of new rules to guide bilateral trade in services, investment, and IPRs. Moreover, the United States could also benefit from liberalization in the Korean market in that it would allow US firms to establish an export platform from which to serve other Pacific Rim markets (Allgeier 1988, 95).

The problem remains how the United States would reciprocate for such

---

45. Some make a virtue out of this necessity, and argue that an FTA with Korea would be a catalyst for a broader FTA in the Pacific Basin. See, for example, Kim (1988).

46. The implications of the new US Trade Act for US–Korean trade relations are reviewed in Schott (1989a).

Korean concessions. In particular, the US negotiators would be hard pressed to commit to the removal of the textile and apparel and steel quotas that hinder Korean exports to the United States. In fact, it is "most probable that the United States would seek to maintain an MFA-consistent bilateral agreement with Korea even in the context of an FTA" (Allgeier 1988, 95). Furthermore, as with Japan, the United States will likely need to maintain flexibility to act against perceived unfair trade practices, especially in semiconductors and other high-technology sectors.

A US–Mexico FTA?

The vision of a unified North American market has held great interest in the United States for many years both as a foil to the EC and as a means for the United States to promote closer relations with its neighbors. The Congress directed the President to study the prospects for a North American Free Trade Area (NAFTA) in the Trade Agreements Act of 1979 (section 1104), and both Presidents Reagan and Bush have supported the *long-term* objective of free trade in the region.

For Mexico, however, the allure of a free trade area has never been great because of the large disparities in economic development in North America. Mexicans are rightly concerned that the burden of adjustment in manufacturing would fall heavily on their industries, while trade in labor services would be impeded by immigration concerns. This has led Mexico's new trade minister, Jaime Serra Puche, to conclude that an FTA is not in Mexico's short-term interest, and that freer trade between the United States and Mexico must be negotiated in gradual increments.[47]

In addition, Mexico has a strong stake in its new membership in the GATT system. Given its strong dependence on trade with the United States, the GATT is now perceived as a way to protect Mexico against the changing trade policies of its neighbor to the north. Interestingly, this perception of GATT is 180 degrees different from that prior to Mexican accession in 1986: Mexico no longer regards GATT disciplines as a threat, but rather as an effective ally in its continuing bilateral relations with the United States.

To be sure, Mexico has already implemented substantial trade reforms unilaterally pursuant to GATT accession and IMF/World Bank programs. The average tariff rate has dropped from 28.5 percent in December 1985 to 11.8 percent in December 1987; imports requiring permits or subject to official prices have also fallen sharply during the period (see Trigueros, this

---

47. For a report on Mexico's policy toward both an FTA and the GATT, see *Financial Times*, 8 December 1988, 5.

volume). Moreover, for anti-inflationary reasons, the peso has been maintained at least temporarily at a relatively high level, which has encouraged imports and increased pressure on the manufacturing sector. Critics within Mexico have charged that these reforms have gone too far too fast, especially since there have been no reciprocal concessions by Mexico's trading partners. In response, President Carlos Salinas de Gortari announced a rollback of some of the tariff cuts as part of the new economic package instituted when he took office in December 1988 (*Financial Times*, 14 December 1988, 3).

Mexico's go-slow approach to further trade liberalization reflects the political realities of negotiating trade liberalization at a time when the debt-service requirement imposes a heavy constraint on internal demand. New liberalization would sharply increase competitive pressures on Mexican industry and generate political opposition. However, the Salinas government is committed to a further opening of the Mexican economy. Such a policy is likely to proceed sector by sector, involving both trade and investment reforms and perhaps privatization of some state-owned enterprises.

Mexico's interest in freer trade with the United States reflects both its trade dependence on the US market and its need to promote export-led growth to generate revenues to service its massive foreign debt. Mexico's trade surplus with the United States averaged $3.8 billion or 57 percent of its global surplus from 1985 to 1987. During that period, about 78 percent of Mexico's exports of manufactures went to the United States (Weintraub 1988, 16). Exports of manufactured goods almost doubled from 1985 to 1987 and now account for almost half of Mexico's total exports. Manufactures have replaced petroleum as Mexico's leading export sector (Weintraub 1988, 13). By 1987 Mexican exports to the United States accounted for more than two-thirds of total exports and contributed 13 percent of Mexican GNP.

The surge in manufactured exports raises a concern about long-term market access, however. Although current US barriers to Mexican exports have been modest—affecting only 5 to 10 percent of goods exported to the United States according to data cited by Trigueros (this volume)[48]—continuation of this export growth would mean that existing controls probably would become binding in the future, and pressures for new barriers would build. Because of this, Mexico shares Canada's strong interest in restraining the growth of US process protectionism, or at least in establishing a contractual basis for consultations on trade policies and measures that could affect Mexican trade interests.

Several recent US–Mexico trade agreements provide a good foundation

---

48. These figures do not include antidumping and countervailing duties, which do not reflect protectionism per se and which would probably not be exempted by an FTA in any event.

for prospective efforts to negotiate freer trade between the United States and Mexico. In 1985, the United States and Mexico signed an agreement on subsidies and countervailing duties, which served as a surrogate for Mexican accession to the GATT subsidies code. This pact helped defuse a number of bilateral subsidy/countervail disputes by imposing discipline on Mexican subsidy programs and by requiring an injury test in US countervail cases affecting Mexican goods. In 1986, the terms of Mexico's accession to the GATT were influenced substantially by bilateral negotiations. Finally, the US–Mexico Framework Agreement, signed in November 1987, set out common objectives and administrative mechanisms to begin the process of bilateral trade liberalization. This process already has yielded three relatively minor agreements to liberalize access to markets for textiles, steel, and beer, wine, and spirits (Weintraub 1988, 37).

More recently, Mexico has started down the same road as Canada by proposing exploratory talks on liberalization in four industrial sectors and four service sectors. Much of the interest is in the expansion of existing quotas affecting Mexican exports of textiles and steel to the United States, along with the resolution or avoidance of problems in the auto and petrochemical sectors. Services and investment issues are also on the agenda, reflecting key US interests in the bilateral relationship. Not surprisingly, agricultural issues so far have received less attention, with only limited discussion under the umbrella of the framework agreement of products such as winter vegetables and melons. Agricultural reform will be a particularly hard nut to crack, given the large population, small average land holdings, and low productivity of the Mexican farm sector.[49]

Such an agenda points to the negotiation of either sectoral agreements or bilateral preferences like the Caribbean Basin Initiative (CBI). Neither result would be consistent with the GATT, and therefore either would require a waiver of GATT obligations under the provisions of GATT Article XXV. Ample precedents exist for waivers under both situations (for example, the US–Canada Auto Pact for sectoral agreements and the CBI for trade preferences).

By contrast, the NAFTA concept or a bilateral FTA seems to be more of a long-run ideal than a near-term policy option.[50] A quick examination of the implications for Mexico of the FTA approach exposes several serious problems for Mexico that have led it to shy away from such options.

First, as already noted, the pace of Mexican liberalization may be con-

---

49. For further discussion of this issue, see Gerardo M. Bueno, "A Mexican View," in Diebold (1988, 119).

50. A variant of the first option is proposed by Guy F. Erb and Joseph A. Greenwald, "An Agenda for Talks on Trade," *Journal of Commerce*, 16 December 1988, 8A.

strained in the near term by the need to generate substantial trade surpluses to contribute to the servicing of Mexico's foreign debt. Attempts to circumvent this problem by staging trade concessions so that Mexico gets a longer time period to phase in its reforms than the United States are unlikely to appease Mexican critics because of the effects such a liberalization schedule would have on production and investment decisions. Moreover, the larger the disparity in the timing of the implementation of concessions between the two countries, the harder it would be to sell the agreement in the United States.

Second, Mexico would be hard pressed to achieve significant liberalization of its policies toward foreign direct investment, which often have led to bilateral disputes with the United States. Recent reforms have not been as extensive as those undertaken by Canada in revamping the Foreign Investment Review Agency, in part because of the development objectives of Mexican government planners and in part because of sovereignty concerns that are likely to be even more sensitive than those raised in the debate about the Canadian energy industries.

Third, Mexico and Canada share many of the same concerns over the US countervailing duty law, and US concerns about domestic subsidies in Mexico—especially in the energy and natural resource sectors—mirror those that have been raised about Canadian policies. Mexico would undoubtedly benefit from commitments similar to those the United States gave Canada regarding ex ante consultation on prospective changes in US countervailing duty law and resort to binding arbitration in bilateral countervailing duty disputes. Given the harsh congressional reaction to those provisions, prompted by the failure to achieve complementary discipline on subsidies, however, it would be difficult for the United States to extend similar assurances to Mexico. Moreover, as in the US–Canada talks, most of the subsidy issues that confront US–Mexico trade are unlikely to be resolvable in the context of bilateral negotiations.

In sum, a US–Mexico FTA or Mexican adherence to the Canada–US FTA is not feasible in the short to medium term. A NAFTA will therefore remain an ideal, not a real policy option, for the next decade or more. Nonetheless, given the strong US interest in Mexico's economic development, further proposals to resolve trade and debt problems are likely to emerge. As demonstrated by its early summit meeting with President Salinas, the Bush administration is committed to a "good neighbor" economic policy with Mexico.

In the trade area, there are possibilities for other types of arrangements that could strengthen the as-yet-skeletal framework of bilateral trade relations and result in freer trade. Mexico would clearly benefit from the introduction of formal consultation and dispute settlement procedures and the establishment of a binational commission similar to that negotiated in the Canada–US FTA. Joint administration may prove difficult, however, in the absence of equivalent obligations and in the absence of similar legal procedures. This issue did not arise in the Canada–US context and thus posed no obstacle to the acceptance of the binational commission.

Moreover, the dispute settlement procedures of the Canada–US FTA were relatively easy to negotiate because of the similar legal procedures and unfair-trade regulations of the partners. This has not been the case with Mexico, although the issue has been moot until recently because of the comprehensive nature of Mexican import controls. However, import liberalization has opened up new trade opportunities, which will require new administrative responses by the Mexican government. New institutional procedures in a bilateral US–Mexico pact could help shape those procedures and build a stronger foundation for the bilateral trade relationship.

A US–ASEAN FTA?

Former US Trade Representative Clayton Yeutter often suggested that a US–ASEAN pact could be the next FTA to be negotiated by the United States. Indeed, since February 1988, a joint study of the feasibility of such an agreement has been conducted by private consultants from both regions. In addition, some ASEAN members were included in initial proposals by Secretaries Baker and Shultz for a Pacific area council modeled after the Organization for Economic Cooperation and Development, although these proposals have lain dormant since the end of the Reagan administration.[51]

ASEAN is the only regional grouping under consideration for an FTA. Interestingly, ASEAN itself is not a free trade area. Rather it is a loose association of six countries,[52] whose political objectives so far have outweighed its efforts at economic integration. Under these circumstances, the United States would have to enter into six FTAs, even though they could have similar provisions (as the EC did with the EFTA countries in the 1970s).

Although ASEAN has existed since 1967, only recently has it begun to take steps toward freer flows of goods and services within the region. Tariff preferences for member countries have been instituted gradually pursuant

---

51. For press reports on these initiatives, see "US–ASEAN Talks End; Trade Study Planned," *Journal of Commerce*, 16 February 1988, 5A; Elaine Sciolino, "Shultz Calls for Free Trade in Asia," *New York Times*, 12 July 1988, D6; and Walter S. Mossberg and Alan Murray, "Departure of Treasury Secretary Baker Would Bring Halt to Initiative in Asia," *Wall Street Journal*, 3 August 1988, 22.

52. Brunei, Indonesia, Malaysia, the Philippines, Singapore, and Thailand.

to the 1977 Agreement on ASEAN Preferential Trading Arrangements (Krause 1982, 13). Although internal trade has grown, the increase pales in comparison to the growth in the total trade of ASEAN members, suggesting that "ASEAN was essentially irrelevant to the expansion of international trade among the members of this group" (Wonnacott and Lutz, this volume).

In the aggregate, the ASEAN countries run a trade surplus with the United States, which has averaged $4.5 billion annually from 1985 to 1987 and represents 2.2 percent of total ASEAN GNP. There is substantial variation among ASEAN countries in their trade ties with the United States, however. Not surprisingly, Singapore, the most open economy, is the largest US trading partner in ASEAN, accounting for about 40 percent of ASEAN exports and imports to the United States in 1987. The Philippines exports the least to the United States, with the exception of Brunei, but is the most dependent on the US market, which takes 36 percent of its total exports.

ASEAN interest in an FTA seems to derive from three main concerns. First, ASEAN members would like to guard against the growth of process protectionism in the United States. Several Malaysian exports already are subject to countervailing duties, and penalties have been threatened against Thai exports pursuant to a section 301 case concerning its IPR laws.[53] Although technically unrelated, the removal of Singapore from eligibility under the US GSP program has also contributed to this concern. ASEAN members hope that an FTA would help resolve current disputes and deflect future cases.

Second, ASEAN exports face perhaps even stronger protectionist pressures in Japan and the EC (Ariff, this volume). The ASEAN nations hope that an FTA will strengthen ties with the United States so as to serve as a buffer against Japan, the leading ASEAN trading partner and their leading provider of foreign direct investment. Moreover, more secure market access in the United States would provide insurance against a rollback of trade with Europe if, in fact, a fortress Europe eventuates.

Third, ASEAN members expect that an FTA would encourage more US direct investment, particularly outside the petroleum sector (Ariff, this volume). The United States already has invested more than $10 billion in the region, both in petroleum and in production facilities. The importance of these offshore plants is reflected in the trade flows: transistors, valves,

---

53. In January 1989, the United States announced it would remove several Thai exports from eligibility for GSP preferences on 1 July 1989 in retaliation for the failure of the Thai government to strengthen its national laws protecting pharmaceutical patents and computer software copyrights held by US firms. The measures were crafted, however, so that they probably will affect only about $27 million, or 1 percent of Thai exports to the United States. See Richard Lawrence, "US Reprisals Against Thailand are Minimized," *Journal of Commerce*, 2 February 1989, 4A.

and related manufactures account for both 23 percent of US exports to ASEAN and 17 percent of US imports from ASEAN.

As with the other countries in the Pacific Rim, the United States has both political and economic interests in improved trade ties with the ASEAN. Overall, the ASEAN relationship has been regarded as a means to reinforce a US bastion in Asia to promote democratic goals and to counter the influence of the Soviet Union and the PRC. The main political objective is stability in the region and the promotion of democratic governments. This is particularly relevant for the Philippines, given its long association with and close ties to the United States. This factor alone may justify a separate pact with the Philippines (although perhaps not an FTA) even if US–ASEAN talks do not go forward.

The United States also has substantial economic interests in the ASEAN countries, including the reduction of high tariffs (except in Singapore) and bilateral or regional accords on trade in services and IPRs. In these areas, however, ASEAN interests are quite diffuse and often conflicting. This factor will complicate efforts to harmonize regional policies and to negotiate bilateral trade reforms.

A US–Australia FTA?

Australia is the outlier among the candidate countries. It is the least dependent on US trade, and it is the only candidate country that runs a trade deficit with the United States. In addition, it is the only country that already has rejected the option of an FTA with the United States, although it might have to reconsider if the United States were to negotiate other FTAs with Australia's main trading partners in the Pacific Rim (Snape, this volume).

Australia's lack of interest in an FTA with the United States stems principally from the product composition and the structure of protection of bilateral trade flows. Australia's main exports to the United States are agricultural products (meat, wool, and shellfish) and crude materials (base metals and petroleum) that often face substantial NTBs. For example, US quotas have caused sharp cutbacks in Australian exports of sugar, which are down about 93 percent in volume terms since 1981 (Stove 1988).

In contrast, Australian imports from the United States generally do not face quantitative restrictions, and Australian tariffs, although high in some sectors, are declining rapidly.[54] Although an FTA covering both tariffs and

---

54. Except for textiles and clothing, footwear, and motor vehicles, tariffs are being phased down to a maximum rate of 15 percent by 1992. Quotas in these four sectors

NTBs could provide reciprocal benefits for both countries, Australian officials were rightly concerned that it would be fairly improbable that US agricultural quotas and VERs (especially on meat and sugar) would be liberalized, and US farm programs revised, to provide preferences for already competitive Australian suppliers to the US market.

While rejecting a bilateral deal with the United States, Australia has followed the US precedent by pursuing a bifurcated approach to trade negotiations. In the GATT, it has taken a forceful role in creating the Cairns Group of agricultural exporting nations, which has developed compromise positions that could bridge the gap between the United States and the EC on agricultural reform. At the same time, however, it has established an FTA with New Zealand (which was signed in 1983 and significantly elaborated in 1988) and is exploring similar arrangements with complementary economies such as Canada and the ASEAN. The Closer Economic Relations (CER) pact with New Zealand, like its cousin in North America, has already yielded significant trade and investment reforms and an agreement on trade in services that could provide an important building block to a GATT accord in that area. All tariffs and quotas on bilateral trade between Australia and New Zealand are to be eliminated by 1 July 1990; in addition, antidumping and safeguards measures will no longer be applied on bilateral trade as of that date.[55]

Nonetheless, Australia has not turned a totally deaf ear to FTA overtures from the United States, for two reasons. First, its exports continue to face the threat of new US NTBs such as quotas on lamb, which were proposed but deleted from the 1988 Trade Act. Second, the negotiation by the United States of other FTAs would discriminate against Australian trade interests in those markets. Some Australian exports to the United States (for example, uranium and zinc) are already disadvantaged by preferences accorded Canada by the Canada–US FTA; similar problems could arise in the Pacific Rim countries (Snape, this volume). If such pacts came under active negotiation, Australia would have to join the queue as a defensive measure. Furthermore, such an event would be perceived as a sign that the Uruguay Round had

---

have been, or are being, replaced by tariffs or tariff equivalents through the use *inter alia* of auctions of import rights (see Bergsten et al. 1987). The binding in GATT of these unilateral tariff cuts is a key Australian concession on the table in Geneva. For current rates on products involved in bilateral trade with the United States, see Snape (this volume).

55. For more detail on the background and history of the CER and the results of the 1988 review, see Lloyd (1988) and *Australia New Zealand Closer Economic Relations Trade Agreement: Documents Arising from the 1988 Review*, Department of Foreign Affairs and Trade, Canberra, Australia, August 1988.

faltered and that the protection of the multilateral system, which has benefited small industrial countries like Australia so well, was eroding.

A Pacific Rim FTA?

This discussion has focused on the pros and cons of bilateral FTAs. However, most of the countries in the Pacific Rim assume that a bilateral FTA with the United States would be only one of several that would be negotiated in the region. Indeed, some Taiwanese argue that an FTA with them could be used as a wedge to spur talks with Korea and Japan toward the formation of a regional pact.

Most other countries, however, are wary of a regional pact involving both the United States and Japan. Although those two countries already dominate Pacific Rim trade, their inclusion in a regional FTA would create a substantial strain on the GATT system, on which all the smaller countries in the region depend.

Even a regional FTA without Japan has a strong downside. As noted above, in most instances the MFN tariff cuts achieved in a regional FTA would benefit the Asian countries in the pact more than the United States. Problems also arise with regard to the star-shaped FTA postulated by Park and Yoo (this volume), with the United States at the center and the Asian candidates at the periphery. Such an arrangement would increase the dependence of the peripheral economies on the center (the United States), while complicating their trade relations with each other. The United States would gain in all their markets, while they would compete among themselves for greater access to the US market. At the same time, a Pacific Rim FTA, with or without Japan, would exacerbate European fears and probably perversely result in strengthening proponents of a fortress Europe and accelerating the devolution of the world trading system into trading blocs.

Furthermore, the history of agreements between developed and developing countries is not encouraging. None have resulted in FTAs; rather they have been limited to the extension of trade preferences on specific products or in specific sectors, and those preferences usually have been one-way for developing country exports in the developed country market (as in the Lomé agreement).

During the Reagan administration, Secretaries Baker and Shultz expressed interest in broader trade and economic cooperation among the Pacific Basin countries, although none openly avowed support for an FTA. Their focus was more on linking trade with other economic issues such as debt and exchange rate management. As such, their proposals ran counter to the efforts of those who sought to use bilateral agreements as a means to concentrate attention on trade policy.

Conclusions and Policy Recommendations

This section reviews the overall results that could be attained through the negotiation by the United States of more FTAs, and examines whether they could meet the four US policy objectives postulated at the start of this chapter. In light of these findings, it sets out policy recommendations with regard to both bilateral and multilateral negotiations.

The Limits of FTAs

The FTA approach has been heralded as a means to achieve substantial trade liberalization on a bilateral basis and to bolster efforts currently under way in the Uruguay Round of GATT negotiations to strengthen the world trading system. At the same time, FTAs have been touted as a more effective way than GATT talks for the United States to exert its negotiating leverage to achieve such results and to reduce its trade deficit; indeed, some give the trade balancing goal higher priority than trade liberalization. Proponents of FTAs thus differ on whether the FTA approach should be a complement to, or a substitute for, the GATT process.

When one looks closely at what would be involved in such prospective FTAs, including the US barriers that might have to be removed and the implications for the world trading system, it is clear that the bilateral approach has its limits. Prospective bilateral agreements—particularly in the Pacific Basin—would not (with few exceptions) achieve the desired results for several reasons.

First, FTAs hold little promise of substantial trade reform. In each candidate country, the main trade concessions are likely to be in the area of tariffs. The more restrictive NTBs, including import licensing and certification regulations as well as discriminatory public procurement policies, are likely to be exempted. The ability of the United States to negotiate reductions in such barriers could be constrained by its own unwillingness to put US NTBs on the table in such sensitive areas as textiles and apparel and steel. The statement by a US trade official that the MFA bilateral with Korea would have to coexist with an FTA is instructive in this regard. So, too, is the experience of the Canada–US negotiations regarding countervailing duty and subsidy policies.

In addition, there are many trade barriers that are not amenable to bilateral solutions. Unilateral or bilateral disarmament will not work if the policies and practices of third countries continue to influence world trade and thus distort domestic markets. Key trade problems regarding agriculture and subsidies require global solutions, as was learned in the Canada–US negotiations.

Furthermore, if the liberalization is limited to specific products or sectors and is applied in a discriminatory manner, the agreement could undercut multilateral efforts and could even have perverse effects for US trade. Most past US efforts to open foreign markets selectively have resulted only in a redistribution of import shares, not overall liberalization, as US suppliers received special preferences to the detriment of other exporters. However, such efforts usually are imitated by other countries seeking their own special deals. In the end, such actions often result in market-sharing arrangements instead of market liberalization—an outcome clearly inferior to the maintenance of the GATT for US trading interests.

For this reason, the United States would not be able to achieve its liberalization goals from even the most extensive possible series of bilateral FTAs. A "tariff-free area"—a distinct subset of an FTA—would be the likely outcome, with major NTBs grandfathered (that is, left intact) as was done with subsidy programs and some agricultural quotas in the Canada–US agreement. The maintenance of such barriers in turn would continue to limit sharply the access of US firms to those markets.

Second, more FTAs are likely to detract from, rather than reinforce, the Uruguay Round negotiations. Except for such areas as services and IPRs, bilateral agreements do not hold much promise as building blocks for GATT accords.

This conclusion contrasts sharply with the assessment of the Canada–US FTA. The reason for the difference is straightforward: the Canada–US pact involved economies that were at comparable levels of development and already were substantially integrated, and countries whose trade laws and regulations were quite similar. Moreover, US objectives focused as much, if not more, on rulemaking as on market access in Canada; these rules could serve as models for prospective GATT accords. By comparison, the reduction of foreign trade barriers is a much more dominant US objective with the candidate FTA countries examined in this study.

Perhaps more importantly, however, it is difficult to maintain the credibility of the FTA option without undercutting efforts in the Uruguay Round. The pursuit of more FTAs would send a clear signal to the candidate countries and others that the United States was disillusioned with the multilateral process and that US support for the Uruguay Round was eroding. In most instances, this perception would trigger a defensive reaction by the candidate countries and maybe others, driven by a fear of growing US protectionism and of a further weakening of GATT discipline, to secure access to the US market by negotiating bilateral FTAs.

Moreover, although the threat of more FTAs between the United States and its trading partners may scare countries back to the GATT bargaining table, it may also prompt perverse bilateral responses. Smaller countries might forsake the GATT talks and rush to join the FTA queue, whereas larger traders such as the EC might build their own trading blocs—indeed, proponents of a fortress Europe are bolstered by US efforts to negotiate outside of the GATT. In essence, rather than keeping their feet to the fire in GATT talks, FTAs would lead the candidate countries to sacrifice their multilateral goals for stability in their bilateral relationship with the United States, because they would perceive that the United States was walking away from the Uruguay Round. At the very least, it would be evident that the United States was diverting scarce resources away from the GATT round.

In other words, prospective bilaterals would promote the idea of trading blocs and prompt the defensive strategies noted above. Such a reaction has already led several small countries to rush to try to join the queue. Meanwhile, the EC has warned that a Pacific area agreement could generate perverse reactions and bolster proponents of a fortress Europe. The formation of blocs then would threaten to become a self-fulfilling prophecy.

Third, FTAs could contribute to the improved management of bilateral trade relations by creating new rights and obligations that perforce require new consultative and dispute settlement mechanisms to supervise the operation of the agreements and to monitor and enforce the parties' rights and obligations. Such mechanisms could also provide a means to preempt potential disputes. The binational trade commission, and the provision for binding arbitration to resolve certain types of disputes, that were incorporated in the Canada–US FTA could be useful models for other FTAs. Such provisions seem to be of particular interest to Japan and other countries in the Pacific Basin. However, the establishment of such formal procedures need not require a full-blown FTA, and could be incorporated instead in a consultative framework agreement.

Although such consultative mechanisms need not conflict with GATT objectives of the partner countries, the existence of various bilateral dispute settlement mechanisms could raise problems with regard to the consistency of rulings. For example, different bilateral panels could put forward conflicting interpretations of US obligations regarding the administration of its unfair-trade statutes.

Fourth, FTAs are unlikely to redress bilateral trade imbalances. The magnitude of the liberalization required of candidate countries to cut their surplus with the United States by a substantial amount is beyond the pale of reciprocal trade negotiations. Moreover, the avowed objective of trade diversion implicit in such agreements has little more than temporary political appeal. Efforts by candidate countries to reduce the bilateral imbalance in the short term yield little in terms of trade improvement or political goodwill. Both require a more sustained performance that can only be achieved through complementary changes in macroeconomic and exchange rate policies by the United States and its trading partners.

Implications for US Trade Policy

Interest in FTAs in the United States has resulted from a general dissatisfaction with US trade policy and the trade deficit, and from a growing discontent with the GATT and the multilateral process. Protectionist pressures generated by the massive US trade deficits have led to questions—particularly in Congress, the US labor movement, and the US business community—as to whether the pursuit of negotiations in the GATT can achieve the results needed to open foreign markets to US exports.

Confidence in the GATT and the multilateral process has eroded substantially in recent years. Indeed, disillusion with multilateralism may be the fundamental explanation for the growth in interest in bilateralism. As in the old joke about the beauty contest, "Having seen A, we choose B." In the same way, critics of the GATT have sought an alternative approach, which could maximize US negotiating leverage and produce results quickly. The success of the FTAs with Israel and Canada, although both are unique for political and economic reasons, suggested that perhaps the "magic bullet" to revitalize US trade policy lay in the replication of such FTAs with other trading partners, even though neither agreement is likely to have a significant impact on the US trade deficit.

The magic bullet is a myth. Trade negotiations—and other trade policy measures, whether pursued unilaterally, bilaterally, or multilaterally—can do little to correct the US trade deficit. Such actions can only complement the more fundamental steps that need to be taken in the area of macroeconomic and exchange rate policy in the United States and abroad to bring the US trade and current accounts back down to a sustainable level over the long term (Bergsten 1988; Cline 1989).

Nonetheless, the question remains whether FTAs are a better approach than the GATT process for the conduct of US trade policy, and whether FTAs could be pursued so as to complement the Uruguay Round negotiations. The answer to both queries is a resounding no.

First, as analyzed in the section on "FTAs and the GATT," it is evident that the much-heralded advantages of bilateral accords over the GATT process are illusory. The same problems that are impeding progress on the multilateral front—the unwillingness of countries to make meaningful and politically difficult concessions concerning their own trade barriers—also would impede bilateral progress. There is nothing specific to the GATT that makes its process more difficult.

Second, it is likely that the pursuit of more FTAs, at least those with the candidate countries examined in this study, would be regarded as substitutes for the multilateral process, not complements to it. The main reason for such countries to pursue an FTA with the United States seems to be to take out an insurance policy against new US protectionism and a perceived US pullback from the GATT.

The FTA approach thus carries several risks. It could undercut US efforts and support for the GATT without achieving significant trade reforms through bilateral or regional arrangements. Indeed, FTAs reduce momentum for MFN tariff cuts by creating vested interests in the partner countries for the preservation of the FTA tariff preferences. Furthermore, failure of the Uruguay Round would greatly complicate efforts to resolve global macro-economic problems, and in turn would exacerbate the debt crisis in the developing countries. The correction of the US trade deficit would then become even more difficult.

Conclusions

The conclusions of this study can be summarized as follows:

☐ The future of US trade policy should be tied to a new GATT, one reinvigorated and strengthened by prospective reforms resulting from the Uruguay Round.

☐ GATT negotiations hold a better prospect for trade liberalization than bilateral FTAs. Moreover, *prospective* FTAs would not reinforce the GATT negotiations; indeed, a continuation of FTA negotiations could undermine the Uruguay Round and contribute to the further erosion of the GATT system.

☐ The pursuit of more FTAs would send a clear signal that the United States was disillusioned with the multilateral process. In most instances, this perception would trigger a defensive reaction by US trading partners, leading them to turn away from the GATT talks and instead to try to secure trade preferences in the US market through the negotiation of an FTA.

☐ The bilateral option is distinctly suboptimal. It affords few, if any, advantages over the multilateral process, and yields small results in terms of trade liberalization. Furthermore, FTAs do not significantly affect the bilateral or aggregate US trade balance.

☐ For these reasons, the continuation of the two-track US approach to trade negotiations, which made sense when it was unclear whether there would be a new GATT round and when the bilateral FTA track was limited to Israel and Canada, would be counterproductive. Exploratory talks and/or the negotiation of more FTAs would undercut US efforts in the Uruguay

Round without yielding significant offsetting benefits in terms of trade liberalization.

- ☐ Although the negotiation of FTAs should be avoided, one exception should be made to the general policy against bilateral accords. The "good neighbor" trade policy should be continued with Mexico because of its beneficial impact on trade and economic development, and limited potential for trade diversion. Bilateral negotiations should seek to liberalize trade in specific goods and services sectors. A waiver of GATT obligations under Article XXV should be sought by both countries.

- ☐ Solutions to bilateral problems raised under section 301 and other provisions of US law—such as those where bilateral negotiations are mandated by the 1988 Trade Act to remove unfair foreign trade barriers—should be sought, whenever feasible, in the multilateral context of the Uruguay Round. Their resolution should be an important test of the success of the round.

- ☐ If the GATT round falters, alternatives to the multilateral process should then be considered. The preferred fallback approach would *not* be bilateral agreements, however. Rather, the United States should then pursue an approach similar to the GATT-plus concept of a decade ago among those of its trading partners willing to reduce trade barriers and adopt new trading rules that go beyond the GATT, on a conditional-MFN basis.

- ☐ FTAs provide at best a third-best option for US trade policy; consideration should be given to FTAs with countries in the Pacific Rim only if the GATT round falters.

Acknowledgments

The author benefited significantly from extensive and insightful comments on earlier drafts by C. Michael Aho, C. Fred Bergsten, Richard N. Cooper, William Diebold, Sylvia Ostry, Amelia Porges, and Paul Wonnacott. Cynthia L. McKaughan provided invaluable research assistance, and Angela L. Barnes and other Institute colleagues helped prepare the manuscript for publication.

References

Aho, C. Michael, and Jonathan David Aronson. 1985. *Trade Talks: America Better Listen!* New York: Council on Foreign Relations.

Allgeier, Peter F. 1988. "Korean Trade Policy in the Next Decade: Dealing with Reciprocity." *World Development*, vol. 16, no. 1, 85–97.

Atlantic Council of the United States. 1976. *GATT Plus: A Proposal for Trade Reform*. Report of the Special Advisory Panel to the Trade Committee of the Atlantic Council, Washington.

Baker, James A., III. 1988. "The Geopolitical Implications of the US–Canada Trade Pact." *The International Economy*, January/February, 34–41.

Balassa, Bela, and Marcus Noland. 1988. *Japan in the World Economy*. Washington: Institute for International Economics.

Baucus, Max. 1988. "Pacific Overture." *The International Economy*, November/December, 70–71.

Bayard, Thomas O., and Soo-Gil Young, eds. 1989. *Economic Relations Between the United States and Korea: Conflict or Cooperation?* SPECIAL REPORT 8. Washington: Institute for International Economics.

Bergsten, C. Fred. 1987. "Economic Imbalances and World Politics." *Foreign Affairs*, vol. 65, no. 4 (Spring 1987), 770–794.

Bergsten, C. Fred. 1988. *America in the World Economy: A Strategy for the 1990s*. Washington: Institute for International Economics.

Bergsten, C. Fred, and William R. Cline. 1987. *The United States–Japan Economic Problem*. POLICY ANALYSES IN INTERNATIONAL ECONOMICS 13, revised edition. Washington: Institute for International Economics, January.

Bergsten, C. Fred, Kimberly Ann Elliott, Jeffrey J. Schott, and Wendy E. Takacs. 1987. *Auction Quotas and United States Trade Policy*. POLICY ANALYSES IN INTERNATIONAL ECONOMICS 19. Washington: Institute for International Economics, September.

Bhagwati, Jagdish. 1988. "The Pass-Through Puzzle That Probably Isn't: The Missing Prince from Hamlet." Unpublished paper, Columbia University, December.

Bradley, Bill. 1988. Speech to the New York Economic Club, New York, 8 December.

Brooks, Roger A., ed. 1988. *The U.S.–Republic of China Trade Relationship: Time for a New Strategy*. The Heritage Lectures. Washington: Heritage Foundation.

Brzezinski, Zbigniew. 1988. "America's New Geostrategy." *Foreign Affairs*, vol. 66, no. 4 (Spring), 680–699.

Chen, Phillip M., ed. 1986. "Politics and Economics of a U.S.–ROC Free Trade Area." *Asia and World Institute Monographs* 42. Taipei: Asia and World Institute, October.

Choate, Pat, and Juyne Linger. 1988. "Tailored Trade: Dealing with the World as It Is." *Harvard Business Review*, January–February, 86–93.

Cline, William R. 1989. *American Trade Adjustment: The Global Impact*. POLICY ANALYSES IN INTERNATIONAL ECONOMICS 26. Washington: Institute for International Economics, March.

Destler, I.M. 1979. "U.S.–Japanese Relations and the American Trade Initiative of 1977: Was This 'Trip' Necessary?" In William J. Barnds, ed., *Japan and the United States: Challenges and Opportunities*. New York: New York University Press, 190–230.

Destler, I.M. 1986. *American Trade Politics: System Under Stress*. Washington: Institute for International Economics, and New York: Twentieth Century Fund.

Diebold, William, Jr., 1952. "The End of the I.T.O." *Essays in International Finance* 16. Princeton, N.J.: International Finance Section, Princeton University, October.

Diebold, William, Jr., ed. 1988. *Bilateralism, Multilateralism, and Canada in US Trade Policy*. Cambridge, Mass.: Ballinger for the Council on Foreign Relations.

GATT. 1988. *Review of Developments in the Trading System*. Geneva: GATT.

Gephardt, Richard A. 1988. "More Free Trade Areas?" Statement before the Institute for International Economics, 31 October.

Hamilton, Colleen, and John Whalley. 1988. "Coalitions in the Uruguay Round: The

Extent, Pros and Cons of Developing Country Participation." *NBER Working Paper* 2751. Cambridge, Mass: National Bureau of Economic Research, October.

Holmes, Frank, Ralph Lattimore, and Anthony Hass. 1988. *Partners in the Pacific.* Wellington: New Zealand Trade Development Board.

Hufbauer, Gary Clyde, Joanna Shelton Erb, and Helen P. Starr. 1980. "The GATT Codes and the Unconditional Most-Favored-Nation Principle." *Law and Policy in International Business,* vol. 12, 59–93.

Hufbauer, Gary Clyde, and Jeffrey J. Schott. 1985a. *Economic Sanctions Reconsidered: History and Current Policy.* Washington: Institute for International Economics.

Hufbauer, Gary Clyde, and Jeffrey J. Schott. 1985b. *Trading for Growth: The Next Round of Trade Negotiations.* POLICY ANALYSES IN INTERNATIONAL ECONOMICS 11. Washington: Institute for International Economics, September.

Kim, Kihwan. 1988. "Maintaining Korea's Competitiveness in a Changing Domestic and Global Environment." Luncheon address to a conference on Japan, Korea, and the United States: Pacific Economic Power in the Coming Decade, cosponsored by the Japan Society and the Asia Society, New York, 6 June.

Kissinger, Henry, and Cyrus Vance. 1988. "Bipartisan Objectives for American Foreign Policy." *Foreign Affairs,* vol. 66, no. 5 (Summer), 899–921.

Krause, Lawrence B. 1982. *US Economic Policy Toward the Association of Southeast Asian Nations.* Washington: Brookings Institution.

Leutwiler, Fritz, et al. 1985. *Trade Policies for a Better Future: Proposals for Action.* Geneva: GATT Independent Study Group, March.

Lloyd, P.J. 1988. "Australia–New Zealand Trade Relations: NAFTA to CER," in K. Sinclair, ed., *Tasman Relations, New Zealand and Australia: 1788–1988.* Auckland, New Zealand: Auckland University Press.

Mansfield, Mike. 1987. "The US and Japan: Promises to Keep." Speech to the 19th Japan–America Conference of Mayors and Chamber of Commerce Presidents, Tokyo, 18 November.

Nakasone, Yasuhiro. 1988. "Japan–U.S. Cooperation: The Asian–Pacific Dimension." Address at the School of Advanced International Studies, The Johns Hopkins University, Washington, 10 May.

Patterson, Gardner. 1966. *Discrimination in International Trade: The Policy Issues, 1945–1965.* Princeton, N.J.: Princeton University Press.

Preeg, Ernest H. 1970. *Traders and Diplomats.* Washington: Brookings Institution.

Republic of China, Council for Economic Planning and Development, Executive Yuan. 1989. *Detailed Action Plan for Strengthening Economic and Trade Ties with the United States.* Taipei, March.

Schott, Jeffrey J. 1983. "The GATT Ministerial: A Postmortem." *Challenge,* May/June, 40–45.

Schott, Jeffrey J. 1988. *United States–Canada Free Trade: An Evaluation of the Agreement.* POLICY ANALYSES IN INTERNATIONAL ECONOMICS 24. Washington: Institute for International Economics, April.

Schott, Jeffrey J. 1989a. "US Trade Policy: Implications for US–Korean Trade Relations," in Thomas O. Bayard and Soo-Gil Young, eds., *Economic Relations Between the United States and Korea: Conflict or Cooperation?* Washington: Institute for International Economics.

Schott, Jeffrey J., and Murray G. Smith, eds. 1988. *The Canada–United States Free Trade Agreement: The Global Impact.* Washington: Institute for International Economics.

Snape, Richard H. 1986. "Should Australia Seek a Trade Agreement with the United States?" *Discussion Paper 86/01.* Canberra: Economic Planning Advisory Council and the Department of Trade, June.

Snape, Richard H. 1988. "Is Nondiscrimination Really Dead?" *The World Economy*, vol. 11, no. 1 (March), 1–17.

Stove, Vincent W. 1988. "Australia Cool to Trade Deal." *Journal of Commerce*, 26 February 1988, 8A.

US International Trade Commission. 1985. *Review of the Effectiveness of Trade Dispute Settlement under the GATT and the Tokyo Round Agreements.* Publication 1793. Washington: US International Trade Commission, December.

US International Trade Commission. 1988. *Pros and Cons of Initiating Negotiations with Japan to Explore the Possibility of a U.S.–Japan Free Trade Agreement.* Publication 2120. Washington: US International Trade Commission, September.

US International Trade Commission. 1989. *The Pros and Cons of Entering into Negotiations on Free Trade Area Agreements with Taiwan, the Republic of Korea, and ASEAN, or the Pacific Rim Region in General.* Publication 2166. Washington: US International Trade Commission, March.

Verity, C. William. 1988. "Remarks before the Council on Foreign Relations." *US Department of Commerce News*, 8 June.

Viner, Jacob. 1950. *The Customs Union Issue.* New York: Carnegie Endowment for International Peace.

Weintraub, Sidney. 1988. "Mexican Trade Policy and the North American Community." *Significant Issues Series*, vol. X, no. 14. Washington: Center for Strategic and International Studies.

Winham, Gilbert R. 1986. *International Trade and the Tokyo Round Negotiations.* Princeton, N.J.: Princeton University Press.

Wonnacott, Paul. 1987. *The United States and Canada: The Quest for Free Trade.* POLICY ANALYSES IN INTERNATIONAL ECONOMICS 16. Washington: Institute for International Economics, March.

2

Is There a Case for Free Trade Areas?

Paul Wonnacott and Mark Lutz

A rose by any other name is still a rose. But the simple messages carried by words are important. Once Lenin had preempted the title "Bolshevik" (one of the majority) and stuck his adversaries with the term "Menshevik" (one of the minority), he had already come close to winning by definition. Who wants to resist the will of the majority?

We come here today to discuss prospective free trade areas (FTAs), but we may, after reflection, want to bury some of them. The most important single observation about FTAs and their close cousins, customs unions,[1] is that they do not necessarily represent a move toward free trade. They do not necessarily cause an improvement in international efficiency; it is possible that they reduce efficiency and real incomes instead. This was the central point in Viner's classic, *The Customs Union Issue* (1950). An FTA may be trade creating, generating additional international trade and improving real incomes. But it also is a discriminatory arrangement. Some countries are in; some are out. Thus, trade may be rearranged and redirected when an FTA is formed. Such trade diversion generally represents a step away from efficiency.

If that is so, why be distracted by preferential free trade groupings? There is a preferable alternative, namely, multilateral reductions in trade barriers on a most-favored-nation (MFN) basis, such as those that have occurred in various rounds of negotiations under the auspices of the General Agreement on Tariffs and Trade (GATT). It cannot, of course, be proved that such reductions in trade barriers lead to an increase in world welfare; indeed,

---

1. In this chapter we often use the term "free trade area" broadly to include customs unions.

Paul Wonnacott is Professor of Economics at the University of Maryland. Mark Lutz is an economist with the International Monetary Fund. The authors present their own views, not necessarily those of their institutions.

the opposite may be the case in the presence of domestic economic distortions. But the general presumption in favor of freer trade on an MFN basis is one of the most robust conclusions to come out of the study of economics in the past two hundred years.

The reason to look at FTAs is that further multilateral liberalization may be difficult because of two well-recognized, interrelated difficulties: the free-rider problem and the convoy problem. During a multilateral negotiation, when concessions are to be extended to all parties, there is a political incentive to hold back, keeping one's own tariff barriers up while hoping to get the advantages of other countries' tariff cuts. The only way to avoid free riding is to make cuts only when every participant is willing to do so. In this case, the least willing participant determines the pace of negotiations; the speed of the convoy moving toward freer trade is limited by the speed of the slowest ship.

For a large country such as the United States, the free-rider problem can be particularly frustrating. The United States has little opportunity to hitch a free ride; if the United States does not go along, a general cut in trade barriers is unlikely. Such frustrations help to explain the greater emphasis that the United States has placed on the bilateral approach in the past decade, either to deal with specific problems—such as the beef, citrus, and microchip negotiations with the Japanese—or to promote a broader reduction in bilateral barriers, such as in the free trade agreements with Israel and Canada. These two agreements lead to the obvious question: should there be others?

To shed light on this question, we begin with the traditional analytic framework, based largely on Viner's distinction between trade creation and trade diversion. We then move on to a number of analytic issues that have been touched upon rather lightly in the literature, but that gain importance once we begin to look at potential new agreements:

- ☐ Is geographical proximity of the members of an FTA important? With the exception of Mexico, any of the prospective free trade associations that the United States might enter would include countries separated by oceans; indeed, some would span the Pacific Ocean.

- ☐ Is it desirable for members of an FTA to be similar in terms of the types of products they produce, or in terms of their income levels?

- ☐ If two countries A and B are already members of an FTA, what are the implications for both A and B of a new agreement between A and C?

- ☐ When a series of agreements is entered, what are the implications for countries left out?

☐ Is it desirable to make exceptions to GATT Article XXIV, which requires that a preferential free trade agreement eliminate trade barriers on substantially all the trade between the members? Under what circumstances might some products be excluded from free trade?

This chapter also addresses the important issue of economies of scale, and presents some tentative evidence on how free trade agreements have affected trading patterns.

One other preliminary matter should be noted. In judging an FTA, our principal criterion of success will be economic success; that is, under what circumstances does an FTA contribute to economic efficiency? But there is another aspect to success: political success. The political side is even more important for FTAs than for most other policy issues. After all, it is a political constraint—the actual or perceived inability to achieve the better economic option of multilateral reductions in trade barriers—that provides the justification for the study of the second-best option of FTAs.

To some extent, economic success and political success are interrelated. Unless an FTA is successful enough politically to be established in the first place and to survive, its potential economic success is not a very important issue. Furthermore, if an FTA results in a large net reduction in efficiency and is thus highly unsuccessful from an economic viewpoint, it is unlikely to survive politically. This is particularly so if economic costs are concentrated in one of the partners and economic gains in another.

Nevertheless, political success and economic success are far from synonymous. The history of protectionism makes it amply clear that inferior economic arrangements may be highly successful politically, and have great survivability.

It is sometimes argued that, with the loss of momentum in the GATT, international rules should be loosened and countries should be free to make any international agreements they find in their own interest. The resulting process may be untidy, but as groups of countries grope toward mutually beneficial arrangements, the overall efficiency of the world economy is likely to increase. The distinction between economic success and political success leads us to reject this argument. While special arrangements that bend the GATT rules may be desirable, they should not be accepted uncritically; the burden of proof is on the proponents. Just as protection can be politically popular, so trade diversion can be politically popular: benefits go to producers with their focused political power, while the costs fall on foreigners and on buyers whose diffused interests are often ignored by those wielding political power. The GATT rules have performed two very useful functions: the commitment to bound duties has provided governments with some shield against domestic groups pressing for protection, and the GATT rules have protected the interests of consumers and third countries.

To recapitulate, we start from three basic premises:

☐ We accept the general case for multilateral free trade, and the presumption that it will result in increased efficiency.

☐ We start with the presumption that a code of international rules—such as those of the GATT—is desirable. A positive case must be made for any departures from the established rules.

☐ We start without any presumption that a prospective FTA will represent a movement toward a more efficient or toward a less efficient economy; it may do either, depending on its detailed effects.

Economic Efficiency: Trade Creation and Trade Diversion

In principle, the correct way to judge the overall economic effects of an FTA is to compare real income under an FTA with the real income that would occur with the status quo. Such a comprehensive approach is difficult, however, which is why Viner's distinction between trade creation and trade diversion remains at the core of customs union theory. This distinction allows us to get some handle on the efficiency effects without doing a complete, comprehensive empirical study.

As a classical economist, Viner concentrated on the costs of production. In general, international trade provides benefits by making lower-cost goods available. But when an FTA is formed, there are two conflicting movements: toward lower-cost sources for some goods, and toward higher-cost sources for others. Specifically, where new international trade is *created*, with partner A now buying goods from partner B that it previously produced at home, efficiency is improved; B's goods will be imported because they are cheaper. On the other hand, if trade is *diverted*, with partner A now buying from partner B the goods that it previously imported from outside countries, then efficiency generally falls. Partner B is generally a higher-cost producer than the outside country; otherwise, A would have imported from B even before the FTA was formed. In practice, of course, an FTA will have both trade-creating and trade-diverting effects. However, this distinction does allow us to make a first pass at the efficiency question: if trade creation dominates, there is a presumption that efficiency will be improved. If trade diversion dominates, Viner concluded that the effect would be a fall in efficiency.

However, the distinction between trade creation and trade diversion represents an oversimplification. There are several grounds on which an FTA may be desirable even if it is predominantly trade diverting.

Less Distorted Consumption

As Meade (1955), Lipsey (1957), and others pointed out at an early stage, trade diversion results from a preferential cut in tariffs. Because tariffs are eliminated, the price to partner A's consumers may well be lower on the products newly imported from partner B, even though B's costs of production exceed those of country C, the previous supplier. The pattern of consumption as a result may be less distorted, and this beneficial effect may more than compensate for the fact that B's costs of production are higher than those of outside countries. By focusing narrowly on the costs of production, Viner missed the possibility of an improved pattern of consumption.

The Meade–Lipsey argument may be extended to intermediate products: again, diversion of trade does not necessarily lead to a decline in efficiency. With duty-free imported inputs from the FTA partner, the improved efficiency of the productive process may compensate for the switch to a less efficient source of imports.

Economies of Scale

Economies of large-scale production provide a second reason why an FTA may improve efficiency even if it is predominantly trade diverting. Even though B's goods were initially more costly than those of outside producers, their costs may become competitive by international standards once B has access to A's market, and is able as a consequence to exploit economies of scale. Even if B remains a higher-cost producer than outside countries, economies of scale may cause a reduction in total costs.

For example, suppose that B produced 100 units of a good for its own home market prior to the establishment of an FTA, at an excess cost of $10 per unit. (That is, B's cost per unit is $10 above the price at which the good is available from countries outside the prospective FTA.) Then, after the FTA is established, B produces 200 units for the combined internal markets of A and B, and its excess costs fall to an average of $4 per unit as a result of economies of scale. Total excess costs in this product fall from $1,000 to $800 as a result of the formation of the FTA. Even though trade has been diverted to a source with higher average costs, there nevertheless has been a gain in efficiency. (In this example, B's *marginal* costs are $2 below the world price.) This possible gain in efficiency was recognized by Viner, but he dismissed economies of scale as not very important. Nevertheless, during the later years of his life, he began to modify his views, and empirical and theoretical work over the past quarter century has identified economies of scale as one of the key issues in FTAs. More will be said on this subject later.

Nontariff Barriers

The idea that trade diversion is economically undesirable is based on the assumption that tariffs constitute the prevailing barrier to trade. If tariffs are in fact the only barrier, then the diversion of trade from an outside source generally does involve higher costs of production, and the probability of lower efficiency. If outside countries were not the lower-cost source, presumably they would not have been used in the first place.

However, as quotas and voluntary export restraints become more prominent features of the protective framework, it is no longer so clear that trade diversion will reduce efficiency. Once a preferential reduction in barriers has been made, partner B may replace an outside nation as the source of supply, but partner B is not necessarily the higher-cost producer; B's low-cost exports may have been restrained by A's quantitative restrictions. If partner B is in fact the lower-cost source, then there will be a conflict between efficiency—which in this case can be promoted by trade diversion—and the safeguarding of the interests of outside nations. Clearly, the gradual replacement of tariffs with quantitative restraints over the past several decades has muddied the analysis of trade diversion; it has provided another reason why trade diversion need not be bad.

Balance of Payments Disequilibrium

Finally, exchange rate misalignments and balance of payments disequilibria may mean that imports with the lowest monetary costs do not measure economic costs accurately, or, in other words, necessarily have the lowest opportunity costs. Perhaps trade discrimination can help to compensate for balance of payments disequilibria. This was the rationale for the scarce currency clause of the International Monetary Fund. It recognized that discrimination might be desirable against countries with an excessively strong balance of payments. Deficit countries might thereby keep relatively open trading relationships with each other, even in circumstances where they were restricting their imports for balance of payments reasons.

The desire to help the United States deal with its trade deficits—and, in particular, to help the United States gain markets at the expense of the Japanese—appears to be one of the motives behind proposals for an FTA between the Republic of China and the United States. There is some frustration that cuts in Taiwan's tariffs, aimed at opening the market to imports from the United States, have led to a flood of Japanese and Korean products instead.[2]

---

2. See, for example, comments by Jerry Liang, President of Goodyear Taiwan Limited, in Brooks (1988, 21).

Although this point can be valid in principle, we would be very uncomfortable about the establishment of an FTA as a way of dealing with trade imbalances. Generally, tariff reductions in an FTA are staged over an extended period—10 years in the Canada–US agreement. It is appropriate to focus on long-run goals when establishing an FTA. It would, for example, have been a mistake to establish the European Community (EC) on the assumption that the "dollar shortage" would be a permanent feature of the international economy, justifying long-run discrimination against US exports.

The scarce currency clause was intended for short-run use, with discrimination to be abandoned as payments balances returned toward equilibrium. If trade discrimination is to be used as a way of dealing with payments imbalances, we would prefer to consider temporary arrangements along the general lines of the scarce currency clause, rather than the establishment of an FTA, unless the FTA will also be desirable on its own merits in the long run, after the payments problems pass.[3]

In spite of these four qualifications, the distinction between trade creation and trade diversion provides a very large first step in the analysis of an FTA. Specifically, it leads to the following conclusions:

First, increases in internal trade among the members of an FTA should not be taken as an indicator of the economic success of the FTA. Such increases are a measure of how *powerful* the effects of the FTA have been, but these effects can be either good or bad. The overall increase in internal trade combines the newly created international trade (which is good) and the diversion of trade from outside sources to partners within the FTA (which is generally bad). To begin to assess the desirability of an FTA, it is necessary to separate the increase in internal trade due to trade creation from that due to trade diversion, as we shall see in more detail toward the end of the chapter.

Second, the distinction between trade creation and trade diversion provides powerful support for GATT Article XXIV—an article that at first seems paradoxical because it says in effect that a partial preferential agreement (such as the old British Commonwealth) is undesirable, while a complete preferential agreement, covering all products, is generally desirable.

The problem with partial agreements, covering some products but not others, is that the dynamics of the negotiating process can lead to an

---

3. The case for a US–Taiwan FTA seems to be based partly on an uncritical acceptance of the assumption that efficiency would be enhanced by a diversion of trade from Japanese to US sources of supply (Brooks 1988, 15). Even where payments imbalances make this true in the short run, it will generally not be true in the long run.

emphasis on trade diversion and relatively little trade creation. To see why, suppose that countries are permitted to get together to make any preferential agreements they wish. A natural way for a country to open negotiations would be something like the following: "Look, we're now importing computer chips from Japan, while you're importing TV sets from Hong Kong. We'll cut our tariffs on your chips—allowing you to displace the Japanese as suppliers to our market—if you will cut your tariffs on our TVs, and thus allow us to come into your market and compete with those unfair, low-wage producers from Hong Kong." Negotiators will be less enthusiastic about tariff cuts that would generate new imports from the partner country, causing a shrinkage of the corresponding domestic industry. Thus, if countries are allowed to pick and choose among products, the negotiating process is likely to be biased, resulting mostly in trade diversion and avoiding trade-creating tariff cuts. In the words of the Snape Report on a possible US–Australia FTA (1986, 91), "there is a tension between what tends to be economically beneficial [that is, trade creation] and what is politically easy." Again, we observe a distinction between economic success and political success, which provides a major rationale for GATT Article XXIV. It not only protects the rights of outside nations; it also helps to ensure efficiency within an FTA itself.

However, the experience of the past quarter century suggests that questions should at least be raised regarding Article XXIV, with its rule that the internal barriers on "substantially all" trade must be eliminated by a customs union or FTA. Specifically, the inclusion of agricultural trade within the EC scarcely seems to have led to greater efficiency of the world economy. Although the Common Agricultural Policy (CAP) fails to meet the other major criterion of Article XXIV—that barriers to imports from nonmember countries "should not on the whole be higher or more restrictive" than those preceding the customs union—the CAP has in fact persisted, with unfortunate effects on world agricultural trade. This suggests a rather uncomfortable conclusion: perhaps more thought should be given to exceptions than in the past. If so, however, closer consultation with outside countries—either through the GATT or more directly—would be needed to provide some assurance that exceptions were not simply an excuse for concentrating on trade diversion. That is a tall order. This point also underlines the importance of progress on agriculture in the current GATT round.

The "substantially all" test may also be questioned because of the way in which free trade groupings have in fact developed. In Europe, the sectoral agreement in coal and steel was from the beginning intended as a stepping stone toward a more general economic and political union (Diebold 1959, 13); in fact, it was soon followed by the establishment of the EC. The US–

Canadian Auto Pact of 1965 likewise preceded the recent comprehensive free trade agreement, although this was more a historic accident than an unfolding plan. The point here is that sectoral agreements can lead to more complete agreements, and should therefore perhaps be accorded a degree of tolerance.

One other development of the past quarter century—namely, the increasing reliance on quantitative restrictions (QRs) rather than tariffs as a protective device—also raises questions about the "substantially all" trade test of Article XXIV. A sector-by-sector negotiation to relax quotas on a bilateral basis should not lead to trade diversion unless QRs are tightened on imports from third countries. Thus, in the event of selective relaxation of QRs, Article XXIV may be replaced by a relatively simple test: is a tightening of QRs on other countries being avoided? If so, then a *prima facie* case can be made that the selective relaxation promotes efficiency, and does not come at the expense of other countries. (Of course, the facts may be unclear. As time passes, it is uncertain what may happen to restraints on third-country goods.) This point has clear implications for the discussions between the United States and Mexico, which may lead to the easing of QRs on selected US imports from Mexico.

Once again, however, the argument can become complex. As noted earlier, QRs mean that we can no longer assume that trade diversion means a switch to a higher-cost, less efficient source. Thus, the test suggested in the previous paragraph—that selective relaxations of quotas not be accompanied by a tightening of quotas on imports from third countries—is a sufficient but not necessary condition for an increase in efficiency. Efficiency might be improved even if third-country quotas were tightened, and trade diverted, but perhaps it is best to tiptoe away from this conclusion. Article XXIV is aimed not simply at ensuring efficiency, but also at protecting the interests of nonmember countries. Regardless of their efficiency effects, preferential relaxations of quotas that cut down third-country exports would create political strains in the international trading system.

To sum up the discussion of GATT Article XXIV: the rule against sectoral agreements generally makes sense. However, sectoral agreements to relax quotas should be an exception to this rule, provided only that QRs on imports from third countries are not tightened. Moreover, a sectoral arrangement may be a precursor to a more general free trade agreement, and may be desirable if the prospective FTA will increase efficiency.

A third conclusion is that an FTA—with each member country free to set its own tariffs—generally dominates a customs union with its common external tariff (CET). The reasons are straightforward. Where trade diversion occurs—with partner A now buying a product from partner B that it previously obtained more cheaply from the outside world—the benefits will go to producers in B while the higher costs will be borne by purchasers in A. With an FTA, partner A can escape these costs by unilaterally cutting tariffs and thus switching the source of supply back to outside nations, with their lower costs. Within a customs union no such unilateral decision is possible; any cut in the CET will require an agreement with the government of B, over the objections of its producers. In brief, the political forces within an FTA are likely to lead to less restrictive trade policies toward outside countries than would occur with a customs union.

This political pressure for unilateral tariff cuts by individual members of an FTA can also occur even where trade diversion has not taken place, and where an intermediate good is still being imported from an outside country after an FTA is established. Within an FTA, drawbacks of duties on intermediate goods must be disallowed; otherwise, there will be inefficient transshipments, with purchasers in each of the countries buying from producers in the partner nations in order to avoid the cost of tariffs on imported inputs. Thus, although drawbacks generally promote efficiency, they do not do so within a free trade association (see Wonnacott 1987, 136–38). Because drawbacks are disallowed, producers facing high tariffs on intermediate imports are at a competitive disadvantage with respect to competitors in the trading partner. With the recent ratification of the Canada–US FTA, there has already been some discussion in Canada over the desirability of cutting tariffs on overseas imports of intermediate products.

To sum up: an FTA is generally superior on economic grounds to either a loose partial preference system or a tighter customs union. This is fortunate, because political considerations favor an FTA rather than a customs union for most of the prospective groupings under consideration. In the Canadian and Israeli cases, a customs union would have been out of the question. The smaller nation could scarcely have expected to make a major input into US trade policy toward third countries, and a customs union thus would have required a politically unacceptable commitment to have their trade policies made in Washington. Here, then, we have a contrast to the earlier conclusion; on this point, political factors are likely to lead to the better economic outcome.

Trade Creation and Trade Diversion: Secondary Criteria

The distinction between trade creation and trade diversion provides a shortcut, a way of coming to a preliminary conclusion without doing a complete study of the impact of a free trade agreement on real incomes. In turn, there is a second level of shortcuts that gives some idea of whether an

FTA is likely to be trade creating or trade diverting without engaging in a detailed examination.

The Height of Trade Barriers

The trade creation/trade diversion ratio is likely to be high, and an FTA therefore desirable, if:

☐ The tariffs of outside countries are high. Most obviously, if outside countries had prohibitive tariffs on all imports, there would be no trade to be diverted.

☐ The tariffs of prospective members are high before the establishment of the FTA. If so, there will again be little trade with third countries to be diverted, and a lot of trade is likely to be created within the FTA.

☐ After the establishment of the FTA, the tariffs on external trade are low.

The first two points mean that the case for FTAs has declined over recent decades as trade barriers have been reduced. We thus have a paradox. As the GATT system has been successful, it has weakened the case for FTAs, but its past successes have made future multilateral successes harder and harder to achieve. The GATT may be running out of steam, causing countries to turn to the bilateral alternative. The success of GATT has at once made free trade groupings less desirable, but more likely to be considered.

Characteristics of the Partners

Trade creation is likely to be great, and trade diversion small, if the prospective members of an FTA are natural trading partners. Several points are relevant:

☐ Are the prospective members already major trading partners? If so, the FTA will be reinforcing natural trading patterns, not artificially diverting them.

☐ Are the prospective members close geographically? Groupings of distant nations may be economically inefficient because of the high transportation costs. This has declined in importance in the past half century, as transportation and communication have become much cheaper and faster.[4]

---

4. On improvements in transportation and communications, see Cooper (1986).

Nevertheless, the farther apart the prospective members, the more critically an FTA should be studied.

Two other characteristics of the members are much more difficult to evaluate:

☐ Are the members competitive or complementary? At first glance, an FTA would seem to be desirable if the members' economies are complementary; then they would be natural trading partners. It is therefore surprising that one of the criteria listed by Viner was that an FTA was more desirable "the *less* the degree of complementarity—or the *greater* the degree of rivalry—of the member countries with respect to *protected* industries, prior to customs union" (Viner 1950, 51, italics in original). This has been the most controversial of Viner's conclusions.

Viner's case for competitiveness can be made as follows. If the countries' economies are similar, they will continue to import third-country goods in which neither has a comparative advantage; trade diversion will be small. On the other hand, if their protected industries are complementary, trade diversion will be great. Complementarity will mean that they can get along with small quantities of imports from third countries. As they cut back on such imports, efficiency will suffer.

The opposite case, that in favor of complementary economies, can be made as follows. If the economies are complementary, there are major differences in comparative advantage among them. This means that, for every dollar's worth of trade that is created, the gains will be large. It is important to look not only at the amount of trade created, but also at the gain for each dollar of new trade.

Thus, the important point would seem to be not simply whether the countries' economies are complementary or competitive. The central issue is the cost structures of the prospective members, relative to the costs of *outside* countries. Complementarity is desirable *if* the countries are close to (or below) world cost levels. Then the gains per unit of trade creation will be large, and the costs per unit of trade diversion small.

☐ Are the countries at similar or different levels of development? Perhaps the most difficult question of all faces the less developed countries (LDCs): if they consider FTAs, should they look to the developed countries, or to other LDCs, as potential partners?

If countries at quite different stages of development join in an FTA, major political strains are likely to arise because of sharply different perceptions. Producers in the developed country may consider the less developed partner an unfair competitor because of its low wages. The less developed country may view the more developed partner as an impossibly stiff competitor because of its more advanced technology and high productivity. Even if the gains are evenly balanced, it is quite possible that each partner will feel aggrieved. The sharp difference in perception is one of the reasons why special arrangements between the developed and the less developed countries have involved mainly unilateral preferences by the developed countries over the past few decades. This, in our view, has not necessarily been the best way to go; unilateral preferences have been based on a rhetorical question demanding the wrong (negative) answer: "How can Brazil possibly compete with Germany in selling into the US market?" In practice, its lower wages may put it in a very good position to do so. But the political problem of widely differing perceptions rules out most FTAs between developed and less developed countries. The poor prospects for political success mean that, for most combinations of developed and less developed countries, it is not worthwhile to undertake a detailed analysis of possible economic success.

For the developing countries, associations with other LDCs have at once major attractions and major disadvantages. The major attraction is the possibility of gaining access to larger markets; this may facilitate the development of manufacturing with its economies of scale. Except in fortuitous circumstances, however, there also may be major political obstacles to success in such associations. The problem might be compared to that of the 19th-century US South, a region that was a net exporter to the world market and suffered economic losses when it was forced to buy highly protected manufactures from the North. In the 19th century, this economic problem was a factor in the secessionist movement. In modern customs unions among developing countries, a similar imbalance in gains and losses has created strains. For example, feelings in some areas that they were not sharing in the gains, but instead were simply paying high prices for their partners' goods, have been a factor in the failure of efforts toward integration in East Africa. In the Andean Pact an attempt has been made to divide the gains more evenly by allocating the right to produce various goods among the various members. But this has tended to undercut the rationale for integration in the first place. For example, when one country is given the right to produce some types of automobiles, with other vehicles allocated to other nations, there is little hope for gaining major economies of scale (Wonnacott 1984).

In summary, the division of gains is a major economic and political problem of almost any association that includes developing countries, whether these countries join with other developing nations or with developed nations. The only exception—where the prospects of political success seem relatively good—are cases in which developing countries already are competitive in world markets for manufactured goods. Success holds open the door to further successes.

Economies of Scale and Market Access

Economies of scale provide one of the keys to success of a free trade association. For example, empirical estimates of the effects of a Canada–US FTA indicated that most of the gains would be derived from greater economies of scale (see, for example, Harris 1985, and Wonnacott and Wonnacott 1967). But while economies of scale offer the promise of major gains, they also introduce dangers. In the presence of economies of scale, many decisions cannot be made on a marginal, gradual basis. Production of specific goods can be undertaken economically only if fairly large quantities are to be made. This means that, within an FTA, it is important not only to reduce trade barriers, but also to have assurances that the barriers will stay down. It would be risky to gear up for sales to the partner's market if these markets might be closed.

It is precisely this problem that drove Canada to initiate free trade talks with the United States. As a result of previous multilateral reductions in tariff rates, Canadian manufacturers could no longer count on a comfortable existence in a protected domestic market; they were increasingly forced to look toward export markets, predominantly those in the United States. But as they did so, they were worried by the prospects of sudden changes in their terms of access, particularly from countervailing duties. Indeed, fear rather than hope seems to have been the most powerful motivator of the Canadian initiative.

On this point, Canadian concerns were only partially eased; the Canada–US agreement sets out improved procedures for consultation and dispute settlement, and provides Canada some protection against future extensions of US law. But Canada's main objectives, namely, a more comprehensive agreement on the use of subsidies and on the application of countervailing duties, remain unfulfilled; the parties have agreed to continue negotiations over the next few years. How this issue is resolved will have a major effect on the attractiveness of the United States as a partner in future free trade negotiations, because the Canada–US agreement would presumably be the starting point for future negotiations between either of these countries and a potential new partner.

In passing, we note that recent developments in international trade theory have underlined both the importance of economies of scale and the tension that they can introduce between the interests of single nations and the common interests of nations as a group. Since the early literature on infant industries, economies of scale have been recognized as providing one of the few intellectually valid arguments for protection. A single nation can, under certain circumstances, gain from the imposition of a tariff in the presence of economies of scale. At the same time, economies of scale greatly increase the common interest in relatively free trade: protection splits the world market up into small, inefficient units. Some recent work has looked in greater detail at the way in which economies of scale can provide a reason for protection (Brander and Spencer 1984), while other work has emphasized the narrowness of the assumptions required to make this case for protection (Horstmann and Markusen 1986).

Outside Countries: Establishing Triangles

Once two countries A and B have a free trade agreement, how does it affect the desirability of a new agreement between one of these countries and another partner, C? And if there are agreements between A and B, and between A and C, will this add to the attractiveness of an association between B and C that will complete the triangular set of agreements?

Consider first the desirability of following up an agreement between A and B with another between A and C. From C's viewpoint, such an agreement may be attractive to recapture markets in A that would otherwise be lost to B. The more trade is diverted by the original FTA, the more attractive membership will become to outside countries. However, where FTAs are having a major trade-diverting effect, C may be put in the difficult position of choosing between a new arrangement with A and maintaining its relationships with the rest of the world. Another option is for C to become involved in direct discussions with A and/or B at an early stage to reduce the negative effects of the original agreement between A and B. This alternative has both political and economic advantages, particularly insofar as it helps C to avoid a dilemma where it feels driven by trade diversion to seek an otherwise undesirable association with A or B.

Now consider the desirability of an overlapping set of agreements for one of the original members, either A or B. Particularly for the smaller partner— Canada in the current example—there is much to be said for approaching new partners. We have already seen how the logic of an FTA may drive Canada to consider unilateral cuts on tariffs on imports from third countries, particularly those on intermediate inputs. If there is an advantage in cutting tariffs anyway, why not try to get something in return, perhaps moving to another comprehensive free trade agreement with, say, the EC?

Furthermore, being at the apex of a triangle has significant advantages for the smaller country. For example, if Canada had free trade agreements with both the United States and the EC, it would have preferential access to both markets: it would have a preference over the United States in selling to Europe, and over Europe in selling to the United States (R. J. Wonnacott 1975). Indeed, from Canada's viewpoint, such an arrangement might be preferable to a comprehensive agreement including the United States, Canada, and the European Community, regardless of its overall economic desirability. Specifically, the preferential access would allow Canadian producers to sell some products at higher prices to the United States on the one hand and to Europe on the other. This would benefit Canadian producers even if it were trade diverting and resulted in lower efficiency and higher costs to purchasers in the importing nations.

Here is an example of the importance of being small. Because of Canada's small size, two overlapping agreements possibly might be stable; the windfalls granted to Canada might be tolerable because they would not be very large in the overall scheme of things. Nevertheless, this does raise a question: why would Europe—or Japan, or other nations—be diverted into negotiations with Canada when the main event is trade with the United States?

For most outside countries, the agreement between Canada and the United States does not make an agreement with the United States significantly more or less desirable, since Canada is relatively small in the overall North American picture. There can be exceptions—such as Australia—where similarities with the Canadian economy lead to fears of trade diversion, a point we already have touched on. Nevertheless, for most third countries, the significance of the Canada–US agreement and the US–Israeli agreement is that they have opened up the question. Having already entered two free trade agreements, the United States has set precedents and a framework for others.

Regional Associations and Changing Trade Patterns

The effects of regional associations obviously can be complicated. We can nevertheless shed some light on their effects by looking at changes in trade patterns. Of course, the limited number of such associations makes it difficult to generalize. Our observations will certainly be ad hoc; we only hope to have risen to what Harry Johnson used to call "systematic ad hockery."

Table 2.1 lists the members of eight regional associations established in the past three decades. Table 2.2 shows how trading patterns have changed, with the associations ranked according to the increase in internal trade among the members after the association was established (exports plus

Table 2.1   Selected regional associations

Association	Year of formation	Member nations
Andean Pact[a]	1969	Bolivia, Chile, Colombia, Ecuador, Peru, Venezuela
Association of Southeast Asian Nations (ASEAN)	1967	Brunei, Indonesia, Malaysia, the Philippines, Singapore, Thailand
Central American Common Market (CACM)	1960	Costa Rica, El Salvador, Guatemala, Honduras, Nicaragua
East African Community (EAC)	1967	Kenya, Tanzania, Uganda
European Community (EC)		
EC6	1958	Belgium, France, Germany, Italy, Luxembourg, the Netherlands
EC9	1972	EC6 plus Denmark, Ireland, United Kingdom
European Free Trade Association (EFTA)[b]	1960	Austria, Denmark, Finland, Norway, Portugal, Sweden, Switzerland, United Kingdom
Latin American Free Trade Area (LAFTA)[c]	1961	Argentina, Brazil, Chile, Colombia, Ecuador, Mexico, Paraguay, Peru, Uruguay
New Zealand–Australia Free Trade Area (NAFTA)	1965	Australia, New Zealand

a. Venezuela joined in 1973 and Chile withdrew in 1976. Data for the Pact include all six members.
b. Finland was granted associate status in March 1961 and is included in the data compiled. In 1972, Denmark and the United Kingdom withdrew from the EFTA and joined the EC.
c. Venezuela joined in August 1966 and Bolivia five months later but are not included in the data compiled.

Table 2.2 Trade patterns of regional associations
(percentage of combined GDP of member nations)

Association and time periods[a]	Internal trade Base	Later / Change	External trade Base	Later / Change	Total trade Base	Later / Change
Readily apparent increases in internal trade						
CACM[b]	1.8	10.0	33.4	33.2	35.2	43.2
1957–60 1966–70		8.2		−0.2		8.0
EC6						
1953–57 1963–67	8.1	13.1	20.0	17.9	28.1	31.0
		5.0		−2.1		2.9
1953–57 1968–72	8.1	17.2	20.0	18.3	28.1	35.5
		9.1		−1.7		7.4
EC9						
1968–72 1978–82	17.6	24.3	17.9	24.0	35.5	48.3
		6.7		6.1		12.8
EFTA						
1955–59 1965–69	6.9	8.7	30.1	27.4	37.0	36.1
		1.8		−2.7		−0.9
Andean Pact						
1964–68 1974–78	0.9	2.4	30.5	38.2	31.4	40.6
		1.5		7.7		9.2
No obvious effect on internal trade						
ASEAN						
1967–71 1972–76	7.0	7.8	37.5	49.9	44.5	57.7
		0.8		12.4		13.2
NAFTA						
1961–65 1971–75	1.7	1.8	28.6	24.8	30.3	26.6
		0.1		−3.8		−3.7
LAFTA						
1956–60 1966–70	1.6	1.6	19.0	13.1	20.6	14.7
		0.0		−5.9		−5.9
EAC[c]						
1968–72 1973–77	6.3	3.9	35.6	34.5	41.9	38.4
		−2.4		−1.1		−3.5

a. Except for EAC and ASEAN, the base period precedes establishment of the regional association. For EAC and ASEAN (both established in 1967), bilateral trade data from the period preceding establishment are not available.
b. CACM has been moribund since the war between El Salvador and Honduras (1969).
c. EAC effectively came to an end in 1977.

Source: International Monetary Fund, Direction of Trade Statistics Database.

imports, measured as a percentage of their combined GDP).[5] We divide the associations into two groups: those whose internal trade has apparently been stimulated by the establishment of the association, and those whose internal trade apparently has not. We include the Association of Southeast Asian Nations (ASEAN) in the second group, even though internal trade did increase by 0.8 percent of combined GDP. The reason is straightforward: the increase in internal trade was dwarfed by the increase in external trade. It seems plausible that the increase in internal trade was due to the general dynamism of the trading sectors of their economies rather than to any strong effect of the association itself. Indeed, these overall data suggest that the formation of ASEAN was essentially irrelevant to the expansion of international trade among the members of this group.

What tentative conclusions does the experience of the various associations suggest?

One is that each of the associations in the first group began with an across-the-board approach, agreeing to complete internal free trade within a specific time period, except for explicitly enumerated items. Each of the associations in the second group used a product-by-product approach. They entered a series of agreements that identified the products for which internal trade was to be liberalized, with the hope that this list could be progressively extended in continuing negotiations. As might be expected from the theoretical analysis, the product-by-product approach was generally associated with a decline in trade with outside countries (with the notable exception of ASEAN). However, something occurred that we would not have anticipated: the product-by-product approach was not conducive to a rapid increase in *internal* trade. Thus, the wisdom of GATT Article XXIV is confirmed. Not only is the across-the-board approach best as a way of avoiding efficiency-reducing trade diversion. It also seems to be best as a way of promoting internal trade. When the product-by-product approach is used, countries are apparently reluctant to suggest specific candidates for internal liberalization. There are, for example, anecdotes about ASEAN countries searching for candidates for internal liberalization, and coming forward with proposals on snowplows and nuclear power plants (Tan 1982).

Second, there appears to be a positive relationship between the expansion of internal trade and similarity of economic structure. The three associations involving countries with the most dissimilar economic structures in terms of composition of GDP and the structure of manufacturing were ASEAN,

---

5. For the East African Community and ASEAN, the IMF data base does not go back before the establishment date of 1967. In these two cases, the base period is soon after the establishment of the regional association, presumably before it had much effect.

the Andean Pact, and the Latin American Free Trade Association (table 2.3), two of which were "below the line" in table 2.2, without any clear increase in internal trade resulting from their associations. (The third association— the Andean Pact—was just "above the line.") These data therefore are generally consistent with the frequently noted phenomenon that similar economies tend to be one another's best customers.

There seems to be no clear association between physical proximity and the development of internal trade. The most successful FTA in terms of rapid development of internal trade was the Central American Common Market, a group of contiguous states. However, the least successful, the East African Community, is also made up of contiguous states. The geographically scattered European Free Trade Association (EFTA) is in an intermediate position.

Geographical proximity is apparently much less important than other factors in determining the outcome of an FTA. However, none of the past agreements include the sort of widespread, trans-Pacific arrangements that may be proposed in the future. If more widespread associations are to be considered, it would be desirable to look more closely at the problems caused by geographic dispersion.

It is, of course, difficult to generalize on the basis of historical experience when there are so few associations to observe. What insights does the experience of individual associations offer?

In the early years of the EC, the rise of internal trade (by 5 percent of the members' combined GDP between the mid-1950s and the mid-1960s) was accompanied by a relative decline in trade with outside nations (which fell by 2.1 percent of GDP, from 20.0 percent to 17.9 percent). That suggests, as a crude measure, that as much as two-fifths (2.1/5) of the new internal trade may have been diverted from outside nations in the short term, with the other three-fifths (that is, $2.9 = 5.0 - 2.1$) representing newly created trade. Put another way, this suggests that trade diversion was roughly 70 percent as great as trade creation (2.1/2.9). Perhaps on this point we should not apologize for our crude measure. More detailed research, reviewed by Mayes (1978), gives widely diverse estimates ranging from − 36 percent to + 167 percent for the trade diversion/trade creation ratio in this early period up to 1967.

Note also that as time passed and the EC became larger, trade diversion no longer showed up in these gross figures; external trade grew as a percentage of GDP. The research surveyed by Mayes confirms that trade diversion declined with the passage of time. Of course, much of the increase in external trade in the 1978–82 period may have been the result of extraneous developments, such as the increase in oil prices and the general reductions in tariffs. However, the EC experience does provide support to Viner's conclusion that trade diversion will be less important as the size of an association increases.

Each FTA is special, but the European Free Trade Association is perhaps the most special of all. In particular, the decline in external trade was apparently not so much the result of the EFTA itself as of the EC, which was developing at the same time (Price 1982, EFTA Secretariat 1980). Trade of the EFTA nations with the EC picked up as some members left EFTA to join the EC, and as the remaining EFTA nations successfully completed bilateral agreements with the EC in 1972.

The experience of the Association of Southeast Asian Nations has already been noted: its overall trade grew very rapidly, but the association itself made little apparent contribution to that growth. This conclusion is confirmed by Arndt and Garnaut (1979, 199), who concluded that "there has been much useful talk but little practical action" in ASEAN.

The aggregate figures of table 2.2 show no increase in internal trade as a ratio of the GDPs of the members of the Latin American Free Trade Association (LAFTA).[6] One reason for the slow growth of internal trade was the weak commitment to reduce trade barriers among the members. In the initial agreement, LAFTA members "did little more than commit themselves to future rounds of negotiations" (Finch 1982, 210). Early negotiations met only limited success, and progress on reducing internal barriers essentially stopped in 1967, amid dissatisfaction of the intermediate and smaller members with the distribution of gains from the association. Wionczek (1970) concludes that the geographical and economic dispersion of the members was a leading cause of LAFTA's difficulties.

The Central American Common Market (CACM) enjoyed the greatest increase in internal trade during its brief existence; internal trade rose by 8.2 percent of the combined GDP of the member states between the late 1950s and the late 1960s. This figure is all the more remarkable because the initial trade was so low, only 1.8 percent of combined GDP. There was also little change in their trade with the outside world, which remained stable at one-third of GDP. Thus, these summary data suggest that the large increase in internal trade was newly created, not simply diverted trade. However, the aggregate trade ratios mask important details, particularly the degree of trade diversion. With changing patterns of protection, there was a major change in the composition of external trade, with a shift of imports from manufactured goods to intermediate products. Trade in manufactures

---

6. However, this table probably understates the growth of both internal and external trade. Because of rapid inflation and sticky exchange rates, internal prices rose more than the prices of traded goods. Our tentative conclusion, however, is that LAFTA would still belong in group B (table 2.2) even if price corrections were made.

Table 2.3 Characteristics of regional association members

	Composition of GDP (percentage)			
Association	Agriculture	Industry	Manufacturing[b]	Services
CACM[c]	30	20	15	51
	(6)	(1)	(1)	(5)
EC6[c]	8	46	33	46
	(3)	(7)	(5)	(5)
EC9[c]	9	42	31	49
	(6)	(9)	(6)	(6)
EFTA[c]	12	38	27	51
	(7)	(6)	(5)	(7)
Andean Pact[c]	20	27	19	53
	(11)	(6)	(8)	(11)
ASEAN[d]	30	23	13	48
	(19)	(6)	(5)	(15)
NAFTA[e]	9	35	NA	56
LAFTA[c]	21	29	21	50
	(9)	(7)	(5)	(5)
EAC[d]	44	15	9	41
	(9)	(3)	(2)	(6)

Figures in parentheses are standard deviations.
a. Percent of manufacturing value added in 1970.
b. Manufacturing is a subcomponent of industry.
c. GDP data are from 1960.
d. GDP data are from 1965.
e. GDP data are from 1971.
NA = not available.

Sources: World Bank, *World Bank Development Report* (1983 and 1987); International Monetary Fund, *International Financial Statistics Supplement on Output Statistics,* No. 8, 1984.

Structure of manufacturing[a]				
Food and agriculture	Textiles and clothing	Machinery and transport equipment	Chemicals	Other
49	14	3	8	26
(9)	(6)	(2)	(6)	(9)
14	11	28	9	38
(3)	(4)	(5)	(1)	(1)
19	13	30	9	43
(8)	(5)	(9)	(2)	(7)
14	11	23	6	46
(4)	(9)	(6)	(1)	(6)
31	21	5	6	38
(11)	(11)	(4)	(2)	(11)
25	10	11	5	48
(13)	(7)	(7)	(2)	(14)
22	10	20	5	43
33	17	8	6	36
(13)	(2)	(6)	(2)	(8)
40	15	6	9	30
(18)	(10)	(6)	(1)	(4)

among the members expanded rapidly. However, there was considerable tension over the location of new manufacturing plants, and this was a factor in the football war of 1969 that marked the effective end of the CACM (for details, see Cline 1978, and Wionczek 1970).

Finally, the East African Community (EAC) presents the most puzzling picture of all. Not only did internal trade decline; it declined *much* more than did overall trade. That community is perhaps best interpreted not as an example of economic integration, but as a not-very-successful attempt to limit the forces of autarky and nationalism that accompanied the dissolution of the British Empire. Political instability had adverse effects both on internal economic growth and on trade among the countries. Disputes among members of the EAC over the division of the gains from trade were a contributing factor in the decline of internal trade (Hazlewood 1979).

Concluding Observations

Looking back, we are impressed once more how complex and slippery are the issues raised by free trade associations. The most valid generalization is that it is very difficult to generalize. We would, however, offer several concluding observations:

☐ The distinction between trade creation and trade diversion remains the key to the evaluation of an FTA, even though the case against trade-diverting associations has been muddied by economies of scale and by the shift toward nontariff barriers as a method of protection.

☐ Likewise, GATT Article XXIV remains a good starting point in judging FTAs. In particular, the experience of recent decades suggests that the across-the-board approach is not only the best way of limiting trade diversion; it also seems the best way of promoting internal trade within an FTA.

Not only are partial arrangements inferior from the viewpoint of the member nations of an FTA; they also undercut the GATT. GATT has well-known limitations, but a central fact should not be overlooked. Under the GATT system, an unprecedented growth of mutually beneficial international trade has occurred. The principle of nondiscrimination, which lies at the heart of the GATT, should not be lightly discarded with new arrangements that do not meet the standards of Article XXIV. The economic and political costs of disintegration of the world into trading blocs could be very high indeed.

☐ Frictions over the division of gains—particularly dissatisfaction over the location of new manufacturing plants— can create major problems within an FTA. This has been a significant problem within the Andean Pact, LAFTA, the CACM, and the EAC. Some members see themselves in a role similar to that of the US South in the 19th century, or the Canadian West in this century. They end up buying high-cost manufactured goods from other members of the FTA, without reaping commensurate gains. That is likely to be a central problem for any FTA among developing countries, especially if the members have dissimilar economies.

☐ We are skeptical of the use of an FTA for balance of payments purposes.

References

Arndt, H. W., and Ross Garnaut. 1979. "ASEAN and the Industrialization of East Asia." *Journal of Common Market Studies*, March, 191–212.
Brander, James A., and Barbara J. Spencer. 1984. "Tariff Protection and Imperfect Competition." In Henryk Kierzkowski, ed., *Monopolistic Competition in International Trade*. Oxford: Oxford University Press.
Brooks, Roger A., ed. 1988. *The U.S.–Republic of China Trade Relationship: Time for a New Strategy*. Washington: Heritage Foundation.
Cline, William R. 1978. "Benefits and Costs of Economic Integration in Central America." In William R. Cline and Enrique Delgado, eds., *Economic Integration in Central America*. Washington: Brookings Institution.
Cooper, Richard. 1986. "The United States as an Open Economy." In R. W. Hafer, ed., *How Open Is the US Economy?* Lexington, Mass.: Lexington Books.
Diebold, William. 1959. *The Schuman Plan*. New York: Frederick A. Praeger for the Council on Foreign Relations.
EFTA Secretariat. 1980. *EFTA—Past and Future*. Geneva: European Free Trade Association.
Finch, M. H. J. 1982. "The Latin American Free Trade Association." In Ali M. El-Agraa, ed., *International Economic Integration*. New York: St. Martin's Press.
Harris, Richard G. 1985. "Summary of a Project on the General Equilibrium Evaluation of Canadian Trade Policy." In John Whalley and Roderick Hill, eds., *Canada–United States Free Trade*. Toronto: University of Toronto Press, in cooperation with the Royal Commission on the Economic Union and Development Prospects for Canada.
Hazlewood, Arthur. 1979. "The End of the East African Community: What Are the Lessons for Regional Integration Schemes?" *Journal of Common Market Studies*, September, 40–58.
Horstmann, Ignatius J., and James R. Markusen. 1986. "Up the Average Cost Curve: Inefficient Entry and the New Protectionism." *Journal of International Economics*, vol. 20, no. 3/4 (May), 225–47.
Lipsey, Richard. 1957. "The Theory of Customs Unions: Trade Diversion and Welfare." *Economica*, vol. 24, no. 93 (February), 40–46.
Mayes, David G. 1978. "The Effects of Economic Integration on Trade." *Journal of Common Market Studies*, September, 1–25.
Meade, James E. 1955. *The Theory of Customs Unions*. Amsterdam: North Holland.
Price, Victoria Curzon. 1982. "The European Free Trade Association." In Ali M. El-Agraa, ed., *International Economic Integration*. New York: St. Martin's Press.

Snape, R. H. 1986. *Should Australia Seek a Trade Agreement with the United States?* Canberra: Economic Planning Advisory Council.

Tan, Gerald. 1982. "Intra ASEAN Trade Liberalization: An Empirical Analysis." *Journal of Common Market Studies*, June, 321–31.

Verdoorn, P. J., and A. N. R. Schwartz. 1972. "Two Alternative Estimates of the Effects of the EEC and EFTA on the Pattern of Trade." *European Economic Review*, November, 291–335.

Viner, Jacob. 1950. *The Customs Union Issue*. New York: Carnegie Endowment for International Peace.

Wionczek, M. S. 1970. "The Rise and the Decline of Latin American Economic Integration." *Journal of Common Market Studies*, September, 49–64.

Wonnacott, Paul. 1984. "Industrial Allocation in the Andean Pact." In Jose Nunez del Arco et al., eds., *The Economic Integration Process of Latin America in the 1980s*. Washington: Inter-American Development Bank, 103–14.

Wonnacott, Paul. 1987. *The United States and Canada: The Quest for Free Trade*. POLICY ANALYSES IN INTERNATIONAL ECONOMICS 16. Washington: Institute for International Economics.

Wonnacott, R. J. 1975. "Canada's Future in a World of Trading Blocs: A Proposal." *Canadian Public Policy*, Winter, 118–30.

Wonnacott, R. J., and Paul Wonnacott. 1967. *Free Trade Between the United States and Canada: The Potential Economic Effects*. Cambridge, Mass.: Harvard University Press.

Comments

Isaiah Frank

Although the subject of both this conference and the chapter by Paul Wonnacott and Mark Lutz is free trade areas, the subject was cast more broadly by Fred Bergsten in his introductory remarks. As he put it, we are really talking about alternatives to the multilateral approach involving some degree of discrimination in favor of the partners and against outsiders. Such arrangements could cover a wide spectrum ranging from consultative and sectoral agreements to full-fledged free trade areas (FTAs) and customs unions. They could be bilateral or plurilateral, and could be limited to countries within a region or comprehend countries in different regions.

The current interest in alternatives to multilateralism, regardless of the specific form they might take, stems, I believe, from four sources: a perception of the inadequacies of the GATT and the slow progress in remedying them in the Uruguay Round; the conclusion of the negotiation of a comprehensive Canada–US FTA; the moves toward a single European market by 1992; and the view that US trade policy needs to be tailored to the diversity of economic systems in other countries and to our special relationships with them.

The widely noted shortcomings of the GATT are of three types. One is the ineffectiveness of a number of the articles as guides to the behavior of GATT members, especially the articles pertaining to agriculture, safeguards, subsidies, and import quotas. A second is the sluggish response in the Uruguay Round to the need to broaden the coverage of the GATT to reflect new realities such as the growing importance of trade in services, the closer links between trade and investment, and the need to strengthen the protection of intellectual property. The third shortcoming is the lack of effective multilateral mechanisms for disciplining the behavior of GATT members and settling disputes among them. All these problems are being addressed in the Uruguay Round. Nevertheless, the slowness of members to respond affirmatively to US initiatives to strengthen and modernize the GATT has led many in the United States to urge consideration of other alternatives.

The Canada–US agreement has been widely cited as a model of how much further countries can go toward the mutual liberalization of trade and investment through a bilateral rather than a multilateral approach. The agreement comprehends not only tariffs and quantitative restrictions but

Isaiah Frank is the William L. Clayton Professor of International Economics at the School of Advanced International Studies of The Johns Hopkins University.

government procurement, standards, trade in services, investment, and other subjects of special interest to the two parties.

The third development sparking an interest in alternatives to multilateralism is the prospect of a fully integrated European market by 1992. The extension of internal liberalization to the movement of capital, investment, government procurement, and the harmonization of tax systems implies a far-reaching advance toward a single European market. Inevitably it has engendered fears that some of the adjustment costs will be transferred to nonmembers of the European Community (EC) in the form of new restrictions and discrimination. This prospect has stimulated proposals for joint defensive measures in the form of new bilateral and plurilateral arrangements among countries outside the EC.

Finally, influential members of Congress and others have been impressed with the argument that the United States needs to tailor its trade policy to the varying ways in which other governments intervene in their economies rather than to assume that they all follow our market-driven economic model. This view has generated proposals for special US trade agreements of varying scope with Japan, Mexico, and other countries, including the centrally planned economies of Europe and Asia that are now undergoing economic liberalization.

Whatever the impetus for new preferential trade arrangements, the chapter by Wonnacott and Lutz is a valuable contribution to our understanding of the nature and consequences of FTAs. In particular, the paper shows how Viner's insightful distinction between the trade creation and trade diversion effects of FTAs is reflected in the drafting of the GATT. Although those concepts are not specifically mentioned, Article XXIV includes two provisions designed to improve the chances that trade creation will dominate trade diversion. The first is that barriers to outsiders may not be raised, so that whatever trade diversion occurs as a result of the agreement is a consequence of the removal of restrictions on trade among members rather than of new barriers against outsiders.

The other provision requires that "substantially all trade" be covered by the agreement, so that countries may not pick and choose among products— a process that would inevitably maximize trade diversion and minimize the painful domestic adjustments implied by trade creation. Although the authors of the paper acknowledge this logic, they raise doubts about the "substantially all" criterion, citing the fact that "the inclusion of agricultural trade within the EC scarcely seems to have led to greater efficiency of the world economy." The problem here, however, is not with the "substantially all" criterion but with the failure of the EC's Common Agricultural Policy to meet the other test of Article XXIV that external barriers not be raised.

It is often said that if trade creation exceeds trade diversion, the free trade area (or customs union) is beneficial. But beneficial for whom? On this question Viner is quite clear. Although the members of the FTA collectively benefit, the outside world cannot gain in the short run regardless of whether trade creation or trade diversion is dominant. The reason is clear: outside countries experience only trade diversion in the short run. The possibility of less distorted patterns of consumption, cited by the authors as mitigating the adverse effects of trade diversion, is an offsetting benefit that accrues only to members and not to outsiders.

How large are the gains from the establishment of an FTA? The authors point out quite rightly that increases in trade among the members should not be taken as an indicator of the economic success of the FTA. One reason is that the increases reflect the combined effect of the beneficial trade creation and the generally harmful trade diversion. But even if one separates the two effects, and determines the net balance between them, one still would not have a measure of the economic or welfare effects. Those are, of course, much smaller than the volume of trade created or diverted, and the difference between the smaller welfare gains and losses is smaller still. Perhaps this point would be worth making toward the end of the chapter, where changes in trade patterns are examined as indicators of the effects of FTAs.

The modest size of the economic effects is undoubtedly related to the static nature of the trade creation–trade diversion framework. It focuses on the consequences of once-and-for-all changes in the allocation of existing resources resulting from the formation of the FTA. The more important results are likely to flow from the growth induced by economies of scale (discussed in the chapter) and the stimulus to competition, investment, and technological progress provided by the enlargement of the market.

When these dynamic effects are taken into account, they may not only overwhelm the static results for the members, but also have positive spillovers for outside countries. In short, whereas in purely static terms nonmembers cannot benefit from the formation of an FTA, in dynamic terms they may well gain in the longer run from a secondary form of trade creation induced by the more rapid growth of the FTA as a market for their exports. This observation is consistent with the data in table 2.2 of the chapter showing that the EC's external trade as a percentage of GDP declined initially but then increased in the more recent period.

Unfortunately, while many estimates have been made of the extremely modest static welfare effects, the task of estimating the more far-reaching dynamic effects is more daunting and rarely attempted. It is like the story of the drunk who looked for his wallet under a lamppost because the light was better there. Similarly, we measure the static rather than the dynamic effects of FTAs because the light is better there.

With tariffs set by the industrial countries now averaging only 5 to 6 percent, it is apparent that the present interest in FTAs is not driven primarily by the prospect of gains from the elimination of the remaining tariffs. Nontariff restrictions, however, remain a major obstacle to trade. According to a recent World Bank study, 27 percent of all imports of the industrial countries are affected by nontariff barriers (Nogues et al. 1986). The desire to avoid quantitative restrictions (QRs) and other nontariff barriers may be a prime reason for the current interest in FTAs. And I agree with the authors' observation that the gradual replacement of tariffs by QRs has muddied the analysis of trade diversion.

From this perspective, the EC may be viewed today more as an FTA than as a customs union. As the principal barriers against imports from nonmembers are QRs rather than tariffs, and as each member maintains its own individual QRs against nonmembers, the EC has effectively become in recent years an FTA rather than a customs union with a common external barrier. Moreover, it is far from certain that the establishment of a "single internal market" by 1992 will encompass the unification of quotas on imports from nonmembers.

Wonnacott and Lutz provide a brief but incisive analysis of free trade associations among developing countries. Their generally pessimistic assessment of the prospects for such arrangements is borne out by the many abortive efforts at regional economic integration in Africa and Latin America. If we set aside the political conflicts among members that have undermined FTAs in East Africa and Central America, for example, the main problem has been a perception of unequal gains: the least industrialized members have felt that they were paying higher prices for their partners' manufactured products without receiving equivalent reciprocal benefits for themselves, and new investment within the integrated market tended to concentrate in the more developed countries.

Efforts to deal with these problems have taken many forms, including stretched-out timetables for liberalization by the economically lagging members, financial assistance to them, and "regional integration planning" involving the assignment to particular members of the exclusive right to produce designated products. This policy, of course, defeated the purpose of integration and usually resulted in inefficient industries catering to captive markets.

Perhaps the principal obstacle to economic integration schemes is that the prospective partners ask the wrong question. Instead of asking whether the benefits will at least equal those of their partners, they should ask whether they would be better off with integration than without it. This may be politically unrealistic, however, and there may have to be at least the perception of a rough equality of benefits.

I conclude with three observations. First, we should not forget that regional arrangements for the liberalization of trade and investment are second-best approaches. They always discriminate against outsiders and can be disintegrating forces in a global economy. Second, the preferred approach is the multilateral one that we have been pursuing through the GATT. To the extent that the GATT needs improvement to adapt it to the new economic realities of the end of the 20th century, we should exert every effort to do so in the Uruguay Round. Third, alternative approaches, whether bilateral or plurilateral, should be judged primarily by the extent to which they enhance rather than undermine the prospects for progress on a multilateral scale. After all, the best free trade area is one that encompasses all trading nations.

Reference

Nogues, Julio J., Andrzej Olechowski, and L. Alan Winters. 1986. "The Extent of Nontariff Barriers to Industrial Countries' Imports," *The World Bank Economic Review*, vol. 1, no. 1, September.

Comments

Martin Wolf

The chapter by Paul Wonnacott and Mark Lutz provides a lucid discussion of the economics of free trade areas (FTAs). I find myself in agreement with almost all of it. The authors argue convincingly for what they consider their most important point: "FTAs and their close cousins, customs unions . . . do not necessarily represent a move toward free trade." Correspondingly, I give strong assent to their remark that "While special arrangements that bend the GATT rules may be desirable, they should not be accepted uncritically; the burden of proof is on the proponents."

Given my broad agreement with the chapter, these comments try to go beyond it to consider two additional questions: what is the United States up to with its FTA policy, and could that policy prove a means for reconstructing the international trading system rather than, as seems likely at present, completing its demolition? First, however, I have two comments on the paper itself.

Martin Wolf is the chief economics leader writer of the Financial Times *(London).*

FTAs Compared With What?

The chapter begins with a restrictive assumption, one that follows naturally from its reliance on Jacob Viner's classic (and fruitful) distinction between trade-creating and trade-diverting FTAs. It assumes that the reference point for comparisons with a proposed FTA is the *status quo ante*.

This assumption takes the authors into deep waters. For example, they note that "as quotas and voluntary export restraints become more prominent features of the protective framework, it is no longer so clear that trade diversion will reduce efficiency." Thus the authors provide an example in which trade diversion is efficient because the FTA relaxes discriminatory restrictions on the lowest-cost supplier. This is an extraordinary case, however, and one in which discrimination is justified, but only because it eliminates the costs of discrimination already in place. Here one is well and truly lost in the land of the nth best.

The key issues are what policies can be altered and under what circumstances. The authors do, it is true, provide some justification for their restrictive assumption that trade cannot be liberalized except via an FTA. Thus they assert that "the reason to look at FTAs is that further multilateral liberalization may be difficult. . . ." The "preferable alternative, namely, multilateral reductions in trade barriers on a most-favored-nation (MFN) basis" is unavailable. But the alternative of unilateral liberalization is not even discussed, though developing countries liberalize unilaterally all the time.

Practical people may well say amen to the presumption that a proposed FTA should be compared with whatever one starts with. But the analysis would be more general (and so more persuasive) if one first understood why this is the only choice and whether economically preferable alternatives have been excluded by this assumption.

Two questions deserve analysis. The first concerns the political economy that limits trade policy to the choice between preferential liberalization or none. The second concerns the conditions in which an FTA might be economically superior for a country to unilateral, or even global, free trade (because of improved terms of trade, including more secure market access).

The second of the two questions is particularly relevant to small countries. It is possible, for example, that an FTA with the United States is better for Canada than any alternative trade policy (because of discriminatory improvements in market access). The same possibility emerges from Howard Rosen's interesting chapter on the US–Israel FTA. Israel has liberalized far more under the FTA than the United States, and even if that were not true, the consequences of that liberalization (including, presumably, the gains) would be some two orders of magnitude larger for Israel than the United

States. How do the economics of such preferential liberalization—especially when there is also Israel's agreement with the European Community—compare with those of unilateral liberalization? Does Israel's fear about security of access in the United States justify the FTA as a first-best policy?

In short, what is needed is both a somewhat more general discussion of the economics of FTAs and an examination of the political processes and ideas that, in the authors' judgment, limit the effective choice to the status quo on the one hand and FTAs on the other. Only then can one determine how enthusiastically FTAs should be pursued.

Article XXIV, FTAs, and Customs Unions

My second set of comments on the chapter concerns the authors' conclusions on GATT Article XXIV as well as on the respective merits of FTAs and customs unions. The authors conclude that Article XXIV of the GATT survives scrutiny rather well, the main advantage being the requirement that "substantially all" trade should be covered. The problem with partial liberalization is that it encourages exceptions to liberalization where adjustment costs and, correspondingly, the gains from trade are largest. It is a good general rule that trade liberalization is more beneficial the more it is across-the-board.

The authors make a number of qualifications to their conclusion. They note that partial agreements have sometimes been stepping stones to more comprehensive ones (the Coal and Steel Community in Europe and the US–Canada Auto Pact are examples). In fact, neither of these cases is compelling. The authors also decry the devastating effect on world trade of the requirement to liberalize agricultural trade within the EC, the price being a high level of external protection. This situation, is, however, an example of the superiority of FTAs over customs unions, not an argument against the "substantially all" requirement of Article XXIV. Under an FTA the Common Agricultural Policy would have been unnecessary. The problem was not the GATT's requirement that substantially all trade be covered, but rather the need of a customs union to agree on a common external barrier, which was then set at the level of the most protectionist member country.

The author's proposition that FTAs are superior to customs unions seems firmly based, but it appears paradoxical, for it implies that the world would be better off with more and smaller countries (countries usually, though not invariably, being customs unions). A full customs union, however, especially one with common mechanisms for decision making, may achieve a far higher level of economic integration than an FTA. Such "jurisdictional integration," as Mancur Olson (1982) has called it, could justify the customs union. Also, a greater number of countries might well mean that there will simply be more protection in the world and so greater disintegration of the world economy.

At the same time, countries may behave differently from customs unions because of the greater diffusion of political power within the latter. Within a customs union, each member country is likely to try to obtain a high level of external protection for its own vulnerable industries and may succeed in achieving this objective in return for similar concessions for its partners. Such logrolling might lead to a far higher level of overall protection than in more centralized states.

FTAs and the United States

The fundamental issue raised by the chapter, however, is why the United States has abandoned well over half a century of adherence to the unconditional MFN principle and now sees discrimination as a solution to its trading woes. This shift is peculiar, far more peculiar than the desire of other countries to enter into FTAs with the United States. It is not made any less peculiar by the authors' observation that one of the justifications advanced for FTAs is the help they may give to the US balance of payments. If such absurdities now motivate trade policy in Washington, anything is possible.

Historically, FTAs have been the economic policy of the uncompetitive and the foreign policy of the weak. The shift of the United Kingdom to a full-blown policy of imperial preferences in the 1930s was an admission of both political and economic decline. Equally, the discriminatory policies of the European Community have their roots not only in fear of competition (initially from the United States, now from the Far East) but also in the limited number of instruments of foreign policy available to it. Should one interpret the movement of the United States in the 1980s toward a trade policy based more on discrimination as a tacit admission of its relative economic and political decline? The answer, unfortunately, is yes.

There have to be strong reasons for such a policy, because FTAs in particular and discrimination in general bring major practical (not to mention economic) disadvantages. First, they create resentment among those discriminated against (a particularly severe problem if the hierarchy of privilege is itself complex, as it has become in the case of the EC). Second, partly for this very reason, they are both vexatious and time consuming to manage— Howard Rosen reveals just how difficult in the putatively simple case of Israel and the United States (see Rosen, this volume).

These are powerful objections. Given that the economic benefits to the United States must be small, why is it following this policy, and in particular why is there active discussion of further FTAs? Three explanations may be advanced for the policy: first and most important, frustration with the GATT; second, imitation of the EC; and, third, the desire to sustain a process of international negotiation for fear that congressional pressure for a still more protectionist trade policy would otherwise become overwhelming.

The shift in US thinking toward FTAs, and more generally toward bilateralism as a principle, rather than a shamefaced expedient, is momentous. As the progenitor and most enthusiastic upholder of the unconditional most-favored-nation principle, the United States may well doom the GATT system in its present form by this defection. A key question is whether the result need be chaos and growing discrimination, or whether the FTA idea could instead be a way of rejuvenating the international trading system.

FTAs and the International Trading System

The United States could act in ways that would make FTAs more manageable for itself and more beneficial to the world as well. Three changes are needed.

☐ The United States should promote just one FTA, not a different one for each partner country. Countries would then apply to join the single FTA, negotiations then being mainly about derogations demanded from the FTA agreement.

☐ In the context of such an FTA, the United States should relax the ever-increasing protection afforded by regulatory trade measures.

☐ The new FTA should be open-ended (in strong contrast to EC arrangements). Thus, any country or group of countries prepared to abide by the rules would be entitled to join.

If there were only one FTA, then there would be only one fault line of discrimination, with countries either preferentially treated or not. This would make managing the FTAs vastly simpler. Otherwise, a change in any one FTA would adversely affect partners in all the other FTAs. This would not merely create bitterness, but would probably necessitate the renegotiation of all the other FTAs, and so on, forever. It would be little less than lunatic for the United States to organize its affairs in this way. After all, when the United Kingdom proposed the European Free Trade Association it did not try to set up a separate arrangement with each partner country.

The second condition is also important, because a commitment to free trade can be nullified by administrative protection. Since dumping is most unlikely under free trade, antidumping action can be abandoned. If at all possible, limits on subsidies should be agreed on by the participants of the FTA together (rather than be countervailed by one country acting on its own). It is worth noting that even the EC has made virtually no use of safeguard arrangements within the free trade area created by its agreement with EFTA.

Finally, the new FTA should be open-ended, for only in that way can it avoid becoming another step toward fragmentation of the world economy into trading blocs and perhaps be the beginning of regeneration instead. An open-ended FTA with the United States as its core could be the basis of a more disciplined and more liberal trading system, to be spun from the GATT's Article XXIV. As such, it would build on (but go further than) the idea of a North Atlantic Free Trade Area, which was popular in the late 1960s and early 1970s.

The GATT is foundering because GATT mercantilism no longer works. The main problem is that the mercantilist concepts implicit in the GATT are in conflict with the principle of nondiscrimination, from which the global system was to be constructed. The mercantilist views trade as war. His country wins with its exports and loses with its imports. The mercantilist will ask, therefore, why his country should be open to a rival that does not, for whatever reason, appear open to imports from his own country. This, he will assert, is unilateral disarmament.

The whole thrust of US policy in the 1980s is to reject such "unilateral disarmament" and insist on bilateral reciprocity instead. This way of thinking also has led to the worry about free riders that now makes liberalization within the GATT so difficult.

One possible response is to hope that economists finally will succeed in dissuading policymakers from their instinctive belief in mercantilism. But it would seem most unlikely that this is going to happen any time soon.

An alternative is to see whether mercantilism can work in a liberalizing direction once more. An FTA with the United States at its heart might be the solution. If trade is war, then a trade agreement is a peace treaty, and an FTA in particular is the "zero option." Among market economies the absence of all barriers—complete mutual disarmament—should be accepted as a fair basis for liberal trade. If it is not, there is probably no basis for orderly trade relations.

The crucial step would be for the United States to invite other countries to join the US–Canada agreement. In the case of failure of the Uruguay Round, such a globalized FTA could serve as a highly constructive fallback position; if agreement were to be reached with Japan and other key East Asian countries, could the EC allow itself to be left far behind? It would even be possible to ask the GATT Secretariat to provide the secretarial services for such an expanding, open-ended FTA.

With such an encompassing vision behind it, the US policy on FTAs may yet be a means of revitalizing the world trading system. Otherwise, being itself a reflection of confused US thinking, the search for FTAs is likely to engender still further confusion in an already decaying international trading system.

Reference

Olson, Mancur. 1982. *The Rise and Decline of Nations: Economic Growth, Stagflation and Social Rigidities.* New Haven: Yale University Press, 1982.

3

The US–Israel Free Trade Area Agreement: How Well Is It Working and What Have We Learned?

Howard F. Rosen

During a state visit in 1983, Prime Minister Yitzhak Shamir and President Ronald Reagan agreed to negotiate a bilateral trade agreement. Negotiations began soon after, and the US–Israel Free Trade Area Agreement (FTAA) was signed in April 1985. The agreement calls for the removal of all tariffs and most other forms of protection imposed by both countries on each other's products within 10 years. Implementation began on 1 September 1985 and is expected to be completed on 1 January 1995.

This trade agreement must be seen within the context of historically strong political, military, and economic ties between the United States and Israel. Since Israel's independence in 1948, the United States has been its most important and visible ally in almost every area of relations, providing both economic and military assistance. The two countries perform joint research and maintain a high level of strategic cooperation.

US relations with Israel are based on strategic, economic, and political interests. The United States considers Israel the only democratic government in the Middle East. Western dependence on imported oil also forces the United States to maintain a significant presence and to be concerned about regional political and military stability.

Middle East affairs also factor into East–West relations, and Israel has played a role in this context. Between 1948 and 1967, Israel was one of the few countries in the world that had active relations with both superpowers. Since the Soviet Union broke off diplomatic relations with Israel following the 1967 Arab–Israeli War, US relations with Israel have strengthened.

US strategic interests in Israel are supported and encouraged by a vocal and politically active domestic Jewish community. This fact, together with

At the time this chapter was written, Howard F. Rosen was an economist in the Research Department of the Bank of Israel, Jerusalem. The views in this chapter are those of the author and not of the Bank of Israel.

the United States' strategic interests in Israel as a strong Middle East ally, have resulted in a "special relationship" between the two nations.

This chapter reviews the US–Israel FTAA. It examines why the agreement was concluded, what is unique about US relations with Israel that led to the agreement, and what we can say about the agreement's short experience to date that may serve as lessons for subsequent agreements. The first section provides an overview of the US–Israel FTAA. The second section reports on how well each country is meeting the objectives it set in negotiating the agreement. The third section examines recent trends in bilateral trade flows between the United States and Israel. The fourth section reviews current discussions between the two partners, and the fifth section suggests specific lessons from this experience.

The US–Israel Free Trade Area Agreement

The US–Israel FTAA includes provisions on goods and services and deals with tariff and nontariff barriers. Products are separated into three lists. Tariffs on those products not included on any of the three lists were reduced to zero on 1 September 1985. On the US side, this affected most of the zero preferences already afforded Israeli exports under the US Generalized System of Preferences (GSP). For Israel, this initial stage corresponded with complete implementation of tariff reductions agreed to during the Tokyo Round of multilateral trade negotiations (MTNs) under the auspices of the General Agreement on Tariffs and Trade (GATT).[1]

Israeli products that benefited from the immediate removal of US tariffs constituted approximately 80 percent of total Israeli exports to the United States in 1984.[2] US exports to Israel in this category comprised a little more than half of US exports to Israel in 1984.[3]

Tariffs on goods in List A were to be reduced to 80 percent of their base rate (defined as the final MTN rate) on 1 September 1985; to 40 percent on

---

1. Initial tariff concessions under the FTAA did not require either the United States or Israel to go beyond previous commitments. Some Israelis suggest that Israel initiated bilateral talks with the United States in order to get something in return for tariff concessions it was obligated to make anyway.

2. These products include prepared grapefruit, citrons, peppers, certain high-fashion apparel, bed sheets, gold bracelets, and certain leather items.

3. These products include maize, millet, sorghum, soybeans, diamonds and industrial diamonds, parts for planes and engines, radio navigation aids, certain electrical equipment and appliances, and valves and tubes. One explanation for the imbalance in the initial round of tariff cuts is that the vast majority of Israeli products already entered the United States duty-free.

1 January 1987; and to be eliminated totally on 1 January 1989. Products on List A account for only 5 percent of Israeli exports to the United States and approximately one-third of US exports to Israel in 1984.[4]

Tariffs on goods in List B were to be reduced by 20 percent of their base rate (defined as the final MTN rate) beginning 1 September 1985, then by another 10 percent of the base rate every 1 January between 1986 and 1992 (except 1991), and finally eliminated completely on 1 January 1995. Products in List B amounted to only 1 percent of Israeli exports to the United States and 3 percent of US exports to Israel in 1984.[5]

Tariff reductions on products in sensitive industries included on List C do not begin until 1 January 1990, and their elimination is to be phased in under mutual agreement by 1 January 1995. Approximately 14 percent of Israeli exports to the United States and US exports to Israel in 1984 were classified as "import-sensitive" and included on List C,[6] which is the only category in which both countries have committed to make equal concessions.

Many of the Israeli products classified in the latter three groups already enjoy duty-free entry into the United States either through most-favored-nation (MFN) treatment under the GATT or under the GSP, regardless of the fact that they will not become officially duty-free under the US–Israel FTAA for several years. However, those products that continue to enter the United States duty-free under the GSP program remain subject to the quantity limits under the competitive need standard.

Goods traded under this agreement must be wholly grown, produced or manufactured, or substantially transformed in the exporting country. The goods must be imported directly from the other country, without transshipment through any third country before arrival in the importing country. Goods must contain at least 35 percent value-added from the exporting country, although 15 percent may be a product of the importing country.

The US–Israel FTAA includes other provisions besides tariff reductions.

---

4. Israeli exports on this list include footwear, pimentos, certain textiles and apparel, and fresh lemons, limes, and oranges. US exports include cigarettes, craft paper and paper board, yarns and fibers, certain heavy equipment, automatic data processing equipment and computer parts, telegraph printing equipment, sound recorders, footwear and leather products, passenger cars, certain textiles and apparel, and electric measuring apparatus and parts.

5. Israeli exports on this list include fresh grapefruits, avocadoes, artichokes, and certain textiles and apparel. US exports include some textile and apparel products, some chemical products, and certain high-technology products.

6. Israeli exports in this category include processed tomato products, certain categories of olives, dehydrated onions and garlic, citrus fruit juices, fresh-cut roses, certain bromine products, and certain gold jewelry (necklaces). US exports include certain horticultural products, unmanufactured tobacco, certain dairy products, refrigerators and refrigeration equipment, aluminum bars, and radio navigational equipment.

Israel agrees to liberalize some of its licensing procedures and to become a signatory to the GATT subsidies code.[7] The agreement also includes a nonbinding commitment to liberalize trade in services between the United States and Israel. This nonbinding commitment is now being negotiated into a binding agreement between the two signatories.

The US–Israel agreement calls for a symmetrical timetable of implementation in each country. The actual classification of products into four categories differs between Israel and the United States, but the timetable of tariff reductions for each group is identical. Since the vast majority of Israeli goods already entered the US market at either zero or no tariff, the implementation of this agreement places higher adjustment pressures on Israel than on the United States.

Performance Under the Agreement to Date

One way to review the US–Israel FTAA is to measure how well each country has been able to meet the goals it set out when negotiating the agreement. These goals can be categorized as mutual and individual.

Mutual Goals

Table 3.1 presents the United States' and Israel's mutual goals in entering into the free trade agreement negotiations. Because these goals are more general than each country's individual goals, it is difficult to measure each country's success in achieving them. Both countries expect the FTAA to promote trade liberalization, increase trade flows, and lead to stronger political relations. These goals are interrelated since it is assumed that closer economic relations will lead to even closer political relations.

The FTAA has been successful in committing the United States and Israel to trade liberalization, although trade flows have yet to increase substantially between the two countries. Both countries have reduced their tariffs according to schedule. The United States has not had much difficulty in fulfilling its commitment, since almost 90 percent of Israeli imports already entered the United States duty-free under the GSP program before the agreement.

Israel's liberalization efforts are somewhat complicated by its having

---

7. Before signing the FTAA, Israel acceded to the GATT government procurement code in June 1983.

Table 3.1 Mutual goals

Goal	Achievement to date
Trade liberalization	Most Israeli products already enter the United States duty-free under the GSP program.
	Israel is reducing tariffs according to schedule. Initial tariff cuts correspond with multilateral obligations. Israel has signed the GATT subsidies code.
Increased trade	There has not been any significant increase in US nonmilitary exports to Israel since 1985.
	Growth in Israeli exports to the United States since 1985 is in line with their performance since 1980.
Political relations	US–Israel relations strengthened during the Reagan administration, despite several points of acute tensions.
	The United States has not attempted to link economic relations with foreign policy objectives, as has been the case with Israeli relations with the EC.

recently completed final tariff reductions under its free trade agreement with the European Community (EC).[8] Together, imports from the EC and the United States account for almost two-thirds of total Israeli imports. Recent tariff reductions are evident in the reduced tariff revenues relative to imports from all sources (the average tariff rate). The average tariff rate on all nontransport durable consumer goods fell from 20 percent in 1978 to 10 percent in 1987.[9] In addition to tariff cuts, Israel met its other obligation under the FTAA and signed the GATT Subsidies Code.

Attempts to measure the trade effects of the FTAA are handicapped by the fact that many of its provisions are yet to be fully implemented. In addition, it will take several years after complete implementation before the

8. Israel signed a free trade agreement with the EC in 1975, under which both parties agreed to completely eliminate their tariffs by 1 January 1989.

9. Government of Israel, *Statistical Abstract*, various issues.

full effects on trade flows between Israel and the United States become evident in the trade statistics.[10]

It is also difficult to isolate a causal relationship between liberalization and increased trade, as many simultaneous factors influence trade, including macroeconomic conditions, exchange rate movements, and nontrade policies implemented over the same period. This caveat takes on additional relevance in this case, since there have been many important macroeconomic changes in the United States and Israel since the agreement was signed.

The US dollar has appreciated moderately against the shekel since 1985, in part because of changes in Israeli exchange rate policy.[11] By contrast, the US dollar has depreciated by approximately 60 percent against the world's major currencies during the same period. Given these exchange rate changes, US exports to Israel have not performed as well as one might have expected based on the performance of US exports to all markets since 1986. US negotiators complain that this difference may be due in part to Israeli nontariff barriers offsetting the liberalizing effects of the tariff reductions. In addition, US exports have had to compete with increasing Israeli imports from the EC, due in part to the final phase-in of tariff cuts under the EC–Israel agreement.

Since the FTAA was signed in 1985, US nonmilitary exports to Israel have not increased significantly (see figure 3.1). Israeli imports from the United States have grown by only 9 percent since 1985, compared to a 33 percent growth in Israeli imports from all sources. More than three-quarters of the growth in imports since 1985 has come from the EC.[12]

Israeli exports to the United States continue to grow as they did throughout most of the early 1980s. More than half of the growth in Israeli exports between 1979 and 1985 was concentrated in exports to the United States (see figure 3.2). Israeli exports to the United States grew more in the three years preceding the agreement than they have since the agreement was

---

10. Only one study of potential trade creation and trade diversion in the Israeli market has been performed to date, and none have been done since the agreement was signed. See Pelzman (1985).

11. As part of the Israeli Economic Stabilization Program, the shekel was fixed to the US dollar, following a large initial devaluation in July 1985. Since July 1986, the Israeli shekel has been pegged to a basket of five major currencies, which includes the US dollar. The value of the shekel in relation to each of the five currencies within the basket fluctuates marginally every day. Israeli exporters complain that given the recent decline in the US dollar relative to European currencies, this policy works against them in the US market. The government devalued the shekel relative to the basket in January 1987, December 1988, and again in January 1989.

12. Except where noted, trade data presented in this paper are taken from Israeli sources. Exports and imports do not include direct military products or diamonds.

Figure 3.1 Israeli imports, 1979–87 (excluding diamonds)

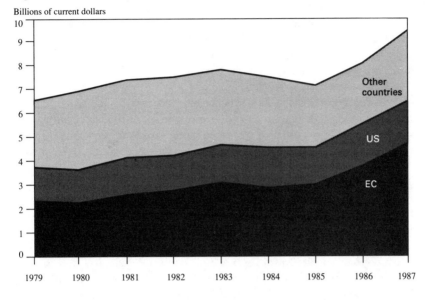

Figure 3.2 Israeli exports, 1979–87 (excluding diamonds)

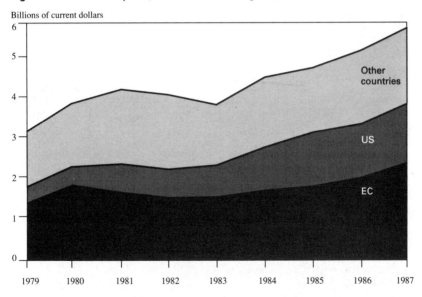

signed. This pattern has shifted since 1985, with half the growth of Israeli exports now concentrated in exports to the EC.

Much of the growth in Israeli exports to the United States in the early 1980s may be attributed to the strong dollar and high US growth rates, which resulted in a doubling of US imports from all sources. On the other side, the growth in Israeli imports from the United States since 1985, together with the relatively much higher growth in Israeli imports from the EC, may be partially due to favorable macroeconomic conditions in Israel resulting from the Economic Stabilization Program introduced in July 1985, which led to a fall in inflation and a pickup in economic growth. As a result of all these factors Israel recorded a trade surplus with the United States in 1986 for the first time in its history.

Overriding the economic objectives of liberalization and increased trade, the United States and Israel see the FTAA as another step toward closer bilateral economic, political, and strategic relations. Although it is difficult to isolate this trade agreement from the context of overall US–Israeli relations, it is part of the complement of official steps to guarantee sound relations between the two countries over much of the past decade.[13]

It is impossible to determine whether the US–Israel FTAA alone has brought the two countries any closer together. Nonetheless, the agreement continues the tradition of special relations that exists between the two nations. In this regard, the political objectives have outweighed the mutual economic objectives that each country had in entering into the agreement.

Israeli Goals

One of Israel's principal concerns in negotiating a free trade agreement with the United States was to formalize and secure the preferences it was receiving under the GSP program (see table 3.2). With growing US trade deficits and rising protectionist sentiment in Congress, Israelis were concerned that the GSP program would be either significantly curtailed or even terminated in

---

13. The initial call for the agreement came during an official visit by Yitzhak Shamir to Washington during the latter part of the Lebanon War in 1983. Despite the political fallout from Israel's involvement in that war, the Pollard spy affair, and the ongoing Palestinian uprising, US–Israel relations strengthened during the Reagan administration. Evidence of these closer ties include the conversion of military loans to grants in 1983, the granting of supplemental economic aid in 1985, the FTAA itself in 1985, the awarding of substantial military contracts under the Strategic Defense Initiative and joint US–Israeli missile development, and the Memorandum of Understanding signed in May 1988, which formalizes bilateral relations in economics, defense, and research.

Table 3.2 Israeli goals

Goal	Achievement to date
Secure tariff concessions.	Israel was able to transfer GSP preferences to the FTAA, obviating concerns about renewal of or quantitative limits on the GSP program.
Expand export markets in United States.	Israeli exports to the United States began to strengthen in 1983, partly in response to macroeconomic factors. Exports since 1985 have continued this trend despite the dollar depreciation.
Reduce import prices and domestic inflation.	Inflation has fallen and stabilized since introduction of the Economic Stabilization Program in July 1985. There is no evidence that this is due to trade liberalization.
Increase productivity in Israeli plants.	There is no evidence of improved productivity attributable to trade liberalization or other factors.
Reduce direct government subsidies in industry.	Israel has reduced both consumption and production subsidies as part of the Economic Stabilization Program. It has resisted major industrial bailouts and pressures for competitive devaluations.
Reduce dependence on foreign aid.	There is no intention at this date to reduce the amount of US economic assistance.
Increase political support from the United States.	Israel believes relations with the United States were strengthened under the Reagan administration and are possibly at one of their strongest points.

1984. Israeli officials therefore decided to seek a separate agreement with the United States to secure these preferences.

Israel's fears were partly justified. The GSP program was extended in 1985, although with several changes. The two most important changes make it easier to "graduate" countries out of the program and introduce sanctions against countries found in violation of workers' rights.[14]

Israel has several economic objectives in achieving free trade with the United States, most of which reflect standard arguments in favor of trade liberalization. Israel depends on exports to help offset its need to borrow from abroad, and imports almost all of its raw materials. Israel hopes that cheaper imports, brought about by freer trade, will help reduce inflationary pressures within Israel and force Israeli industry to become more efficient and competitive, thereby reducing the burden on government to assist Israeli industry and allowing Israel to reduce its dependence on foreign economic aid. Lowering inflationary pressures at home, reducing dependence on foreign aid, and stimulating Israeli industry through exports are all seen as necessary conditions for promoting long-term economic stability and prosperity in Israel.

Israel's political situation introduces another dimension to the traditional arguments in favor of trade liberalization. The Arab boycott of Israeli goods, in place since 1948, means that Israel must seek potential markets beyond its neighbors; this forces higher transportation costs and makes it more difficult for Israeli industry to market its products. To help offset these distortions, Israeli trade policy has sought to secure access to its two largest markets, the EC and the United States.

It is still quite early to find strong evidence that the US–Israel FTAA has helped Israel meet these economic objectives. It is also difficult to isolate the effects of the FTAA on developments in the Israeli economy. Given these two caveats, several interesting indicators remain to be considered.

Except for a gap between 1981 and 1983, Israeli exports have been increasing steadily throughout the decade. Much of this increase is due to a growth in Israeli exports to the United States; this growth predates the implementation of the FTAA. Since 1985, many Israeli exporters argue, the potential gains from initial implementation of the US agreement have been

---

14. Israel's decision to negotiate a separate agreement preserving its trade preferences appears to have been warranted by these program changes. Given its size, the changes in "graduation" provisions made it easier for Israel to lose its GSP preferences. More importantly, Israel already has been affected by changes in worker rights provisions. The Arab-American Anti-Defamation League has filed a complaint against Israel for alleged worker rights violations in the West Bank. The ITC held a hearing on their complaint, and a final determination is expected by the summer of 1989.

eroded by the effects of recent exchange rate movements in Israel and abroad and by rising input costs in Israel.

The Israeli economy has been relatively stable since the Economic Stabilization Program was implemented in July 1985. Inflation has been less than 20 percent in each of the last three years, after reaching nearly 1,000 percent in May 1985. This comprehensive program complemented favorable world macroeconomic conditions, including the depreciation of the dollar and the fall in oil prices and world interest rates, as well as strong US economic growth. It is interesting to note that Israeli nonoil imports rose more sharply than exports after the stabilization program was introduced. Part of this increase in imports may be associated with domestic growth and recent tariff reductions mandated by the Israel–EC agreement.

There does not seem to be any early evidence that the recent trade liberalization has had any significant effect on Israeli productivity, although one hopes that productivity growth will result from structural changes in Israeli industry due to competition from cheaper imports and increased export opportunities. However, it is much too early to see any clear evidence of these structural changes within the economy.

The Israeli government has been reducing subsidies on consumption and production in recent years.[15] These reductions are motivated primarily by concern over growth in government spending and less as a result of international commitments. The Finance Ministry, in an effort to hold down government outlays, is trying to hold off pressure for new bailout programs to financially troubled industries. There is now also some interest within Israel to privatize selected government-owned industries.[16] On the other hand, Israeli exporters have demanded compensation for the government's recent exchange rate policy, which has not allowed the shekel to weaken sufficiently against the dollar to offset domestic inflation and maintain their competitiveness in the US market.

Another Israeli argument in favor of the FTAA is that increased exports could help reduce Israel's dependence on foreign economic aid. This shift away from aid toward trade cannot occur overnight; in the meantime, US aid remains at its 1986 level in current dollars. There is also little evidence of any major policy changes that would reduce Israel's dependence on foreign assistance.

It remains too early to judge how well Israel has been able to meet its

---

15. This is hard to measure since there is little data on the extent of government subsidies.

16. A study commissioned by the Israeli government recommended a list of government companies that should be privatized. It will probably take some time before serious efforts toward privatization are undertaken.

Table 3.3   US goals

Goals	Achievement to date
Strengthen relations.	US–Israel relations remain strong despite the Lebanon War, the Pollard affair, and the recent Palestinian uprising. Pro-Israel support did not translate into additional Jewish votes for Reagan in the 1984 presidential election.
Increase US exports to Israel.	US exports to Israel have been relatively flat, competing with increased imports from the EC, which may be a result of final tariff reductions under the EC–Israel agreement.
Remove disadvantage due to Israel–EC agreement.	The FTAA redresses the disadvantage, but there is no evidence yet that this has translated into changes in trade patterns. The matter is further complicated by recent exchange rate movements.
Promote multilateral negotiations.	Bilateral agreements have been used as an argument that there are alternatives to multilateral negotiations, in part to help advance the Uruguay Round.
Facilitate extension of GSP.	Use of pro-Israel forces helped get legislation with FTAA and GSP extension through Congress.

economic objectives in signing the US–Israel FTAA, given the difficulty in isolating its effects on the economy. However, Israel appears to have met its initial political objectives. It preserved and transferred its preferences under the GSP program to what Israel considers to be a more secure arrangement. In addition, the FTAA is now part of the close web of cooperation that defines the special relationship between the United States and Israel.

US Goals

Purely economic considerations were less important in initial US support for the FTAA (see table 3.3), in part because of the relative size of the United States and the relative importance of trade between the United States and

Israel. Israel accounts for only a little more than 1 percent of US exports and less than 1 percent of US imports.[17] The United States' primary economic concern in negotiating the FTAA was to correct a disadvantage that its products faced as a result of Israel's FTA with the EC—a disadvantage that has been corrected only partially to date.

Israel's free trade agreements with the United States and with the EC differ in several respects.[18] The US agreement is more comprehensive than the initial EC agreement, in terms of both products and trade barriers covered. The EC–Israel agreement was originally negotiated in 1975, and final tariff reductions were implemented on 1 January 1989. The US agreement was negotiated 10 years later, and both countries have only recently begun to implement the required tariff reductions. In addition to tariff differentials, US products must fight against established European strongholds in the Israeli market for consumer electronics, automobiles, and household equipment.

The United States' overriding objectives in signing a free trade agreement with Israel were political. Within the context of the United States' special relationship with Israel, the Reagan administration hoped to demonstrate its pro-Israel position before the 1984 presidential election. Although this agreement and other efforts did not translate into more Jewish votes for Reagan in 1984, these steps led many Israelis to see President Reagan as one of the most pro-Israel American presidents since 1948.

In the area of broader trade policy concerns, the prospect of a bilateral trade agreement with Israel helped support US Trade Representative William E. Brock's threat, following his disappointment and frustration with the 1982 GATT Ministerial meeting, to negotiate directly with any willing partner.[19] American trade officials saw a bilateral agreement with Israel as an "easy" test case with no major consequences for the US trade balance. If successful, it would make it easier to negotiate other agreements. On the other hand, the threat of a shift in US trade policy from multilateral to bilateral was thought to be helpful in getting other countries to cooperate in US efforts to launch GATT negotiations. It is impossible to prove what effect Brock's statements on bilateral trade agreements had on bringing the relevant parties to begin the Uruguay Round. Notwithstanding these diffi-

---

17. International Monetary Fund, *Direction of Trade Statistics*, various issues.

18. For a more complete discussion, see Rosen (1988).

19. In a speech delivered at the Institute for International Economics hours after he returned from the subsequent GATT Ministerial in 1984, Ambassador Brock suggested that the United States was willing to speak about trade liberalization with any country that came forward, as had the Israelis and Canadians.

culties, a new GATT round of trade talks has begun, which shifts back somewhat the focus of US policy toward multilateral negotiations.

Although this was not one of the original objectives in negotiating a free trade agreement with Israel, the Reagan administration was able to use the FTAA as a means of getting congressional approval to extend the GSP program. By combining the free trade agreement and the GSP extension in the same legislation, the administration was able to use pro-Israel support to help overcome congressional opposition to the GSP program.

The United States has met many of its political objectives in negotiating the free trade agreement with Israel but does not appear to have been as successful in meeting its economic goals with the same speed, largely because of the longer time lags associated with meeting these economic goals. Little evidence to date indicates that the FTAA has significantly increased the US market share in Israel. It will probably take some time to see any significant increase in US imports into Israel, in part because of remaining Israeli barriers.

Recent Developments in US–Israel Trade Flows

Israel is much more dependent on the United States for exports and imports than the United States is on Israel. Total Israeli exports reached approximately $8 billion and imports were $11.4 billion in 1987.[20] Exports to the United States amounted to $2.4 billion, or one-third of total Israeli exports, yet only approximately ½ percent of total US imports. US exports to Israel were $1.8 billion in 1987, 16 percent of Israeli imports and less than 1 percent of total US exports. Israel recorded trade deficits with the United States until 1986, when Israeli exports to the United States grew faster than US exports to Israel, reversing the trend and resulting in a trade surplus in Israel's favor.[21]

Exports to the United States tended to dominate Israel's export performance during most of the period between 1980 and 1985, before the FTAA was implemented. The US share of Israeli exports grew from approximately 15 percent of total exports between 1979 and 1982 to approximately 25 percent of all exports between 1982 and 1987. Israeli exports to the United States, as measured in current dollars, grew in every year between 1979 and 1987, except 1982, the peak of the US recession, and 1986.[22] Israeli

---

20. Includes diamonds.

21. Does not include military goods.

22. The decline in Israeli exports to the United States in 1982 may have been in

exports to the United States were particularly strong between 1983 and 1985, during which period they outperformed total Israeli exports.[23] Since 1986, when the shekel was linked to a basket of currencies and no longer solely to the US dollar, Israeli exports to the United States have begun to slow down.

Imports from the United States averaged approximately one-fifth of total Israeli imports between 1979 and 1987. Imports from the United States grew in every year except 1982 and 1985, and outperformed the growth in total Israeli imports only in 1981, 1983, and 1984. During this period imports from Europe outperformed imports from the United States in every year. Indeed, the growth in imports from the EC accounts for three-quarters of total Israeli import growth since 1985.

A closer look at US–Israel trade flows at a more detailed product level suggests some other trends. An average of 57 percent of Israeli exports to the United States are concentrated in manufactured goods, although these exports account for only 30 percent of Israeli manufactured goods exports to the entire world. Furthermore, manufactured goods represent three-fourths of the growth in Israeli exports to the United States since 1982.

Machinery and mechanical appliances became the dominant force behind the significant growth in Israeli exports of manufactured goods to the United States beginning in 1982. These exports have been growing steadily since then, at an average rate of 40 percent per year. Israeli exports of machinery and mechanical appliances to the United States have been growing rapidly since 1982, while similar exports to the EC have remained relatively level. Furthermore, the important growth in machinery and mechanical appliance exports has been to non-US, non-EC markets. Most of this growth occurred between 1983 and 1986. Volatility in transport equipment exports, primarily due to the high value of the products, explains the sharp increase in manufactured goods exports in 1985 and the decline the following year.

Israeli exports of food products to the United States, which comprise only 5 percent of total exports to the United States, are highly concentrated in prepared foodstuffs. This differs from the pattern of Israeli exports to the EC, which is more heavily concentrated in fresh food exports.

Jewelry and chemicals account for another quarter of Israeli exports to the United States, although they have not contributed much to the growth

---

response to the worldwide recession, which started in the United States. US imports from all markets fell by 7 percent in that year.

23. This period was characterized by an overvalued dollar and witnessed a doubling of US imports from all markets. During this period US imports from all countries grew at an average rate of 8 percent per year, while Israeli exports to the United States grew at an average rate of 20 percent per year.

in Israeli exports to the United States. On the other hand, textile exports constitute less than 5 percent of Israeli exports to the United States, although they have grown steadily at a moderate rate since 1981.

There are not many changes in the composition of Israeli imports from the United States since 1979, with 80 percent of imports concentrated in manufactured goods (56 percent) and food products (24 percent). Food products explain most of the increase, and subsequent decrease, in imports between 1980 and 1982. Growth in imports of manufactured goods explains most of the increase in Israeli imports from the United States between 1982 and 1984.

Manufactured goods that Israel imports from the United States are highly concentrated in machinery and mechanical appliances, which account for one-third of the total. These imports have grown steadily since 1979 without any apparent slowdown, but account for a declining share of the increase in Israeli imports from the United States.

The story since 1987 is less clear. Imports of nonmanufactured goods grew strongly, while trade in manufactured goods actually experienced some decline. This may reflect a shift toward higher manufactured goods imports from the EC after final implementation of the EC–Israel FTA. This concern initially led the United States to negotiate its own preferential agreement with Israel. It is still much too early to determine whether the US–Israel agreement will correct any implicit preference given to European exports to Israel due to the EC–Israel agreement.

Current Discussions Concerning the US–Israel FTAA

One of the most important aspects of the US–Israel FTAA is the establishment of a system of bilateral negotiations. This mechanism allows each country to discuss its complaints with the other partner. The agreement calls on the United States and Israel to hold bilateral discussions at least once a year, with additional meetings called as necessary.

Recent discussions between the United States and Israel have focused on complaints about each other's trade practices that allegedly have impaired the benefits expected from the agreement. Although these discussions are still in their formative stages, the two countries' complaints do suggest some fundamental differences in the way the United States and Israel manage their trade policies.

US trade negotiators complain that there are still many nontariff barriers that discourage the entry of American products into Israel. The most important is Israel's purchase tax, which is imposed on wholesale transactions, with rates differing by product. In the case of imports, for which there is not usually a wholesaler, the purchase tax is paid directly by the importer. For those products where there is no domestic substitute, or where the domestic substitute is exempt from the tax, the purchase tax serves as nothing more than a tariff. Purchase tax rates are substantially higher than tariff rates, making it a steeper barrier than tariffs.

The core of the American complaints against Israel's purchase tax is the method in which it is calculated and the exemption of certain products. Since the importer pays the purchase tax, the Customs Bureau claims it must add something to the product's base value to take into account the wholesaler's estimated markup, in order not to place domestic producers at a disadvantage. The United States argues that this additional percentage, and the manner in which it is calculated (called *tama* in Hebrew), discriminates against imports.

The United States also claims that the Israelis arbitrarily set the value of goods upon which their customs officials calculate the import tariff (called *haramah* in Hebrew). In addition, the United States contends, import licenses and standards are being used to prevent the entry of imports.[24]

The Israelis, on the other hand, argue that the US introduction of the customs user fee, even in a GATT-approved format, should be considered a new tariff, and therefore deemed illegal under the FTAA. The Israelis also argue that changes in the way the United States adheres to its "buy national" requirements deny entry to Israeli exports. The Israelis claim that constant changes in these regulations impede small exporters in the US market.

More generally, Israel complains about "process protectionism," arguing that US trade policy is too steeped in a vast array of constantly changing laws. Israeli officials argue that the vast body of US trade law places Israel at a disadvantage, since they must spend time and energy monitoring the benefits negotiated in the FTAA in light of subsequent changes in US trade law. As an Israeli official recently wrote, "Every time Congress passes a new trade law, these laws become more complex and more pro-US industry."[25]

In the past, Israelis have also argued that Canada received certain provisions in its free trade agreement with the United States that American negotiators refused the Israelis. For example, the US–Israel FTAA provides for nonbinding arbitration between the two countries for dispute settlement. The Canadians, on the other hand, received binding arbitration in their agreement in selected cases.

---

24. Israel is not a signatory to the GATT codes on import licensing or customs valuation.

25. Pinhas Dror-Alon, "FTA: Bilateral and Reciprocal," *Jerusalem Post,* 13 July 1988. Dror-Alon is the Economic Affairs Minister at the Israeli Embassy in Washington.

In late 1988, an emergency meeting between US and Israeli trade officials attempted to settle some of these matters before they were taken to dispute settlement. Under severe pressure from the United States, Israel agreed to revise its method of calculating the purchase tax and to phase out purchase tax exemptions on 41 categories by 1995.[26] How these changes will affect US–Israel trade remains to be seen.

Lessons From the US–Israel FTAA

The experience of the US–Israel FTAA suggests four lessons for US trade policy and future bilateral agreements. The first relates to Israel's move from the GSP to a bilateral agreement with the United States. The second addresses Israel's complaint that it could have negotiated a better deal. The third lesson concerns the triangular relationship that results from Israel's two free trade agreements with the EC and the United States. The fourth lesson focuses on the dissimilarities between the two countries.

Lesson 1: Life After GSP

The US–Israel FTAA allows Israel to preserve and even extend the preferences it received under the GSP program. In fact, as noted above, one of Israel's primary objectives in entering into negotiations was to make these preferences more secure. The result of this agreement is that Israel effectively has become the first country to mature from the GSP to its own bilateral agreement. Other countries that have been graduated from the GSP have lost those trade preferences and inherited the full gamut of obligations under the multilateral trading system. The special nature of the relationship between Israel and the United States best explains this development.

Without Israel, there are now fewer obstacles to reform or even terminate the GSP program. Given this prospect, the United States must decide what to do about countries that currently receive GSP preferences. In most instances, GSP "graduates" are expected to cope without any special preferences (as is the case for Korea and Taiwan). A second option is to negotiate some form of continued trade preferences for recent graduates. These preferences could be bilateral, as in the case of Israel. A third option is to develop another program similar to the GSP that offers unilateral trade preferences to developing countries. The Caribbean Basin Initiative is an example of this option.

---

26. "Israel Agrees to Lift Disputed Trade Barriers," *Financial Times,* 8 November 1988.

Since the vast majority of Israeli products were already entering the United States at zero tariff under the GSP, Israel effectively secured the preferences it was already receiving in exchange for opening its markets to US products. In return Israel agreed to significant liberalization of its relatively closed market—an arrangement that places most of the domestic adjustment burden on the Israeli economy. This shift in adjustment burden from the United States onto Israel appears to contradict one of the GSP program's foundations. By graduating countries in this manner, the United States is asking those countries with adjustment difficulties to incur yet a heavier adjustment burden.

The US–Israel pact could be a useful model for reducing the number of countries that receive special preferences while at the same time promoting liberalization with the hope of increasing market access for US products. The special relationship between the United States and Israel made it convenient to do this through a bilateral agreement, but this may not be as easy to achieve, or even preferable, with other countries.[27]

Lesson 2: MFN Status for Bilateral Agreements

The Israelis have complained in the past that the Canadians got a "better deal" than they themselves did in their negotiations with the United States. The United States refused to agree to binding arbitration as part of the dispute settlement mechanism; the Israelis settled for nonbinding arbitration instead. Three years later, the Canadians treated their demand for binding arbitration as a "deal breaker." Approaching the final deadline for completing negotiations, the United States relented and included a provision for binding arbitration in the US–Canada FTA. This concession led to an Israeli demand for equal treatment, and a call to amend their treaty with the United States to include a similar provision.

This episode raises many questions concerning bilateral agreements in general. Is there such a thing as most-favored-nation status with regard to bilateral agreements? Should every negotiating partner receive the same deal? If one country is able to achieve a concession that was not part of previous agreements, should other countries expect their agreements to be updated? Can bilateral agreements be flexible enough to get around this problem? The apparent implication of the US–Israeli and US–Canada agreements is that the tough concessions offered in the final rounds of negotiations become the opening bargaining position in subsequent bilateral

---

27. In the case of other countries that have been graduated unilaterally from the GSP, no agreements have been negotiated, and the United States consequently increased tariffs on certain of their products.

talks. If this MFN policy is not followed, does the United States then strategically decide in which order to negotiate bilateral trade agreements, so that it does not have to make the same painful concessions to more important trading partners?

It appears that no country's trade policy process, especially in a small country, can handle this kind of additional burden and at the same time give proper attention to MTNs. In addition, countries should not risk the chance of obtaining similar concessions in successive bilateral agreements.

Lesson 3: Triangular Trade Policy Objectives

The US–Israel agreement must be seen within the context of each country's broader trade policy objectives. As one of its creators, the United States has been one of the strongest supporters of the multilateral trading system. The US–Israel agreement was the first US experiment with a comprehensive bilateral trade agreement. As discussed earlier, part of the US motivation in negotiating this agreement may have been to start another round of multilateral trade negotiations. On the other hand, the US–Israel agreement set a precedent for bilateral free trade agreements, allowing the United States to actively pursue and achieve a free trade agreement with Canada.

The Israelis argue that they need bilateral agreements with their two largest markets because of the Arab boycott of Israeli products. They argue that since they cannot trade with their neighbors they must have secure, reliable access to overseas markets. The pressure for secure export markets is exacerbated by Israel's need to increase exports to help offset large capital imports and meet its debt payments. Since the United States holds the vast majority of official Israeli debt and continues to provide large amounts of economic aid, the United States has an interest in helping Israel find export markets to enable Israel to stabilize its economy and meet its international financial obligations.

The United States found it necessary to negotiate a free trade agreement with Israel to correct the disadvantage its exporters faced in Israel resulting from the EC–Israel FTA. US willingness to negotiate a bilateral agreement thus was in part a third-country response to trade policies between two other trading partners. Similar pressures for third-country actions already have been evidenced in European and Japanese responses to the Canada–US Free Trade Agreement and the US and Japanese responses to internal market reforms in Europe pursuant to the 1992 process.[28] Bilateral agree-

---

28. Small countries face the same problem, but their size makes it more difficult for them to respond effectively.

ments, as in the case of the United States and Israel, are not the only solutions.

A side effect of bilateral agreements is that they increase the amount of trade that is primarily governed by agreements other than those agreed to multilaterally. Approximately 60 percent of Israel's current trade is now covered under the two bilateral agreements.[29] This reduces Israel's incentives to support a strong multilateral system and serves as an example to other small countries, at the same time that the United States is trying to bring them into the GATT fold.

Lesson 4: Matching the Partners

The US–Israel agreement is unique in that it involves two very different countries, in terms not only of economic size but also of political maturity. US GNP was approximately $4.5 trillion in 1987 compared with Israel's $31.5 billion. Israel depends more on trade, and specifically on the US market, than the United States depends on trade or Israel's market. The United States is a large industrialized country with a developed economy, which is not as heavily dependent on international trade. Israel, on the other hand, is a small and less mature economy, heavily dependent on trade, with a developing industrial sector. The US policymaking process is transparent, formal, and sophisticated. Israel's economy is dominated by government intervention, yet many of the policymaking operations are still quite unsophisticated and inflexible.

Bilateral agreements accent differences between the two partners. These differences are less important in multilateral trade negotiations, as there are more players complicating these differences. A review of current discussions concerning the US–Israel FTAA suggests that these differences can be quite important in a bilateral agreement.

Israel, like many other less advanced, open economies, does not rely heavily on traditional trade policy tools, such as tariffs and quotas, in protecting the domestic market from imports. Policy implementation is much more ad hoc and discretionary. Israeli trade policy may be determined by the Ministry of Industry and Trade, but the real battles are fought at the border with custom officials who unilaterally reject import licenses and arbitrarily estimate a product's import value when calculating a tax. Such practices explain why US complaints concerning Israel's implementation of the FTAA are very specific and focused on nontariff barriers.

---

29. This includes diamonds. The share of trade covered by the EC and the United States, excluding diamonds, is much higher.

Israeli complaints against the United States tend to be more generally focused on the policymaking process than on its implementation. Israel, again like other small countries, argues that it cannot keep up with constant changes in US trade policy, as well as master the skills needed to confront the web of legalities that characterizes US trade policy.

Current discussions between the United States and Israel suggest that the US–Israel FTAA may have been easier to negotiate than to maintain. The opposite may well be the case with the US–Canada agreement. US and Canadian trade flows are much more substantial and similar across products, affecting more workers and industries and touching on many sensitive areas, thereby prolonging negotiations. On the other hand, a long history of settling trade disputes, in addition to other similarities in their economic policymaking processes, may make the US–Canada agreement more resilient to occasional frictions.

Differences between the two partners are actually highlighted in a bilateral agreement and can undermine the success of any such arrangement. These differences need not be restricted to size and dependence on trade, but go beyond to include measures of the economies' stability and flexibility, the structure of their trade, and their policymaking process. The more compatible the partners, the more likely is the agreement to succeed.

Conclusion

The US–Israel FTAA is a product of the special relationship between the two countries. Based on the performance to date, the agreement gets high marks for meeting each country's political objectives but gets low grades for not fully achieving the economic goals each country sought. Israel's primary objective in negotiating a bilateral agreement with the United States was to preserve its trade preferences under the GSP program. Israel also hopes that the agreement will buttress anti-inflation programs at home, expand export markets abroad, and reduce Israel's dependence on foreign economic assistance. The United States views this agreement as part of its long history of strong economic, military, and strategic relations with Israel. The United States also wants to correct the disadvantage its exports face in the Israeli market due to the Israel–EC free trade agreement.

Notwithstanding the unique nature of this agreement, the US–Israel FTAA suggests four general lessons for future bilateral agreements and US trade policy. First, bilateral agreements may be a method of graduating countries from the GSP program—while continuing to liberalize trade between the two countries. Second, maintaining a system of bilateral agreements creates several difficulties, starting with acquiring similar concessions in all agreements. This raises strategic issues of how a country chooses to negotiate bilateral agreements. Third, bilateral agreements between two US trading partners may place the United States on the defensive and dictate changes in US trade policy. Fourth, differences between trading partners may affect how well bilateral agreements can be negotiated and maintained. The brief experience of the US–Israel Free Trade Area Agreement sheds some light onto each of these areas and raises many other issues for further study.

References

Blair, Peggy. 1985. "A US–Israel Free Trade Area: How Both Sides Gain." *Papers on US–Israel Relations* 9. Washington: American Israel Public Affairs Committee.

Government of Israel. 1985. *Guide to the Israel–US Free Trade Area Agreement.* Washington: The Economic Office, Embassy of Israel, and New York: The Government of Israel Trade Center, June.

Hirsch, Se'ev, Igal Ayal, and Shlomo Kalish. 1987. "Israel as a Bridge to the United States and the European Economic Community." Working Paper 926/87. Tel Aviv: Israel Institute of Business Research, March.

Israel–American Chamber of Commerce and Industry. 1986. *The FTA Directory: User Guide to the US–Israel Free Trade Agreement,* August. Tel Aviv and Washington: Israel–American Chamber of Commerce and Industry.

Novik, Nimrod. 1985. *The United States and Israel: Domestic Determinants of a Changing Commitment.* Boulder, Colo.: Westview Press.

Pelzman, Joseph. 1985. "The Impact of the US–Israel Free Trade Area Agreement on Israeli Trade and Employment." Discussion Paper 85-08. Jerusalem: The Maurice Falk Institute for Economic Research in Israel, June.

Rosen, Howard. 1988. "Major Developments in Israeli Trade with the United States and the European Community." Typescript, April.

US Congress. House. Committee on Ways and Means. 99th Cong., 1st sess. 1985. *United States–Israel Free Trade Area Agreement, Hearings,* 6 March.

US Congress. House. Committee on Ways and Means, Subcommittee on Trade. 98th Cong., 2nd sess. 1984. *Proposed United States–Israel Free Trade Area, Hearings,* 22 May and 13–14 June.

US Congress. Senate. Committee on Finance. 99th Cong., 1st sess. 1985. *Proposed United States–Israel Free Trade Agreement, Hearings,* 20 March.

US Congress. Senate. Committee on Finance, Subcommittee on International Trade. 98th Cong., 2nd sess. 1984. *Proposed Free-Trade Area with Israel, Hearings,* 6 February.

United States. Office of the President. 1985. *Establishment of a Free Trade Area Between the United States and Israel.* Message from the President of the United States, 29 April.

4

Strengthening Japan–US Cooperation and the Concept of Japan–US Free Trade Arrangements

Makoto Kuroda

Up to now the history of trade talks between Japan and the United States has been one of "coping with friction." In the 1960s the friction was principally over textiles, in the 1970s over steel and television sets, and in the 1980s over automobiles, machine tools, and semiconductors. In the 1980s the flames of friction have extended to farm products, as reflected in the controversy over the list of 12 agricultural items submitted by the United States to Japan. The issue over beef and oranges, on which the two countries recently reached an agreement in the direction of import liberalization, is still fresh in everyone's memory.

I am reviewing the history of trade friction not merely to recall the old wounds inflicted on the relationship between Japan and the United States, but as a reminder that these problems in fact occurred as trade expanded between our two countries. The amount of trade between Japan and the United States was in the vicinity of $115 billion in 1987, a nearly 19-fold increase over the level recorded 20 years ago. This rate of increase is much greater than the 10-fold increase in trade recorded during the same period between the United States and the European Community (EC)—the amount of trade between them was $155 billion in 1987. When thinking of the trade imbalance between Japan and the United States, some people tend to believe that only Japanese exports are expanding. But recently Japanese imports of US products have been expanding more noticeably than Japanese exports to the United States. US exports to Japan from January to October 1988 increased by about 36 percent over the same period a year before, as compared to only a little more than 6 percent for Japanese exports to the

Makoto Kuroda is former Vice Minister for International Affairs, Ministry of International Trade and Industry, Japan.

United States. Japan–US trade is expanding at a blistering pace on both sides of the Pacific.

Bilateral trade expands simply because it brings profits to both sides, and we should be fully aware of the fact that trade friction is a by-product of the plus-sum game called trade. Thus, intensification of trade friction is an indication of the increased interdependence of Japan and the United States, and should not be looked upon with too much pessimism. The important thing is to decide how to deal with this friction without embittering the overall relationship, because expansion of trade is precisely what brings about economic development in our two countries.

Japan achieved rapid economic growth under the postwar global economic policies implemented by the United States. It now has the second largest GNP in the free world, surpassed only by the United States. Together, Japan and the United States accounted in 1987 for a little less than 50 percent of the free world's GNP. The former US Ambassador to Japan, Mike Mansfield, has said that "the US–Japan relationship [is] the most important bilateral relationship in the world—bar none" (Mansfield 1988).

As a result, the intensification of friction between Japan and the United States not only aggravates the bilateral relationship but may very well have a negative effect on the world economy. As two of the biggest economic powers, Japan and the United States have reached that stage in their relationship at which they should seriously consider how they can contribute to the development not only of their own economies, but of the world economy as well, while effectively dealing with friction. From this perspective, Japan and the United States have an enormous obligation to build a new bilateral relationship.

What would this new bilateral relationship look like? To quote Ambassador Mansfield:

Given that economic competition will, and should, continue between the two countries, we need to cease this nickle-and-diming approach that we have fallen into and find a more collaborative, broader and longer range method of resolving our individual trade differences. . . . One idea worth looking at is the concept of a free trade agreement between the U.S. and Japan (Mansfield 1988).

The ambassador has advocated the necessity of examining the concept of a Japan–US free trade arrangement for many years, but since the end of 1987, Rep. Sam Gibbons (D-FL), the chairman of the House Ways and Means Subcommittee on Trade, and former Senate Majority Leader Robert Byrd (D-WV) have made similar statements. At his meeting in the United States with Prime Minister Takeshita in January 1988, the former Senate majority leader proposed that the two countries examine the pros and cons of establishing a free trade area between Japan and the United States, and later submitted with other senators a set of revised provisions obligating the government departments concerned to hammer out a framework for strengthening Japan–US ties.

The chairman of the Senate Finance Committee, Lloyd Bentsen (D-TX), instructed the US International Trade Commission (ITC) to conduct a survey on the merits and demerits of opening talks on a Japan–US free trade agreement. The ITC report was submitted to Congress in September 1988 (US ITC 1988). Before that, in January 1988, Professor Milton Friedman and 10 other economists placed an ad in the *Washington Post* urging the United States and Japan to begin talks on the establishment of a free trade zone between the two countries. The merits and demerits of the concept are gradually beginning to take shape, thanks to the ITC report and other research findings.

I believe the concept of free trade arrangements discussed here should be studied as one possible avenue of building a new comprehensive, collaborative relationship between two of the world's biggest economic powers. In carrying out such research, we should consider some areas that are covered in the Canada–US Free Trade Agreement, but we should also look into areas that go beyond the coverage of that pact. Unlike the United States and Canada, there exist important social and cultural differences between Japan and the United States. Moreover, as the two leading economic powers in the world, Japan and the United States exert enormous influence on the world economy as well as on each other. A prospective six-point agenda is set out below:

☐ Gradually removing border measures such as tariffs and quotas in all industries, including manufacturing and farming

☐ Removing barriers to economic activities in new areas addressed by the Uruguay Round, such as services, investment, and intellectual property rights, and establishing necessary rules

☐ Establishing a mechanism for dealing with disputes when they unfortunately occur

☐ Harmonizing systems in such areas as certification, standards, and competition policies

☐ Enhancing policy coordination, including macroeconomic policies, for maintaining and developing a sound world economy

☐ Exploring ways to engender joint responsibility for world economic security.

Let us now examine the impact that this new framework of cooperation would have on the Japan–US relationship.

Removing Commodity Trade Barriers

Since 1985, the yen–dollar exchange rate has fluctuated in a range roughly between 120 and 260 yen to the dollar. Given such wide fluctuations and the fact that Japan and the United States have already lowered their tariff levels for industrial products to 2 percent and 4 percent, respectively, industrial product tariffs as border measures have been losing their *raison d'être*.

On the other hand, nearly 30 percent of the value of Japan's exports to the United States is said to be subject to some form of restriction, such as voluntary export restraints (VERs). However, not a few people argue that most VERs are losing their significance. Even in agriculture, the dispute over the GATT's 12 items plus beef and oranges having been settled, liberalization has seen great progress. I believe the environment is becoming more conducive to efforts to remove other border barriers, while agreeing to keep exceptions to a minimum, within a medium- or long-term time frame as has been done in the Canada–US Free Trade Agreement.

With regard to agricultural trade, it should be pointed out that Japan is today the world's number one importer of foodstuffs (its food imports reached $22.4 billion in 1987); that the United States exports more food to Japan than to any other country in the world (26 percent of all food the United States exported in 1987 went to Japan); and that Japan depends on the United States for 30 percent of its food imports.

Removing Barriers and Establishing Rules in New Areas

We can expect further expansion in trade in services, which is becoming an increasingly important part of international economic activity. The economy will be further activated through the avoidance of unnecessary friction over intellectual property rights, and smooth investment activities. As for establishing new rules in these areas, if leading cases can be examined between Japan and the United States, this may greatly stimulate the efforts being made to establish multilateral rules in the new fields, at the Uruguay Round and elsewhere.

The service sector is one that is expected to play a leading role in postindustrial society. It is also an area in which the United States is strongly competitive since it is closer to the postindustrial stage than any other country in the world. I have long been one of those who hold the view that the US current account would be much stronger if we had an accurate grasp of services trade. Thus it will also be important to improve trade statistics so that they accurately reflect the trade flow in services as well.

Dealing With Disputes

As the standard-bearers of free trade, Japan and the United States should endeavor to strengthen GATT procedures and actively make use of them. However, just as bilateral coordination is the assumed first step even in the way GATT deals with disputes, it would be desirable if the trade frictions that unfortunately occur at times could be calmly dealt with on the basis of rules agreed upon bilaterally. Needless to say, the spirit of GATT should be fully respected, and any mechanism that violates it should not be tolerated.

Harmonization of Systems

It is not surprising that countries with different social, cultural, and historical backgrounds should have different systems and institutions. Hence, it is not surprising that there should be friction over differences in the distribution systems of Japan and the United States and over the way antitrust laws are enforced in the two countries. The important thing is not to stress the differences between the two countries, but to pinpoint those differences that constitute a hindrance to commodity and services trade and together to work out a way to remove the differences and achieve institutional harmony. Because the institutional differences are the result of accumulated historical and cultural differences, it is a mistake to insist on the rightness of one or the other side. What is important is to harmonize the pertinent institutions on both sides, or those of a third party, by capitalizing on the merits of each system.

Although the Japanese system is often criticized for being peculiar, when we examine systems on an international level, we sometimes find that the American system is also peculiar. A typical example is the United States' patent system. To acquire preferred status, the United States adopts the principle of granting patents on the basis of when a particular invention was made; Japan and the EC countries, on the other hand, adopt the principle of granting patents on the basis of when the application for a particular patent was made. The former method is seriously flawed—and has been criticized internationally—since it is extremely difficult to ascertain objectively when an invention is made, thus discriminating against inventions made outside the United States, and so patents were not granted at the time of invention.

Another difference between the system of granting patents in the United States and those in Japan and the EC is that, under the US system, the period of patent protection is reckoned not from the date of application but from the time a patent right is granted. This approach causes the protection period, including the inspection period, to be horrendously long when there are delays in the procedures for granting patent rights. In this age of rapid technological progress, the granting of such an extremely long period of protection has come under fire as unreasonable. That is why I have stressed the importance of achieving harmony by capitalizing on the merits of each system.

Economic Policy Coordination

There seems to be a general consensus among American economists that most of the trade imbalance between Japan and the United States is due to the lack of macroeconomic policy coordination. On the basis of such thinking, Japan has endeavored to continue its policy of expanding domestic demand, while the United States has endeavored to take concrete steps to reduce its budget deficit. Helped by this bilateral macroeconomic policy coordination and by US export efforts as well as Japanese import efforts, the US and Japanese trade imbalances are being rectified. Further macroeconomic policy coordination will be indispensable to solidify this favorable trend. But in this case, since the elasticity of US imports with respect to GNP is quite high by international standards, the importance of adopting proper measures to prevent an increase in imports and to tackle the budget deficit should be borne in mind.

Furthermore, it is necessary to coordinate efforts even in implementing such policies as strengthening industrial competitiveness. We should not forget that, for the United States to further expand its exports, it is necessary to encourage investments for expansion of plant and equipment capacity and for research and development. There are many outstanding enterprises in the United States, and Japanese enterprises have learned much from them. But it is said that in the United States the production sector of the economy is taken lightly, and that as a result most of today's bright people are absorbed by Wall Street. If this is true, some countermeasures will have to be taken.

Joint Responsibility

The economic system of the postwar era was built by the United States, which possessed unsurpassed economic and military power. It was under that system that Japan and Europe were able to achieve economic growth. History demands that Japan, as an economic power second only to the United States, bear its share of responsibility in managing the world economy and, together with the United States and the EC, help support the world economic order.

Japan is bound by its constitution to espouse pacifism, and most Asian countries do not want Japan to spend too much on a defense buildup. Therefore, Japan is restrained from contributing to the world militarily. Nevertheless, it is perfectly possible for Japan to assume its share of responsibility in solving the problems of accumulated debt, energy, the environment, and other global matters. For instance, if Japan can help resolve the accumulated debt problem of Latin America, and contribute to its economic recovery, the countries in that region will once again become important markets for US exports, thus contributing significantly to reducing the trade deficit of the United States.

With regard to a comprehensive framework of cooperation between Japan and the United States, some US leaders hold the view that a permissible range of balance of trade goals should be established with an eye to solving the trade imbalance between the two countries. This view is wrong. A typical expression is found in a recent *Foreign Affairs* article by former Secretaries of State Henry Kissinger and Cyrus Vance (1988). A similar view is found in the bill submitted by Senator Max Baucus (D-MT) calling on the government to hold talks aimed at concluding a wide range of economic and trade agreements with Japan (US Congress 1989). I mention them here because I have always respected these three leaders, and I wholeheartedly agree with them that it is necessary to create a comprehensive framework for cooperation between Japan and the United States.

Although it is true that a US–Japan free trade agreement would not ensure the correction of the trade imbalance, it is not appropriate to try to rectify trade imbalances bilaterally in any event. It is contrary to the basic spirit of the GATT to create a bilateral framework for correcting imbalances. To engage in trade activities that include setting balance of trade goals amounts to a denial of free business activities and of the system of free trade. Thus, imposition of various quantitative restrictions to maintain such goals would greatly increase administrative costs and lead to an ultimate collapse of the international economic order. Furthermore, if the two countries agree on the basic idea that trade is carried out to improve the economic well-being of both the importing and the exporting country, then it is clear that the adverse effects of artificially manipulating the volume of trade would have to be borne by those who demand the products that are traded. It is obvious that the advocacy of government-managed trade directly contradicts the respect for the market mechanism that the United States has always espoused.

What impact will the new collaborative relationship between Japan and the United States have on third countries? In the first place, even if the concept of free trade is considered as a new framework of cooperation, it should be examined as a framework that is fully open to third countries. As for our relationships with the developing nations, it will be worthwhile to examine the possibility of introducing a unilateral element like that found in the Lomé Convention. Thus, as long as the framework is kept open, the impact on third countries will be minimal. If serious trade diversion should still occur, efforts should be made to somehow reduce such diversion, including multilateral measures. Through this process or others, the impact on third countries should be fully examined.

Looking at this issue more carefully, I believe that removing border measures, such as the tariffs between Japan and the United States in the manufacturing sector, would not necessarily have a substantial impact on third countries. As noted earlier, the tariff level for manufactured products is already extremely low, almost negligible considering the substantial fluctuations of exchange rates in recent years. Moreover, considerable preferential duties are now granted by Japan and the United States to developing countries. More and more observers are beginning to say that even the necessity of imposing voluntary export restraints on exports to the United States has been diminishing as production by US subsidiaries of Japanese companies expands. With regard to agriculture, farm trade accounts in many countries for a diminishing proportion of their trade as a whole, and so it should be possible to further minimize the problem, provided the new framework is kept open to third countries.

To begin with, the removal of border measures does not necessarily occupy a large part in the new cooperative framework between Japan and the United States. Besides, we can expect trade to expand greatly not only for the United States and Japan, but also for the rest of the world, if the economies of Japan and the United States can be revitalized in a healthy manner through the new framework. Particularly in new fields, it will be possible to expand new frontiers of global economic activities, provided trading rules are examined. In addition, the main framework will have a significant effect in stabilizing the world economy if the relationship between the two countries can be stabilized by effectively dealing with the unavoidable cases of friction connected with their greater interdependence. The world economy would be even more integrated if a similar concept of cooperation could be promoted with the EC, which will be more unified in 1992.

Conclusion

The first priority of the world economic order should be strengthening the GATT. Thus, we should exert our maximum effort to promote the Uruguay Round. There is no doubt that countries like Japan, which is not well endowed with raw materials, are the greatest beneficiaries of the GATT's multilateral free trade system.

However, it is also true that, as economic interchange accelerates, more friction unique to the Japan–US relationship will occur. We cannot turn a blind eye to these unique problems, which is why bilateral cooperation is so vital. Some express concern that such a bilateral scheme would dampen the enthusiasm for multilateral negotiations, but both multilateral and bilateral approaches are aimed at stimulating the economic activities of the United States, Japan, and the rest of the world. And it is fair to say that the multilateral and bilateral approaches will enhance each other—indeed, each will end up accelerating the other approach—if they proceed in a proper manner.

Of course, it will not be easy to realize a new framework of cooperation between Japan and the United States. For instance, it might be difficult to avoid political resistance from industries forced to make structural adjustment. Moreover, Japan and the United States, as the two leading economic powers, have a responsibility to act with a global perspective and to examine fully their relationship with any third country that may be influenced, however slightly. We will need to fully disclose to third countries the kind of collaborative framework that will be brought forth. The Japan–US framework of cooperation will not aim to form an economic bloc that may undermine the advantage of third countries. Rather it will aim to contribute to the growth of the world economy through stable development of the Japan–US relationship. Thus, if diversion of trade from third countries should bring about an unresolvable state of affairs, it may be necessary to consider granting those third countries the same preferential treatment that Japan and the United States share.

The two economic powers that currently account for just under 50 percent of free world GNP do not seem to have many vehicles to fulfill their responsibility for the growth of the world economy. The cost would be enormous if Japan and the United States should choose to go their separate ways—for example, by adopting protectionism or promoting the formation of economic blocs. Increased cooperation is the only road available to the Japan–US relationship.

It is hoped that clarifying the close relationship of interdependence that already exists between Japan and the United States in a systematic way, and indicating the framework of medium- and long-term cooperation between our two countries in a clear-cut manner, will help keep at bay the unnecessary friction that protectionism tends to trigger, thus bringing about economic growth in the two countries and engendering growth in the world economy. The greatest obstacle to such mutual cooperation is the lack of mutual trust that individuals in our two nations harbor, although I think that much of this distrust is based on misunderstanding. Like Bobby Kennedy and George Bernard Shaw before me, who asked not why but why not, I ask why not let us discuss how two of the largest economic powers should associate with each other to their hearts' content and with full awareness of the great responsibility they bear for the world economy.

In the future, we should strive to build a new collaborative framework and create a more forward-looking relationship of coordination and cooperation, instead of repeating the history of coping with friction. That indeed is the path that will fill the "trust gap," the biggest hindrance to Japan–US relations, and allow our two countries to contribute significantly to the world economy.

References

Kissinger, Henry, and Cyrus Vance. 1988. "Bipartisan Objectives for American Foreign Policy." *Foreign Affairs*, vol. 66, no. 5, Summer, 899–921.

Mansfield, Mike. 1988. "The United States and Japan: Facing the Pacific Century." Presented at the United States/Japan bilateral session, Tokyo, 31 August.

US Congress. Senate. S. 292. *Congressional Record*. 101st Cong. 1st sess., 1989. Vol. 135, pt. 8.

US International Trade Commission. 1988. *Pros and Cons of Initiating Negotiations with Japan to Explore the Possibility of a U.S.–Japan Free Trade Agreement*. Publication 2120. Washington: US International Trade Commission, September.

Comments

Robert Z. Lawrence

The environment for US–Japanese trade has improved. For the time being at any rate, trade frictions between the United States and Japan are likely to be much lower than they have been over the past few years. The weaker dollar has improved the competitiveness of US products, and the United States has now passed a new trade law, so that Congress will turn its attention away from trade matters. At the same time, Japan has made substantial progress in shifting its economy toward domestic-led growth, and significant progress has been made on such US–Japan trade issues as imports of beef and citrus and technological cooperation. The discussion over US–Japan trade policy can now turn from short-term concerns to longer-term strategic issues.

We must keep in mind, however, that over the next few years crucial decisions will be made in two other negotiating forums, namely, the multilateral trade negotiations in Geneva and the deliberations in Brussels on a single European market. New initiatives in US–Japan trade relations must be sensitive to their potential impact on these other initiatives.

In several quarters, people are beginning to advocate free trade negotiations between the United States and Japan. Two major arguments favor such an approach.

First, there is widespread recognition that current approaches to US–Japan trade problems are far from perfect. Sectoral negotiations bring out tensions because they require the government in the importing nation to "give away" the advantages of its producers without obtaining offsetting gains in another area to build up popular support. For example, Japan is asked to "sell out" its rice farmers to provide access for US farmers. True, the Japanese consumers gain, but this gain is diffused, whereas the costs are concentrated. Multisectoral approaches, however, could be more politically palatable because there are winners to offset the losers. A more open US steel market could be traded for a more open Japanese rice market, for example.

Second, some argue that by playing their bilateral cards right both the United States and Japan can influence the negotiations in Europe and at the GATT in a more favorable direction. The carrot of progress toward multilateralism requires reinforcement with the stick of complementary approaches along bilateral lines.

Robert Z. Lawrence is a Senior Fellow at the Brookings Institution.

The basic point I will make here, however, is that a move toward a US–Japan free trade area (FTA) would probably be too little too soon. What we should be doing now is coming to an agreement on the long-term goals of US–Japan trade relations. These goals should continue to be in the direction of open markets. Before discussing how these goals should be achieved, however, it is necessary to consider the desirability of an alternative: the managed approach to US–Japan trade.

Managed Trade

Some Americans now advocate that the United States strive for a system of managed trade. America's huge market and the threat of reciprocal treatment, they argue, will increase our leverage. Other nations, Japan in particular, allegedly take advantage of the open US market while reserving local markets for domestic firms. Instead of unrealistically assuming that nations can be induced to follow liberal practices, the United States should accept the diversity in the international system and bargain over results, not rules. We should exact foreign sales in return for access to our market. Cyrus Vance and Henry Kissinger argue for a quota on aggregate US–Japan trade; Lester Thurow suggests, in fact, setting a quota for Japanese exports to the United States that would be auctioned quarterly; Clyde Prestowitz would like to run US–Japan trade like the international airline agreement.

In my view, however, the United States should not abandon the goal of a liberal trading system. If we lead the world toward a new system of managed trade, all countries will lose, and in fact the United States would be hurt more than its trading partners. A managed trade system will benefit those countries best able to manage their economies centrally, and the United States is not one of them. Aside from the inefficiencies inherent in such a system, it will not improve trading conditions for the United States. By limiting the quantity or dollar value of goods foreign nations can sell in the United States, we raise the incentive for them to charge us as high a price as possible. If foreign governments can use US help to limit competition among their exporting firms, those firms can act like monopolists to maximize profits. Given the ability of the Japanese Ministry of International Trade and Industry (MITI) to guide its firms, the Japanese would collude effectively. The United States, however, would be less likely to allocate its products strategically and more likely to do so on political grounds.

We have seen in numerous cases that managed trade hurts the United States by worsening our terms of trade. The United States is, in fact, the best proponent of Japanese industrial policies. We strengthen the hand of MITI by forcing them to organize cartels and by upgrading Japanese exports within and between product categories.

So I think trying to move toward a managed system would be a great error. Contrary to the forecasts of those who would manage US–Japan trade, we are seeing, as a result of the impact of the strong yen, major changes taking place moving Japan in a direction toward more openness. These changes need to be encouraged.

A New Initiative

The United States and Japan should agree to aim for economies that are open to the rest of the world—not simply to each other, but economies that in turn are part of a single world market. We should lay out what kinds of policies are required to take us there and establish a framework for establishing priorities and moving us to this goal over the next two decades. If we keep this goal in mind, then we can explore what kinds of steps we can take bilaterally to bring such an arrangement closer.

I agree with many of the things Mr. Kuroda has said. At the same time, while I advocate setting in motion the development of a consensus, and a common vision in our two countries is required, I am less enthusiastic about putting current emphasis on an FTA, which could run the risk of confusing form with substance.

In his provocative book, *Trading Places*, Clyde Prestowitz argues that Japanese and Americans have very different conceptions about what makes a market open. He quotes the president of Revlon as saying that in Japan everything is prohibited unless expressly allowed, while in the United States everything is allowed unless expressly prohibited. Prestowitz argues that because we are so different we should simply give up on talking about rules and instead negotiate about results. I think we need to agree on what we mean by "open," and I am very encouraged by the Maekawa Report, which says "in order to make Japan more internationally open, policies based upon market mechanisms should be implemented from the viewpoint of 'freedom in principle, restrictions only as exceptions.' " That is exactly the goal I am talking about.

So I am very sympathetic to moves toward liberalization. At the same time, I am not naive. A free trade agreement that is hastily negotiated could set back the goal of achieving markets that are genuinely open.

For the present we must accept that we still have very different institutional arrangements in our economies—and not just those imposed by governments at the borders. We have very different industrial structures, government–business relations, regulations, and distribution systems. A traditional FTA would deal primarily with traditional border barriers. But I suspect that while the removal of border barriers would leave the US market open, this is less likely to be the case with Japan. I do not believe, therefore, that an

FTA arrangement that deals mainly with tariffs, quotas, and other formal border barriers would be sufficient.

This means our problem is much more complex. It leads me toward trying to actually construct a single market—a much more ambitious objective because it requires extensive harmonization—or mutual recognition of regulatory regimes.

But trying to achieve this goal is a much bigger task than negotiations over a few general rules of the game. Indeed, one of the dangers of an FTA approach would be the illusion that we can achieve liberalization on the cheap. We have seen the EC initiative involving eight years of work and 300 measures, and the US and Japanese economies are even more different.

We should therefore forgo the notion that we can eliminate trade frictions. I agree with Mr. Kuroda that trade frictions are actually a barometer of interdependence—that is, of increasing trade and investment—itself a very positive force. They are inevitable. If we keep our objectives in mind, we will realize that the way in which we have tried to relieve the frictions has often been in conflict with what should be our goal, which is not to avoid frictions but to achieve open markets. You cannot resolve Japanese agricultural protectionism without major political costs, regardless of what else is in the package.

There also will be significant transactions costs. The United States cannot deal with Japan with a US Trade Representative's staff the size of the current one. The resources the US government has provided for negotiations are appalling. We cannot do these things on a shoestring. The FTA approach offers the illusion that the United States can run US–Japan trade relations cheaply. In whichever direction we move, the United States will have to spend more on improving its trade bureaucracy.

Mr. Kuroda mentions the lack of trust in the hearts of the people of Japan and the United States, which he feels is brought about by misunderstanding. I think he is correct, and that it would be a mistake to establish an FTA until these perceptions change. One key aspect will be the achievement of positive results by foreign firms who sell in Japan. Japan has made progress, but until we have major groups with strong interests in selling in Japan we will not have the conditions for reaching such an agreement. A second problem is the perception that an FTA is something Japan would do for the United States and not something that is in its own interest. Until there is a deep Japanese desire for an open home market, an FTA is a mistake. The Canada–US agreement or arrangements with Mexico would not succeed if seen as US initiatives.

Nor am I sure a bilateral dispute settlement mechanism between our countries would be desirable. I think the GATT can be very beneficial. I applaud Japan for now using the GATT to question European actions, and

I think we should bring each other to the GATT rather than try unilateral or bilateral mechanisms.

I also differ with Mr. Kuroda about the implications of such an agreement for other trading partners. Japan, Korea, and other Asian countries all produce substitute products. Trade diversion would be quite considerable. Japan's and America's other trading relationships would be threatened.

I also am not sure what Mr. Kuroda means by saying "participation by other countries would be welcome even if the scope of participation would be limited." Would we let the Koreans enter just in electronics, or the Argentines just in wheat?

Finally, I question whether actually going ahead with a US–Japan arrangement in the next few years would help the Uruguay Round or contribute to an open Europe. If we moved too fast on a comprehensive approach, we might dramatically tilt the Europeans toward a fortress Europe and the GATT toward failure. Like nuclear deterrence, a bilateral US–Japan stick has a value as long as it is not used.

I believe in a new framework for the US–Japan relationship, but not an FTA. We should be committed to restructuring our economies to become open components of a single world market at some time in the future. Let us try, for example, to agree on issues in which we can set an example for the rest of the GATT. Now that Japan is organizing voluntary restraint arrangements with Korea and others in textiles, we both could improve our behavior. Let us agree in the future that we will conduct safeguard actions in our two countries and use only tariffs rather than quotas.

I heartily endorse the idea Mr. Kuroda has suggested of mutual recognition of standards. We could make progress here independently of other areas. Similarly we should make progress in reaching understandings on our national approaches to investment rules. But again these understandings should be viewed as models for a more open system, to apply wherever possible to all countries willing to reciprocate. Thus, the United States would define more clearly its national defense exception and rules for registration.

We need a broad framework for our relationship that could include agreement on a set of long-term objectives such as eventually having a single market, and perhaps on a date of 2000 or 2010. This definitional period should not be confined to governments but should include unions, trade associations, and firms as well. Let us have a binational vision of the kind MITI is so famous for, but let us not commit ourselves to a particular, hastily negotiated agreement.

Comments

Clyde Prestowitz

For over 30 years trade frictions between the United States and Japan have been growing more frequent and more serious. Many attempts have been made to color these problems. Just as today multilateralism and the Uruguay Round are seen as the solution, so in years past the launching of the Tokyo Round was hailed as the magic key to trade tranquillity. Later, the Strauss–Ushiba agreement, which was an attempt at a comprehensive, overall settlement, was highly praised. Indeed, it was Ambassador Mike Mansfield, one of the main proponents of the current free trade area idea, who stated at the conclusion of Strauss–Ushiba that the Japanese market was now open and that all problems between the United States and Japan had been removed.

Later still, the Trade Committee, the Sub-cabinet Group, the Trade Facilitation Committee, the Industrial Policy Dialogue, and the High Technology Working Group dealt with a series of individual issues. The efforts of these groups were punctuated by the presentation of a series of "market opening packages" by Japan, apparently oblivious of the fact that the presentation of each new package merely belied the promise that the previous one had finally opened the Japanese market.

At the same time, on the American side there was the conclusion of a series of voluntary export restraints (VERs) and other market-restricting agreements that demonstrated clearly that under pressure the United States would not put its money behind its free trade rhetoric.

The current proposal is being presented as a new idea that will avoid the inevitable bitterness of issue-by-issue slogging by taking a comprehensive, overall approach. But this is not at all a new idea. Indeed, the irony is particularly rich here. In the early 1980s the United States, in various forums, urged Japan to make a comprehensive effort to open its markets. The Japanese response was to ask for specifics: just what markets and what procedures had to be opened? The American attempt to be concrete in response inevitably led to issue-by-issue sparring.

Again, in 1984, fearing precisely the bitterness that has since come to pass, the US Department of Commerce and the US Trade Representative (USTR) proposed a comprehensive approach aimed at achieving certain overall results. This time the overall approach was rejected by the other

Clyde Prestowitz is a Senior Associate at the Carnegie Endowment for International Peace and formerly was Counselor of the US Department of Commerce.

agencies of the US government, which insisted on the famous MOSS (market-oriented sector-specific) talks in preference to the Commerce/USTR proposal, which was seen as an attempt at market management.

Even as MOSS was being launched, however, another kind of market management aimed at an overall solution was being launched with great fanfare and high praise. This was the coordinated devaluation of the dollar, which involved massive intervention and coordination of the exchange markets, perhaps the most important ones of all.

Now that MOSS has made only very marginal gains at the cost of much rancor, and devaluation has barely dented the trade deficit at the cost of halving America's relative wealth, we are being presented with a new overall strategy. But is it new or simply "déjà vu"?

What Is a Free Trade Agreement?

Discussion to date has been sufficiently vague, perhaps purposely so, that it is not clear exactly what is being proposed. However, there are three broad possibilities. Most often discussed is something like the Canada–US free trade pact. The main focus of attention is tariffs, quotas, and other classes of border measures, along with harmonization of certain administrative procedures. A second, less discussed alternative would be an attempt to achieve comparable market openness in the two countries by dealing also with the informal barriers to trade that arise from business practices, industry structure, and industrial policies. A third alternative would be a comprehensive renegotiation of the entire US–Japan relationship, including trade, investment, technology, and defense.

What Is the Problem?

In US–Japan trade, there are always two problems. One is the trade problem itself, which includes the US deficit, the impact of import surges on depressed industries, and the effect of industrial and national security policies on advanced industries. The other is the political problem that arises from the trade problem. This problem is largely a question of the reaction of the US Congress and the business community to pain caused by import surges or perceived unfairness of one kind or another. Many observers do not believe the trade problem is a problem, and thus see the political issues as the major ones.

Recently, however, a third aspect has come to the fore. The balance of world power is shifting from the United States to Japan. That is not necessarily sinister, but it is significant. Historically, the United States has uncoupled trade from other aspects of its relations with Japan. It was able to do this because of the luxury of overwhelming superiority, but that luxury is gone. Uncoupling has always been preferred in order to avoid harming overall relations. It may now be the case, however, that it is precisely the uncoupling that harms the relationship.

What Is the Solution?

The easiest approach, and therefore the one most discussed and most likely to be executed, is something that mimics the Canada–US pact. Tariffs could be reduced to zero, quotas removed, and administrative procedures harmonized. Unfair US trade procedures probably also would be relaxed. Of course, just as with Canada, difficult issues such as rice or industries deemed critical to national security probably would be postponed or excluded.

The result could be presented as a spectacular success. Removal of tariffs on 10,000 items and "opening" of markets worth billions of dollars could be announced. It could be said, under the bicycle theory of trade negotiations, that momentum had been maintained. This strategy is aimed primarily at dealing with the political side of the trade problem. Zero tariffs and billions of dollars of new trade opportunities are calculated to make Congress feel good.

The rice case aside, there still remains a problem. Tariffs and quotas are not significant influences on US–Japan trade. Taking a tariff to zero sounds good, but if it is from 2 percent the change is meaningless. As such, this approach would have little effect on trade. It would not reduce the bilateral deficit, nor would it remove the factors behind the charges of unfair trade and the countercharges of lack of effort.

In fact, the result would be the following:

□ US exports to Japan would not increase significantly.

□ Japanese exports to the United States would continue to grow and might even surge in response to removal of VERs and of the double restraint arising from fear of political repercussions, as well as from relaxation of unfair US trade laws.

□ US industry would continue to operate at a disadvantage to Japanese industry in terms of market opportunities, but it would no longer be seen to have a justifiable complaint, because by definition the markets would be "open." All blame then would be heaped on US management for "not trying hard enough."

Ultimately, the inequity of this approach and the lack of results would be perceived. Congress and business alike would come to believe they had been deceived, and trade tension would rise again. This approach is not a solution, it is "déjà vu."

Implicit in the adoption of the second strategy is the belief that there is a real trade problem. This approach is an effort to deal with it substantially by going beyond border measures to deal with structural and social barriers to trade.

While noble in concept, this strategy is doomed because it is nothing more than MOSS on a grand scale. Take just one example. Strengthening protection of intellectual property is high on everyone's list of trade priorities. There have been many US complaints about Japan in this regard. Much discussion has focused on supposed inadequacies in Japanese patent law and differences in US and Japanese procedures.

In fact, Japanese patent law is not the problem. Japan's law is the same as Germany's, and we have no problem with Germany on patents. Japanese procedures are sometimes idiosyncratic, and in some cases it is difficult to resist the conclusion that they were influenced by considerations of industrial policy. But the real problem is not procedures either. It is the weakness of Japan's judicial system. As a practical matter, someone whose patents are being infringed in Japan knows that his chances of obtaining redress via the Japanese courts are very small. Consequently, he tends to enter into disadvantageous licensing arrangements as the lesser of two evils.

But is the United States really going to insist on reform of Japan's judicial system as part of a free trade arrangement? To ask the question is to answer it. The Canada–US pact took years to negotiate and postponed most of the difficult problems—and that was between the world's two most similar nations. MOSS essentially failed on a small scale. Relying on MOSS will fail on a grand scale, and its failure again will exacerbate tensions. While perhaps more sincere, the second strategy also is "déjà vu."

This leaves the third approach, a comprehensive restructuring of the entire relationship. Such a negotiation would do away with the implicit assumption of US mentorship that still guides the relationship. It would recognize that linkages among trade, investment, security, and political relationships can no longer be denied. Most important, it would recognize that fundamental differences in the two societies mean that the same procedures and rules will lead to very different results in the two countries. Since expectations are that similar processes should give roughly similar results, the opposite of the expectation will always engender suspicions of unfairness.

Comprehensive restructuring of the relationship would recognize this and focus more on results and less on procedures. This kind of an approach is not "déjà vu"; it is truly new, and it should be undertaken. If the label "free trade arrangement" provides a convenient cover for it, that is all to the good. However, the negotiators should be under no illusions. This very necessary restructuring is not going to be a free trade agreement à la the EC or the Canada–US pact. It will be an accommodation between the world's two greatest powers.

5

More Free Trade Areas: A Korean Perspective

Yung Chul Park and Jung Ho Yoo

Interest in customs unions and free trade areas (FTAs) has been renewed these days as a free trade agreement has been reached between the United States and Canada, and as European countries attempt to form an economic union on the continent. More FTAs are being contemplated in the United States, and this prospect is of keen interest to many in the private sector. If the United States succeeds in persuading other trade partners to establish bilateral FTAs, it will eventually create a free trade area that resembles a star, in which the United States trades freely with all partners that agree to bilateral free trade, while other countries continue to maintain trade restrictions among themselves.

The Canada–US agreement is pathbreaking, holding many significant implications for the future of global trading arrangements. If it encourages similar FTAs in different regions of the world, the Canada–US FTA could serve as an intermediate step toward the ultimate objective of a much more liberalized global trading system.

In this respect, the proliferation of FTAs could both complement and supplement the Uruguay Round of trade negotiations. Some aspects of the bilateral agreement between the United States and Canada could serve as a model for multilateral trade negotiations. Most of all, the Canada–US FTA could help the negotiating parties of the Uruguay Round break out of the stalemate on a number of contentious issues such as agriculture and service trade liberalization.

There is also the possibility that the Canada–US FTA may develop into, or acquire some of the features of, a customs union or common market in

Yung Chul Park is Professor of Economics at Korea University. This chapter was written during his tenure as Visiting Professor in the Department of Economics at Harvard University and Research Associate at the Harvard Institute for International Development. Jung Ho Yoo is a Senior Fellow at the Korea Development Institute in Seoul.

which the United States and Canada harmonize their policies with regard to the rest of the world. This development, however unlikely it may be, will produce strong incentives for other groups of countries to form similar unions, thereby dividing the world economy into a number of economic blocs.

This chapter analyzes the implications of FTAs for bilateral as well as multilateral trade relations from the perspective of a small, open economy, the Republic of Korea. The case for a bilateral FTA must in the end be based on a better understanding of whether such an arrangement would help improve the allocative efficiency and welfare of the two partner countries. The first section is devoted to an examination of this question, focusing on how an FTA affects trade patterns in a setting where intermediate inputs are traded and taxed. In particular, the possibility of trade suppression and trade reversal effects is discussed. Also discussed are some of the advantages the center country may enjoy in comparison with other partners in a star-shaped FTA. The next section considers some of the economic forces that could steer the Canada–US FTA into a customs union. Against this background, arguments for and against a bilateral FTA between Korea and the United States are analyzed. Concluding remarks are presented in the final section.

The Effects of an FTA on Trade Patterns

This section considers the effects of an FTA on the trade between the partner countries inside the FTA and between the partner countries and the countries outside the FTA. We attempt to anticipate what may happen to trade patterns as FTAs are formed between the United States and other countries. In particular, we first discuss the effects of an FTA on trade when intermediate inputs are traded and taxed. Second, we consider the impact on trade patterns if the United States should form independent bilateral FTAs with a number of countries.

In the following discussion it is assumed that goods are produced by combining factors of production and intermediate inputs. The intermediate inputs are required in fixed physical quantities per unit of output, whereas the value-added part of a good is produced by factors of production. Factor abundance and technology determine how factors are combined and how efficient the factors are in producing the value-added part. Under these assumptions, if there were no tariffs or subsidies, the cost of the intermediate inputs of a given good would be the same for all countries. Then the unit cost of a good would differ between countries because the cost of the value-added part differs, and a country's comparative advantage among goods would be determined by factor abundance and technology. Goods exported by a country would be those in which the country has comparative advantage. In this chapter we do not further discuss determination of comparative advantage but merely assume that a pattern of comparative advantage is given.

Trade Suppression

Since Viner's pioneering study it has been well established that a customs union or FTA has trade-creating or diverting effects as it removes import tariffs. Less well known is the trade-suppressing effect whereby the domestic production of a partner country inside an FTA replaces imports of a good from the outside. Viner mentions the possibility of such an effect in the larger market of a customs union, as economies of scale operate to lower the partner countries' unit costs in some industries below the levels attainable in their own individual markets (Viner 1950, 45).

These effects of trade creation, diversion, and suppression that Viner considered concern the goods from which import tariffs are removed. They would be the only effects of a customs union or FTA on trade patterns if all traded goods were final goods—that is, if they were used only by investors and consumers. But traded goods also are used by producers as intermediate inputs. Thus, tariff removal not only affects the demand for the tariff-removed goods, but also affects the supply price of other goods in the production of which the tariff-removed good is used. For this reason, if intermediate inputs are traded and taxed, an FTA can have other effects on trade patterns than those mentioned above.

One of the possible outcomes of an FTA is trade suppression that occurs as the importing country's domestic production replaces some or all imports from a low-cost country outside the FTA. The trade suppression can occur with respect to all goods that require inputs of the tariff-removed goods. Tariffs on imported inputs raise the unit cost of the final goods; tariff removal would mean a reduction in the cost of intermediate inputs to producers of the final goods. Thus, as the partner countries of an FTA remove import tariffs on goods traded between them, the domestic producers in these countries will be able to lower the prices of their final goods to become more competitive vis-à-vis the outside producers, against whom the tariffs and other trade barriers remain unchanged. As a result, some trade suppression will take place.

This outcome, unlike Viner's trade suppression, does not require increasing returns to scale. It also differs from Viner's concept in that it concerns the trade in goods other than those from which import tariffs are removed.

In fact, the trade suppression effect is expected to be a commonplace phenomenon for all goods that require intermediate inputs of tariff-removed goods in their production.

It is possible in extreme cases that the trade suppression may result in a trade reversal. What causes the trade suppression is the reduction in input costs due to the tariff removal. If the cost reduction is large enough, a country that used to be an importer of a final good before formation of an FTA may become an exporter afterward.

However, a trade reversal can happen only if the situation before the FTA is unusual. Since the final good used to be imported despite the tariff, the trade reversal requires that the reduction in intermediate input costs after the FTA is formed be greater than the tariff on the final good. Only then will the country be able to outcompete other countries under no tariff protection, and export the good. This is a case of negative effective protection of the final good before the FTA and restoration of competitiveness hidden under a tariff structure afterward.

The Center Country's Advantage

A second possible outcome of a star-shaped FTA, when intermediate inputs are traded and taxed, is another form of trade suppression. It is similar to the first in that domestic production replaces a country's imports after an FTA is formed, but it differs in that the replaced imports originate from the partner country in an FTA and not from the outside.

To explore the possibility of this type of trade suppression, suppose that the simplest form of a star-shaped FTA is established: a three-country (A, B, C) world where country A forms two separate FTAs with countries B and C so that A becomes the center country. Further suppose that there are goods 1, 2, and 3, and that country A exports good 1 to the other two countries; country B exports good 2 to the other two; and country C exports good 3 to the other two.

Under this setting, we are investigating the possibility of trade suppression where country A replaces its imports of good 2 from B with domestic production. The star-shaped FTA will remove A's tariffs on imports of goods 2 and 3 and B's import tariff on good 1 from A. Thus, after the star-shaped FTA is formed, A's producers will see its cost of intermediate inputs drop. The greater the drop, the more competitive A's producers become vis-à-vis B's producers. If the sum of A's tariffs on goods 2 and 3 were sufficiently large to enable A's producers to lower the price of good 2 by more than B's producers after the star-shaped FTA is formed, then A's domestic production will replace some imports of good 2 from B.

However, it should be noted that country A's removal of the tariff on good 2 alone cannot make A's producers more competitive. Although the tariff removal makes it possible for A's producers to lower the price of good 2 by a fraction of the tariff, depending on how important good 2 is as an intermediate input in its own production, it can reduce B's supply price in A's market by the tariff itself. Hence, the removal of the tariff on good 2 will make B more competitive relative to A. In contrast, A's removal of the tariff on good 3 can increase A's competitiveness in good 2 relative to B. This tariff removal provides A's producers with a reduction in input costs that is not available to B's producers. Therefore, trade suppression is possible in which the center country A's domestic production replaces imports from a partner country in a star-shaped FTA.

It is also conceivable that trade suppression can lead in an extreme case to trade reversal. In the above example, country A may start exporting good 2 to country B in the star-shaped FTA. Suppose that the tariffs on intermediate inputs were so high that A's producers of good 2, although more efficient than their counterparts in B in producing the value-added part, were not competitive enough to be able to keep the imports off the domestic market even under the tariff protection. If this were the case, the star-shaped FTA would make A's producers competitive again by removing those tariffs, possibly turning A into an exporter of good 2. Again, this is a case of an FTA restoring the comparative advantage hidden under a negative effective protection.

Lastly, a peculiar form of trade diversion is possible in a star-shaped FTA whereby the center country becomes an importer and an exporter of the same good at the same time. This possibility is not a result of the presence of intermediate inputs as were the possibilities of trade suppression and reversal. It arises because of the rules of origin of FTAs and the center country's advantage in market access of having to pay no import tariffs when exporting to the partner countries.

The possibility of trade diversion can be seen using the above example of a three-country world. If, after the formation of a star-shaped FTA, country A still imports good 2 from B, while also domestically producing some of the good, the unit cost of good 2 must be the same in both A and B. This makes B unable to compete with A in C's market, since B has to pay the import tariff to enter the market whereas A does not. A conceivable outcome in this situation is a transshipment of B's good 2 through A to C, although the rules of origin would prevent it. Thus, if A's unit cost exceeds B's but not by more than C's import tariff, B must be exporting good 2 to A, and at the same time A will be able to outcompete B and export good 2 to C. In this case, country A will be both exporting and importing the same good at the same time. We have seen that an FTA can give rise to trade suppression, as tariff removal lowers the cost of intermediate inputs while the input costs remain the same for the producers outside the FTA. We have also seen another form of trade suppression, very similar to this, in the relation between the center country and other partner countries in a star-shaped FTA. For imports from all the partner countries of individual FTAs, the center country removes its tariffs. Each partner country also removes its tariffs on imports from the center country. Thus, the reduction in intermediate input costs is greater for the producers in the center country than for those in the other partner countries. For this reason, in a star-shaped FTA, trade suppression is possible whereby the center country's domestic production replaces the imports from the partner countries.

This competitive disadvantage from the partner countries' point of view can be overcome by unilateral removal of their own import tariffs. However, there is another disadvantage that the partner countries cannot easily overcome: the disadvantage of having to pay import tariffs to enter markets that the center country enters freely. This gives rise to the possibility of the center country becoming an importer and an exporter of the same good at the same time. This peculiar trade diversion reveals the inefficiencies of a star-shaped FTA and poses some practical problems, which are discussed in the following section.

Peculiar Trade Diversion

Two issues arise in connection with the peculiar trade diversion that can occur in a star-shaped FTA. One is whether the disadvantage is of the same degree for all partner countries, and, if not, what determines the degree. The other is the policy question of what can be done about the inefficiency involved in the trade diversion.

Regarding the partner countries' disadvantage, the following generalization seems warranted.

Proposition: The closer a partner country is to the center country in basic economic conditions, such as factor abundance and technology, in a star-shaped FTA, the greater the country's disadvantage in price competition relative to the center country in a third market in the FTA.

The reason is that the closer the two countries are in basic economic conditions, the more influential are the import tariffs in determining the countries' relative competitiveness in a given good.

Suppose that, in the above example, country B is very close to country A in basic economic conditions, and consider the competition between A and B in a given good in a third partner's market. The value-added component of a unit cost, which is determined by factor abundance and technology, cannot differ significantly between the two countries. Therefore, the difference in unit cost between A and B will depend more on the other component of unit cost, namely, the cost of intermediate inputs. Since the cost of intermediate inputs differs between countries only because of the tariffs on them, the difference in import tariffs will be the primary determinant of the difference in unit costs between A and B.

Hence, the more similar the two countries' basic economic conditions, the greater the effect of tariff removal on the difference in a good's unit cost between them. The star-shaped FTA removes a greater number of import tariffs on intermediate inputs for the center country than for the other partners. Moreover, market access differs between the center and the partner countries. In entering the markets of the countries other than A and B in the FTA, A does not pay import tariffs whereas B has to. For these reasons, the greater the similarity between A and B in basic economic conditions, the more likely it is that the star-shaped FTA will make A more competitive than B in a third partner country.

The second issue concerns the inefficiency involved in the peculiar trade diversion in the star-shaped FTA. Obviously, the trade diversion involves inefficient use of resources from the perspective of all countries in the FTA. The center country can be both an importer and an exporter of the same good at the same time, but no country can be both an efficient and an inefficient producer at the same time. This unusual outcome can arise, on the one hand, because of the center country's advantage and the other partner countries' relative disadvantage in market access in the star-shaped FTA and, on the other hand, because of the FTA's rules of origin.

The difference in market access between the center country and the other partner countries is likely to have a greater significance than the disadvantage implied by the peculiar trade diversion. In a star-shaped FTA, all markets of the partner countries are in effect integrated from the center country's point of view. For each of the individual partner countries, only its own market and the center country's market are integrated. The difference in size between these "integrated markets" will undoubtedly provide the center country with a better opportunity to benefit from the economies of scale. The effect is likely to be a strengthened export competitiveness for the center country vis-à-vis its partners.

Together with the peculiar trade diversion, this result may give rise to the perception that only the center country benefits from the star-shaped FTA. However, in the case of a star-shaped FTA with the United States as the center country, this perception needs to be weighed against the generally accepted proposition that, when trade is liberalized between a large and a small country, the latter gains more than the former. In any case, the partner countries can partially offset this relative disadvantage in exportation by unilaterally removing their own tariffs on intermediate inputs imported from other trade partners, as noted earlier. Then the unit costs will be lowered and their goods will become more competitive. However, the disadvantage is also due to the higher barriers that a partner country faces, which the center country does not, in exporting final goods to the other partner countries in the FTA, and to this extent the disadvantage remains. Thus, it seems that the disadvantage cannot be fully overcome unless each partner country forms bilateral FTAs with the other partners as the center country does, or all the trade partners form an integrated FTA among themselves.

It is possible, however, to approximate the effect of turning the star-shaped FTA into an integrated FTA without really doing it. This can be done by changing the rules of origin among the partner countries. Rules of origin are intended to prevent imports of an outside country's goods passing through a partner in the FTA. If in each of country A's bilateral FTAs the rules of origin are made less stringent on those goods originating from A's partner countries and reexported by A, the partner countries' disadvantage vis-à-vis A in exportation can be considerably lessened. For example, if country C does not apply any rules of origin on the goods imported from A that originate from B, then B will have no disadvantage in exportation vis-à-vis A in entering C's market. If A's partner countries collectively abolish the rules of origin altogether for the goods imported from A but originating from any of the partner countries in the star-shaped FTA, they practically eliminate all the disadvantage. The result is the same as forming an integrated FTA whose member countries do not levy tariffs on goods coming from each other, except that there will still be an inefficient transshipment of goods from one partner country to another through the center country. That this inefficiency remains shows how much more inefficient the star-shaped FTA is when rules of origin are strict.

A Korea–US FTA: Issues and Prospects

The Canada–US Free Trade Agreement is a historic development with many important implications for the future of the world trading system. No doubt many countries are poring over the language of the agreement to determine what it means for their future trade relations with both Canada and the United States. To a small economy like Korea, which depends on trade for growth and development and which has developed strong and extensive economic and security ties with the United States, the FTA makes the future trading environment more uncertain and makes it more difficult to develop a consistent trade policy and position in negotiations with its trading partners in a bilateral or a multilateral framework.

Although the two countries are 6,000 miles apart and separated by an ocean, more than 30 percent of Korea's trade has been with the United States. Korea is seeking, as did Canada, expanded as well as secure access to the United States market. However, Korea can expect neither to reach a free trade agreement with the United States that is as extensive as the Canada–US agreement nor to work out one as easily.

Although the United States is by far Korea's most important trade partner, the Korean public is highly skeptical about the possibility of establishing an FTA between the two countries. Aside from the usual dependency rhetoric, Korea will find it difficult to accommodate US demands on agriculture and services trade; without extracting a concession on this longstanding issue, the United States will have little interest in an FTA with Korea. Furthermore, many in Korea have voiced concern that an FTA with the United States could be perceived as a means of correcting the bilateral current account imbalance, although there is no reason to believe that liberal trade will solve what is essentially a macroeconomic problem.

If, however, any of the other Asian countries that compete with Korea in the North American market were to successfully establish an FTA with the United States, Korea would be forced to change its position. A crucial question is whether Korea could afford to remain outside of such a star-shaped economic union. Would such a proliferation of FTAs facilitate the ongoing Uruguay Round of trade negotiations, with the expectation of strengthening and expanding the GATT system? This question is important because, as a small trading nation, Korea will gain more from successful trade liberalization through multilateral than through bilateral negotiations. To answer these questions, one must begin with a careful examination of the effects of the Canada–US FTA on Korea's trade relations not only with the two countries, but also with other countries.

Since it is a bilateral trade agreement, the Canada–US FTA does not cover trade with other countries. It establishes a free trade area, not a customs union. As such, both countries are free to pursue their own independent trade policies with respect to all other countries. This will not be the case in reality, however. Instead, the two contracting parties will find it much more advantageous and in fact necessary to coordinate their trade and industrial policies vis-à-vis third countries. This could have several effects. It may strain rather than strengthen the economic relations between a country like Korea on the one hand and Canada and the United States on the other; it may interfere with the process of the Uruguay Round of trade negotiations; and in the end it could drive other countries to form an economic union among themselves, thereby dividing the world economy into several economic blocs.

From Korea's perspective, it appears that the Canada–US FTA is not likely to directly affect Korea's trade relations with either country or the rest of the world. Canada accounts for only a small fraction of Korea's exports (3.4 percent) and imports (2.2 percent), and because the two countries' exports differ greatly, the competition between Korea and Canada in the United States or other markets is not very keen. Korea will experience, at least in the short run, some trade diversion as a result of the Canada–US FTA. However, to the extent that the two countries coordinate their trade and industrial policies more closely than before, other countries—especially those engaged in bilateral trade negotiations with either the United States or Canada—may find themselves conducting trade negotiations not with these countries independently, but with a North American union.

In their trade negotiations with the rest of the world, the United States and Canada will face strong internal pressures to form a common position and support it jointly. This will obviously strengthen the bargaining position of both countries. Furthermore, the two countries' trade policies after forming an FTA may become less liberal, as the experience of the European Community's Common Agricultural Policy suggests. Specifically, the closer coordination of trade policy between the two countries necessitated by the FTA is likely to make Canada pursue a more protectionist policy. This probability will increase if the United States is not able to reduce its current account deficit to a manageable level and turns to trade restrictions to protect its industries.

To clarify this line of reasoning, let us suppose that, through bilateral trade negotiation between the United States and Korea, Korea makes a trade concession by removing quantitative restrictions on a commodity that the United States exports. Suppose further that Canada also exports this commodity to Korea, but a similar concession is not extended to Canada because Canada is not involved in the US–Korea negotiations. Irrespective of its relation with the United States, Canada will protest against such a discriminatory trade policy. After joining the United States in an FTA, however, Canada's disadvantage stemming from such discrimination becomes more evident. The situation is similar to that of the star-shaped FTA already discussed, and a trade diversion similar to that peculiar case may occur. Because of their advantage in market access, US exporters will be able to sell more and could take away Canada's share of the Korean market.

This expansion will in turn allow US exporters to exploit economies of scale and help reduce the production costs of the goods in question. Depending upon the size of the market, the cost reduction could be large. For instance, suppose that the United States succeeded in extracting a concession from Japan instead of Korea. The resulting cost advantage could enable US producers to penetrate the Canadian market, or increase their exports to Canada if they exported before formation of the FTA. Under this circumstance, Canada could choose either of the following two policy options: it could undertake strong retaliatory action that it normally would not in the absence of the FTA, or it could ask the United States to support Canada in receiving a similar concession by coordinating their negotiations.

Under the bilateral FTA the pressures on the United States and Canada to coordinate their trade policy toward third countries could cause Canada to pursue more protectionist policies in the event that the United States raises tariffs or puts quotas on imported products. US protection against the third country will, other things being equal, lead to an increase in US producer prices. Under the Canada–US FTA, Canadian producers, given the price differential generated by US protectionist policies, may be able to export to the United States. This development may not have taken place without the protectionist measures by the United States, and it negates much of the effects of such actions. As Richard Harris points out, such a situation cannot persist very long.[1] Sooner or later the US producers will demand that Canada pay its fair share for the benefits of the protection. Thus, Canada would be forced to protect its market to the same degree, or a harmonized system of protection would be needed to replace the two independent systems.

There is a widespread fear throughout Asia that the trade disputes between the United States and some of the Asian countries with which its has large trade deficits will intensify as long as the United States remains unable to correct its trade imbalances. As it has done in the past, the United States may have to resort to protecting its market and to impose retaliatory measures on its Asian trade partners. With the Canada–US FTA now in effect, how will Canada modify its trade policy toward the Asian countries if the tension between the United States and Asian countries does escalate? Will it remain an independent bystander? Will it come out in support of the US actions and go so far as to take similar actions? At this stage one can only speculate, but our argument on the possibility of coordinating trade policy between the two countries suggests that Canada will not be able to stay out of the fray.

The specter of the emergence by 1992 of a fortress Europe with closed doors to Asian traders has encouraged and generated strong interest in a movement toward Asian economic integration. Although at present the

---

1. Harris (1988) argues that the difficulties in administering the rules of origin also will favor harmonization in trade policy.

nature, purpose, and potential members of such a system are at best ambiguous, the proponents of integration argue that the Pacific Asian region has the resource base, growth potential, and complementarity in trade necessary to support economic integration. As a small, open economy seeking diversified export and import markets, Korea does not support the establishment of a formal economic union over a multilateral free trading system. However, if the Canada–US FTA develops the characteristics of a customs union, and the two countries act in unison in their economic relations with third countries, the proponents of Asian economic integration will gain increased support, especially if the two countries' trade policies are perceived to be unfair.

Although Korea has shown stronger interest in the Uruguay Round than in past rounds of trade negotiations, it also realizes the limitations of multilateral negotiations and has engaged in dual-track negotiations, one with the United States and another within the framework of the current GATT round. Now that the United States has expressed interest in the possibilities of more FTAs, using the Canada–US FTA as a prototype, Korea is once again thrust into a position where it must consider the conditions under which it could contemplate an FTA with the United States.

What are some of the important advantages Korea could gain by forming an FTA with the United States? What would be the disadvantages and obstacles that could make such an agreement impossible? Above all, removal of US trade barriers would mean secure access to the largest market in the world for Korea's manufacturing sector, and thus Korean producers would have no handicap in benefiting from economies of scale. Given that 95 percent of Korea's exports are manufactured goods and that roughly 40 percent go to the United States, the importance of secure access to the US market cannot be overstated.

Also, in managing trade relations with the United States, Korea would do much better with an FTA than without it. Currently, all trade disputes regarding Korean exports to the United States are settled according to US laws and procedures. Korea's voice is not much stronger in settling the disputes regarding US access to Korean markets. The fact that virtually no Korean interest can be represented in the dispute settlement is a source of suspicion and makes the outcome less acceptable to Koreans, regardless of the fairness of the process. If an FTA establishes a dispute settlement mechanism agreed to by both sides and a binational commission to supervise the operation of the FTA, as provided in the Canada–US Free Trade Agreement, trade disputes will be much less likely to produce any spillover effects in other areas.

As a way of handling current trade issues, comprehensive FTA negotiations would be superior to the ongoing piecemeal approach that deals with one or a few items at a time whenever a problem arises. All issues of concern to both parties could be brought to the negotiating table, including the issues of trade in manufactures, agricultural trade, services trade, protection of intellectual property rights, trade-related investment issues, and so on. The negotiations can deal with visible trade barriers as well as invisible barriers related to such issues as national treatment, government procurement, and technical standards. The likelihood that a fair balance can be achieved between Korean and US interests is greater in negotiations where all issues can be collectively dealt with than in the current piecemeal negotiations under the threat of section 301.

There need not be too much reservation on the part of Korea about negotiating agricultural and services trade within the context of an FTA with the United States. First, with or without an FTA, Korea has to deal with these bilateral issues, and is in fact currently negotiating with the United States. Also, the Uruguay Round, which Korea was the first to support among the developing countries, addresses essentially the same agenda. Second, an FTA would be illegal under GATT regulations unless it removed "substantially all" trade barriers. A give-and-take approach across broadly defined sectors may be Korea's best chance to promote its national interest in its external transactions with the United States.

Korea's position—if it stays out of an FTA while its competitors form FTAs with the United States—should worry Korean exporters. Perhaps the most worrisome possibility is the combination of a severe world recession and very strong protectionism everywhere. An FTA with the United States would then make the difference between secure access to the market and an unprecedented restriction of market access. The United States has been exploring the possibility of forming more FTAs with other Asian countries, including Taiwan and Japan. Since Taiwan is one of Korea's major export competitors in the US market, Korea would have no choice but to seriously consider establishing an FTA with the United States, if Taiwan succeeded in negotiating a similar agreement. In the unlikely event that Japan joined the United States in an FTA, Korea would again find itself in an extremely vulnerable position on the outside.

The effect of a US–Taiwan FTA on Korea would be obvious. Significant trade diversion would take place. Both Korea and Taiwan can be characterized as labor-abundant developing countries. In terms of factor abundance and level of technology they are much closer to each other than either one is to the United States. Naturally, the two countries compete with each other in the US market for similar kinds of products. Hence, an FTA between the United States and Taiwan would imply a weakening competitiveness for Korea vis-à-vis Taiwan for a wide range of export products. Not only is the product range wide, but US tariffs and nontariff barriers on many of the products are high, as they tend to be on labor-intensive, standard-technology products. Thus, Korea's loss of US market share to Taiwan could be very serious.

An FTA between the United States and Japan, with Korea outside, would be no less threatening. Korea, the United States, and Japan form an interesting trilateral trade relationship. Korea imports much of its capital equipment from Japan; in producing newly expanding export products, such as consumer electronics and automobiles, Korea has been heavily dependent on Japan for the supply of high-technology components. A simple expression of the trilateral relationship is that Korea imports capital equipment and intermediate inputs from Japan, produces the value-added, and exports final goods to the United States.

The immediate impact on Korea of a US–Japan FTA would be trade diversion and suppression as discussed above. On the one hand, as tariffs are removed on imports of final goods from Japan that used to be imported from Korea, Japanese producers would be able to produce value-added at a higher cost than Korean producers, by an amount equal to the value of the tariff, and still be competitive with Korean exporters in US markets. On the other hand, since Japanese intermediate inputs would be available to US producers without tariffs, US producers would be able to produce value-added at a higher cost than Korean producers, by the amount of the cost saving, and still be competitive with Korean producers. Thus, US imports from Korea would be likely to be replaced to some extent by imports from Japan and domestic production in the United States.

The long-run effect of an FTA between the United States and Japan would be a considerable slowdown in Korea's process of catching up with Japan in the US market. As Korea accumulates capital and makes technological progress, the product composition of Korean exports will resemble less that of a typical developing country and more that of an industrial country, especially that of Japan. In the anticipated competition between Korea and Japan in the US market, Korea would be at a serious disadvantage if it were left outside the US–Japan FTA. Unthinkable though it may be, Korea would have to deal with two economic superpowers with common interests and objectives in their external trade.

Although there are many reasons to support an FTA with the United States, opposition is expected to be very strong in Korea. First, although the export industries in the manufacturing sector would welcome the idea of an FTA, virtually all the other sectors of the economy would be wary of the possible adverse impact of competition from US firms. The agricultural and financial sectors are good examples.

In addition, an FTA with the United States may work at cross-purposes with two of Korea's policy objectives. First, an FTA would be inconsistent with Korea's aim to diversify its export markets. Over the last two years, Korea has been more successful in penetrating the Japanese markets. If this trend continues, Japan is likely to provide an export market for Korea not far behind the United States in size. At the same time, Korea has actively sought to improve its relations with China and the East European countries, in an effort to reduce its heavy dependence on both the United States and Japan. This effort has had considerable success. Second, Korea has sought to upgrade its industrial structure and the product composition of its exports. Korea has encouraged investment in more capital- and technology-intensive industries, where Japan and the United States currently enjoy a dominant market share, as a future source of export earnings. The short- and long-term effects of an FTA with the United States on this policy objective are not very clear.

A more important constraint may be Korean nationalism. The establishment of an FTA with the United States could easily be portrayed as a compromise of national sovereignty, as the Canada–US FTA has been in Canada. Unlike Canada, Korea is vastly different from the United States in terms of culture, society, and politics. It would not be surprising if there arose strong opposition to an FTA with the United States based solely on an unwillingness to become more closely tied to that country.

In this regard, the present circumstances do not seem particularly propitious for initiating discussions on an FTA. The US share in Korea's total exports was roughly 26 percent in the early 1980s. That share climbed to a peak of 40 percent in 1986 and began to decline in 1987. The dependence of Korean exports on the American market is deemed too high. An FTA with the United States is rightly expected to increase that dependence.

Despite all these arguments for and against an FTA between Korea and the United States, it is undeniable that, as long as such an arrangement complements the efforts to strengthen and broaden the multilateral trading system and improve the allocative efficiency and welfare of the two countries, it deserves a more careful analysis.

The economics of FTAs basically favors an agreement between Korea and the United States. The two countries are very different from each other in their abundance of capital, labor, and land, and also in their level of technology. These complementary economic conditions give rise to large differences in unit costs for the same goods. According to Viner, large differences in unit costs help a bilateral FTA create trade, whereas a high degree of complementarity in industrial structure hampers it. However, the complementarity in industrial structure between Korea and the United States is not so high as to severely restrict trade creation.

The case in favor of an FTA becomes stronger when trade in intermediate inputs is taken into consideration. With tariffs on intermediate inputs, the trade pattern is likely to be more distorted than when only final goods are traded. A case in point is negative effective protection. Hence, an FTA will make the pattern of comparative advantage more pronounced in trade between the two countries. Exports will expand where one country has a comparative advantage, and more resources will be pulled into those industries in which the country has a comparative advantage.

If a bilateral Korea–US FTA were formed and became part of a star-shaped FTA with the United States at the center, the relative disadvantage for the partner countries, as discussed in the previous section, would not be too great for Korea. As was shown in that section, the partner country's relative disadvantage is smaller if its basic economic conditions are highly complementary to those of the center country, as they are in the case of Korea and the United States. Therefore, the limited effects of a bilateral FTA, removing tariffs and other barriers on merchandise trade between the two countries, speaks in favor of the establishment of an FTA.

Conclusion

As a small and resource-poor country, Korea depends heavily on its trade with the rest of world for its industrialization and economic growth. It is very important for Korea that world trade remain free and that the trading system be strengthened.

For the past ten years or so, the integrity of the world trading system has been threatened from within by the rapidly changing patterns of comparative advantage among countries and by the inability of the advanced industrial countries to make the necessary structural adjustments to the changing patterns of trade. In addition to the old problems, new issues have arisen, such as services trade, that the system is ill-equipped to handle. Perhaps more importantly, the system has been strained by the global macroeconomic imbalances that have been developing since the early 1980s.

Free trade agreements alone are vastly inadequate as a way of coping with, and finding solutions for, these old and new problems. Multilateral negotiations such as the Uruguay Round, following the most-favored-nation principle, would be the best approach. Yet it is risky to rely on that route alone, and bilateral free trade agreements may be able to assist the multilateral approach.

Korea also may find it advantageous to reach a free trade agreement with the United States similar to that between the United States and Canada under certain circumstances such as a severe recession in the world economy combined with strong and widespread protectionism abroad. An FTA between the largest economy in the world and one of the most dynamic and rapidly growing would mean secure access to that large market for Korea and greater benefit from international division of labor for both. As we have seen, when the partner countries are dissimilar in their basic economic conditions, an FTA tends to promote both free trade and the international division of labor. What worries many in Korea is that the United States may view a bilateral free trade agreement as a remedy for its external imbalance, which is essentially a macroeconomic problem. Imbalances in the US external accounts did not necessarily increase because the rest of the world indulged in more unfair trade practices or because US access to other markets was restricted. As a subset of trade policy, free trade agreements cannot be a substitute for better management of macroeconomic policies. A star-shaped FTA, as discussed above, will have the effect of shifting a large share of world trade to bilateral trade between the partner countries. The trade problems that need to be solved may actually intensify, as the star-shaped FTA will increase the need for US industries to adjust to changes taking place in the rest of the world.

Our analysis also demonstrates that in a star-shaped FTA the center country—for example, the United States—which maintains multiple independent FTAs with each of the partner countries, benefits most as it achieves economies of scale from an enlarged and integrated market. This advantage does not exist for the other partners. This bias in favor of the center country may encourage the partner countries to negotiate FTAs among themselves, thereby leading to an expanded FTA. On the other hand, it is conceivable that this bias could discourage other countries from joining a star-shaped FTA. If Korea, for instance, were to form a bilateral FTA with the United States, it would be in Korea's interest to negotiate FTAs simultaneously with other countries that maintain FTAs with the United States. The cost of forming a number of bilateral FTAs simultaneously or in succession would be enormous, and this burden may discourage Korea from joining.

Also, one cannot dismiss the possibility that the Canada–US FTA and, for that matter, other future bilateral FTAs could develop into or acquire the characteristics of a customs union, where the contracting countries coordinate their trade and industrial policies with respect to the rest of the world. In such an event, other countries in different parts of the world may find it advantageous to establish similar FTAs among themselves to deal more effectively with the North American FTA. The world economy may then become divided into a number of competing economic blocs—a development that should be guarded against.

However, despite their discriminatory nature, there may be a strong driving force for more open trade through FTAs, if they include partners of widely different basic economic conditions. Outside countries that compete with one of the partners inside the FTA are likely to lose their export markets if they stay out of the FTA. Division of labor and economies of scale will benefit the partners of an FTA. If the opposite is the case—that is, if an FTA includes only countries with similar economic conditions—the effect may just be an expansion of the area under protection for the industries of the partner countries. There will be benefits from economies of scale, but the benefit from division of labor will be minor or absent.

References

Harris, Richard G. 1988. "CAFTA and Future North American Trade Relations". *International Economic Program Working Papers* DP 88–10. Toronto: University of Toronto, June.

Viner, Jacob. 1950. *The Customs Union Issue.* New York: Carnegie Endowment for International Peace.

6

Feasibility and Desirability of a US–Taiwan Free Trade Agreement

S.C. Tsiang

The persistent large trade imbalance between Taiwan and the United States since 1981 has created certain tensions and frictions between the two countries. There is a constant fear on the part of Taiwan of retaliatory protectionist measures being imposed by the deficit country, the United States. When the news reached Taiwan of the formation by the United States of a free trade area (FTA) first with Israel and then with Canada, the government authorities wistfully thought that if a similar agreement could be concluded between the United States and Taiwan, then the worries of protectionist retaliation could be eliminated once and for all. At first that remained just wishful thinking. Later on, however, American officials and senators and representatives began to show interest in FTAs with the Pacific Rim countries, including Korea and Taiwan. However, their main goal seems to be to negotiate a free trade agreement with the most formidable trading nation, Japan.

Such news was received enthusiastically in Taiwan. To be sure, the benefits to be obtained from an FTA with the United States appeared enormous. Taiwan is heavily dependent on trade with the United States. It exported nearly 60 percent of its GNP in 1987, and 44 percent of those exports went to the US market. In the same year, Taiwan's imports equaled 33 percent of its GNP, of which 22 percent came from the United States. On the other hand, the United States, whose GNP is about 36 times that of Taiwan, is not very dependent on external trade. In 1987, it exported only 6 percent of its GNP, and only about 3 percent of its merchandise exports went to Taiwan. Thus, one would think that the United States probably would not be very interested in an FTA with Taiwan.

However, there are two reasons why the United States might be interested in an FTA with Taiwan. First, there is the persistent trade imbalance with

S.C. Tsiang is the President of the Chung-Hua Institution for Economic Research in Taiwan.

Taiwan. Second, Taiwan could be used as a wedge to break into other countries in the Pacific Rim, a vast and vigorously growing area of the world. That is, if Taiwan can be first brought into an FTA with the United States, providing its products duty-free treatment in the US market, all other countries in this area that are in close competition with Taiwan would suddenly face increased competition and would stand to lose their former shares in the US market to Taiwan's products. Furthermore, in Taiwan's import market, their exports would face increased competition from American exports, which would enjoy duty-free status. This would have the effect of inducing some reluctant countries in the area to join the FTA.

Thus, if the United States is really interested in inducing, say, Japan to join an FTA, and Japan is rather reluctant, a good strategy would be to negotiate an agreement with Korea and Taiwan at the same time. If one of the smaller countries agreed to join, the other one and Japan would be strongly pressured to join also.

The Benefits to Taiwan of an FTA With the United States

Free trade areas are very similar to customs unions, which were much discussed in connection with the formation of the European Community. According to the classic analysis of this subject by the late Jacob Viner, the benefits to be derived by the member countries are from the "trade creation effects" of the union. On the other hand, there might be some losses arising from the "trade diversion effects" of the union, which would shift some imports from their original, cheaper sources of supply to higher-cost sources that now receive duty-free treatment. As to the countries that are excluded, there can be only one fate, namely, to endure some trade diversion at the expense of their own exports.

From the point of view of a single country, however, trade creation in its favor may include trade diversion from outside countries. Thus, a country's increased exports to the partner country's market after the formation of an FTA would include: (1) the replacement of imports from third countries that do not enjoy the duty-free treatment; (2) the increase in demand in the partner country induced by the cheaper supply prices with the removal of tariffs; and (3) the replacement of the partner country's own domestic products that are unable to compete on that account. The first source of increased exports is probably the most important and elastic, at least in the short run. In the strict cosmopolitan sense, however, it does not constitute true trade creation at all, because it increases the exports from one country at the cost of reducing the exports from other countries, which are actually cheaper sources of supply but are unable to compete because of tariff discrimination. It therefore represents the trade diversion that Viner pointed

Table 6.1   Taiwan's major exports to the United States, 1987

Tariff code	Merchandise	Export value (millions of $US)	Taiwan's market share (%)	Chief competitor's market share (%)[a]	Tariff rate (%)[b]
38	Apparel	2,638	14.7	36.7	20.1
64	Metal products	720	17.0	28.9	4.4
65	Metal products	1,229	24.0	22.4	5.3
67	Machinery	2,767	9.4	56.4	3.8
68	Electrical products	4,239	9.5	53.4	4.8
70	Footwear	3,301	24.1	29.0	9.6
72	Instruments	1,489	15.0	38.1	4.0
73	Sporting goods	2,133	30.9	39.1	6.3
77	Rubber and plastic products	1,188	18.0	27.2	4.4

a. The chief competitors are Japan, Korea, Hong Kong, and Singapore.
b. Tariff rates are effective tariff rates measured by the ratio of the tariff actually paid to the dutiable import value.

Source: Tariff Schedule of the United States Annotated Data Tape.

out to be detrimental to the welfare of the importing country and of the world as a whole (especially to that of the countries whose products are the victims of replacement).

The great enthusiasm with which the idea of forming an FTA with the United States is greeted in Taiwan is probably due largely to the expectation of such easy expansion of its exports in substitution for exports from outside countries. The reason for this expectation may be observed from table 6.1. However, this expectation is perhaps too wishful and unrealistic. As noted above, the United States has made it known that it is interested in negotiating a free trade agreement with Taiwan along with a group of Pacific Rim countries that have shown remarkably fast growth capability. Its final goal is certainly not to stop at an FTA with Taiwan alone. Even if Taiwan is in fact the first country on the Asian Pacific Rim to form an FTA with the United States, Taiwan surely will not enjoy the monopoly of duty-free importation into the US market for long, because the threat of Taiwan's exports cutting into their own shares of the US market very likely would induce other Asian Pacific Rim countries also to join an FTA with the United States. It certainly does not seem wise to be left out of all the major free trade blocs that are forming in the world, for then all one gets is trade diversion from all sides at one's own expense.

The expansion of exports to be expected from an FTA with the United States should be estimated more realistically as consisting only of the increase in aggregate demand for imports in the United States due to the price reduction when tariffs are eliminated, and the reduction in competing domestic supplies in the United States due to the removal of protective tariffs. In this respect, the disparity in the relative size of the Taiwan and US economies works in Taiwan's favor, because a small percentage change in the aggregate demand or supply due to a price change would mean quite a big absolute change compared with Taiwan's exports. Of course, the aggregate increase in demand would have to be shared with other countries in the FTA.

The most important benefit to be expected from an FTA with the United States is the future assurance of free access to the enormous US market, free from the contingent risk of incurring protectionist measures or the demand for voluntary export restraints. Such assurance of free entry into the huge open market would enable the entrepreneurs in a small country to find individual niches where they have a comparative advantage and expand into a scale of operation large enough to enjoy all the economies of modern technology. To enable domestic industries to operate efficiently is, therefore, the most weighty benefit to be obtained from an FTA with the United States in the long run.

Of course, we must be prepared to accept the counterpart losses concomitant with these benefits. To be able to concentrate on lines of production with comparative advantages implies having to give up lines of production with comparative disadvantages that would be swept away by foreign competition when protective tariffs are abolished. This, however, is often politically difficult to accept by the negotiating countries, even though in the long run such a more rational reallocation of resources would be beneficial to the country concerned.

Thus, in Taiwan, even a recent liberalization of the import of turkey meat from the United States led to a demonstration of chicken farmers in the streets of Taipei. Taiwan is a very congested island, with as many as 540 persons per square kilometer, compared with 26 persons per square kilometer in the United States. Furthermore, Taiwan being quite mountainous, only one-fourth of the land area is cultivable. Thus, agriculture, except those lines where utmost freshness of the product is important, has in general lost all comparative advantage vis-à-vis imports from the United States. When Taiwan forms an FTA with the United States, a country with abundant agricultural land, it must consider whether its agriculture is to be retained or abandoned.

Many politicians in Taiwan believe that a country must to some extent be self-sufficient in food production to survive any emergency, and they would insist on a certain degree of protection for agriculture, especially for the basic crop of sustenance, rice. At present, the price of rice in Taiwan is almost three times as high as the world market price. In negotiating an FTA, therefore, agriculture surely will be a stumbling block.

However, it is not impossible to overcome this problem. In negotiating an FTA with Japan and Korea, the same difficulties over heavily protected agriculture certainly will be encountered. Perhaps the United States will tolerate some exceptions to full free trade principles in the case of agriculture. Otherwise, it might be rather difficult to reach agreement with those two countries in an FTA negotiation.

I think Taiwan's national security consideration might be taken care of by adequate storage of food instead of by protecting food production through rice support prices that are several times higher than the world market price. Much savings in national resources can be achieved in that way. If more firm guarantees of Taiwan's security could be obtained from the United States, this change in strategy would be more readily acceptable. Besides, letting the artificially propped-up agricultural sector shrink would also solve the present problems of skyrocketing prices of urban real estate and urban congestion, and the increasing difficulties of obtaining industrial sites for new industries in Taiwan.

The Benefits to the United States of an FTA With Taiwan

From the point of view of the United States, the direct benefits of an FTA with Taiwan appear relatively much less significant, since the United States is far less dependent on trade with Taiwan than Taiwan is dependent on the United States. As noted above, in 1987, while 44 percent of Taiwan's exports went to the US market, only 3 percent of US exports were sent to Taiwan. That does not necessarily imply that the absolute gains to be obtained by the United States will necessarily be smaller than the gains accruing to Taiwan, because the average existing tariffs on US exports to Taiwan are generally considerably higher than those confronting Taiwan's exports to the United States. This is clearly shown in table 6.2, which lists the major types of US merchandise exported to Taiwan in 1987 and their shares in Taiwan's import markets, as well as the import tariff rates applied.

Moreover, for several items, mainly agricultural and forestry products, US exports dominate Taiwan's import market, sometimes overwhelmingly. For example, the US share of imports of oil seeds is 84.1 percent, of grains 79.7 percent, of tobacco 79.5 percent, of papermaking materials 55 percent, and of leather 49.8 percent. In most cases, the US dominance is partly the result of trade preference policies adopted by the government of Taiwan, such as

Table 6.2   Major US exports to Taiwan, 1987

Tariff code	Merchandise	Export value (millions of $US)	US market share (%)	Japan's market share (%)	Tariff rate (%)[a]
10	Grains	454	79.7	0	12.89
12	Oil seeds	433	84.1	0	4.66
24	Tobacco	132	79.5	0.2	44.59
27	Mineral products	386	10.6	1.6	3.15
28	Inorganic chemicals	196	40.7	25.7	3.99
29	Organic chemicals	703	33.3	23.4	5.00
38	Miscellaneous chemicals	134	29.3	33.3	9.82
39	Artificial resins and plastic materials	239	26.5	45.0	6.72
41	Leather	248	49.8	15.1	0.81
44	Wood products	151	15.5	2.3	2.25
47	Paper-making materials	211	55.0	1.2	0.97
55	Cotton	164	23.8	4.6	1.20
71	Precious metals	378	47.6	10.5	0.36
73	Basic metals	192	9.3	61.4	10.38
84	Machinery	697	15.4	50.2	10.11
85	Electrical products	1,060	21.7	53.5	11.12
87	Vehicles	114	9.3	54.8	35.27
90	Instruments	215	29.1	46.2	7.22

a. Tariff rates are weighted-average tariff rates effective February 1988, with the weights given by the import values of 1987.

Source: Monthly Statistics of Trade, Republic of China.

giving exclusive rights to the United States to import, banning importation from major competing countries, and sponsoring "Buy American" trade missions. Imports from the United States benefiting from such policies will probably not respond very sensitively to further elimination of tariffs alone. However, many agricultural imports are still subject to controls and restrictions—for example, rice, poultry, and sugar—and could respond to the abolition of those controls.

For most manufactured products, however, US exports are dominated by Japanese exports. If tariffs are removed on US products alone, imports of those products can certainly be expected to increase considerably. However, this would be a case of trade diversion, which would be detrimental to the welfare of Taiwan as it would induce Taiwan to switch some of its imports from a cheaper source to a more expensive source of supply. Moreover, Taiwan would lose the tariff revenue collected from dutiable Japanese imports that are replaced by duty-free American imports.

Such substitution effects, however, will last only as long as Japan remains outside of an FTA. Thus, the substitution of American exports for Japanese exports in the Taiwan market, as well as the substitution of Taiwan exports for Japanese exports in the US market, would serve to goad Japan into the fold, if the formation of a Pacific Rim FTA is what the United States has in mind.

Thus the long-run benefits to be expected from the formation of an FTA between the United States and Taiwan should be those that would accrue from the formation of a large FTA covering the United States, Canada, and the Asian Pacific Rim countries. The benefits from free trade and specialization according to each country's comparative advantage should be enormous, and there should be ample possibility to expand each country's chosen industries of specialization to a scale large enough to enjoy the full extent of economies of large-scale production.

There should be, however, a full understanding of the nature of the FTA on the part of all participating countries. Free trade inevitably will lead to selection of surviving industries in each country by international competition. Therefore, after a country voluntarily joins the FTA, there should be no more complaints that foreign labor is robbing the employment opportunities of domestic workers, or that foreign agricultural imports are ruining domestic agriculture and even spoiling the domestic real estate market. In that respect, we may do well to bear in mind the implication of the famous Stolper–Samuelson theorem that free trade is to some extent equivalent to free factor movement in its effects on factor prices. It is the duty of economists to persuade the public and the politicians that in the long run the general welfare will be increased by the international division of labor.

However, the problem of autarky and concerns about national self-sufficiency in times of emergency remain very difficult to reconcile with the formation of an FTA unless it is accompanied by the simultaneous conclusion of a mutual security treaty. Otherwise, concerns with national defense in times of emergency always would be a stumbling block to the formation of an FTA.

Furthermore, we may do well to remember that an FTA will not necessarily solve the problem of trade imbalances. That would still have to be solved by exchange rate adjustment and by adjusting the balance between national expenditure and national product in each country. The establishment of free trade without any tariff barriers and restrictions, however, would greatly increase the elasticities or sensitivity of responses to any exchange rate or expenditure adjustments, and thus make the correction of any trade imbalance easier to achieve. With the elasticities of demand for imports and of supply of exports increased, a relatively small change in the exchange rate will be enough to correct a relatively large imbalance in trade.

A word of caution is necessary with regard to the trade imbalance induced by the imbalance between national expenditure and national product. This kind of imbalance in trade cannot be easily corrected by mere exchange rate adjustments or by the formation of an FTA. It is simply caused by the spillover into foreign markets of excess national expenditure. The exchange rate adjustment operates by the principle of "expenditure switching," but does not operate to eliminate or reduce the excess expenditure. Thus, if the first-round effect of an appropriate exchange rate adjustment succeeds in eliminating the trade deficit temporarily by switching some foreign and domestic demand away from foreign goods and toward domestic goods, while the deficit country does nothing to curb its own expenditures, then the extra demand thus shifted back onto domestic goods certainly would aggravate the state of excess demand in the domestic goods markets. Prices would rise in those markets, and the rise of these domestic prices would then cancel out the original exchange rate adjustment that brought about these shifts.

That is why the current imbalance in US trade, which is caused by its enormous budget deficits and extraordinarily low private savings, cannot be remedied solely by exchange rate adjustments. Although the United States has succeeded in browbeating those of its trade partners that have developed trade surpluses into appreciating their currencies by 45 percent or more, its trade deficit is still far from being eliminated. Unless the root cause of the trouble, that is, the tendency of the United States to overspend its national income, is eradicated, the imbalance in its trade will not be cured with or without FTAs. It is, therefore, very important for us not to entertain any unrealistic expectations about the efficacy of an FTA, lest when disappointed we also lose faith in what it really can do.

7

A Free Trade Agreement With Australia?

Richard H. Snape

Much of the trade policy of the United States in recent years has been driven by concern over bilateral trade imbalances and perceptions of foreign unfairness with respect to industrial targeting, subsidized exports, protection of intellectual property, and rights of establishment. Broad bilateral agreements have been motivated by political factors (with Israel and the Caribbean Basin) or by proximity combined with a very high volume of trade (with Canada). If these factors define criteria for US interest in a trade agreement, then Australia is not really a candidate.

The United States does not have a substantial trade deficit with Australia; indeed there is a two-to-one excess of exports over imports. Few Australian exports to the United States are subsidized or dumped, and Australia competes in primary commodities more than in computers or clothing. Australia's import barriers, although still relatively high by OECD standards, are generally in the form of GATT-conforming tariffs rather than nontariff barriers, and currently are being reduced. Intellectual property is protected, and the door to US investment is quite open. Furthermore, the volume of trade is not high by the standards of the United States, and the countries are separated by the world's largest ocean.

Viewed from Australia, the situation seems a little different—apart from the ocean. The United States is the largest source of imports, just ahead of Japan, and the second largest destination, well after Japan, for exports. US tariffs are generally low, but there are some substantial nontariff barriers on products of major export interest to Australia. US farm product subsidies

Richard H. Snape is Professor of Economics at Monash University in Melbourne, Australia, and Editor of the World Bank Economic Review *and* The World Bank Research Observer. *This paper draws on Snape (1986). Nothing in this paper should be interpreted as representing the views of the World Bank or of the Australian Government, which commissioned the earlier study.*

often erode Australian sales in third countries. The trade deficit (goods and nonfactor services) with the United States is equal to 87 percent of the total trade deficit, which in turn is about 2 percent of GDP.[1] In some quarters in Australia there is a view that the playing field could be leveled somewhat.

A trade agreement between Australia and the United States, then, is likely to be of much more economic consequence to Australia than to the United States, unless the US government saw such an agreement as a strategic move in a larger trade plan. (One particular instance of this could be if Australia sought a free trade agreement with Japan, which is in many ways a more natural partner than the United States.) But despite the rather small overall consequences of trade with Australia, products of major export interest to Australia touch areas of particular political sensitivity in the United States. Although the United States has proposed liberalization in some of these areas in the context of the Uruguay Round negotiations, implementation of such liberalization is likely to be strongly resisted within the United States. Without it there would be little attraction to Australia in a "free" trade agreement.

This chapter addresses first the pattern of trade and trade barriers between the two countries, the consequences of removing these barriers, and the areas in which particular problems are likely to arise. It then considers some wider implications of the pursuit and achievement of such an agreement.

Trade Flows

Imports by the United States from Australia are highly concentrated in a small number of commodity groupings. Table 7.1 shows that just two of the two-digit Standard International Trade Classification (SITC) categories account for 44 percent of the total imports. Apart from the anonymous "special transactions," Australia's exports are predominantly primary products. For these products, as for exports as a whole, the United States is a major market. For three of the two-digit categories (meats, metalliferous ores, and textile fibers) Australia is a major supplier to the United States (as it was for sugar before protection for the US industry put a virtual end to that), but overall it is insignificant.

On the import side, the data in table 7.2 show much greater product diversity. Among the 14 main commodity groupings, the United States supplies more than 20 percent of Australia's imports of all but three.

The United States supplies a larger proportion (22 percent) of Australia's

---

1. This may be compared with a trade deficit, similarly defined, of about 2.7 percent of GDP in the United States.

Table 7.1   Main imports by the United States from Australia, 1986

SITC (Revision 2)	Product	Value (millions of $US)	Australian share of US imports (%)	US imports from Australia as share of world imports from Australia (%)
01	Meat and meat preparations	654	25	48
28	Metalliferous ores	612	27	17
93	Special transactions	281	3	69
33	Petroleum and petroleum products	234	0.6	40
68	Nonferrous metals	139	2	10
03	Fish and fish preparations	105	2	27
26	Textile fibers	101	20	5
67	Iron and steel	94	1	32
52	Inorganic chemicals	66	2	26
79	Other transport equipment[a]	55	1	67
06	Sugar and sugar preparations	53	4	13
All other commodities		480	0.2	4
All commodities		2,874	0.7	12

a. Other than road vehicles.

Source: United Nations, *COMTRADE Data Base.*

imports than it does of world imports as a whole (about 11 percent). In contrast, Australia supplies a smaller proportion of the United States' imports (about 0.7 percent) than it does of the imports of the world (1.2 percent). But despite the bias of Australia's exports away from the United States, the US market is, of course, of major importance to Australia: 2 percent of

Table 7.2 Main imports by Australia from the United States, 1986

SITC (Revision 2)	Product	Value (millions of $US)	US share of Australian imports (%)	Australian imports from US as share of world imports from US (%)
75	Office machines	650	42	4
93	Special transactions	641	63	16
79	Other transport[a]	506	63	5
87	Precision instruments	456	39	6
74	General industrial machinery	322	25	4
89	Miscellaneous manufactured goods	304	22	5
72	Specialized machines	299	24	4
71	Power generating equipment	228	31	3
77	Electrical machines	215	17	2
78	Road vehicles	182	9	1
51	Organic chemicals	140	26	3
58	Plastic materials	135	50	3
33	Petroleum and petroleum products	114	10	4
59	Chemical materials	100	37	3
All other commodities		1,077	11	1
All commodities		5,369	22	2

a. Other than road vehicles.　　　　　　*Source:* United Nations, *COMTRADE Data Base.*

Australia's GDP is exported to the United States, whereas only 0.1 percent of the GDP of the United States is exported to Australia.

Tables 7.3 and 7.4 present data for products at a more disaggregated level. From table 7.3 it can be seen that there are only five products at the three-digit SITC level for which US imports from Australia exceeded $100 million in 1986: beef, alumina, special transactions, crude petroleum (mainly imported by Hawaii), and wool. In general the dependence of Australia on the US market is very high—61 percent for boneless beef, 55 percent for alumina and for crude petroleum, 44 percent for the "beach sands" ores, 32 percent for shellfish, 56 percent for iron and steel plates, and 69 percent for special transactions, for example. In a few products Australia is a major supplier of the United States: alumina (81 percent of total US imports), boneless beef (53 percent), beach sands ores (61 percent), greasy wool (66 percent), and wheat gluten (51 percent), but in all others Australia is of minor significance.

Table 7.4 presents similar data for Australian imports from the United States: only imports valued at approximately $60 million or more have been included. The United States is the dominant supplier of two-thirds of the products listed, with shares up to 80 percent (for aircraft). In contrast to Australian exports to the United States, none of the United States' major exports to Australia is a primary product, with the exception of refined petroleum products, of which it is a minor supplier.

Trade Barriers

Tariffs

Tables 7.5 and 7.6 contain data on the tariff and nontariff barriers facing some of the main traded commodities, specified at the very disaggregated level of the tariff line. The tariff data are the tariff levels that are applicable in late 1988; however, the Government of Australia announced that all tariffs that currently are above 15 percent will be reduced to 15 percent, and all those between 10 percent and 15 percent reduced to 10 percent, progressively over a four-year period beginning in mid-1988 (Statement of the Australian Treasurer, 25 May 1988). Clothing, textiles, footwear, and motor vehicles are not covered by these decreases, but the progressive reductions of very high levels of protection that are already in progress for these products are to be accelerated. In addition, a revenue duty of 2 percent on all imports has been removed.

Even after these reductions, the tariffs of the United States will be lower

Table 7.3 Main products imported by the United States from Australia, 1986

SITC (Revision 2)	Product	Value (millions of $US)	Australia (%)	Sources of US imports of product		US imports from Australia as share of world imports from Australia (%)
				Main supplier[a]	%	
011	Meat; fresh, chilled, or frozen	653	36	Canada	27	49
(01112)	Bovine meat, boneless	(625)	(53)	(New Zealand	28)	(61)
287	Base metal ores and concentrates, n.e.s.	603	50	Guinea	9	34
(28732)	Alumina (aluminum oxide)	(494)	(81)	(Surinam	5)	(55)
(28793)	"Beach sands" ores[b]	(70)	(61)	(South Africa	15)	(44)
931	Special transactions	281	3	Canada	32	69
333	Crude petroleum	225	1	Mexico	14	55
268	Wool and animal hair	100	51	New Zealand	20	6
(2681)	Sheep's or lamb's wool, greasy	(62)	(66)	(New Zealand	20)	(5)
036	Shellfish, fresh, frozen	99	4	Mexico	16	32
674	Iron and steel, universal, sheet, plate	70	2	Japan	32	40
(67491)	Other sheets and plates[c]	(59)	(4)	(Japan	50)	(56)

684	Aluminum	57	2	Canada	44	8
524	Radioactive material	54	4	Canada	30	34
061	Sugar and honey	52	5	Dominican Republic	15	13
971	Gold, nonmonetary, n.e.s.	48	1	Canada	43	9
792	Aircraft	46	1	Canada	29	87
683	Nickel	46	9	Canada	52	38
686	Zinc	31	6	Canada	50	20
592	Starch, inulin, gluten, etc.	28	7	New Zealand	27	52
(59212)	Wheat gluten	(16)	(51)	(Canada	30)	(70)
784	Motor vehicle parts and accessories	28	0.2	Japan	45	36
112	Alcoholic beverages	19	0.6	France	24	42
714	Engines and motors, n.e.s.	19	0.6	France	40	53

n.e.s. = not elsewhere specified.
a. Other than Australia.
b. Ores and concentrates of molybdenum, niobium, tantalum, titanium, vanadium, and zirconium.
c. Not universals, not tinned, not high carbon or alloy.

Source: United Nations, COMTRADE Data Base.

Table 7.4 Main products imported by Australia from the United States, 1986

SITC (Revision 2)	Product	Value (millions of $US)	Sources of Australian imports of product			Australian imports from US as share of world imports from US (%)
			US (%)	Main supplier[a]	%	
931	Special transactions	641	63	UK	13	16
792	Aircraft	502	80	France	8	6
752	ADP equipment	428	43	Japan	27	4
874	Measuring, control instruments	368	40	Japan	16	6
759	Office, ADP mechanical parts, accessories	206	58	Japan	23	4
749	Nonelectrical machines, parts, n.e.s.	127	31	Japan	18	5
892	Printed matter	127	35	UK	34	7
723	Civil engineering equipment	114	35	Japan	33	6
713	Internal combustion piston engines	103	26	Japan	48	3
784	Motor vehicle parts, accessories, n.e.s.	103	23	Japan	43	1

598	Miscellaneous chemical products, n.e.s.	84	38	UK	25	3
728	Other machines for specific industries	79	22	West Germany	21	4
872	Medical instruments, n.e.s.	75	45	West Germany	15	6
515	Organic-inorganic compounds, etc.	69	33	UK	9	6
764	Telecommunications equipment, parts, accessories, n.e.s.	69	11	Japan	50	6
641	Paper and paperboard	68	13	Finland	17	4
782	Vehicles, special motor vehicles, n.e.s.	67	12	Japan	74	3
(7821)	Vehicles for transport of goods	(67)	(12)	(Japan	75)	(3)
898	Musical instruments, parts	67	30	Japan	32	6
743	Pumps, n.e.s., centrifuges, etc.	65	27	Japan	21	6
334	Refined petroleum products	62	9	Saudi Arabia	27	3
882	Photographic and cinema supplies	60	32	Japan	28	4

n.e.s. = not elsewhere specified.
a. Other than the United States.

Source: United Nations, *COMTRADE Data Base.*

Table 7.5 Tariff and nontariff barriers facing major Australian exports to the United States, 1988

Harmonized tariff no.	Product	Tariff	Nontariff barriers
0202.30.60	Beef; frozen, boneless	4.4 cents/kg	Monitoring, VERs
2818.20	Alumina	0	
0306.12.00	Lobsters	0	
1701.11.00	Sugar	1.5 cents/kg[a]	Import quotas
2844.30.20	Uranium compounds	0	Threatened
5101.11.20,40	Wool, greasy or fleece washed	5.5–6.6 cents/kg clean	
7207–7209	Sheets of iron and steel	5.1–6%	VERs
7606	Aluminum bars, plates	3.0%	
7502	Unwrought nickel	0	
2614.00	Titanium ore	0	
7901.11,12	Unwrought zinc	1.5%, 19%	Threatened
7901.20	Zinc alloys	19%	
0404.90.10	Casein	0.44 cents/kg	Threatened
2844.10	Uranium oxide	0	Threatened
2711.11.00	Natural gas	0	
2709	Crude petroleum	5.25–10.5 cents/ barrel	
1109.00.90	Wheat gluten	8.0%	
0204.30.00	Lamb	1.1 cents/kg	Monitored, other barriers threatened
0406.30.20	Cheddar cheese	16%	Import quotas
5105.21,29	Wool tops	7.7 cents/kg + 6.25%	Threatened

a. Approximate

Source: US Tariff Schedule and other sources for tariff rates.

than those of Australia on most products. Among items of major export interest to Australia, the tariff on sugar is 1.5 cents/kg, but this is almost irrelevant because of other barriers to imports. Sheets of iron and steel face tariffs of 5 to 6 percent (but again other barriers exist), wool a tariff of 5.5 or 6.6 cents/kg, wool tops 7.7 cents/kg plus 6.25 percent, zinc alloys 19 percent, and wheat gluten 8 percent. Nearly all other items of export interest to Australia (except cheese) bear tariffs of 6 percent or less. Furthermore, nearly all the US import tariffs of interest to Australia are bound under the GATT at post-Tokyo Round levels. In contrast, relatively few of Australia's tariffs are bound under the GATT at any level, although such binding of the recently announced reductions is being advanced as a negotiating chip in the Uruguay Round.

Nontariff Measures

The situation is somewhat different with respect to nontariff barriers and other measures. Perhaps the most important Australian nontariff barriers for the United States are the arrangements for automobiles and components. Import quotas on motor vehicles were removed in April 1988, and the tariff was reduced to 45 percent, to fall to 35 percent by 1992. Australian content and export promotion remain, although the protective effects have been reduced. Also of relevance to US exports could be a recently introduced preferential scheme for pharmaceutical firms undertaking research and development in Australia. Import quotas still remain for clothing, textiles, and footwear, although their planned removal has been accelerated. Production subsidies for some products remain in place (see below), and a foreshadowed plan for communications equipment appears to have a protective element (Industries Assistance Commission 1988, Appendix 6).

On products of major export interest to Australia, actual or threatened nontariff barriers are common and constraining. Beef imports are monitored and are frequently subject to "agreed" restraints. Restrictions on lamb imports were part of early versions of the recent US trade bill, and although they were removed from the bill, a provision under which lamb imports are to be monitored remains. It is fairly clear that restraints would be imposed if US lamb imports were to increase rapidly. Sugar was until recently a major export but has now been virtually eliminated by protection, by the response of corn sweeteners to this protection, and, to a lesser extent, by preferences for other producers (Maskus 1987; Cameron and Berg 1987). Australia has taken action recently under the GATT against the US sugar import policy. Imports of basic steel and steel mill products are restrained by means of voluntary export arrangements, while steel imports have also been the subject of antidumping and countervailing duty inquiries. Most dairy products (and in particular cheese) face quantitative restrictions. Restrictions on imports of wool tops were part of the recently vetoed textiles bill.

While the United States does not currently have nontariff barriers on imports of nonferrous ores and metals, such barriers existed on lead and zinc ores and metals from 1958 to 1965 (Hufbauer, Berliner, and Elliott

Table 7.6 Tariff and nontariff barriers facing major US exports to Australia, 1988

Harmonized tariff no.	Product	Tariff[a]	Nontariff barriers
8471.10–99	ADP machines	0	
8802.11–50	Aircraft	0	Domestic airline policy administered by restriction on imports of large commercial aircraft[b]
8708.10–99	Parts and accessories for motor vehicles	25–45%	Motor vehicle content requirements
8473.30	Parts for ADP machines	0	
8701.90.19	Agricultural tractors	0	
4901.10–91	Books, etc.	0	Restriction on pornography
ex 8433	Mowers, haymaking machinery, balers, other harvesters	15%	
ex 8433	Combine harvesters, parts	0	
8803.10–90	Parts for aircraft	0	
ex 8429–30	Road rollers, graders etc. (tracked), parts	0–25%	
ex 8430	Diamond drilling machines	20%	
8431.43	Parts for drilling machines	10%	
ex 8429–31	Road rollers, graders etc. (wheeled), parts	0–30%	
Various	Electrical measuring and checking instruments	0	
ex 8407–09	Motor vehicle engines and parts	15–45%	Motor vehicle content requirements

a. Tariffs may be waived when there is no competitive domestic production. See text for recently announced changes in tariffs.
b. This policy is under review.

Source: Australian Tariff Schedule and other sources.

1986, 355–61), and the possibility of them being reintroduced remains (Baldwin 1985, chapter 2). This possibility constrains the actions of exporters and potential exporters. Similarly, uranium has been a sensitive and restricted import in the past and remains sensitive. There has also been considerable pressure from copper producers to restrict imports of copper,[2] and from clothing and textile interests to include developed country exporters in the restrictive provisions of the Multi-Fiber Arrangement. (In restricting the exports of developing countries under the Multi-Fiber Arrangement, the exports of Australian wool are indirectly affected.) An antidumping action in the past against Australian canned fruit has discouraged exports of this product.

Government Procurement

The essence of the GATT code relating to government procurement that was negotiated in the Tokyo Round is to extend the provisions of the GATT to cover government purchases of goods. It applies to goods for which the contracts exceed 150,000 SDRs. While the United States is a signatory, Australia is not. The Australian government's practice, at least at the national level, is to give explicit preference for Australian production above that provided by other tariff and nontariff barriers. It may be briefly and roughly summarized as giving a 20 to 25 percent preference for Australian content in nonmilitary contracts, which is not consistent with the GATT Government Procurement Code. (This preference will probably be subjected to critical examination in light of the recently announced reductions in protection referred to above.) As US government policy is not to award supply contracts to those countries that have not signed the code, Australia probably has lost sales of nickel and zinc for coins. Defense contracts have a higher and uncertain degree of preference for Australian content (Industries Assistance Commission 1988, 76). Even though the United States is a party to the procurement code, access to supply contracts at all levels of government has proved difficult for producers in other countries, as evidenced by the prominence of the issue in the negotiations for the Canada–US Free Trade Agreement.

---

2. Australia's exports of copper to the United States are small, but exports to other destinations would be affected if exports from other countries are excluded from the United States.

Offsets

Since 1970 the Australian government has implemented an offsets policy with the stated objective of securing Australian access to foreign technology and markets. Successful foreign tenderers for government contracts, above a threshold level, have been "encouraged" to place orders in Australia for a proportion of the value of the contract. The main industries that have benefited from direct offset orders are aerospace, electronics, and communications. In 1986 the Australian government raised the threshold to approximately $US 2 million, built some flexibility into the required proportion of 30 percent, and tightened somewhat what had been rather weak enforcement. As state governments have been operating offset arrangements independently, in March 1988 the federal program was extended to embrace state government purchasing on the same basis. Exemption from offset requirements can be secured by agreements to undertake research and development in Australia and/or to export.

Safeguards

Australia and the United States are major users of safeguards procedures against both so-called fair and unfair trading practices of other countries, both using procedures that for the most part conform with the provisions of the GATT. Table 7.7 shows the United States to be the world's largest user of countervailing duties, while Australia is the third largest. Australia is the main user of antidumping actions and together with the United States accounted for 60 percent of all such actions in the years 1980–86. In those years Australia targeted the United States with 44 of 112 antidumping actions and the only countervailing duty action. Neither country has been a major target for safeguard investigations by the other relating to "fair trade" (Article XIX of the GATT, or section 201 of the US trade act). Exporters in both countries are wary of the propensity of competitors in the other to claim unfairness, and an agreement on this issue could be of mutual benefit.

A "law of similars," or tariff concessions when there is no domestic production of a commodity that is covered by a broad tariff category, is a major feature of the Australian tariff system. Mainly because of this provision, about two-thirds of Australian imports actually enter duty-free. While the removal of the tariff concession for particular goods when a domestic producer is threatened is not generally referred to as a safeguard provision, it has a similar effect, particularly when, as it was until the late 1960s in Australia, it is combined with a made-to-measure tariff system that ensures "adequate" protection for domestic production.

Table 7.7 Countervailing duty and antidumping actions, 1980–86[a]

Action	Australia	United States	All countries
Countervailing duty actions against:			
Australia		2	2
United States	1		1
All countries	20	281	460
Antidumping actions against:			
Australia		2	3
United States	44		112
All countries	416	350	1,288

a. Initiated actions; not all yielded positive findings.

Source: Finger and Olechowski (1987), Tables A8.2 and A8.4.

Subsidies

US agricultural price support programs have long been of concern because of their tendency to limit or close the US market to Australian imports—restricted access being the means by which such price support usually is implemented, at least in part—as have the effects on other markets of the export of subsidized US surpluses. While in recent times there has been dispute as to whether Australia's traditional export markets have been invaded by subsidized US exports, such disputes have a limited life, for subsidized exports to any market in the longer run can be expected to depress prices on the world market as a whole. Australian price support for agricultural products of export interest to the United States has been modest, except for tobacco, the estimated effective rate of protection of which has decreased from more than 100 percent in the early 1980s to 24 percent in 1986–87 (Industries Assistance Commission 1987, 201; 1988, 174). Production subsidies continue in Australia for some steel products, but were due to expire at the end of 1988; among other products of interest to the United States, there are subsidies on book production (20 percent of production costs, and declining so as to end in 1993), computers (20 percent of value added, ending in 1990), textile yarns and products (various rates, ending in 1993–96), metalworking machine tools and robots (20 percent of value added, ending in 1991), and cultivating and harvesting equipment

Table 7.8 Services trade between Australia and the United States, 1986–87
(millions of $Aust)[a]

	Australia's exports (credits)	Australia's imports (debits)
Nonfactor services		
Shipment	25	154
Other transportation	335	289
Travel	449	412
Other	276	614
Total	1,085	1,469
Factor services		
Property income		
Reinvested earnings	94	275
Other	492	3,076
Labor and other	38	32
Total factor services	624	3,383
Total services	1,704	4,852

a. Over the relevant period $Aust 1 exchanged for about $US 0.7.

Source: Australian Bureau of Statistics, *Balance of Payments, Australia,* 1986–87 (Canberra, Catalogue No. 5303.0).

(about 10 percent of the factory selling price ending in 1990) (Industries Assistance Commission 1988, table A8.2).

Services

Few data are available on bilateral trade flows in services, or for services trade as a whole for that matter. Table 7.8 contains balance of payments data indicating that while Australia exports to the United States more than it imports of tourism and "other transportation," there is a deficit in nonfactor services, as well as a five-to-one deficit in factor services. More than a quarter of all Australia's payments on foreign capital accrue to the United States, whereas of the much lower investment income earned abroad by Australians, about 21 percent accrues in the United States.

Sea Transport

Australia and the United States both allow their shipping companies to join shipping cartels, or "conferences." But as a product of trade practices legislation in the United States the liner conferences to and from that country are open conferences; that is, they may be joined by any shipping company without the consent of existing members. Both countries receive national treatment in the other with respect to shipping between the two countries, and there is little explicit discrimination against other countries. In 1984 the Australian government introduced a policy requiring federal government departments to offer their liner cargoes first to Australian ships "where Australian ships can provide a reasonably competitive service at normal Conference rates" (Department of Transport 1986, 113). The US government requires that some US cargoes (such as foreign aid shipments) be carried by US ships. Neither country has signed the United Nations Code of Conduct for Liner Conferences, which would give each country's ships the right to carry 40 percent of the trade between them.

Both countries effectively reserve, at very high cost, coastal shipping (cabotage) for ships owned and manned by their own nationals—for the United States this protection extends to the building of the ships also. Thus, international trade in the coastal shipping service is virtually prohibited. Within Australia this restriction of trade is currently being examined, and it is likely that less restrictive trade barriers will be introduced. The strength of political forces in the United States on maritime matters is indicated by its late exclusion from the Canada–US Free Trade Agreement.

Aviation

Bilateral reciprocity is the essence of trade in international aviation between the two countries, as between most others. With respect to passenger traffic, one Australian airline flies to the United States, and two US carriers fly to Australia. Local traffic in the other's country is strictly limited. Although the United States has greatly deregulated its domestic air transport in recent years, the deregulation has not been extended to international carriers in the domestic market—Qantas does not have domestic carriage rights within the United States (or, for that matter, in Australia) other than for its international passengers. The United States is more open to foreign investment in domestic airlines, however, and an Australian airline (Ansett) is the largest single shareholder in one of the smaller US carriers, America West.

Banking

Investment in banking is covered in the section on investment below. Australians are now free to place banking business abroad, in contrast to the situation before December 1983, when there was a blanket prohibition, with exceptions. US residents are not restricted in transacting with foreign banks.

Broadcasting and Motion Pictures

There are no restrictions in either the United States or Australia on residents receiving broadcast transmissions from abroad. There are restrictions in Australia, however, on the incorporation of foreign material in what can be transmitted locally on both radio and television, in the form of Australian content requirements. While neither country has content requirements or other discriminatory restrictions on the screening of motion pictures, subsidies on the production of motion pictures in Australia have been important in the last 15 years or so.

Telecommunications

As in many other countries, but not the United States, telecommunications in Australia is a state monopoly. The definition of telecommunications in the laws that confer this monopoly is broad and essentially covers all transmitted communication. For significant international trade in telecommunications as such to take place, access to the distribution system is essential. While in Australia the reception of beamed messages from abroad is permitted, retransmission is regulated. Barriers to trade thus exist at the point of access to the distribution system.

Intellectual Property

The United States and Australia protect intellectual property in a similar manner, the main exception having been removed in 1986 with the lapse of the manufacturing clause of the US Copyright Act, which, in various forms for almost a century, had made the selling in the United States of books printed abroad a risky business.

Movement of Factors of Production

Capital

Currently there are no Australian restrictions on Australians' borrowing or investing abroad. While foreigners are able to undertake portfolio investment in Australian enterprises freely, direct investment is controlled. Acquisition of substantial interests in businesses with assets of more than approximately $US 4 million ($US 2.4 million for rural properties) is subject to government permission, as is the investment of more than $US 8 million in new enterprises. There are tighter controls on mining and real estate (particularly existing residential real estate), and there is a virtual prohibition on foreign ownership in aviation, radio, television, and newspapers. Borrowings by foreign governments in Australia are prohibited. Australia has a branch banking system; having issued 16 new banking licenses after an international competitive tender four years ago (mergers among the preexisting Australian-owned banks have formed four major "old" banks), it is unlikely that the government will issue further licenses in the foreseeable future.

While restrictions on foreign investment in Australia have been eased significantly in recent years, the current regulations still provide far less than national treatment. The United States is more liberal in its treatment of foreign capital, despite recent rhetoric, although foreign investment in domestic aviation and radio and television broadcasting is restricted. Take-overs are the subject of national security provisions in the 1988 trade bill, and on occasion they have run into problems with state governments.

Labor

Visa and entry laws restrict services trade between the two countries, as between all countries. (We are, of course, addressing only temporary movement from one country to another. Migration raises other issues.) In general, Australia admits only executive and professional, technical, or other specialist staff for temporary residence with employment. Only top managers are granted an initial four-year visa; others who qualify for entry receive an initial two-year visa, which is renewable if the applicants have particularly valuable expertise. Manual or relatively unskilled workers are generally not eligible for visas that permit work. Within professional categories a number of restrictions and practices act as trade barriers, recognition of foreign qualifications being particularly important. Also important are practices throughout the entertainment industry in Australia that, for example, restrict the number of foreign opera singers and foreign actors in Australian films, require payment to an Australian production company when a foreign crew is filming in Australia, and so on.

The United States also restricts the supply of services from temporary labor, both at the point of entry and in terms of recognition of foreign qualifications, and like most other countries discriminates against the relatively unskilled. Although legislation may permit the entry of foreign construction teams, for example, very few are used. Mexico has been an important source for fruit pickers, for example, although legislation has tightened significantly in this area. Foreign doctors encounter similar difficulties in Australia and the United States in terms of recognition of qualifications; accountants in the United States (but not in Australia) require state certificates, which generally are not issued unless a US accounting education has been received, and similar requirements exist in other professions. Practices similar to those in Australia exist with respect to foreign "stars" on Broadway.

Australian firms with interests in the United States have experienced difficulties and delays in obtaining visas for Australian executives to be stationed in the United States, and no doubt similar problems have arisen in the opposite direction.

Effects of a Free Trade Agreement

As with any preferential trade agreement, a free trade agreement between the United States and Australia would bring trade diversion as well as trade creation, for services trade as well as for trade in goods. A model designed to capture these effects for goods trade has been developed by Sam Laird, previously of UNCTAD but now at the World Bank, and was run for Australian–US trade two years ago (Snape 1986). Of necessity the assumptions underlying such an exercise are fairly heroic, and the results should not be interpreted as any more than indicative of relative magnitudes. It was assumed that tariffs were removed by both the United States and Australia and that tariffs and not nontariff barriers were the binding restraints. (Further assumptions and specification of the model are contained in Snape 1986, chapter 2 and appendix II.) The results (which should not be aggregated because general equilibrium effects are not taken into account) are presented in tables 7.9 and 7.10. Although the calculations relate to data of the early 1980s, the general picture is unlikely to have been changed greatly by developments since then, although as Australian tariffs have declined the effects on Australian imports would be smaller.

For Australia's exports it can be seen that the only three products (at the

three-digit SITC level) for which there is export expansion of more than
$US 5 million are restricted by existing nontariff barriers, so that tariff
reductions on their own would be almost irrelevant.[3] Although there are
significant proportionate increases in exports of some other products, the
amount of trade involved is very small.

Turning to the exports of the United States to Australia, as tariffs were
significantly higher in Australia the effects of their reduction are much
greater. Although imports of two of the listed products are restricted by
nontariff barriers, these two products do not dominate the imports of
Australia in the way that the potential import expansion of the United States
is dominated by nontariff barriers. The recently announced tariff reductions
in Australia will lower the export expansion that the United States could
expect from a preferential reduction of tariffs by Australia.

These calculations clearly show why Australia, in the absence of any
action by the United States on nontariff barriers, is unlikely to be interested
in a trade agreement. (As noted earlier, there are products of export interest
to Australia, besides those listed in table 7.9, that are restricted by nontariff
barriers or threats thereof.) The trade creation on the side of imports probably
yields an efficiency gain for Australia, but this gain and more could be
achieved by a unilateral (or multilateral) tariff reduction rather than the
bilateral reduction being considered here. Trade diversion yields an economic
cost, one that can be justified if the demand for exports expands sufficiently
(and if this expansion could not otherwise have been obtained without a
preferential barrier reduction). But without a reduction of US nontariff
barriers, the expansion of demand for Australia's exports would be paltry.
Furthermore, as virtually every US tariff of concern to Australia is bound at
current (post-Tokyo Round) levels, there is no scope for the binding of US
tariffs to be a quid for Australia's quo.

So it is to the nontariff barriers to trade in goods and services that one
must look for the possibility of a bilateral trade agreement that is likely to
be attractive to Australia, or to an agreement being a possible route to a
more beneficial multilateral or plurilateral agreement.

A range of possibilities exists in relation to nontariff barriers. At one end
of the spectrum would be an open door for Australian imports and for them
to be sold at internal US prices. Although this is what has been agreed
upon for Canadian beef under the Canada–US Free Trade Agreement (but
not for some other Canadian agricultural products or for Israeli agricultural

---

3. For meat and sugar the projected expansion of imports probably is underestimated
significantly. This is due to an assumption, made for all commodities, of imperfect
substitution between alternative sources of supply, and the assumed substitution
elasticity is probably much too low for these products.

Table 7.9   Estimated trade creation and diversion effects of an elimination of US tariffs facing products imported from Australia, 1983[a]

SITC (Revision 1)	Product description	Value of actual trade (millions of $US)	Tariff[b] (%)	Trade creation[c] (%)	Trade diversion[c] (%)	Total creation and diversion (millions of $US)
061	Sugar and honey	83	(17.1)[d]	(17)[d]	(9)[d]	(21)[d]
011	Meat; fresh, chilled, or frozen	573	(2.1)[d]	(2)[d]	(...)[d]	(13)[d]
674	Universals, plates and sheets of iron or steel	50	(7.2)[d]	(12)[d]	(...)[d]	(5.9)[d]
861	Scientific, medical, optical measuring and control instruments	27	5.7	11	1	3.1
599	Chemical materials and products, n.e.s.	35	3.6	4	...	1.4
841	Clothing, except fur clothing	4	10.1	32	3	1.3
719	Machinery and appliances– non-electrical, parts	17	3.9	7	1	1.3
726	Electrical apparatus for medical purposes, radiological appliances	4	11.6	29	5	1.3
262	Wool and other animal hair	79	5.2	2	...	1.3
684	Aluminum	28	3.0	...	...	0.9
733	Road vehicles other than motor vehicles	11	3.4	1	...	0.8

Table 7.9   (Continued)

SITC (Revision 1)	Product description	Value of actual trade (millions of $US)	Tariff[b] (%)	Trade creation[c] (%)	Trade diversion[c] (%)	Total creation and diversion (millions of $US)
513	Inorganic chem-icals—ele-ments, oxides, halogen salts (including alumina)	540	0.1	. . .	. . .	0.8
024	Cheese and curd	7	(10.2)[d]	(10)[d]	(. . .)[d]	(0.8)[d]
894	Perambulators, toys, games, and sporting goods	4	4.9	17	1	0.7
541	Medicinal and pharmaceuti-cal products	9	4.1	7	. . .	0.6

n.e.s. = not elsewhere specified.
a. Total effects at the three-digit SITC (Revision 1) level, aggregated from tariff lines. Included are the 15 most important products in terms of total trade creation and diversion.
b. Trade-weighted tariff average.
c. Expressed as a percentage of imports from Australia.
d. Nontariff barriers restrict imports of these products.
Ellipsis indicates less than 0.5 percent.

Source: Snape (1986). Data drawn from *GATT Tariff Line Tapes for Tariff and Trade Values* (Geneva: GATT). The model was developed and run by Sam Laird.

products under the free trade agreement with that country), Australian beef production is probably more of a threat to US beef producers than is Canada's. (Canadian beef imports have not been subject to restriction when beef import restraints have been in operation for other countries.) So such access could not be achieved without considerable political cost in the United States: the domestic political consequences of the overtures made by the United States at the Uruguay Round agricultural negotiations have yet to be tested. Similarly for sugar, the threat of Australian imports to the

Table 7.10 Estimated trade creation and diversion effects of a preferential removal of Australian tariffs facing products imported from the United States, 1981[a]

SITC (Revision 1)	Product description	Value of actual trade (millions of $US)	Tariff[b] (%)	Trade creation[c] (%)	Trade diversion[c] (%)	Total creation and diversion (millions of $US)
719	Machinery and appliances—nonelectrical goods	436	10.9	10	8	77
732	Road motor vehicles	363	(9.4)[d]	(13)[d]	(6)[d]	(70)[d]
718	Machines for special industries	387	8.0	7	3	37
629	Articles of rubber, n.e.s.	31	18.4	85	16	31
893	Articles of artificial plastic materials, n.e.s.	31	19.1	82	17	30
581	Plastic materials, regenerated cellulose, and resins	142	8.9	12	6	26
729	Other electrical machinery and apparatus	184	5.3	10	3	25
722	Electric power machinery and switchgear	99	10.7	14	10	23
894	Perambulators, toys, games, and sporting goods	34	17.1	48	15	22
653	Textile fabrics, woven, excluding narrow, not cotton	53	(16.3)[d]	(28)[d]	(11)[d]	(21)[d]

Table 7.10 (Continued)

SITC (Revision 1)	Product description	Value of actual trade (millions of $US)	Tariff[b] (%)	Trade creation[c] (%)	Trade diversion[c] (%)	Total creation and diversion (millions of $US)
714	Office machines	341	1.4	4	1	18
698	Manufactures of metal, n.e.s.	34	17.9	29	14	15
641	Paper and paperboard	97	9.2	11	4	14
657	Floor coverings, tapestries, etc.	20	47.2	45	26	14
724	Telecommunications apparatus	43	11.3	24	8	14

n.e.s. = not elsewhere specified.

a. Total effects at the three-digit SITC (Revision 1) level, aggregated from tariff lines. Included are the 15 most important products in terms of total trade creation and diversion.

b. Trade-weighted tariff average.

c. Expressed as a percentage of imports from the US.

d. Nontariff barriers restrict imports of these products.

Source: Snape (1986). Data drawn from *GATT Tariff Line Tapes for Tariff and Trade Values* (Geneva: GATT). The model was developed and run by Sam Laird.

whole price support system in the United States would appear to rule out open access for Australian exporters.

A possibility is for preferences for Australia to be given within the existing nontariff barriers. For beef and sugar again there would be major problems if any significant benefit were to be given to Australia at the expense of other suppliers. In beef, Australia potentially is such a large supplier that significantly expanded access would have a major impact on other exporters; unrestricted access for Australia could drive quotas (when they are implemented under the US arrangements) for other suppliers to zero. In sugar, total imports have declined significantly in recent years, and again unrestricted access for Australia would have major impacts on other suppliers. However, imports are declining so rapidly that there will soon be none left to divert. A meaningful action by the United States would require substantial reduction in the domestic sugar price support, a notoriously sensitive subject for almost the whole 20th century (Krueger 1988).

The Canada–US agreement shows the inventiveness that can be tapped where nontariff barriers and subsidies are involved, and it is pointless to attempt to run through all the possibilities where barriers exist already. A move of some importance for Australia could be a guarantee that nontariff barriers would not be imposed where they currently do not exist—to clear them out of the wings in which they are waiting. Similarly, agreement with respect to the export to third countries of subsidized products could be valuable, although the agreement with Canada could extend no further on this than that:

Each Party shall take into account the export interests of the other Party in the use of any export subsidy on any agricultural good exported to third countries, recognizing that such subsidies may have prejudicial effects on the export interests of the other Party (Article 701.4).

For services there are two guides as to the direction negotiations could take: the agreements that the United States has with Israel and Canada on the one hand and the Closer Economic Relations Trade Agreement between Australia and New Zealand on the other. There is a marked difference in approach, one that is relevant for the negotiations on services in the Uruguay Round, as well as for any possible trade agreement between Australia and the United States. The agreement with Canada contains a positive list of covered services (a service is not covered by the agreement unless it is listed), grandfathers existing restrictions on these services, and prohibits new restrictions on them. It makes provision for the movement of some forms of professional labor, and for investment. The Australia–New Zealand agreement, in a protocol signed in August 1988, takes the negative list approach—all services are liberalized except those listed.

Although it is possible in principle for the two approaches to give the same result, in practice the latter is generally a more liberal approach to trade policy, particularly over time as new forms of service develop. While the parties have until March 1989 to add exceptions to the list, the initial exceptions relate only to some aspects of aviation (partly because of obligations under the Chicago Convention), posts and telecommunications, broadcasting, and, for Australia, some forms of insurance, banking, and government preferences for Australian consultants. The agreement is subject to the foreign investment policies of the two countries, but is much more liberalizing than the US agreements (as are the provisions relating to goods also). Labor already flows freely between Australia and New Zealand.

An agreement between Australia and the United States that followed the Australia–New Zealand agreement in services could be important in itself, and particularly for the smaller partner, but it could be more important as a demonstration to others of thorough liberalization of services trade. But the Canadian agreement suggests that a much more limited approach would be forthcoming from the United States, one that would give modest gains and have modest political costs.

Safeguard actions are another area of potential negotiation, and again the agreements with Canada and New Zealand can give an indication of the possibilities. The Canada–US agreement retains safeguard action both with respect to injury to an industry from increased imports ("fair" trade, that is, along the lines of GATT Article XIX) and with respect to injury caused by dumping or subsidies. The agreement imposes a time limit on the former type of safeguard action, and excludes the partner from global action when exports of the partner do not contribute significantly to the injury. For dumping and subsidies, existing rights of retaliation are retained, but a binational panel is to be established to rule on disputes. These are quite modest developments given the importance attached to the subject, particularly by the Canadians.

The Australia–New Zealand agreement goes much further. From July 1990 for trade between the parties, Article XIX-type safeguard measures and antidumping actions are to be abolished. The trade ministers have also agreed that their governments will not give production or export subsidies on goods exported to the other country. Again it is the Canada–US agreement that gives an indication of the likely possibilities for a US–Australia agreement.

It is likely that the United States would require Australian acceptance of the GATT Procurement Code as a condition of a free trade agreement. As noted above, this would conflict with the Australian government's procurement and offsets policies. Under the agreement with New Zealand, the Australian government treats New Zealand content in tenders as being Australian. The Canada–US agreement embraces the GATT Procurement Code and lowers the threshold to $US 25,000, but it does not extend it beyond goods, or to government below the federal level. Although there is obviously scope for liberalization in procurement, and particularly by Australia, it is an area of sensitivity.

Relation to Other Agreements

Any trade agreement between Australia and the United States could be expected to conform to the provisions of Article XXIV of the GATT, as do the agreements with Canada and New Zealand, although most "free trade" agreements in fact do not appear to do so. This requirement could imply that nontariff barriers would have to be addressed.

With respect to other agreements, the United States could be embarrassed in relation to its Caribbean Basin Initiative if it were to give preference to

Australian sugar, and possibly beef. More important, however, would be the implications for the free trade agreement with Canada.

Australia competes in the US market with Canada in a number of products: in particular, some nonferrous metals, uranium, and (potentially) beef. The US agreement with Canada thus discriminates against Australia with respect to these products. Removal of this discrimination by the United States through negotiation of a similar agreement with Australia could be regarded by Canadians as an erosion of concessions for which they have paid. Such is the problem at the heart of discriminatory trade policies. For nonferrous metals the main implications arise in Canada's exemption from a 19 percent tariff on some types of zinc—a strong discrimination against Australia. For uranium, to give Australian uranium producers the same guarantee that has been given to Canada (Annex 902.5 of the agreement) of exemption from any restriction that may be imposed on the enrichment of foreign uranium would be a major benefit for Australian producers.[4] Although Canadian beef has not been strongly competitive with Australian beef in the past, the formalization of exemption of Canadian beef from restrictions provides preferential incentives for Canadian producers, to which they may respond, that would be removed by similar treatment for Australian beef.

The safeguard provisions of the agreement with Canada also contain the potential for discrimination against Australia. Under these provisions, the United States can discriminate against non-Canadian products if US producers claim injury from imports as a whole, rather than imports from Canada in particular.[5] While this could affect any product, the history of restrictions on nonferrous metals and the competition between Australian and Canadian producers in these products suggest that this discriminatory safeguards provision could be of importance in relation to nonferrous metals.[6]

---

4. It may be argued that the guarantee to the major foreign supplier to the United States of exemption from any restrictions on the enrichment of foreign uranium serves to guarantee access for minor suppliers such as Australia also. Two contrary points may be noted: (1) from time to time countries have restricted imports from relatively minor suppliers of a product when a major foreign supplier has not been restricted, and (2) costs of production, etc., change over time, and Canada may not always be the major supplier to the United States that it is now.

5. The relevant provisions are Article 1102, 1 and 4: "... a Party taking such [GATT Article XIX] action shall exclude the other Party from such global action unless imports from that Party are substantial and are contributing importantly to the serious injury or threat thereof caused by imports. For [these] purposes ... imports in the range of five percent to ten percent or less [sic] of total imports would normally not be considered substantial. ... In no case shall a Party take [such] an action ... that would have the effect of reducing imports of such a good from the other Party below the trend of imports over a reasonable recent base period with allowance for growth."

6. For many nonferrous metals Canada is a much larger supplier than Australia, and

As far as Australia's trade agreements are concerned, New Zealand manufacturers that export to Australia could feel strong competitive pressure if free access were to be granted to the United States, and, like Canadians, New Zealanders could argue that the benefits for which they have paid by their concessions have been undermined.

Broader Issues

There is a strong argument that the interests of all countries, but particularly the smaller countries of the world, are best served by a liberal, nondiscriminatory, multilateral trading system. There is not a great deal of economic gain for the United States in a free trade agreement with Australia alone, and, somewhat paradoxically, there would be some significant domestic political costs in the United States if such an agreement were to be of any substantial benefit to Australia. So for the United States the attraction, if any, would lie in the political sphere, or for such an agreement being one of a series of bilateral agreements, perhaps expanding into a more liberal "trading club" than the GATT or than the GATT is likely to become. The wider the membership, the more likely that the trade creation gains will outweigh the trade diversion costs.

As far as Australia is concerned, the risks of damage to the multilateral system are somewhat greater—the big and powerful can look after themselves rather better, section 301 or its equivalent in hand. Australia has a big stake in US (and European and Japanese) markets being open, not just to direct exports from Australia, but also for indirect exports—for example, for imports from Asian exporters who in turn import Australian raw materials. Bilateral approaches to trade policy can risk the closing off of these multilateral benefits. On the other hand, if the rest of the world is forming trade blocs and negotiating bilateral agreements, Australia could well be out on its own. The Canada–US agreement, the shift of the United States away from its postwar leadership against preferential arrangements (Snape 1988), and the significant danger of an inward-looking Europe after 1992, warn that such a scenario is quite possible. If it develops further, there would be little choice but to seek bilateral or trading bloc deals, and there is a good case for joining early rather than late.

---

it may be judged unlikely that safeguard actions would be taken against minor suppliers if the major foreign supplier is excluded from them. Against this view, the two points noted in footnote 4 relating to uranium may be reiterated.

Acknowledgments

Sam Laird has been most helpful in supplying current data from the UN *COMTRADE Data Base* for this chapter. Paul Meo, Greg Wood, and Roger Freney have provided very helpful comments.

References

Baldwin, Robert E. 1985. *The Political Economy of U.S. Import Policy.* Cambridge, Mass.: MIT Press.

Cameron, Laurie A., and Gerald C. Berg. 1987. "The U.S. Sugar Program: An Historical View." Presented at the Western Economic Association Annual Meeting, Vancouver, July.

Department of Transport. 1986. *Liner Shipping Report: An Industry Task Force Review of Australia's Overseas Liner Shipping Legislation.* Canberra: Australian Government Publishing Service.

Finger, J. Michael, and Andrzej Olechowski, eds. 1987. *The Uruguay Round: A Handbook on the Multilateral Trade Negotiations.* Washington: The World Bank.

Hufbauer, Gary C., Diane T. Berliner, and Kimberly A. Elliott. 1986. *Trade Protection in the United States: 31 Case Studies.* Washington: Institute for International Economics.

Industries Assistance Commission. 1987. *Annual Report, 1986–87.* Canberra: Australian Government Publishing Service.

Industries Assistance Commission. 1988. *Annual Report, 1987–88.* Canberra: Australian Government Publishing Service.

Krueger, Anne O. 1988. "The Political Economy of Controls: American Sugar." NBER Working Paper no. 2504. Cambridge, Mass.: National Bureau of Economic Research.

Maskus, Keith E. 1987. "The International Political Economy of U.S. Sugar Policy in the 1980's." Presented at the Western Economic Association Annual Meeting, Vancouver, July.

Snape, Richard H. 1986. *Should Australia Seek a Trade Agreement with the United States?* Discussion Paper no. 86/01. Canberra: Economic Planning Advisory Council.

Snape, Richard H. 1988. "Is Non-Discrimination Really Dead?" *The World Economy,* vol. 11, no. 1 (March), 1–17.

Comments

Anne O. Krueger

When I agreed to discuss the papers on possible free trade areas (FTAs) between the United States and Australia, Korea, and Taiwan, I expected to learn about the economies of the latter three countries and the most important ways that FTAs would impact upon them.

Interestingly, I learned even more than I expected, but not about Australia, Korea, and Taiwan. Each of the authors did a very competent job of considering the impact on his country of a possible FTA with the United States. But what emerges from the three chapters is striking, and it raises some basic questions about the whole FTA approach. What I learned has to do with American policy, not with the specifics of Australia, Korea, or Taiwan.

The bottom line that emerges clearly from the three chapters, considered jointly, is perhaps the best and clearest case for the GATT that can be made. Simultaneously, the papers make clear that so-called free trade areas—at least as considered here—are not in fact free trade areas but rather agreements that at best provide assurances to American trading partners that protectionism will go no further with them.

Let me explain why these conclusions emerge so clearly. Richard Snape provides a first-rate analysis of the Australian situation: he doubts that an FTA between the United States and Australia has much to offer Australia because the major commodities for which Australia has an interest in obtaining greater access to the American market are subject to nontariff barriers whose removal is probably politically infeasible. He recognizes that a genuine FTA, with removal of these barriers, would be of great value to Australia, but does not consider that a realistic option. Incidentally, Australia's trade barriers against American imports (both tariff and nontariff) are negligible. One final point worth noting: Snape observes that even if the United States were willing to consider lowering some of its politically sensitive nontariff barriers in return for an Australia–US FTA, Canadians might well object since concessions on those products are presumably part of what the Canadians "won" in their bargaining with the United States.

For Korea, Park and Yoo develop a model in which a "center" country forms free trade areas with several trading partners. Their central concern is that any one of the partners might be at a disadvantage in competing with the center—in any market—because the center would have access to

Anne O. Krueger is the Arts and Sciences Professor of Economics at Duke University.

all markets while the individual partner countries' producers would have only restricted access to the others' markets. Of course, any individual trading partner of the center country could offset any such disadvantage by opting for free trade; in any event, most countries have procedures for rebates of duties paid on imported inputs.

However, my concern here is not with the specifics of the model: what is important is that Park and Yoo correctly assume that they cannot analyze a possible Korea–US FTA without knowing how many other countries there will be within the FTA, and which countries they would be. It is self-evident that if the United States formed FTAs with either Japan or Taiwan or both, it would be extremely detrimental to Korea to remain outside it. The authors clearly believe that finding a bilateral dispute settlement mechanism, modeled along the lines of that proposed in the Canada–US agreement, would provide perhaps the greatest benefit to Korea, as contrasted with the current situation, where American courts and procedures decide bilateral issues (predominantly through proceedings under section 301 of the Trade Act of 1974).

Professor Tsiang's chapter makes the same point for Taiwan: he is at a loss to know how to analyze the specifics of an FTA without knowing what the trade relations between the United States and Japan would be. Having surveyed the issues, he concludes that a genuine move toward freer trade between Taiwan and the United States would be most welcome, but he notes that, for such an area to work, "both partners" would have to understand that excuses such as "cheap foreign labor" could no longer be used to rationalize protection.

Two themes emerge from these chapters. First, none of the authors seems to expect the United States to abandon its protectionism; the most they hope for is some change in the dispute settlement process (about which more below) and a promise of no further increase in protection. Second, each of the authors recognizes that there are significant differences in the effects of FTAs, depending on who else has one.

Turning to the first theme, it cannot be denied that a bilateral dispute settlement process would constitute a net benefit, and possibly a considerable one, to American trading partners. Possibly even more important might be the eschewal of further protectionist measures. But what emerges clearly is that FTAs, as they are discussed in these chapters, are not envisaged as FTAs normally are: no one is talking about the absence of protectionist barriers, the eschewal of safeguards or antidumping provisions, or the abandonment of the panoply of trading rules. They are discussing some undertakings that would modify the ways in which trade law is administered and the selective removal of some trade barriers in America's trading partners. That is a far cry from the original conception of a GATT-plus, under which members of the FTAs would respect their GATT obligations to all countries and then go on to additional undertakings among themselves.

However, the second theme is equally disturbing. If it is true that the United States is bargaining, with Canada for example, for removal of trade barriers from selective sectors in return for preferential access to, say, the American meat market, what will then happen if the United States proceeds to bargain with Australia or some other country, and offers the same preferential access to that country? Clearly, the value of the concession to Canada would be reduced. Would not Canadians have a right to complain, as Snape deftly points out? Clearly, the same sort of considerations would apply to Taiwan, Korea, or Japan if one of those negotiated and entered an FTA before the other two.

Possibly even more disturbing, however, is the prospect of a bilateral dispute settlement mechanism with each FTA partner. Obviously, the Canadian–American Commission would be making and interpreting trade law as it went; so, too, would the Korean–American Commission. It is not at all clear how any degree of consistency would be assured over time. That in itself could give firms in one trading partner a significant advantage over those in another, and create major problems for American importers and exporters. The major beneficiaries would be American lawyers specializing in international trade.

The obvious answer to the problems raised by the bilateral approach is that trade relations should be multilateral. Park and Yoo suggest that this means that all countries entering into the FTA should first sit down together and work out multilateral rules. But the broader question is, why eschew the GATT? Even casual consideration of the complexities of one-at-a-time bilateral negotiations demonstrates forcefully the need for a multilateral approach.

I conclude that the American discussion of FTAs—not genuine, no-restrictions and no-trade-barriers FTAs, but the kind that require 16 months to negotiate and consist of 900 or more pages—is doubly tragic: it uses the language of free trade to perpetuate protectionism, and is simultaneously highly unrealistic since it cannot possibly be extended one country at a time over a large number of countries. Possibly even worse, it distracts attention from the current Uruguay Round of multilateral trade negotiations. Although American rhetoric has indicated that the bilateral and multilateral approaches are "parallel track" pursuits, consideration of the issues raised in the Australian, Korean, and Taiwanese papers suggests that the bilateral approach is a major distraction from the Uruguay Round, and reduces the commitment to it just at a time when that determination is most needed.

8

The US–ASEAN Free Trade Area Option: Scope and Implications

Mohamed Ariff

The economies of the United States and the Association of Southeast Asian Nations (ASEAN) are quite different in many obvious ways, and it is precisely these differences that render US–ASEAN economic relations mutually rewarding. However, the underlying common denominator is that both are market economies that have been ardent supporters of the liberal trading system. The United States has long championed the cause of free trade, although it seems to have succumbed in recent years to growing domestic protectionist pressures. The United States is not regarded as a protectionist villain in the ASEAN region, unlike the European Community (EC) or Japan. It nevertheless appears that it is the United States that has been turning on the most protectionist heat recently, as evidenced by the growing number of trade bills in the US Congress. Growing protectionist fevers in the developed countries in general, and the United States in particular, are of grave concern to ASEAN countries, which depend heavily on trade.

It is clearly in the interest of both the United States and ASEAN to have a liberal world trading system that is subject to multilateral rules and disciplines. The intention of the United States to liberalize trade has never been in doubt, although the US position has been blunted somewhat, partly by protectionist forces at home and partly by the lack of reciprocity abroad. The ASEAN countries did not participate actively in the previous multilateral trade negotiations (MTNs), but they are now prepared to play an active role in the GATT process. The Uruguay Round of GATT talks is generally viewed as a last-ditch effort to save the multilateral trading system. Although it would be premature to judge the possible outcome of the Uruguay Round at this juncture, there seems to be no basis for high expectations. The

---

Mohamed Ariff is a professor of economics at the University of Malaya in Kuala Lumpur.

Uruguay Round will probably turn out to be the most successful MTN so far, but it is unlikely to iron out all the issues that threaten the world trading system.

It is generally agreed that a liberal trading system cannot be created in the absence of a hegemonic power. The US role as the torchbearer of free trade was largely associated with its position as a hegemon in the international arena. It now appears that US hegemony has significantly declined in the face of the growing importance of Japan and the EC (Krause 1988). There has also been considerable erosion in the will of the United States to play the leadership role in the GATT system.

The ASEAN countries are no more than marginal players in the multilateral trade negotiations. The implication is that there is very little that ASEAN can do to save the multilateral trading system, no matter how prepared they are to stretch themselves.

It may be discerned from all this it would not be safe for trade-dependent countries like the ASEAN nations to hinge themselves precariously to the multilateral trading system. This is not to deny that the multilateral approach can offer the first-best solutions. Pragmatism, however, forces most countries to look out for fallback positions. It is in this context that one might view bilateral and plurilateral arrangements as alternatives to the multilateral approach.

An alternative scenario would therefore be one in which the world is divided into trading blocs through bilateral or plurilateral arrangements. Already there are several regional groupings that are seemingly consistent with the GATT system. It is reasonable to surmise that the world will see more of these should the Uruguay Round fail.

Viewed in this light, a linkup between the United States and ASEAN is by no means a wild proposition. For the United States, it is mainly a question of extending the special bilateral relations that it already has with several other countries such as Canada and Israel. For ASEAN, it is essentially a question of taking a bold step beyond the present bilateral arrangement it has with the United States as a "dialogue partner." Although a US–ASEAN free trade area (FTA) is not in the cards yet, it represents an interesting policy option that merits serious consideration.

This chapter explores the scope of a possible FTA between the United States and ASEAN and examines the implications of such an arrangement. Admittedly, the present exercise aims to be no more than a think piece. Accordingly, the analysis is qualitative, while the approach is somewhat normative.

US-ASEAN Economic Relations: A Profile

The political economy of an FTA between the United States and ASEAN will be influenced greatly by the nature and character of the current bilateral relations between them. It is therefore important to take at least a cursory look at the structure of bilateral transactions between the United States and ASEAN, particularly those aspects that may have a direct bearing on the question of an FTA.

Economic relations between the United States and ASEAN have progressed remarkably over the years. US–ASEAN trade increased 25-fold in less than 20 years, from $945 million in 1967 to $23.5 billion in 1985. The trade balance more often than not has been in ASEAN's favor. It is also noteworthy that ASEAN is the United States' fifth largest trading partner, after the EC, Canada, Japan, and Mexico, whereas the United States is ASEAN's second largest trading partner, after Japan. Trade relations between the United States and ASEAN are clearly asymmetrical in the sense that the United States is far more important to ASEAN than ASEAN is to the United States.

The composition of trade flows exhibits considerable diversity and complementarity. ASEAN exports to the United States consist mainly of primary commodities and a variety of light manufactures (DeRosa 1986), as is consistent with the resource endowments of the region. Evidently, ASEAN countries have a comparative advantage in resource-intensive and labor-intensive products. In contrast, the bulk of US exports to ASEAN are chemicals and transport equipment—goods that are technology and capital intensive (DeRosa 1986). The bilateral trade pattern thus seems to conform roughly with the traditional Heckscher-Ohlin trade theory.

The above observation, of course, does not mean that US–ASEAN trade is free from distortions. Nor does it imply that there have been no trade frictions between the United States and ASEAN. Administered forms of US protectionism have affected several ASEAN exports, particularly sugar, textiles, and apparel. Recent US antidumping investigations and countervailing duty (CVD) impositions also have affected several ASEAN exports.[1] US agricultural subsidies for soybeans, corn, and rice have caused problems for ASEAN rice, corn, and palm oil exports in third-country markets (Ariff

---

1. Although ASEAN countries are less affected by CVD and antidumping actions than other East Asian countries, the specter of potential CVD actions does haunt them. The United States imposed a 17.7 percent CVD on Malaysian iron rods in April 1988. Several other Malaysian products are under CVD investigations. There were US CVD cases against Indonesian and Malaysian textiles and Thai rice, but the results of these investigations revealed that the subsidy levels were below 0.5 percent in all three cases.

and Tan 1988). Nonetheless, it appears that US protectionism has had very little dampening effect on ASEAN exports (Ariff and Hill 1985). It also appears that trade regimes in ASEAN countries—with the exception of Singapore and Brunei—are generally far more restrictive than that of the United States, as shown by the comparative figures relating to tariff rates and nontariff barriers (tables 8.1 and 8.2). Besides, ASEAN exports seem more vulnerable to protectionism in the markets of the EC and Japan than in that of the United States (Ariff and Hill 1985).

In addition to merchandise trade, there has been considerable trade in services between the United States and ASEAN, but no one really knows the magnitude of such flows.[2] Presumably ASEAN, with the possible exception of Singapore, has a sizable services deficit with the United States. The largest services imports of ASEAN from the United States appear to be freight and insurance, and travel and tourism (Yuan 1988). Apparently, the United States has a clear comparative advantage in a wide range of services, although that does not necessarily mean that ASEAN has a comparative or an absolute disadvantage in all categories of services.

The United States is also a major source of foreign investment to ASEAN. American investment in the region exceeds $10 billion (Kintanar and Tan 1986), and ASEAN accounts for about one-fifth of the total US direct investment in developing countries. However, ASEAN is less important to the United States as an investment destination than are Canada, Europe, and Latin America (Yuan 1988). Japanese direct investment in ASEAN exceeds that of the United States, accounting for about 20 percent of the total foreign capital stock compared with a 4 percent share for the United States (Pangestu 1986).

The United States has been an important dialogue partner of ASEAN since the inception of the dialogue process after the ASEAN Bali Summit in 1976. The dialogue sessions have helped solve many bilateral problems. Nonetheless, there are still some thorns in ASEAN–US relations. ASEAN is extremely unhappy about soaring protectionism in the United States, especially the growing number of trade bills before the US Congress; about the lack of US support for international commodity agreements and price stabilization schemes; about the low level of US investment outside the petroleum sector; and about the slow pace of technology transfer by American transnational corporations. On the other side of the coin, the United States is concerned about inadequate enforcement of patent and intellectual property rights in the region; about ASEAN barriers to services trade and investment; and about the slow pace of ASEAN regional integration.

---

2. Bilateral data on services trade are available only for Thailand.

Table 8.1 Average ASEAN and US ad valorem tariff rates (percentages)[a]

SITC category	ASEAN countries					United States	
	Indonesia	Malaysia	Philippines	Singapore	Thailand	Pre-MTN	Post-MTN
Primary commodities (0–4)	29.1	9.0	30.0	0.5	23.2	*	*
Manufactures (5–8)	33.1	12.1	29.8	0.5	29.1	6.4	4.4
Chemicals (5)	18.9	10.1	21.2	0.0	15.4	4.5	2.7
Basic manufactures (6)	36.8	11.2	33.3	0.0	29.6	6.4	4.6
Machinery, transport, equipment (7)	26.7	12.9	22.5	0.4	20.4	5.2	3.5
Miscellaneous manufactures (8)	49.8	14.2	42.3	1.7	50.9	9.6	6.6

SITC = United Nations Standard International Trade Classification; MTN refers to the Tokyo Round.

a. Specific tariff duties and various special ASEAN countries' import surcharges are excluded from the averages. ASEAN tariff rates refer to the following years: 1980 (Indonesia), 1981 (Malaysia), and 1983 (Philippines, Singapore, and Thailand).

* Very few of the US primary commodities were subject to the general tariff-cutting formula in the Tokyo Round; and therefore their tariff rates were not included in the US Trade Representative's report used to compile this table.

Source: Campbell and DeRosa (1988).

Table 8.2 Nontariff barriers in the ASEAN countries and the United States, circa 1983[a]

Trade category	ASEAN countries (% frequency)[b]					United States	
	Indonesia	Malaysia	Philippines	Singapore	Thailand	% Frequency	% Import coverage[b]
All categories	11.4	6.4	17.6	6.5	8.8	7.0	43.0
Fuels	1.7	0.0	32.6	0.0	2.6	94.0	100.0
Agriculture	13.9	12.7	24.1	11.9	9.3	6.4	24.0
Manufacturing	11.3	2.1	12.2	5.4	6.7	6.9	17.1
Textiles	20.2	0.2	0.0	1.3	3.5	30.8	57.0
Footwear	0.0	0.0	0.0	20.0	0.0	5.4	11.5
Iron and steel	13.8	1.2	96.9	0.0	3.1	22.8	37.7
Electrical machinery	13.8	0.0	2.3	3.5	2.6	0.6	5.2
Vehicles	18.9	41.9	29.2	3.7	40.0	1.3	34.2

a. The ASEAN data cover only quantitative restrictions, while the US data encompass all forms of nontariff barriers. ASEAN data refer to the following years: 1980 (Indonesia), 1981 (Malaysia), and 1983 (Philippines, Singapore, and Thailand). US data refer to 1983. ASEAN statistics are simply averages of frequency rates by detailed trade product categories. US statistics are trade-weighted averages.
b. Frequency rates indicate the proportion of total number of customs product categories affected by nontariff barriers, whereas import coverage rates indicate the proportion of total value of imports affected by nontariff barriers.

Source: Campbell and DeRosa (1988).

Analytic Framework

Against this backdrop one can conduct an analysis of an FTA involving the United States and ASEAN. The costs and benefits of such an FTA, in terms of both allocative efficiency and distributive justice, will hinge crucially on the kind of FTA structure one has in mind. It is not clear at this stage what form the US–ASEAN FTA could possibly take, if any at all. It would be naive to think that the United States will be prepared to extend to ASEAN the same kind of special relations it has with Israel and Canada. The former is heavily determined by politics, while the latter is largely influenced by geographical proximity. ASEAN is a region of considerable strategic importance to the United States, which seems to regard ASEAN as the bastion of democracy and the defender of the capitalistic system in Southeast Asia. This accounts for the favorable attitude of the United States toward ASEAN. Economic considerations provide an additional motivation for closer ties, given the American investment and trade interests in the region.

At this stage, one can only resort to adopting the textbook model of a free trade area, which involves a grouping of two or more countries that agree to abolish all trade barriers among themselves, while allowing the individual countries to pursue independent trade policies with respect to third countries. A US–ASEAN FTA based on such a model is not inconceivable, since it is theoretically possible for the United States and ASEAN to grant free entry to each other's products, while each remains free to adopt whatever policies it chooses toward third countries. This autonomy with respect to trade with third countries also can mean freedom to enter into similar arrangements with other countries. Seen in this light, the extension of the FTA arrangement in a *bilateral* fashion by either side is not fundamentally inconsistent with the textbook FTA model. However, this will render the analysis far more complex, as the benefits and costs of a US–ASEAN FTA cannot be considered in complete isolation from, say, US–Mexico or ASEAN–Japan FTAs. Thus, for example, the negative effects of a US–ASEAN FTA may be blunted, if not neutralized, by the creation of an ASEAN–Japan FTA.

Despite this complication, the Vinerian classification of the static effects of a customs union into trade creation, trade diversion, and consumption effects still make considerable sense in the present context (Viner 1950). Theory tells us that trade creation (which involves a shift from a high-cost domestic source to a low-cost partner source) represents a gain, while trade diversion (by which is meant a shift from a low-cost third-country source to a high-cost partner source) entails a loss. The FTA would be judged beneficial if trade creation outweighs trade diversion. The consumption effect must be positive, as there are no common external tariffs, and the consumers will be paying less than before. According to this line of reasoning, an FTA would be considered economically sound only if the net result of all such effects is positive.

However, it has been pointed out that trade diversion need not imply a welfare loss if there is sufficient intercommodity substitution in addition to intercountry substitution (Lipsey 1960). In addition, it has also been argued that scale economies could also undo trade diversion in the long run. To all these considerations one must add the various long-term dynamic effects.

An Evaluation

The following assessment of possible gains and losses that may result from a US–ASEAN FTA is not based on any quantitative estimation of costs and benefits. The primary objective is merely to identify the sources of possible gains and losses and to indicate roughly the relative strengths of positive and negative factors in an ordinal fashion.

Bilateral trade liberalization under an FTA will certainly result in increased trade flows between the United States and ASEAN, given the fairly elastic demand for their products in each other's markets. Increased trade flows may take the form of increased interindustry and intraindustry trade. Now that the ASEAN countries are rapidly industrializing themselves, the scope for intraindustry trade under an FTA seems enormous. Increased bilateral trade flows, however, may not lead to an increase in world welfare. Much would depend on whether the additional trade is due to trade creation or trade diversion. This, in turn, would depend largely on whether the US and ASEAN economies are competitive or complementary.

The more competitive the economies, the greater the trade creation, since an FTA would allow the more efficient partner to replace the higher-cost domestic source. The higher the cost differential between domestic and partner substitutes, the greater the gain in terms of improved resource allocation (Makower and Morton 1953). Yet, it is quite obvious that the US and ASEAN economies are very different, especially in terms of natural resource endowments and factor proportions. This seems to suggest that the comparative advantage of the United States would differ greatly from that of ASEAN—hence the basis for the current trade flows between the two. That is attested by the commodity composition of US–ASEAN trade (Campbell and DeRosa 1988). ASEAN's comparative cost advantage seems to lie in natural resource-intensive and skilled and unskilled labor-intensive products, whereas the United States seems to have a comparative advantage in capital-intensive and technology-intensive activities. All this amounts to saying that the US and ASEAN economies are complementary rather than competitive.

Just as competitiveness between the US and ASEAN economies means that US and ASEAN products would compete with each other in a trade-creating manner, the complementarity of their economies implies that ASEAN and US products would compete in each other's markets, not with each other, but with third-country products in a trade-diverting fashion. Thus, American products would replace Japanese and EC substitutes in the ASEAN markets, while ASEAN products would replace substitutes from, say, Korea, Taiwan, Hong Kong, Mexico, and Brazil in the US market. There is little basis for expecting replacement of American products by ASEAN substitutes in the US market or replacement of ASEAN products by American substitutes in the ASEAN market. *A priori* reasoning therefore would lead us to the conclusion that trade diversion effects would dominate.

It is quite clear that bilateral FTAs cannot provide the first-best solution in the sense that they cannot maximize world welfare. One can therefore only view an FTA as a second-best alternative. If the alternative to the multilateral trading system is mercantilism or, worse still, autarky, bilateral FTAs will prove to be a superior option. Much therefore depends on what we compare FTAs with.

Other factors also should be considered. What may be bad from the global point of view may not be so from a national or regional viewpoint. What is ASEAN's loss in terms of trade diversion (replacement of its imports by US substitutes) is a gain to the United States. By the same token, what is a loss to the United States in terms of its imports being diverted to ASEAN is a gain to ASEAN. Moreover, trade diversion may result in lower consumer prices, especially where protectionist barriers against third countries remain high and cost differentials between "partner" and "foreign" products are not large. Under such circumstances, there can be a significant gain in the form of improved consumer welfare.

In other words, it is quite possible that a US–ASEAN FTA would result in a net gain for the grouping as a whole, although it may not lead to an increase in world welfare. The distribution of this gain between the United States and ASEAN would depend largely on the relative size of the markets, production patterns, and the protection profiles of the United States and ASEAN, not to mention their abilities to exploit the new opportunities.

The US economy is considerably larger than that of ASEAN, not only in terms of geography, demography, and resource endowments, but also in terms of purchasing power and consumption patterns. A bilateral FTA arrangement with the United States would give ASEAN exports a tremendous advantage in terms of US market penetration. Reciprocity will provide similar market access for US products in ASEAN, but it cannot ensure complete symmetry in terms of market penetration, given the vast difference in market size. It appears that ASEAN's gain in this regard will be significantly larger than that of the United States.

The production pattern in the United States, relative to the size of its domestic economy, appears to have a narrower base than that of ASEAN. That is, the degree of specialization in the United States is considerably higher than that of ASEAN. Some ASEAN countries have established broad-based patterns of production behind protectionist walls. The more specialized the economy, the greater the loss from trade diversion and the smaller the gain from trade creation. Thus, on this count too, it appears that ASEAN would enjoy a larger share of the gain than the United States from a bilateral FTA.

Despite growing US protectionist pressures, the profile of US protection still remains relatively low compared with that of ASEAN, especially in terms of tariffs. The higher the level of initial tariffs, the greater the benefit from tariff elimination. It then would follow that ASEAN would benefit more than the United States from an FTA.

An FTA is not a zero-sum game, as the gains of one party need not be at the expense of the other. However, the preceding analysis leads us to the conclusion that ASEAN will benefit more than the United States from such a bilateral scheme. However, this analysis has concentrated on the static effects of FTAs. It is pertinent to take into account some of the salient dynamic effects, which are more difficult to come to grips with. Economies of scale that result from production for a wider market can be significant, especially for ASEAN's heavy industries, which are constrained at present by the small domestic market. There are also important implications for capital movements. If we consider international trade and international capital movements as substitutes in Mundellian fashion (Mundell 1957), an FTA should result in reduced bilateral investments. However, to the extent that investment plays a complementary role, investment in support activities should increase on both sides under an FTA.

At least in theory, establishment of an FTA amounts to giving member countries' products duty-free access on a reciprocal basis, which represents a discriminatory arrangement. This is tantamount to granting unlimited generalized system of preferences (GSP) facilities to one another, albeit on a reciprocal basis. If the past experience of ASEAN in attracting foreign investment to take advantage of the GSP facility is anything to go by, a US–ASEAN FTA would open a new channel for third countries to invest in ASEAN activities aimed at the huge US market. Here again, ASEAN stands to gain more than the United States.

It is also relevant to consider the terms-of-trade effects of a bilateral FTA between the United States and ASEAN. Trade diversion may force third countries to reduce prices, especially if supplies are inelastic. It is almost certain that the terms of trade of member countries would improve vis-à-vis third countries (Mundell 1964). Thus, there is a basis for thinking that there would be sizable terms of trade gains for the United States and ASEAN against third countries under the FTA, especially since the combined US–ASEAN market is large enough to have an impact on world prices. However, it is hard to tell whether ASEAN's terms of trade with the United States would improve or deteriorate under the FTA. Much would depend on the reciprocal demand.

By and large, whichever way we look at it, the scale seems to be tilted in favor of ASEAN. The United States gain will be mainly in terms of political mileage. This will help the United States reestablish itself as a hegemon in Southeast Asia and satisfy the US "obsession" with reciprocity in trade concessions. It is in the US interest to have an ASEAN grouping that is economically viable and sound, so that it can contribute to the stability of the Southeast Asian region, which is of strategic importance to the United States. There is no better way for the United States to have a strong influence in the region than through trading arrangements. Thus, even if the US–ASEAN FTA means an economic loss to the United States, it may be taken as a price to pay for the political advantage resulting from it. However, that the scale is tilted in ASEAN's favor does not necessarily mean that the United States must suffer a loss; to repeat, an FTA is not a zero-sum game.

In the final analysis, ASEAN has very little, if any, to lose in *economic* terms from all this, since what is seemingly a cost in the short run may well be a gain in the long run.[3] Thus, for instance, an FTA may force some painful industrial and structural adjustments in ASEAN countries as its products face stiff competition in the home market from American exports. In the process, marginal and inefficient firms in ASEAN countries will have to quit the scene. To be sure, this is not a bad thing, and, in fact, this is precisely what trade creation is all about. It may, however, cause political difficulties at home. Ironically, it is politically more difficult to "sell" a trade-creating FTA than a trade-diverting one, although it is the former and not the latter that makes economic sense.

There also will be a substantial loss of government revenue for those ASEAN countries that depend on tariffs for their revenue. This loss, however, does not necessarily represent a loss to their economies, as the forgone revenue could be passed on to the consumers in the form of lower prices.

However, there are dangers that a US–ASEAN FTA may thwart the development of industries in which ASEAN countries have potential or

---

3. There are, however, serious political implications that should not be lost sight of. The bilateral FTA arrangement will bring ASEAN firmly within the US sphere of influence. This might mean that ASEAN countries would become client-states of the US commercial empire.

latent comparative advantage. This may well be the case in certain service industries, where some protection on infant industry grounds may be warranted. It would, however, be naive to think that ASEAN has such comparative advantage in a wide spectrum of service industries. To say the least, there is no rational basis for ASEAN to exclude services trade from the FTA altogether. On the contrary, it can be argued that free access to the US market for ASEAN's labor-intensive services can help promote the development of ASEAN's services sector. One difficult area may be financial services, especially banking. Total free trade with the United States in this sector may weaken the grip of ASEAN central banks on their domestic financial markets and blunt their monetary policy instruments. The danger lies in the theoretical possibility that the headquarters of American banks in New York will be calling the shots rather the central banks in ASEAN capitals. Such risks may be significantly reduced through institutional arrangements, however.

For ASEAN, a bilateral free trade arrangement with the United States, *ceteris paribus,* would mean increased dependence on the US economy rather than increased interdependence, given the sheer dominance of the US economy. The implication is that ASEAN economies may become increasingly vulnerable to US policies and economic cycles. However, it may be counterargued that such vulnerability exists even now and cannot be avoided by any open economy. This represents a price ASEAN countries will have to pay for the advantages that accompany a bilateral free trade arrangement with the United States. However, the price can be minimized through appropriate macroeconomic stabilization policies, and by strengthening existing economic links with other countries and establishing new links.

It has been implicitly assumed in this discussion that the free trade area would be confined to the United States and ASEAN, and that neither party would enter into a similar arrangement with other countries. This need not be the case. As a matter of fact, the United States already has similar bilateral arrangements with Canada and Israel, as noted earlier. There are strong possibilities that the United States may establish bilateral FTAs with several other countries, including Japan, Korea, Taiwan, Australia, and Mexico. Likewise, ASEAN may enter into bilateral free trade arrangements with other countries as well. All these will no doubt add to the complexity of the analysis, but they do serve to strengthen the case for the US–ASEAN FTA.

If the United States establishes bilateral FTAs with, for example, Japan, Korea, Taiwan, Australia, and Mexico, in addition to Canada and Israel, the US–ASEAN FTA will mean that ASEAN products will have to compete in the US market not only with US products but also with those of these other countries. This extension of competition will help maximize the gains from trade creation and minimize the losses from trade diversion insofar as the United States is concerned. Should ASEAN also enter into bilateral free trade arrangements with Japan, Korea, Taiwan, and Australia, American products will have to compete with the products of these countries, as well as those of ASEAN, in the ASEAN market, thereby increasing ASEAN's gains from trade creation and reducing its losses from trade diversion. The dynamic benefits referred to earlier will show a manifold increase by the presence of a multiplicity of interconnecting bilateral FTAs.

If we extend this line of reasoning to its logical end, we cannot escape the conclusion that those who will be disadvantaged most by all this will be those countries that do not participate in the FTA process. Nonparticipants will be discriminated against, and their products will be subject to "unfair competition" in FTA markets because of preferential tariff cuts. Economic considerations then will compel them to join the bandwagon. All this may seem unfair or unjust because it is utterly discriminatory and totally contrary to the principle of multilateralism. But, quite paradoxically, the greater the number of countries involved in interconnecting bilateral FTAs, the closer the world is to global free trade. The real danger lies in the process stopping short, leaving the world divided into several economic blocs.

Seen in this perspective, the US bilateral initiatives with Canada, Mexico, Japan, Korea, Taiwan, Australia, and ASEAN appear to be the initial steps toward a Pacific economic bloc. A US–ASEAN FTA would constitute one of the important building blocks of a Pacific Community.

In the preceding analysis, ASEAN was taken for granted as if it were a single entity, which it certainly is not. ASEAN comprises six member countries that have successfully avoided regional "integration." ASEAN is no more than a loosely structured "association." Although some progress has been made in terms of regional economic cooperation with respect to intraregional trade and industrial cooperation, ASEAN's long-term goals still remain undefined even after 21 years of existence. ASEAN has rejected the customs union format and regards the common market idea as too far-fetched. Even the concept of a full-fledged FTA seems too elusive for ASEAN. Under these circumstances, it would indeed be embarrassing for ASEAN to talk about an FTA with the United States when it does not have an FTA established among its own members in the first place.

To be sure, it is not absolutely necessary for ASEAN countries to have an ASEAN FTA in order to participate in a US–ASEAN FTA. The latter arrangement will serve to expedite the free trade process within ASEAN. However, the absence of the ASEAN entity gives rise to a technical problem: the US would have to enter into six FTAs with six ASEAN countries. ASEAN has never signed an agreement with a third party on a collective basis. Although ASEAN countries have collectively negotiated with third countries, all agreements have been signed only individually. Agreements on GSP and on textiles and apparel under the Multi-Fiber Arrangement with the EC, the United States, and Japan provide outstanding examples of ASEAN's individual approach. Such an approach is still possible even in the case of a US–ASEAN FTA, but the process can be very untidy and unwieldy. A neat solution would be for ASEAN to first declare itself an FTA and then enter into a bilateral FTA with the United States on a collective basis.

Conclusion

The tone of this paper is somewhat theoretical in nature rather than empirical. Theoretical reasoning based on conventional tools of analysis in the US–ASEAN context suggests that a bilateral FTA between the United States and ASEAN would be mutually beneficial, although the bulk of the benefits might accrue to ASEAN rather than the United States. However, it is not apparent whether a US–ASEAN FTA would lead to an increase or a decrease in world welfare. In any case, a bilateral FTA is clearly inferior to a multilateral regime of free trade, which undoubtedly represents the first-best solution (Cooper and Massel 1965). A policy suggestion then follows that the United States and ASEAN should not abandon multilateral approaches and resort to bilateral FTAs instead.

One might, however, question the wisdom of comparing a US–ASEAN FTA with the first-best alternative. The Uruguay Round will not achieve significant trade liberalization on all items in the current multilateral trade negotiation agenda, and it may end up with much less. Such considerations argue in favor of a fallback position such as the US–ASEAN FTA option. In the event of a collapse of the multilateral trading system, all countries will be the losers, but the smaller countries like ASEAN will be the most adversely affected. Thus, the US–ASEAN FTA option would make considerable sense, especially to ASEAN. Presumably, ASEAN has valid reasons to be wary of the growing regionalism in Western Europe, where efforts are under way to establish a fully integrated market by 1992, the implications of which are not favorable for ASEAN exports. ASEAN may find some comfort by resorting to a bilateral FTA with the United States.

Be that as it may, it would be more appropriate to look upon a US–ASEAN FTA option as a supplement to, rather than a substitute for, the multilateral trading system to the extent that it conforms to the GATT provisions under Article XXIV. Assuming that multilateral approaches are not abandoned altogether, nonpreferential tariff cuts on a most-favored-nation (MFN) basis by ASEAN and the United States will help minimize the negative effects of the bilateral FTA.

Furthermore, it would be misleading to view a US–ASEAN FTA in isolation. The merits of bilateral FTAs become more apparent if they are considered in relation to one another than if they are looked at separately. To put it differently, the case for a US–ASEAN FTA would become stronger if the United States and ASEAN entered into similar bilateral arrangements, especially with common trading partners.

The preceding analysis suggests that, in the case of a US–ASEAN FTA, ASEAN would stand to gain more than the United States, although the gain would be less than that under a nondiscriminatory multilateral trading system. That the ASEAN could have a larger share of the gains resulting from a US–ASEAN FTA does not, however, constitute a *prima facie* case for ASEAN to opt for a bilateral FTA with the United States; such an arrangement clearly would be inferior to what the multilateral trading system can offer. The primary source of gain from the FTA would be the tariff reduction. A nonpreferential trade liberalization on an MFN basis would mean that the tariff-cutting country can enjoy all the FTA advantages without having to suffer the disadvantage of trade-diverting effects associated with preferential tariff reduction.

However, ASEAN may have little choice in this regard. It would be futile for ASEAN or any other single entity to pursue MFN tariff cuts if the rest of the world—particularly the major players—do not. The danger is that ASEAN may be alienated if more and more countries join the FTA bandwagon.

In other words, no bilateral FTA should be considered as a substitute for the multilateral trading system, as it is unambiguously a poor substitute. However, FTAs make better economic sense if there are more players in the game. The larger the number of countries, the stronger the positive effects and the weaker the negative effects of preferential arrangements. Thus, for instance, if ASEAN were to form an FTA with the United States, American products would displace Japanese and European products in the ASEAN market in a trade-diverting fashion. If, however, the United States also formed bilateral FTAs with the EC and Japan, while ASEAN too entered into similar arrangements with the EC and Japan, ASEAN would not suffer trade diversion.

In the final analysis, both the United States and ASEAN would be far better off under the multilateral system. Nondiscriminatory trade liberalization still represents the best policy. One should not therefore abandon the multilateral approach in favor of a bilateral preferential approach. All this notwithstanding, one may seriously consider, as a last resort, a bilateral FTA, following the age-old dictum, "If you can't beat them, join them."

References

Ariff, Mohamed, and Hal Hill. 1985. *Export-oriented Industrialization: The ASEAN Experience*. Sydney: Allen and Unwin.

Ariff, Mohamed, and Loong-Hoe Tan, eds. 1988. *The Uruguay Round: ASEAN Trade Policy Options*. Singapore: Institute of Southeast Asian Studies.

Campbell, B., and Dean DeRosa. 1988. "Increasing Protectionism and Its Implications for ASEAN–U.S. Economic Relations," in Loong-Hoe Tan and N. Akrasanee, eds., *ASEAN–U.S. Economic Relations: Changes in the Economic Environment and Opportunities*. Singapore: Institute of Southeast Asian Studies.

Chia, Siow Yue. 1986. "ASEAN Manufactured Exports to the United States," in A. Kintanar, Jr. and Loong-Hoe Tan, eds., *ASEAN–U.S. Economic Relations: An Overview*. Singapore: Institute of Southeast Asian Studies.

Cooper, C. A., and B. F. Massel. 1965. "A New Look at Customs Union Theory," *Economic Journal*, vol. 75, December.

DeRosa, Dean. 1986. "ASEAN–U.S. Trade Relations," in A. Kintanar, Jr., and Loong-Hoe Tan, eds., *ASEAN–U.S. Relations: An Overview*. Singapore: Institute of Southeast Asian Studies.

Kintanar, A., Jr., and Loong-Hoe Tan, eds. 1986. *ASEAN–U.S. Economic Relations: An Overview*. Singapore: Institute of Southeast Asian Studies.

Krause, Lawrence B. 1982. *US Economic Policy Toward the Association of Southeast Asian Nations: Meeting the Japanese Challenge*. Washington: Brookings Institution.

Krause, Lawrence B. 1988. "Economic Trends in the United States and Their Implications for ASEAN," in Loong-Hoe Tan and N. Akrasanee, eds., *ASEAN–US Economic Relations: Changes in the Economic Environment and Opportunities*. Singapore: Institute of Southeast Asian Studies.

Lipsey, Richard G. 1960. "The Theory of Customs Unions: A General Survey," *Economic Journal*, September.

Makower, H., and G. Morton. 1953. "A Contribution Towards a Theory of Customs Union," *Economic Journal*, March.

Meade, James E. 1956. *The Theory of Customs Unions*. Amsterdam: North Holland.

Mundell, Robert A. 1957. "International Trade and Factor Immobility," *American Economic Review*, June.

Mundell, Robert A. 1964. "Tariff Preferences and the Terms of Trade," *The Manchester School of Economics and Social Studies*, vol. 32.

Pangestu, M. 1986. "The Pattern of Direct Foreign Investment in ASEAN: United States vs Japan," in A. Kintanar, Jr., and Loong-Hoe Tan, eds., *ASEAN–U.S. Economic Relations: An Overview*. Singapore: Institute of Southeast Asian Studies.

Viner, Jacob. 1950. *The Customs Union Issue*. New York: Carnegie Endowment for International Peace.

Yuan, L. T. 1988. "ASEAN–U.S. Trade in Services: An ASEAN Perspective," in Loong-Hoe Tan and N. Akrasanee, eds., *ASEAN–US Economic Relations: Changes in the Economic Environment*. Singapore: Institute of Southeast Asian Studies.

9

A Pacific Free Trade Area?

Peter Drysdale and Ross Garnaut

Vigorous expansion of trade, investment, and other economic ties within the East Asian and Pacific economy has been crucially important to the region's extraordinary growth in recent decades. This expansion has taken place without the framework of formal regional institutional arrangements that fostered integration across the Atlantic among the original OECD countries (Crawford and Okita 1976, 34). It is an impressive example of market integration around institutional and legal barriers to trade, capital movements, and other forms of economic interchange.[1] Integration has proceeded despite persistent political resistance to the domestic structural implications of internationally oriented growth. As this growth has occurred, some barriers have been lowered, others have been introduced anew or raised, and many remain.

This paper takes as the central objective of international economic diplomacy in the Pacific region, the preservation and enhancement of the conditions for continued economic growth. The international system that has supported this vigorous trade expansion is under threat from several directions: tensions between the United States and Japan (and to a lesser extent between the United States and Taiwan and Korea) over large trade imbalances; the prospects of increased economic introversion in Europe as 1992 approaches; the accommodation of new patterns of comparative advantage in the newly industrializing countries (NICs) of Asia as they

---

1. Cooper (1974, 2–4) makes the useful distinction between "market" and "institutional" integration.

Peter Drysdale is Professorial Fellow and Executive Director of the Australia–Japan Research Centre, Research School of Pacific Studies, Australian National University. Ross Garnaut, former Australian Ambassador to China, is a Senior Fellow in the Department of Economics, Research School of Pacific Studies, Australian National University, and a consultant on Australia–East Asian relations to the Australian Prime Minister and the Minister for Foreign Affairs and Trade.

compress into a few years the adjustments necessary after a decade of rapid economic growth; and the new challenge of managing the emergence of China, with its partially reformed centrally planned system, as a major player in Pacific economic relations. Peace and political stability depend upon a relatively open economic environment, offering China realistic alternatives to autarky at a crucial point in its political history, and providing similarly reliable alternatives for the states of Indochina, the Soviet Union, and North Korea at a time of opportunity for reducing longstanding sources of conflict.

The central objective is thus a conservative one: to preserve the present system of relatively open economic relations in the Pacific, however imperfect it may be. We would add as second and third objectives the reduction of barriers to intra-Pacific trade, and the reduction of barriers to trade with major economies outside the region, particularly the European Community (EC). This chapter examines whether these objectives would be enhanced by the formation of a free trade area (FTA) encompassing the market economies of the Western Pacific, together with the United States and Canada.

One question that must be addressed is whether the central, conservative objective can be achieved without progress on the second and third objectives. Frustration at the lack of progress in reducing Northeast Asian and European barriers to trade, especially in agricultural products, has been an important element in the corrosion of political support in the United States and elsewhere for the multilateral system. We can expect this frustration to intensify if the Uruguay Round delivers disappointing results.

Trade and other economic relations among the market economies of the Pacific have been characterized by high intensity and rapid growth. They are thus a convenient group of economies to consider in the context of an FTA. The role of the People's Republic of China must also be discussed as a trading economy similar in scale of total trade to Taiwan or Korea. China is experiencing similarly rapid growth, is specialized in labor-intensive manufactured exports as have been the other Northeast Asian economies, and is oriented toward the Pacific in its foreign economic relations. Thus, when for brevity we refer to "the Pacific region," we include the United States, Canada, the Western Pacific market economies, and the People's Republic of China. Later we make separate reference to the circumstances of Mexico, which lacks close economic ties across the Pacific but trades intensively with the United States, and to the centrally planned economies of the Western Pacific, which as yet have only slender economic links with their neighbors.

Pacific Trade and Growth

In recent decades, East Asian economies have experienced stronger sustained growth than the world has previously known. From the mid-1950s, Japan grew at a rate that more than doubled output each decade until, by the time of the first oil shock in 1973–74, its production per capita was close to that of some of the established industrialized nations. Since the mid-1970s, Japan's growth has been less spectacular, but has remained above the average for the advanced economies.

The four Asian NICs started their rapid growth later, in the early 1960s, and from lower bases than Japan, but on average have grown even more rapidly. Three of them—Taiwan, Singapore, and Hong Kong—already have surpassed the average per capita output in the lower-income OECD countries. Korea, starting from a lower base, still seems likely to attain the living standards of the less prosperous OECD economies before the end of the century.

In the other principal ASEAN economies—Indonesia, the Philippines, Thailand, and Malaysia—growth has been less consistent and more modest, but has comfortably exceeded average performance in the developed and developing economies alike since the late 1960s. Finally, over the past decade, China has joined the ranks of the high-growth East Asian economies. It has been exceeding its own goal of doubling real output each decade.

One result of these developments has been a historic shift in the center of gravity of world production. In the early postwar period, when the liberal GATT trading system was being established, North America accounted for one-half of world GNP, and East Asia, devastated by war and civil strife, for only a few percent. By the early 1960s, the North American share of world production was still extremely large at around 40 percent, whereas East Asia's share had increased to 9 percent. By the early 1980s, North America's share of world GNP had fallen to 27 percent, whereas East Asia's had more than doubled to 19 percent. These trends have continued, and it seems likely that in the 1990s East Asia will contribute as much as North America to world GNP, with the two regions accounting for more than one-half of world output.[2] These shifts in the locus of world economic power

---

2. These data rely on World Bank, *World Tables 1987*; United Nations, *Monthly Bulletin of Statistics,* various issues; Council for Economic Planning Development, *Taiwan Statistical Data Book,* 1987. Data for the centrally planned economies are in terms of net material product. These are the standard measures of GDP used by the World Bank and other international agencies. We are aware that they do not provide perfect measures of the relative output of goods and services in different economic systems. See Summers and Heston (1984). When adjustments have been attempted for

have implications for the leadership and management of the international trading system.

A rapidly expanded share of trade in output has marked East Asia's growth in recent decades. The early years of rapid growth were associated with powerful specialization in the export of labor-intensive manufactures, but patterns of export specialization then progressed rapidly into more capital-intensive production as living standards improved. Growth in trade has been geographically focused in the Pacific region. These trends, and some reasons for them, are illustrated in tables 9.1 and 9.2.

Table 9.1 demonstrates the vast potential for intra-Pacific trade based on differences in relative endowments of natural resources, labor, and capital. The theory of changing comparative advantage in economic growth postulates that a poor country initially has comparative advantage in natural resource-based products; that growth of the capital stock causes comparative advantage to shift toward labor-intensive manufactures and services if the country's per capita natural resource endowment is poor, but not otherwise; and that continued growth, reflected in higher per capita income, will cause comparative advantage to shift successively into more capital-intensive manufactures and services.[3]

The history of the Pacific economies demonstrates this pattern. Wide variations in per capita natural resource endowments, represented crudely by population density in table 9.1, suggest a high degree of complementarity between Australasia and North America, on the one hand, and East Asia, particularly Japan and the Asian NICs, on the other. The large variations in per capita income provide opportunities for trading capital-intensive for labor-intensive manufactures. Moreover, the ascension of Japan and several of the NICs into the ranks of relatively high-income economies is opening rich new opportunities for intra-industry specialization in trade in technologically sophisticated goods and services, especially among the adjacent economies of Northeast Asia.

A distinctive feature of high growth in East Asia has been the rising shares of foreign trade in production, as the economies of the region put to good use the potential gains from trade deriving from their widely different relative resource endowments. East Asian and Pacific trade is growing more rapidly than world trade. The dollar value of two-way trade between Europe

---

measurement imperfections, they have had the effect of substantially raising East Asia's share of world GDP, especially because they ascribe much higher levels of production to China.

3. For an approach to the application of the theory of changing comparative advantage to East Asia, see Garnaut and Anderson (1980).

and North America increased slightly more than sixfold between the beginning of the 1970s and 1987; meanwhile Japan–North America trade increased almost tenfold; trade between Japan and the NICs of Northeast Asia increased 18-fold; and trade between North America and the Asian NICs jumped more than 48-fold in the same period.[4] Already the East Asian and Pacific region accounts for 37 percent of total world trade.

The huge economic transformation in East Asia has brought with it a major shift toward the Pacific and away from the Atlantic as the focus of world trade. Table 9.2 documents changes in the geographic structure of Pacific and world trade flows between 1965 and 1987. Over this period, the Pacific share in world trade grew from around 30 percent to almost 37 percent. Intraregional trade grew from less than 50 percent to around 63 percent of Pacific countries' trade, a proportion approaching that of Europe's: in 1987, intraregional trade amounted to 71 percent of Western Europe's total trade. Pacific countries' trade with each other is almost twice as large as their share in world trade. For Australia, Northeast Asia other than Japan (i.e., Korea, Taiwan, and Hong Kong), ASEAN, and China, the share of other Pacific countries in export and import trade is commonly higher, around 70 percent of their total trade.

Barriers to Pacific Trade

The trade expansion that has supported East Asian growth and structural change represents a historic achievement of the international system. Nevertheless, old and new barriers have prevented realization of substantial additional gains from trade among the Pacific countries.

Rapid economic growth has generated rapid change in comparative advantage, both in the East Asian economies and in their trading partners. The general record of structural adjustment in response to changing comparative advantage has been a good one—as attested by the expansion and change in commodity composition of trade. But there are important examples of governments in East Asia and elsewhere in the Pacific intervening to block the structural implications of growth.

The major instances of high protectionist barriers dissipating potential gains from intra-Pacific trade have occurred in large industries, which were rapidly losing comparative advantage as a result of economic change in Northeast Asia. Principal examples in goods-producing industries include foodstuffs in Japan, Korea, and Taiwan, and labor-intensive commodities

---

4. Data drawn from International Monetary Fund, *Direction of Trade Statistics*, 1988.

Table 9.1 Resource endowments, sectoral shares of total trade, and "revealed" comparative advantage in developed and developing Pacific Basin countries, 1986[a]

	Australasia[b]	North America[c]	Japan	China	Asian NICs	Other ASEAN	Industrial market economies	Developing economies[d]
Population density (persons/km²)	2.4	13.8	326.6	110.2	507.0	95.4	24.0	53.0
GNP per capita ($US)	11,157	17,158	12,840	300	3,308	647	12,960	610
Real GNP per capita growth rate. 1965–86 (%/year)	1.7	1.7	4.3	5.1	6.8	4.0	2.3	2.9
Sectoral shares of total trade (%)								
Agriculture								
Exports	47	18	1	22	7	34	14	22
Imports	8	9	26	10	14	13	14	16
Fuels, minerals, and metals								
Exports	35	10	1	16	6	35	8	35
Imports	7	12	41	4	16	15	17	11

Light manufactures								
Exports	3	5	10	45	47	14	11	25
Imports	15	14	8	14	18	11	13	14
Heavy manufactures								
Exports	15	67	88	17	40	17	67	20
Imports	70	65	25	72	52	61	56	59
"Revealed" comparative advantage								
Agriculture	3.3	1.2	0.1	1.6	0.5	2.3	0.9	1.4
Fuels, minerals, and metals	2.2	0.7	0.1	1.0	0.4	2.3	0.6	2.2
Light manufactures	0.3	0.4	0.8	3.4	3.1	1.1	0.9	1.6
Heavy manufactures	0.3	1.1	1.6	0.3	0.8	0.3	1.2	0.4

a. Exports and imports refer to export and import shares, respectively. "Revealed" comparative advantage is defined as the ratio of the share of a commodity group in total exports for a country or group of countries to that commodity group's share of world exports.
b. Australia and New Zealand.
c. United States and Canada.
d. Excludes high-income oil exporters.

Sources: Peter Drysdale, *International Economic Pluralism: Economic Policy in East Asia and the Pacific* (New York: Columbia University Press, 1988), updated from the International Monetary Fund; and World Bank, *World Development Report* (New York: Oxford University Press, 1988).

Table 9.2 Pacific and world trade shares, 1965 and 1987 (percentages)

Reporter	Australasia[a] 1965	1987	Japan 1965	1987	Other Northeast Asia[b] 1965	1987	ASEAN 1965	1987	China 1965	1987
Australasia	6.2	8.2	14.4	24.8	1.9	7.2	1.3	6.7	4.5	3.9
	5.6	7.6	9.3	20.4	1.1	4.7	2.0	5.4	0.6	1.7
Japan	5.0	2.9			6.1	10.2	8.8	7.2	3.2	3.8
	8.0	6.4			1.0	6.8	6.9	13.8	2.9	5.2
Other Northeast Asia	3.8	1.9	9.5	11.8	1.4	3.8	6.4	5.4	1.1	12.2
	2.2	2.6	23.0	27.8	0.9	3.1	3.8	7.7	21.3	18.3
ASEAN	3.7	2.6	24.0	21.9	3.4	7.9	2.9	16.8	2.2	2.4
	2.1	3.2	27.9	24.9	2.2	5.7	5.0	16.1	4.5	4.2
China	2.1	0.9	15.9	16.2	28.8	34.9	7.1	5.9		
	13.3	3.6	19.0	23.7	1.0	19.8	3.1	4.8		
North America[c]	3.1	2.1	6.8	10.0	1.4	4.0	1.5	3.2	0.3	1.4
	1.7	1.0	9.1	19.2	1.5	6.3	2.0	3.8	0.1	1.5
Pacific total[d]	3.7	2.5	7.3	9.5	2.9	7.7	2.9	6.1	1.1	3.4
	3.6	2.8	9.3	17.6	1.4	6.6	3.0	6.9	1.6	3.9
Western Europe	2.2	0.8	0.8	1.7	0.5	1.1	0.7	1.1	0.5	0.7
	2.2	0.6	1.2	4.6	0.5	1.5	0.6	1.2	0.4	0.6
Middle East	3.0	1.1	13.6	23.7	0.6	3.5	0.9	6.6	0.4	0.4
	1.5	2.0	5.4	12.4	0.5	3.6	0.2	2.7	0.9	2.1
Mexico	0.4	0.2	8.2	5.9	0.2	0.9	0.4	0.4	0.3	0.3
	1.3	0.3	2.5	7.3	0.1	0.9	0.0	0.2	0.0	0.1
Latin America[e]	0.2	0.4	4.0	6.2	0.2	1.3	0.2	0.7	0.8	1.2
	0.6	0.6	3.8	8.0	0.2	2.1	0.2	0.8	0.0	0.8
Rest of world	1.0	0.5	4.3	6.7	0.6	1.6	0.5	1.3	1.4	2.6
	1.4	1.4	6.0	9.0	0.6	2.7	0.7	2.8	1.1	3.8
World total	2.4	1.4	3.9	5.8	1.2	3.6	1.3	3.1	0.8	1.8
	2.4	1.5	4.4	10.2	0.7	3.6	1.3	3.5	0.8	2.1

For each country or region, exports are given in the first line, imports in the second.
a. Australia and New Zealand.
b. Korea, Taiwan, and Hong Kong.

Sources: International Monetary Fund, *Direction of Trade Statistics;* International Economic Data Bank, Research School of Pacific Studies, Australian National University.

	Partner												
North America		Pacific total		Western Europe		Middle East		Mexico		Latin America		Rest of world	
1965	1987	1965	1987	1965	1987	1965	1987	1965	1987	1965	1987	1965	1987
13.3	14.4	44.8	68.2	44.4	19.8	1.7	4.5	0.5	0.2	1.2	1.4	7.9	6.1
25.8	23.3	45.1	63.8	45.3	29.4	4.6	2.9	0.1	0.2	0.5	1.2	4.4	2.7
35.7	41.4	58.9	65.7	14.2	20.9	3.8	4.0	0.5	0.6	5.9	3.7	17.2	5.7
35.3	26.5	54.5	58.2	9.4	15.9	13.9	14.1	1.9	1.1	9.2	4.3	13.0	6.7
34.6	37.2	57.0	72.2	28.6	18.2	2.5	3.1	0.2	0.2	2.0	2.0	9.8	4.6
19.6	17.2	70.7	76.8	20.6	14.8	1.6	3.5	0.3	0.3	1.6	1.9	5.5	2.8
29.3	23.4	65.6	74.7	25.1	15.6	0.8	2.8	0.0	0.0	0.8	0.9	7.6	5.3
23.8	16.4	65.5	70.1	24.8	18.1	2.9	7.6	0.3	0.1	0.6	1.0	6.2	2.6
1.1	8.7	55.0	66.7	23.5	11.4	3.2	6.5	0.0	0.0	0.3	1.2	17.9	14.3
7.5	14.6	44.0	66.7	27.3	20.7	2.0	0.9	0.2	0.2	7.5	2.9	19.3	8.9
29.6	38.3	42.7	58.9	31.4	22.7	3.0	3.6	3.3	4.5	13.3	11.0	9.7	3.9
36.2	27.9	50.5	59.7	25.2	22.8	1.8	2.7	2.3	4.4	16.8	10.6	5.6	4.2
28.6	35.2	46.8	64.5	29.4	20.4	2.9	3.7	2.4	2.1	10.1	6.1	10.8	5.2
32.9	24.8	51.9	62.5	24.6	20.7	4.0	5.0	1.8	2.7	12.5	7.2	7.0	4.5
9.5	9.8	14.3	15.2	65.0	71.4	3.0	3.8	0.5	0.2	4.1	2.1	13.7	7.5
13.5	7.6	18.4	16.2	57.8	70.7	4.8	2.8	0.3	0.3	5.5	2.4	13.6	7.8
7.9	15.2	26.3	50.5	53.7	37.4	9.1	4.5	0.0	0.0	1.7	4.2	9.1	3.5
18.2	14.2	26.8	36.9	47.3	55.6	13.7	4.7	0.0	0.0	0.8	0.7	11.4	2.2
64.2	76.7	73.6	84.3	9.4	13.3	0.1	0.0			8.5	2.1	8.4	0.2
68.4	77.5	72.3	86.1	24.5	12.8	0.0	0.1			2.6	0.5	0.7	0.5
38.2	53.3	43.7	63.2	34.7	27.1	0.4	0.5	0.2	0.1	17.0	7.2	4.2	1.9
42.0	45.3	46.8	57.5	30.0	28.0	1.5	4.4	0.7	0.7	19.4	8.2	2.3	2.0
8.0	13.7	15.8	26.3	57.2	61.1	2.9	1.4	0.1	0.1	1.3	1.0	22.8	10.1
15.9	9.3	25.7	29.0	49.6	58.5	2.3	2.2	0.4	0.0	2.4	1.2	20.1	9.2
17.2	21.1	27.0	36.9	50.6	49.3	3.0	3.5	1.0	0.9	6.5	3.8	13.0	6.5
21.1	15.8	30.7	36.8	45.4	48.9	4.3	3.7	0.7	1.2	7.8	4.3	11.8	6.3

c. United States and Canada.
d. Australia, New Zealand, Japan, other Northeast Asia, ASEAN, China, North America, and the Pacific islands.
e. Includes Mexico, the Caribbean, and other Latin American countries.

Table 9.3 Selected Pacific countries' agricultural protection, 1980[a] (percentages)

Commodity	Australia	United States	Japan	Korea	Taiwan
Rice	−12	3	192	156	135
Wheat	−6	−18	261	33	81
Barley	−14	−5	307	90	73
Sugar	−1	45	141	n.a.	−3
Beef	−1	5	100	67	76
Agriculture	−2	0	85	117	52

a. These figures are rates of agricultural protection, defined as the percentage by which the producer price exceeds the border price. The estimates shown are the weighted averages for 12 commodities, using production valued at border prices as weights.

n.a. = not applicable

Source: Anderson and Hayami (1986), tables 2.5 and 2.6.

(textiles, clothing and footwear, and consumer electronics) and standard-technology manufacturing industries (metals, motor vehicles) in North America and Australasia.

The outstanding example of barriers to intra-Pacific trade is that of Northeast Asian agricultural protection (table 9.3). In the period covered by the table, Australia had negative protection for all agriculture. The United States imposed no protection on average for agriculture, but high protection for sugar in the first half of the 1980s. The introduction of the export enhancement program and other agricultural assistance in recent years has modified this picture, while leaving average US assistance to agriculture at moderate levels in international terms. Japan, Korea, and Taiwan, by contrast, provide extraordinarily high levels of assistance for all types of agriculture, and for the commodities that are of greatest importance in Pacific trade. The major liberalization of Japanese beef imports announced in 1988 will significantly moderate protection levels for that commodity.

Among the Pacific countries not represented in table 9.3, New Zealand provides virtually no assistance to agriculture, following major liberalization initiatives since 1984. Canada generally provides low protection to agriculture, although dairy products and to a lesser extent sugar are exceptions (Hathaway 1987, 91). China and the ASEAN countries have highly distorted agricultural sectors but at current international prices probably a lower level of net assistance. In the case of China—important among other reasons for being the world's largest producer and consumer of grains and a range of other foodstuffs and agricultural raw materials—there may be little or no net assistance to the foodstuffs that are most important in current consumption, but high protection for meat and other high-quality foodstuffs that are increasingly important in consumption as incomes rise. By comparison, the European countries provide a very high level of assistance for agriculture, but one that is well below the levels in Japan, Korea, and Taiwan (Hathaway 1987).

The general pattern of protection in manufacturing is more complex and less easily summarized. Average tariff levels are now low in the United States, Canada, and Japan, although by no means negligible in all commodities.[5] Low nominal tariff rates nevertheless provide substantial effective protection for some metals and metal products where little value is added in the manufacturing process.

Average rates of nominal tariff protection on all industrial products are much higher in Korea (23.5 percent) and Taiwan (13.8 percent).[6] Highly protected categories in Korea include machinery and transport equipment (21.4 percent), chemicals (21.4 percent), and miscellaneous manufactures (28.2 percent). In Taiwan, highly protected categories include textiles (16 percent), machinery and transport equipment (14.5 percent), and chemicals (14.2 percent).

Australia and New Zealand for some years have had the highest average tariff levels on manufactured goods of all OECD countries (Anderson and Garnaut 1987). Recent policy initiatives have reduced rates substantially, but averages remain high by OECD standards, although lower than for Korea and Taiwan. After the implementation of recently announced liberalization measures, tariffs in Australia will remain very high only for passenger motor vehicles (up to 35 percent) and textiles, clothing, and footwear (up to 55 percent; Keating 1988). New Zealand's tariffs remain especially high for a similar range of goods.

The proliferation of nontariff protection devices during and since the mid-1970s recession has caused tariffs to be a most unreliable guide to manufacturing protection levels. Over this period we have seen the United States introduce major nontariff protective devices in textiles, apparel, footwear, steel, automobiles and motorcycles, and consumer electronic goods (tele-

---

5. For example, US tariffs average 18.2 percent for textiles, and 10.6 percent higher for hides and leather. See General Agreement on Tariffs and Trade, *Tariff Escalation* (note by the Secretariat prepared for the Commission on Trade and Development, Forty-First Session, July 1980).

6. These data exclude petroleum products. They are unweighted average tariffs calculated using 1987 data from local tariff schedules.

vision and radios; Hufbauer and Rosen 1986). Recent policy initiatives have left Australia and New Zealand relatively clear of nontariff barriers for manufactured goods. In Australia, quantitative restrictions in the form of tariff quotas (the main nontariff barriers) now apply only to textiles, clothing, and footwear. These restrictions are being phased out in an announced series of steps ending in 1995.

Contrary to international perceptions, Japan has the cleanest import system for manufactured goods among OECD countries; official nontariff barriers have almost no effect on trade.[7] The relatively low proportion of manufactured goods in Japanese imports, and low import penetration ratios in manufactured commodities in which other developed countries are major importers, have led protectionist interests in North America, Europe, and Australasia, and sometimes officials and independent commentators in those same countries, to postulate a major role for nonofficial barriers, perhaps with official sanction. It is true that the Japanese distribution systems contain a powerful conservative bias, delaying the emergence of large-scale imports well beyond the time when imports appear to have become competitive. However, such biases are not unique to Japan (Itoh 1988). Moreover, the evidence since the appreciation of the yen in 1985 suggests that, despite long lags, normal competitive pressures operate for Japan. Japan's imports of manufactured goods from the Asian developing countries have been increasing at around 50 percent annually since 1985. The share of manufactures in Japanese total imports also has been increasing rapidly over this period, although not so strongly from the United States (table 9.4).[8]

Nontariff barriers are high for manufactured goods in Korea and Taiwan, although liberalizing steps are being taken in both economies. Manufacturing production in China and the ASEAN countries is highly distorted by protection in the forms of high tariffs, quantitative restrictions, and local content schemes. In China and the Philippines this is exacerbated by exchange controls, and in China a large proportion of production is still being allocated at arbitrary prices through state corporations.

Recent attempts to measure protection in the other ASEAN countries have produced estimates as high as 109 percent effective protection for import-competing manufacturing in Indonesia, 36 percent effective protection for all manufacturing in the Philippines, and 50 percent (Corden method) or

---

7. One hopes that recent discussion of dumping issues with Korea does not lead to the marring of this good record.

8. This issue has been addressed, somewhat inconclusively, in recent contributions from Lawrence (1987) and Saxonhouse and Stern (1988). For a good review of the discussion, see Takeuchi (1988).

Table 9.4 Share of manufactured goods in total imports, Japan, 1979–88[a]
(percentages)

Year	Share in all imports	Share in imports from United States	Share in imports from Australia
1979	26.0	42.3	8.8
1980	22.8	44.1	9.2
1981	24.3	45.3	10.0
1982	24.9	47.4	8.6
1983	26.6	52.4	10.5
1984	29.8	52.0	11.7
1985	31.0	55.2	12.9
1986	41.8	60.7	18.0
1987	44.1	56.1	22.5
1988			
January	45.0	56.4	29.0
February	48.8	61.9	26.1
March	47.7	56.0	23.9
April	49.9	55.1	33.0
May	48.6	54.1	26.6
June	48.2	56.3	23.0
July	46.8	52.9	25.9
August	49.2	51.6	26.0

a. Manufactured goods comprise the categories of "Chemicals," "Machinery and Equipment," and "Others." Petroleum products are not included.

Source: Japan Tariff Association, *The Summary Report on Trade of Japan,* various issues.

71 percent (Balassa) effective protection on importable manufacturing in Thailand. Average effective protection in Malaysia is probably close to the low end of the ASEAN spectrum for manufacturing as a whole, but the most recent estimates suggest very high levels for such large categories as nondurable consumer goods (85 percent), consumer durables (173 percent), and machinery (39 percent).[9]

Each of the other ASEAN countries has attempted major liberalization efforts over the past decade. There has been some modest progress, partic-

9. See Pangestu and Boediono (1987, 25)—these estimates exclude rice milling and sugar refining; Tan (1987, 65); Akransanee and Ajanant (1987, 94); and Hock (1987, 120).

ularly in Indonesia and Thailand, and some retrogression. The general picture of variable and extremely high protection remains.

China and the ASEAN countries (other than Singapore) would benefit greatly from participation in international trade negotiations that provided incentives toward liberalization on the export side and rationalization of their import regimes. Indeed, the extension of East Asian high growth on a sustained basis to these important countries would seem to require such initiatives, which would also help sustain growth elsewhere in the region.

Among the other higher-income Pacific countries, protective barriers are highest in foodstuffs, textiles, clothing and footwear, and motor vehicles. They create significant distortions in the production of domestic electrical equipment, iron and steel, and—because of tariff escalation—nonferrous metals. However, at a time when macroeconomic frustrations in the United States have been generating aggressive reactions against all of the successful economies in East Asia, one should not forget that two economies in the region, Singapore and Hong Kong, have by far the cleanest import systems in the world, with barely a hint of restriction against trade in goods and relatively few barriers to trade in services.

Table 9.5 presents world trade in commodities in which some Pacific countries have high levels of protection. A striking feature of the data is the tendency for Pacific countries' exports to be heavily concentrated in commodities against which other Pacific countries impose high barriers to trade.

Textiles, clothing, and footwear accounted for a third of the total exports of Korea, China, and Hong Kong in 1986, a quarter of the exports of Taiwan, and a high proportion of ASEAN manufactured exports. Significantly, if intra-EC trade is excluded from the total, Pacific countries account for more than one-half of total world exports in these commodities. Despite high levels of protection (matched by similarly high barriers elsewhere), Pacific countries account for a similar proportion of world imports.

A similar pattern emerges for trade in other commodities in which Pacific trade barriers are high. Again excluding intra-EC trade, Pacific countries account for two-thirds of world motor vehicle exports. Among agricultural commodities, Pacific countries dominate world markets for wheat, feed grains, and rice, and supply half of the world's exports of beef. The proportion is lower for sugar, in which tropical developing countries outside the Pacific are the important suppliers.

This pattern has not emerged by accident. In the process of rapid economic growth in East Asia and changing comparative advantage throughout the region, all Pacific countries have moved to protect those industries in which they have most profoundly lost comparative advantage as a result of East Asian growth. From these data we can draw the strong conclusion that, should Pacific countries reduce their assistance to their most highly protected industries on a nondiscriminatory basis, the associated export expansion is likely to be concentrated in other Pacific countries simply on grounds of competitiveness.

There is certainly considerable scope for further trade expansion by Pacific countries through measures that provide more confident market access and that reduce the trade barriers that limit the realization of the potentially strong complementarity within the region. Given the low resistances to regional trade reflected in regional trade concentration, the reduction of trade barriers on a most-favored-nation (MFN) basis, in a way that does not offend Pacific countries' global trading interests, is likely to mean that most new suppliers of imports will come from within the region rather than from non-Pacific countries.

The growth of East Asian and Pacific markets has made the major contribution to world trade growth over the last two decades, and especially over the past decade. Table 9.6 reveals that, net of intra-European trade, around 50 percent of world trade growth in this period has been in the Pacific market.

Table 9.7 shows that Pacific markets have absorbed two-thirds of the strong growth in East Asia's exports over the past two decades. East Asian import growth itself has absorbed one-third of the total. The United States' role as a market was especially important in the decade after the mid-1970s recession, but has slowed since the macroeconomic adjustments of 1985. Europe's role as a market, although much smaller, remained too significant for East Asian countries to ignore as a focus of trade policy interest. It also is noteworthy that Japan absorbed a significantly higher proportion of other East Asian exports in the recent period of lower US imports.

The mutual trading interests among Pacific countries, together with the strong commitment to trade-oriented development strategies among the developing countries of the region, provide a likely springboard for trade and other foreign economic policy measures to accommodate the trade and development needs of all the countries within the region. They will also strengthen the global system of commitments to an open international trade regime.

Origins of the Pacific Free Trade Area Proposal

The growth of the East Asian economy and of Pacific economic interdependence, the shift of world economic power away from Europe and the Atlantic toward East Asia and the Pacific, and the changed status of Japan and the United States in world affairs have all encouraged suggestions for a new focus in relations among Pacific economies (Crawford 1968, 10).

Table 9.5   Pacific commodity exports and imports, 1986[a]

Country/region	Textiles, clothing, and footwear		Domestic electrical equipment		Road motor vehicles		Iron and steel		Nonferrous metals	
	Value	%	Value	%	Value	%	Value	%	Value	%
United States	3,605	1.8	510	0.3	18,514	9.1	1,081	0.5	1,841	0.9
	31,386	8.2	2,573	0.7	69,421	18.2	9,556	2.5	7,976	2.1
Canada	733	0.9	99	0.1	23,916	28.3	1,749	2.1	3,232	3.8
	3,795	4.8	614	0.8	21,696	27.3	1,386	1.7	812	1.0
Australasia	351	1.3	50	0.2	184	0.7	439	1.6	1,615	6.0
	2,147	7.0	278	0.9	2,562	8.4	666	2.2	213	0.7
Japan	6,242	3.0	1,799	0.9	52,993	25.4	12,706	6.1	1,567	0.8
	5,520	4.6	104	0.1	1,398	1.2	1,762	1.5	3,655	3.1
Korea	10,740	31.0	583	1.7	1,514	4.4	1,971	5.7	143	0.4
	947	3.0	119	0.4	378	1.2	1,344	4.3	702	2.2
China	10,725	34.4	129	0.4	15	0.1	141	0.5	212	0.7
	2,572	7.9	145	0.4	1,402	4.3	4,411	13.5	570	1.7
Taiwan	10,234	25.9	601	1.5	616	1.6	566	1.4	132	0.3
	565	2.4	58	0.2	587	2.4	1,112	4.6	781	3.3
Hong Kong	8,228	41.7	624	3.2	2	0.0	16	0.1	37	0.2
	8,201	23.2	280	0.8	482	1.4	880	2.5	528	1.5
ASEAN	4,388	6.6	242	0.4	191	0.3	479	0.7	1,264	1.9
	2,644	4.2	220	0.4	1,606	2.6	2,611	4.2	585	1.4
Pacific[d]	55,254	7.7	4,636	0.7	97,947	13.7	19,285	2.7	10,048	1.4
	57,856	7.3	4,403	0.6	99,706	12.5	23,764	3.0	16,102	2.0
World	142,815	7.2	11,751	0.6	194,610	9.8	68,696	3.5	38,916	2.0
	147,744	7.2	12,022	0.6	192,318	9.3	71,261	3.5	40,817	2.0
Pacific share in world (%)	38.7		39.4		50.3		28.1		25.8	
	39.2		36.6		51.8		33.3		39.4	
Less intra-EC trade (%)	52.4		56.9		67.1		38.5		33.7	
	52.1		53.0		68.5		45.4		51.2	

For each country or region, exports are given in the first line, imports in the second.

a. In millions of US dollars, and percentages of country or region's total imports or exports.

0 denotes a value less than $500 thousand.
0.0 denotes a share less than 0.05 percent.

Sources: United Nations trade data; International Economic Data Bank, Research School of Pacific Studies, Australian National University.

Unmilled wheat		Unmilled feedgrains[b]		Rice		Sugar[c]		Beef		Total Commodities
Value	%	Value	%	Value	%	Value	%	Value	%	(millions of $US)
3,006	1.5	3,265	1.6	621	0.3	0	0.0	606	0.3	204,654
27	0.0	102	0.0	38	0.0	821	0.2	1,258	0.3	381,362
2,041	2.4	503	0.6	0	0.0	35	0.0	143	0.2	84,381
0	0.0	79	0.1	42	0.1	195	0.2	187	0.2	79,631
1,915	7.2	427	1.6	58	0.2	454	1.7	1,446	5.4	26,749
4	0.0	7	0.0	10	0.0	24	0.1	4	0.0	30,471
0	0.0	0	0.0	0	0.0	1	0.0	2	0.0	209,081
886	0.7	2,358	2.0	4	0.0	338	0.3	553	0.5	119,424
0	0.0	0	0.0	0	0.0	54	0.2	0	0.0	34,702
425	1.4	397	1.3	0	0.0	183	0.6	0	0.0	31,518
2	0.0	393	1.3	104	0.3	37	0.1	34	0.1	31,158
607	1.9	88	0.3	43	0.1	40	0.1	91	0.0	32,720
0	0.0	0	0.0	20	0.1	30	0.1	0	0.0	39,486
125	0.5	466	1.9	1	0.0	32	0.1	81	0.3	24,023
0	0.0	0	0.0	0	0.0	1	0.0	0	0.0	19,734
21	0.1	24	0.1	112	0.3	37	0.1	67	0.2	35,366
1	0.0	384	0.6	802	1.2	484	0.7	3	0.0	66,531
545	0.9	150	0.2	119	0.2	183	0.3	67	0.1	62,399
6,964	1.0	4,973	0.7	1,606	0.2	1,221	0.2	2,236	0.3	715,949
2,658	0.3	3,674	0.5	365	0.1	1,860	0.2	2,243	0.3	798,199
11,328	0.6	10,147	0.5	2,743	0.1	4,840	0.2	8,182	0.4	1,984,670
12,112	0.6	10,947	0.5	2,758	0.1	4,916	0.2	8,338	0.4	2,062,575
61.5		49.0		58.5		25.2		27.3		36.1
21.9		33.6		13.2		37.8		26.9		38.7
78.7		67.4		69.4		28.4		51.4		46.7
27.7		44.9		15.2		41.6		49.2		49.3

b. Unmilled barley, maize, rye, oats, and other cereals (excluding wheat and rice).
c. Raw beet and cane sugar, refined sugar, etc., and molasses.
d. Comprises the countries specified above and the Pacific island states.

Table 9.6   Contributions to growth in world trade, excluding intra-EC trade (percentages)

Country/region		Share in world trade			Contribution to world trade growth		
		1965	1975	1986	1965–75	1975–86	1965–86
Australia	X	2.1	1.7	1.4	1.6	1.1	1.3
	M	2.3	1.4	1.5	1.2	1.6	1.4
Japan	X	6.0	8.3	13.6	9.0	17.7	14.4
	M	5.6	8.4	7.4	9.2	6.6	7.6
China	X	1.2	0.9	2.0	0.9	2.9	2.1
	M	0.9	0.9	2.0	0.8	2.9	2.1
Other Northeast	X	1.1	2.2	6.1	2.6	9.1	6.6
Asia[a]	M	1.8	2.9	5.6	3.2	7.6	6.0
ASEAN	X	3.1	3.3	4.3	3.3	5.2	4.5
	M	3.2	3.4	3.9	3.5	4.2	3.9
East Asia total	X	11.3	14.8	26.1	15.7	34.8	27.6
	M	11.5	15.6	18.9	16.7	21.3	19.6
North America[b]	X	24.9	20.7	18.8	19.6	17.4	18.2
	M	19.9	19.0	20.5	18.7	35.6	29.4
New Zealand and	X	0.8	0.5	0.5	0.4	0.5	0.4
other Pacific	M	1.0	0.7	0.5	0.6	0.4	0.5
Pacific total[c]	X	39.1	37.6	46.7	37.2	53.6	47.4
	M	34.6	36.7	49.3	37.2	58.8	50.8
EC	X	23.5	21.9	22.0	21.4	22.2	21.9
	M	27.7	23.2	20.5	22.0	18.5	19.8
Middle East	X	5.2	11.4	4.9	13.1	−0.2	4.8
	M	3.4	6.0	4.7	6.8	3.8	4.9
Rest of world	X	32.2	29.1	26.4	28.3	24.3	25.8
	M	34.3	34.1	25.4	34.0	19.0	24.5

X = exports; M = imports.
a. Korea, Taiwan, and Hong Kong.
b. United States and Canada.
c. Australia, New Zealand, Japan, other Northeast Asia, ASEAN, China, North America, and the Pacific islands.

Source: International Economic Data Bank, Research School of Pacific Studies, Australian National University.

Table 9.7 The contribution of major markets to East Asian export growth in real terms, 1965–88[a]
(percentages)

Country/region	Share					Contribution[b]				
	1965	1975	1985	1987	1988[c]	1965–75	1975–85	1985–88	1965–87	1965–88
Japan	6.4	10.7	9.2	8.0	11.0	12.9	8.1	14.7	8.2	11.5
East Asia	23.9	32.5	33.6	32.1	33.7	36.8	34.4	33.8	33.1	34.7
North America	30.9	23.0	33.8	34.2	29.2	19.1	41.7	19.7	34.6	29.0
Pacific[d]	59.4	59.2	70.5	68.8	65.1	59.1	78.7	54.2	69.9	65.7
EC	15.2	13.9	11.7	15.8	16.7	13.3	10.1	27.0	15.9	16.9
World	100.0	100.0	100.0	100.0	100.0	100.0	100.0	100.0	100.0	100.0

a. East Asia is defined to include Japan, Korea, China, Hong Kong and ASEAN. Taiwan is not included. The unit value index for exports from all Asian developing countries except Taiwan and China was used as a deflator. The 1987 and 1988 data were deflated by data available for the first three quarters of 1987.
b. Defined as the increase in East Asian exports to each region as a proportion of the total increase in East Asian exports.
c. Data for 1988 are estimates of annual exports based on performance in the first quarter of 1988.
d. East Asia, North America, and Oceania.

Sources: International Monetary Fund, *Direction of Trade Statistics,* various issues; United Nations, *Monthly Bulletin of Statistics,* 1988.

A PACIFIC FTA?   235

Prominent in this discussion has been the notion of a developing community of interests in the Pacific and the recognition of advantages in closer regional economic cooperation. Until recently, however, the debate about what forms of institution building might best serve the interests of Pacific countries in managing and further developing their already substantial economic inter-relationship has eschewed the idea of European-style integration. It is illuminating to recall the context in which the idea of a Pacific free trade area first emerged and of its revival as a focus in trade diplomacy.

Although the growth of East Asian and Pacific economic interdependence did not originate in the establishment of formal regional institutional arrangements, two important elements in the nexus of political and com-mercial history in which it took place can be easily identified. The first is the role played by GATT in postwar recovery and growth; the second is the dominance of the United States throughout this formative period.

First, postwar trade and economic growth flourished within the framework of the GATT-based international trading system under US leadership. The GATT-based trade regime grew out of the Atlantic Charter and the Mutual Aid Agreements of the wartime period and served well the cause of reconstruction and liberalization of trade and economic activity for the first few decades after World War II (Finlayson and Zacher 1981). It provided the essentials of a global trade regime—far from comprehensive in its coverage of commodities or commercial interests (as some hoped the aborted plan for an International Trade Organization might have been), yet hugely supportive of trade expansion and world economic recovery and growth generally (Keohane and Nye 1977). This was critical to countries in East Asia and the Western Pacific that did not immediately or directly benefit under the initial rules and terms of GATT. But it also directed and limited trade and economic growth in some areas.

Second, the United States dominated the Pacific economy during that period. American leadership, regional as well as global, was comprehensive and hegemonic, combining strategic, political, and economic interests. In this period the Pacific alliance against the Soviet bloc in the Cold War era was conceived and established.

The GATT framework (and, importantly, Japan's eventual accommodation within it under the aegis of the United States) and the Pacific security alliances provided the underpinnings for the confident development of trading links within the East Asian and Pacific economy.

The idea of a community of Pacific countries associated in some form of regional arrangement began to emerge in the mid-1960s, principally in business and academic circles and later, tentatively, in official quarters (Drysdale and Patrick 1979). Interest in this idea was motivated by the desire to preserve the opportunities for internationally oriented economic development that had generated such spectacular results, both against corrosive pressures generated by that growth itself and against emergence of economic introversion in Europe associated with the entrenchment and expansion of the EC.

Then as now, the United States–Japan relationship was the most important single relationship within the Pacific region. However, Australia and Japan were already developing a quite significant bilateral economic relationship, which grew out of commercial initiatives in the mid-1950s. In their subsequent reactions to the changing international economic environment, both countries moved toward closer involvement with each other. Nothing illustrates this better than their response to the emergence of the EC and the problem of global market access in the mid-1960s (Drysdale and Patrick 1979, 18–21).

Australia responded to the damaging effects of the EC's Common Agricultural Policy on its prospects for growth, which had been based on expanding its traditional markets for agricultural exports, by intensifying the development of new markets in Japan, the Pacific, and East Asia (Crawford and Okita 1976, 25–30). Japan's response to the emergence of a discriminatory bloc in Western Europe and increasing dependence on raw materials from the region was to encourage closer economic relations with its main Pacific trading partners, and to pursue a line of commercial diplomacy designed to counter the effects of intensified European protectionism by developing an alignment of interests within the Pacific economy (Kojima 1971, chapters 1 and 3; for a review of the historical context of these developments, see Arndt 1987, 79).

The first detailed proposal for a Pacific regional economic association emerged in Japan and took the form of a free trade area scheme. The rationale advanced for institutional integration, involving discriminatory treatment in international trade, was based upon analysis of the effects of the formation of the EC upon the five advanced industrial countries of the Pacific and upon the relations between them and the developing countries of Asia and the Pacific (the "extended Pacific area"). The starting point in this argument was that "each time a shock was felt from outside the five Pacific countries, the necessity for closer Pacific integration was felt more seriously" (Soesastro 1983, 28).

The proposal for a Pacific free trade area, consisting of the Pacific five as full members and incorporating East Asian developing countries as associate members enjoying nonreciprocal tariff concessions, was primarily a reaction to the establishment of the EC. The EC was destined, it was felt, to have a huge impact not only on international trade and investment flows, but also on world economic influence. The EC's elimination of internal tariffs in 1968 added to fears of an increasingly inward-looking and self-sufficient

European bloc damaging to Pacific interests in global market access.[10] The logic of Pacific economic integration was urged, both in response to the threat of institutional integration in Europe and as a vehicle for realizing the potential of the East Asian and Pacific region. The completion of the Kennedy Round of negotiations in 1967 gave tactical point to the Pacific FTA proposal (Soesastro 1983, 28–31).

The most important factor working against the earlier Pacific FTA proposal was the global interest in US commercial diplomacy. The United States could not participate easily or sensibly in discriminatory regional trading arrangements through a grouping of either European or Pacific countries; this course would have been quite incompatible with its stature in world trade at that time, and contrary to the main thrust of its approach to international trade policy.[11] Moreover, the Pacific five included countries of disparate size and lacked the degree of integration required to make the dismantling of protective measures within the group politically or economically feasible (Arndt 1967).

Nonetheless, the foreign economic policy interest that underlay the Pacific FTA proposal, although perhaps overambitious and of limited immediate policy relevance, contained the seeds of a useful approach to important problems that were emerging in the growing economic and other relations among the diverse economies and societies of the East Asian and Pacific region (Drysdale 1969). The huge growth of trade, investment, and aid relationships among the countries of East Asia and the Pacific was spawning not only opportunities but quite predictable policy problems that would be managed less and less well within established bilateral arrangements or by individual countries unilaterally. In this context the first airing of a Pacific FTA proposal provided a useful impetus to the evaluation of other ideas directed toward the objective of closer Pacific economic cooperation.

In the two decades that followed, interest in Pacific economic cooperation came to focus heavily on building institutions that were functionally related to the economic interests of individual Pacific countries and to the region as a whole, and on the evolution of support for an open global economic regime within which East Asian and Pacific countries could continue their economic expansion. In 1980, a meeting in Canberra saw the establishment of the Pacific Economic Cooperation Conference (PECC) (Drysdale 1988,

---

10. The original contribution to this discussion was made in Kojima and Kurimoto (1966). Under the Foreign Ministry of Takeo Miki in Japan, the first Pacific Trade and Development Conference was organized in Tokyo in January 1968 at the Japan Economic Research Center to evaluate Kojima's proposal. See Drysdale (1984).

11. Parts of the argument in this section are drawn from Drysdale (1988), especially chapter 8.

chapter 8). The PECC meetings, which involved government officials, industry leaders, and researchers, led to productive exchanges on trade policy issues. They were part of the intellectual background to an early call for a new round of multilateral trade negotiations in December 1983, and for consultations among the officials of several Western Pacific countries, in preparation for what became the Uruguay Round of trade negotiations.

Such mechanisms are evolving because an infrastructure of regional consultation and cooperation is necessary to develop common Pacific positions; because of the region's growing industrial might and economic interdependence; because reduction of policy uncertainties offers large potential gains through a stronger framework for regional economic relations; and because they assist the communication of the diverse policy objectives of very different countries and of smaller and weaker economic partners in the Pacific. Growing knowledge among Pacific countries of each other's institutions and policy practices strengthens the level of mutual confidence in national economic policies and reduces psychological and political barriers to the movement of commodities and capital and the relocation of production, all of which can serve to enhance international welfare.

Free Trade Areas Resuscitated

In the contemporary international economic policy environment, serious challenges to East Asian development ambitions have again emerged in the area of trade policy. A characteristic of industrial transformation in the East Asian countries is that their trade growth has required the taking over of market shares from established exporters, first in labor-intensive manufactured goods, as Japan did from Britain and Europe in both the prewar and postwar periods, and as the East Asian NICs have done from Japan and more recently from one another (Garnaut and Anderson 1980; Drysdale 1988). Arrangements that limit or discriminate against this type of trade growth and transformation, by ossifying established trade shares, frustrate East Asian development ambitions, adversely affect Pacific trade interests, and thereby limit the growth potential of the world economy.

The thrust of the GATT trade regime and other international institutions established after World War II was toward the establishment of an open trade regime that embodied, importantly, the principles of "nondiscrimination," "predictability," "transparency," and "openness" (Dunn 1983, 109; Crawford 1968; Snape 1984, 17). These principles steadily gained expression in successive GATT reviews and rounds of trade liberalization, in the unconditional MFN rule, in the adoption of tariffs as the principal and "acceptable" form of trade protection, and in the "binding" of tariff rates to negotiated levels.[12] In applying these principles and rules the architects of the GATT sought to avoid the experience of trade restrictions, bilateralism, and uncertainty of the intrawar years and develop a confident global framework within which the benefits of trade liberalization would flow to all from the action of a relatively small number of major trading nations (Dunn 1983, chapter 5).

A trading system incorporating these principles and rules was of particular importance to smaller countries seeking economic growth through trade expansion. One of the great achievements of the United States and multilateral commercial diplomacy in the postwar period was undoubtedly the accommodation of Japan within the GATT's MFN trading framework, despite the initial application of Article XXXV, which permitted many trading nations to discriminate against Japan until the 1960s. Without appeal to the GATT principles and the GATT framework, Japan would hardly have been able to achieve so smoothly its economic growth and trade expansion of the first few decades after the war. An open international market where trade discrimination is constrained by general adherence to the MFN rule allows the accommodation of new and competitive suppliers, for whom trade is central to economic growth and industrialization. And so, in the postwar period, the GATT regime has facilitated a major transformation in the geographic structure of world trade and the emergence of the East Asian economy.

The main "internal" influence on the trade policy interests of the East Asian and Western Pacific countries continues to lie in the economic relationships of these countries with the United States. The United States is a major market for manufactured goods from the region. The Northeast Asian countries in particular are likely to see more value in trade liberalization if it includes the United States. For its part, the United States has shown an increasing interest in the Western Pacific as the region has grown in importance, and the share of US trade with the region has increased. Thus far, as is evident even with respect to Japan, the United States has tended to approach trade relations with particular East Asian countries in a case-by-case, bilateral manner, the results of which have not always been consistent with the MFN principle.

In the preliminaries to the new GATT round, the United States shifted toward a trade diplomacy based on the conditional MFN approach, seeking

---

12. Snape (1984, 17) notes that Harry Johnson says of nondiscrimination, "That principle has absolutely nothing to recommend it on grounds of either economic policy or the realities of international commercial diplomacy," but nevertheless endorses it as the best principle available. See Johnson (1976, 30–31).

"free trade solutions" to its trade policy problems.[13] The agreement with Israel and the negotiation of a free trade arrangement with Canada were important targets in this policy approach, as was the much-heralded Caribbean Basin Initiative. There seems to be strong interest within the United States in entering closer economic arrangements with Mexico, thus moving toward a North American FTA. There are also suggestions for some sort of FTA between the United States and the Western Pacific countries (ASEAN, Australia, and others). On the face of it, these US suggestions seem not to be aimed at the ultimate establishment of a Pacific FTA but rather at setting up bilateral mechanisms between the United States and some Western Pacific countries on a different, separate footing from US bilateral dealings with Japan. Whichever is the case, the Western Pacific countries have been given reasons to consider an FTA in the Pacific.

Problems in the United States–Japan Relationship

For the Pacific countries, international trade diplomacy still revolves around the management of the economic relationship between the United States and Japan.[14] This is the most important relationship within the Pacific economy, and one of the most important in the world. Pacific trade and commercial policies by the mid-1980s had become focused sharply upon the serious imbalances between the United States and Japan, which provided one motivation in the evolution of a new FTA approach to Pacific trade diplomacy.

Heightened tension in the management of the United States–Japan relationship in the first half of the 1980s resulted mainly from serious miscalculations in the macroeconomic policies of both countries and the lack of effective macroeconomic policy coordination. This was a recurrent problem from the late 1960s on, but extreme imbalances, focused on rising US current account deficits and Japanese surpluses, emerged very rapidly between 1981 and 1985. The main adjustments for both Japan and the United States had to be on the macroeconomic front, and those adjustments were set in motion, rather belatedly, after the Plaza Agreement of September 1985 forced the matter through a shift in exchange rates (Drysdale 1988, chapter 9).

---

13. For background to this policy approach, see Hay and Sulzenko (1982), Cline (1982), and Wonnacott (1984).

14. Among the best reviews of developments in the US–Japan relationship during this period is Patrick (1987).

These developments in the United States–Japan relationship were of some consequence for the shape of Pacific trade diplomacy. Both countries were diverted into attempts to resolve their global trade imbalances by action directed at each other, both negative and positive, in the form of specific restrictions or surcharges and bilateral market access arrangements. Specific trade issues came to dominate the policy approach. A related development and a danger for the Western Pacific and other countries was that the United States' targeting of Japan and Japan's obsession with the United States led both parties to negotiate bilateral deals that damaged third parties and undermined confidence in the whole trading system.

The cry of "specific reciprocity" as the guiding principle for trade and commercial policy became ever stronger in the United States over this period. Specific reciprocity (the careful equilibrium of benefits country by country and sector by sector in which market-sharing arrangements are the goal and tit-for-tat is a legitimate strategy) contrasts with the uncertain benefits of diffuse reciprocity (such as is embedded in the GATT system, where multilateral negotiations and agreements foster a set of rules and norms under which reciprocity seeks an overall balancing of concessions).[15]

"Strategic trade policy" and "fair trade" are the intellectual and political slogans heralding this new American policy environment.[16] In the 1980s, the Reagan administration clung to the rhetoric of diffuse reciprocity, although the political process increasingly demanded the practice of specific reciprocity. The political process and eventually the intellectual argument targeted on Japan to justify the retreat from support for a global regime based upon multilateral agreements and diffuse reciprocity.[17]

---

15. Robert O. Keohane (1986) sets out the distinction between specific and diffuse reciprocity most clearly. Stephen D. Krasner (1986) takes up the distinction to rationalize a strategy of specific reciprocity in US dealings with Japan.

16. Grossman and Richardson (1985) provide a recent review of this literature. Among the more important contributions in the international relations literature that have encouraged this interest is that by Axelrod (1983).

17. For example, Krasner (1986, 789), sees Japan as an economy that "defies external penetration . . . Japanese institutions, both public and private, are linked in a dense network of reciprocal obligations," and he goes on to say that "it is extremely difficult for new actors to pierce this network. . . ." He concludes: "If domestic-political-economic structures vary, then similar universal rules such as those codified in the GATT, can have very different behavioral outcomes. Tariff reductions in a market-oriented system like the United States will offer more opportunities to foreign producers than similar reductions in Japan, because buyers are more likely to consider only the costs and benefits of a specific transaction rather than to also incorporate assessments about past and future relationships with prospective suppliers. Diffuse reciprocity will not work even in the absence of conscious efforts at exploitation by the Japanese. The difference between the domestic structures of these two states guarantees that a universal open system based upon diffuse reciprocity will leave the United States with the 'sucker's payoff.' "

In the negotiations preparatory to the extension of an international systemic public good, such as are involved in changes to the trade regime through a new GATT round, interplay between the interests of specific reciprocity (among the major groups of trading nations) and diffuse reciprocity (the application of generalized rules and norms of behavior) is a natural if not essential ingredient. The first step in the process addresses the free-rider problem among the principal players, encouraging all of them to join in the exchange of concessions; the second delivers "stable, beneficial arguments in complex multilateral situations" involving domestic politics and international relations as well as economic interests (Keohane 1986, 19–27).

Certainly Japan's role in trade liberalization and international negotiations on other commercial, exchange rate, and macroeconomic policy issues is central to Pacific economic policy, but it will only support broader Pacific policy objectives if it finally eschews specific reciprocity in dealings with the United States and does not neglect third-country interests. The idea, with which Ambassador Mansfield has been associated, of a United States–Japan FTA is therefore not a sensible ultimate goal.

The question in this context is whether third-country interests are encompassed sufficiently within the Pacific framework to make the idea of a broader Pacific FTA attractive. The short answer must be that Japan's interests (as well as those of the East Asian NICs) now extend well beyond any group of Pacific countries that could readily or easily join a Pacific FTA. The importance of the European relationship, the delicate development of interdependence with China, the emergence of the Soviet bloc, and the opportunity for the emergence of Vietnam and North Korea from their past isolation are only some of the factors that extend East Asia's third-country interests and commitments to the multilateral trade and economic system.

Response to Free Trade Area Proposals

One possible response to US expressions of interest in special trade relations with various Western Pacific countries is to negotiate a Pacific FTA that covers the United States, Canada, and some combination of the Western Pacific economies. Would such a response help the key strategic objectives identified earlier: the shoring up of the system of imperfectly open trade in the Pacific; the reduction of barriers to intra-Pacific trade; and the reduction of European barriers to Pacific trade?

A free trade area is more likely to bring net benefits the larger its size. We have observed that the Pacific accounts for slightly less than one-half of world production of goods and services, and is likely to account for a higher proportion in the future. The Pacific countries are more important to each other's trade and potential trade than these output figures alone would suggest. The exceptionally high complementarity discussed earlier, and the economic advantages of intense Western Pacific trade that derive from location, point to an increased likelihood that a Pacific FTA would generate net benefits for its members and, less powerfully, for the world as a whole.

Trade barriers in Pacific countries are highest in precisely those commodities in which the comparative advantage of other Pacific countries is strongest: protection in Japan, Taiwan, and South Korea against agricultural exports from Australasia and North America; protection in Australasia and North America against labor-intensive exports from China, the East Asian NICs, and other ASEAN countries, and against exports of a range of more capital-intensive standard-technology products, especially motor vehicles from Japan and the East Asian NICs. This increases the likelihood of net gains from a Pacific FTA that is not subject to important exemptions.

The last qualification is important. In practice, FTAs and customs unions have been replete with exceptions, at least in their early years; where they have not, the establishment of the area has been associated with increased barriers to trade with the rest of the world. This outcome is driven by an important asymmetry in the political economy of protection policy between the highly focused opposition to trade creation by established interests in protected industries together with the highly focused support of established interests in trade diversion, on the one hand, and the diffuse beneficiaries from trade creation on the other (Anderson and Garnaut 1987, chapter 4). Hence the tendencies toward higher protection against the rest of the world that can be observed early in the existence of the US, Canadian, Australian, and European customs unions, and the proliferation of exceptions in the Australia–New Zealand and Canada–US FTAs. The realities of the political economy of protection make it impossible to ignore the likelihood that, in a Pacific FTA, the process of negotiation and compromise would favor trade diversion over trade creation.

Nor can we presume that all Pacific countries would seek to participate in negotiations to establish a Pacific FTA. China, with its partially reformed price system, is not now in a position to accept the obligations of participation in a "clean" FTA. It would be possible in principle to negotiate a range of commitments by China to open trade that led in the direction of more open and even freer trade. But the presence of special rules of thumb to govern China's trade relations with the Pacific would invite the proliferation of commitments short of free trade by other participants, especially but not limited to developing countries. Yet to exclude China would carry considerable costs and could retard China's progress toward more open trade relations, thus reducing the chances of ultimate success in the whole modernization program. Trade diversion from China within a smaller Pacific FTA would generate tensions and retaliation that would carry their own costs. And if China continued to grow strongly despite these new obstacles, over time a progressively smaller proportion of opportunities for profitable intra-Pacific trade would be covered by the FTA, thus weakening the presumption of net benefits for members and the world as a whole.

Nor is it likely that the ASEAN countries would accept membership in a clean free trade area. Governments in Indonesia, the Philippines, Malaysia, and even Thailand have all compromised heavily in implementing trade liberalization programs over the past decade (Findlay and Garnaut 1987, 271–73). Attempts at intra-ASEAN liberalization have yielded much more trade diversion than trade creation. Despite the attraction of open access to North American and Australasian markets, it is unlikely that the ASEAN states would agree to participate fully. To exclude ASEAN and to expose its members to trade diversion in favor of other Pacific economies would reduce the gains from Pacific integration, and set back the hesitant process of trade liberalization in the ASEAN economies themselves. To welcome ASEAN membership on a nonreciprocal or incompletely reciprocal basis would invite the proliferation of exceptions elsewhere.

We defined our first objective as the preservation of the relatively but imperfectly open trading environment that supported the productive extension of rapid growth in East Asia in recent decades. This objective seems to argue against any integration process that runs a severe risk of setting back severely the prospects for internationally oriented growth in China and the ASEAN states.

Now let us presume for analytical purposes that it were possible to wave a magic diplomatic wand and embark on a process of negotiation that actually delivers a clean and comprehensive Pacific FTA. Would such a process help or hinder the reduction of barriers to trade between Pacific countries and trading partners in the rest of the world?

The process of establishing a Pacific FTA would require a huge concentration of political and administrative effort in all the member countries. This would inevitably divert attention from wider trade policy objectives in the international system. The effort would follow perceptions of failure in the Uruguay Round and disillusionment with the multilateral trading system. But disappointment with the GATT-based system would not in itself demonstrate that an imperfect system of wider international trading relations could not get worse.

It is not clear how a commitment to a Pacific FTA, involving substantial trade diversion away from the rest of the world in the best of scenarios, would facilitate the negotiation of lower trade barriers with the EC. Possibly, the threat of such developments would focus European governments more clearly on the need for success in the Uruguay Round. But action to implement this threat would at best have the effect of suspending progress on the negotiation of reciprocal liberalization with Europe during a long transitional process.

Similarly, the diversion of trade policy-making resources into the development of a Pacific FTA, and the diversion of trade from the rest of the world, would weaken the region's capacity to respond to early stirrings of interest in internationally oriented development in the Soviet Union and Indochina, and the tentative signs of possible future stirrings in North Korea that can be read into recent statements on Korea from the Soviet Union. For the foreseeable future, the expansion of trade relations between the Pacific countries and these centrally planned economies is of minor importance in narrow economic terms. But it would be foolish to diminish the potential for reduction in political tension and the threat of war, and eventually reduction in military expenditures, that would over time be associated with constructive Pacific responses to these economies' interest in closer economic relations.

The United States at least would be mindful of Mexican and other Latin American interests in the process of Pacific integration. The accommodation of these interests would further increase the likelihood of special arrangements and exceptions within a Pacific FTA.

It may seem that the liberalization of trade in services appears more likely to be susceptible to treatment under the aegis of the FTA approach. The obstacles to international competition in services do not arise mainly through fiscal mechanisms, as they do with tariffs on commodities. They take the form of government monopoly of services (e.g., in communications); government controls on entry or capacity (in aviation); prescriptions of qualifications for entry (in professional services); or rules on domestic content (in the media). Some of these restrictions involve international agreements on rights or conditions of operation. These may appear easier to press through arrangements such as the Australia–New Zealand Closer Economic Relations Trade Agreement. However, although their multilateral negotiation may be difficult at this point, they are not likely to be treated easily within the framework of a Pacific FTA (as the Canada–US experience attests). Indeed, the complexities of service trade liberalization would seem equally amenable to negotiation within the framework of broader MFN-type trade and commerce agreements, alongside commodity trade issues.

We conclude that efforts to establish a Pacific FTA are not consistent with Pacific countries' interests in more effective movement toward global trade liberalization. Discriminatory trade arrangements within the Pacific region, and discriminatory treatment of Japan by the United States and other Western Pacific countries, or of other Western Pacific countries by Japan and the United States, are inconsistent with East Asian and Pacific trade policy interests and are likely to damage the growth performance of other countries in the region. If, on the other hand, the FTA suggestion were not intended to involve trade discrimination within the Pacific, it may provide an impetus for accelerating movement toward liberalization on an MFN basis, both in the region and elsewhere. The important requirement in such discussions would be to avoid any acceptance of the discrimination against non-Pacific countries implied by the term "free trade area," and to work toward finding areas of reciprocal concessions that can be offered on an MFN basis. But how can we reconcile this approach with recent tendencies within US trade policy and, more broadly, with the reduced willingness of the United States to continue to provide liberal leadership to the multilateral trading system?

The Diminished Hegemon

The diminished relative position of the United States in the Pacific and world economies is an inevitable result of American success in international economic policy during the postwar period. The United States has prospered exceptionally in the liberal trading system of which it was the chief sponsor. This same system has sponsored more rapid growth in smaller, and initially much poorer, American allies and trading partners as they have taken advantage of opportunities to expand the gains from trade. This is exactly what a priori analysis would have led us to expect if we had known that the postwar mechanisms were going to work well. Yet in the place of self-congratulation in the United States, we see recrimination and the adoption of attitudes and policies that threaten to undermine the liberal international system.

Some analysts have sought to explain the changed US approach in a theory of the hegemonic leader in the supply of an international public good, the open multilateral trading system. As by far the largest economy in the early postwar system, and by implication the largest beneficiary of it, the United States needed and was prepared to play a leadership role in supplying the public good, while letting free riders in Europe, Australasia, Japan, and the developing countries escape the burden of accepting symmetric market access obligations.[18] But the relative decline of the United States in world production and trade in the subsequent decades has diminished US preparedness to carry the costs of leadership. To restore the

---

18. For a discussion of this idea, see Bhagwati (1987, chapter 3).

system requires the emergence of a new hegemon, willing and able to carry these costs. But there is none in sight.

This line of analysis poses a problem for economists. The required leadership in the maintenance of an open system may carry some adjustment costs, but conveys an overall benefit, presuming that the hegemon does not so dominate world markets that a diminution of the extent of its trade can improve its terms of trade sufficiently to outweigh the allocative costs of reduced specialization. In circumstances of hegemonic decline, the expectations of the leader gaining from free trade, even if its trading partners impose protection, are even larger, since variations in its own level of trade will be even less influential in determining relative prices. Symmetrically, the small country's imposition of barriers to trade, far from being a free ride, imposes costs that, if anything, are greatest when its relative size is least.

Bhagwati (1987) has sought to rationalize observed tendencies in the international system by supposing that the United States earlier was acting as the leader in a different sense by permitting "justifiable asymmetries" of obligations on a temporary basis. As the temporary circumstances ended with recovery in Europe and growth in the Western Pacific, the United States demanded reciprocity of access. There are problems with this logic if a rationale is sought in the calculation of national economic interest. However, two possible ways in which the United States might rationally have been pursuing national interest come to mind. First, the introduction of distortions in trade, to the cost of the United States itself and its partners in the international system, might be rationally calculated to force partners to drop their own trade distortions. This is the expressed objective of the massive retaliation against European agricultural subsidies through the US export enhancement program.[19] It is incidental to this argument that the retaliatory instruments chosen by the United States imposed proportionately higher costs on innocent bystanders. The key test of rationality is whether the retaliation was well judged to force liberalization elsewhere. If the realities deny good prospects for such a response in Europe, the retaliation can only damage US interests.

Second, the descent into bilateralism seems to have had some success in enhancing US interests at the expense of third parties through trade

---

19. Colleagues at a recent seminar at the East Asian Institute at Columbia University pointed to the parallel between the Reagan administration's export enhancement program, directed at the EC, and the military buildup, directed at the Soviet Union. At high short-term costs to the United States, these commitments imposed costs on adversaries to provide a congenial environment for negotiations on reciprocal disarmament. The effectiveness of each strategy depends on a series of fine judgments.

diversion. The United States has been able to pursue this approach in agriculture, where protection is commonly provided by administered import quotas that may be allocated so as to discriminate between suppliers. This might convey a narrow and short-term benefit to the United States alone, but this benefit would be somewhat offset by the indirect cost to the United States of losses borne by other allies and trading partners.

This consideration has been important recently in US bilateral initiatives aimed at increasing American shares of East Asian commodity markets. An important example involved the Japanese beef trade. In response to US demands for greater access to the Japanese market, beef import restrictions have been altered to allow more US imports, but this liberalization has been at the expense of third countries, particularly Australia. In the four years before 1983, the US share in the volume of Japanese beef and offal imports rose from 31 percent to 44 percent, while the Australian share fell from 62 percent to 49 percent. The total import volume rose by less than 10 percent during the period (Anderson and Hayami 1986). This policy approach was turned around in the settlement with Japan in July 1988, when Japan reformed its beef trade system in a manner consistent with the important GATT principles of transparency and nondiscrimination. Coal markets have been affected similarly, but to a lesser degree, through different mechanisms.

Both in the massive retaliation against European subsidies and in the bilateral initiatives, any case for action in the narrow US national interest would have been as strong in earlier times as in recent years. It is not obvious how the relative decline of the United States in world production and trade would have strengthened the economic case for action in recent times.

The key to understanding the new US attitudes to the international trading system lies not with anything happening mainly in that system itself, but in the polity's incapacity to come to grips with profound macroeconomic imbalances. Other countries' protection policies are blamed for a payments imbalance that has its origins in domestic budgetary policy. The problem for other countries in managing the US challenge to the liberal system is that large-scale trade liberalization in East Asia and Europe is incapable of contributing in a major way to curing the US current account problems. There would seem to be no reliable prospect for addressing current international trade tensions independently of US progress in moderating domestic demand, in pursuit of balance in current external payments.

This is where hegemonic decline may be important. The US polity, wounded by macroeconomic difficulties, has lost tolerance for the weaknesses in the trade policy performance of others, independently of rationally calculated national advantage. The increase in relative size and strength of others is important principally for its effects on political reactions at all levels in the United States.

A Pacific Approach to Liberalization

How then can the United States' partners in the Pacific respond to these powerful new currents in trade policy in a manner consistent with nondiscriminatory liberalization?

First, realization of the fragility of the system provides a strong incentive to work toward success in the Uruguay Round. It is a dangerous time to take risks and liberties with the multilateral system. The US administration and the wider US polity are likely to judge success initially in terms of progress on agriculture. The EC, Japan, and the Western Pacific developing countries would be wise to calculate carefully the cost of inadequate movement on agriculture, beyond the usual cost of foregone gains from trade.

Disappointing progress in the GATT round will herald a highly dangerous period for the international trading system. This will be a time to rechannel interest in a Pacific FTA into renewed, regionally based efforts to strengthen the multilateral system.

The strategic problem in pursuing discussions under the FTA umbrella will be to maintain a focus on nondiscrimination and to find areas of reciprocal concessions that are capable of sustaining US interest in the discussions. From the viewpoint of the Western Pacific countries, the most important concessions by the United States would relate to access to the US markets for manufactured goods in which East Asian countries are most competitive.

For the United States to extend such concessions on an MFN basis would not, with the exception of steel, have a strong impact on US–Europe trade. The areas of greatest Japanese competitiveness do not now coincide closely with those of European competitiveness in the US market. In fact, initial US concessions to Japan could simply consist of the removal of trade arrangements such as voluntary export restraints that discriminate against Japanese goods. However, concessions relevant to the East Asian developing countries would affect US trade with Latin America if offered on an MFN basis. Thus, it would be sensible for the United States to engage Latin American countries in the process of reciprocation alongside the discussions with the Pacific nations.

The main areas of concession that could be offered to the United States by the Western Pacific countries are agricultural trade liberalization and liberalization of access to trade in services. The involvement of the United States in trade negotiations would make significant progress in agriculture more feasible, both because of US interest in that area and because of the significance for Northeast Asian countries of the concessions that the United States would be able to offer in exchange. The Western Pacific developing countries would find advantages in increased access for labor-intensive manufactures, and more secure access for more capital-intensive, standard-technology manufactures in developed country markets.

Although the United States may have benefited from its country-by-country bilateral bargaining over access to East Asian commodity markets in the past, the benefits have been severely limited by the quantitative restrictions on overall agricultural trade. Movement toward more liberal agricultural trade would benefit Australasia, for example, relative to the United States by removing present discrimination, but would yield substantially greater gains to all agricultural exporters (including the United States) than have been achieved in existing bilateral dealings. Hence, Australia's initiative in forming the "Cairns Group" of efficient agricultural exporters has sought to engage the United States and other agricultural exporters in the negotiation of a more general and phased liberalization of the agricultural trading system.[20]

The approach suggested here draws its prospects for success from the tendency for barriers to intra-Pacific trade to be highest in commodities and markets in which other Pacific economies are competitive suppliers. The incentive for participation, beyond the realization that the liberal trading system is in peril, is the opportunity to shape the agenda. The nondiscriminatory nature of concessions avoids carrying the high costs of exclusions of the kind involved in a Pacific FTA. China and the ASEAN countries need not be excluded by their incapacity to make comprehensive commitments to intra-Pacific free trade, so long as they are able to offer liberalization that contributes substantially to trade expansion. The "Pacific Round" would be entered at a time of crisis, and the developed countries and NICs would be aware of the severe consequences of failure to make substantial progress.

There would remain the problem of resentment in the US polity toward any free ride for European agriculture. There would be pressures for the United States to take its "massive retaliation" to a conclusion alongside the Pacific Round.

A much better strategy, should the EC persist in its current positions, may be to regionalize the retaliation and its costs in the context of the Pacific Round. The fiscal burden could be shared by the developed countries, or by countries with per capita incomes above a specific level. The burden sharing would be fiscally and psychologically helpful in the United States. The fiscal commitments would be greatly unwelcome elsewhere in this

---

20. See, for example, *Australia and Pacific Cooperation*, Second Report of the Australian National Pacific Cooperation Committee, Canberra, July 1987, 9; and Stoeckel and Cuthbertson (1987, chapter 2).

region, but would need to be weighed against the benefits of strengthening the multilateral system and of genuine liberalization within that system. In Japan, they would need to be judged alongside other, politically more difficult pressures for burden sharing with the United States. In Canada, Australia, and New Zealand, they would be partially compensated by the alleviation of what has been in recent years a major sectoral problem, generated by the unilateral implementation of the US export enhancement program. In the current fiscal circumstances of the United States, regional burden sharing, especially the participation of Japan, would substantially enhance the credibility of the retaliation. It is hoped that such retaliation would never actually be required.

The central concept of a regional round of negotiations directed toward multilateral concessions, but focused on issues of high regional interest, has been discussed from time to time over the past decade. It made sense, and still does, only as a complement to the primary goal of a successful GATT round. Its feasibility has been enhanced in recent years by the practice of regional cooperation in a wide range of trade policy matters, including in preparation for the Uruguay Round.[21] It seems to us that a response to failure in the Uruguay Round along these lines would hold out rather better prospects than a Pacific FTA for holding the line on corrosion of the multilateral system, promoting intra-Pacific liberalization, and securing progress on reduction of barriers to trade between Europe and the Pacific.

Acknowledgments

We gratefully acknowledge the assistance of Jeremy Whitham, Prue Phillips, Diane Elias, David Lawson, James Jordan, Elyse Tanoye, Kim Lan Ngo, and Minni Reis in preparing data, gathering background information, and word processing.

References

Akrasanee, Narongchai, and Juanjai Ajanant. 1987. "Thailand: Manufacturing Industry Protection: Issues and Empirical Studies." In Christopher Findlay and Ross Garnaut, eds., *The Political Economy of Manufacturing Protection: Experiences of ASEAN and Australia*. Sydney: Allen & Unwin.
Anderson, Kym, and Ross Garnaut. 1987. *Australian Protection: Extent, Causes and Effects*. Sydney: Allen & Unwin.

---

21. See Garnaut (1981). When Australian Prime Minister R. J. L. Hawke called for a new round of multilateral trade negotiations in a speech in Bangkok in December 1983, he referred to a regional round along the lines suggested here as a fallback should efforts fail to launch and to implement a new round.

Anderson, Kym, and Yujiro Hayami, eds. 1986. *The Political Economy of Agricultural Protection: East Asia in International Perspective.* Sydney: Allen & Unwin.

Arndt, H. W. 1967. "PAFTA: An Australian Assessment." *Intereconomics*, 10, 271–76.

Arndt, H. W. 1987. *Economic Development.* Chicago: University of Chicago Press.

Axelrod, Robert. 1983. *The Evolution of Cooperation.* New York: Basic Books.

Bhagwati, Jagdish. 1987. *Ohlin Lectures.* Boston: MIT Press.

Cline, William R. 1982. *"Reciprocity": A New Approach to World Trade Policy?* POLICY ANALYSES IN INTERNATIONAL ECONOMICS 2. Washington: Institute for International Economics, September.

Cooper, Richard. 1974. "Worldwide versus Regional Integration: Is There an Optimal Size of the Integrated Area?" Yale University, New Haven. *Economic Growth Center Discussion Paper* 220, November.

Crawford, J. C. 1968. *Australian Trade Policy, 1942–1966.* Canberra: Australian National University Press.

Crawford, John, and Saburo Okita. 1976. *Australia, Japan and Western Pacific Economic Relations: A Report to the Governments of Australia and Japan.* Canberra: Australian Government Publishing Service.

Drysdale, Peter. 1969. "Japan, Australia, and New Zealand: The Prospect for Western Pacific Economic Integration." *Economic Record*, 45, no. 111, September, 321–342.

Drysdale, Peter. 1984. "Pacific Trade and Development Conference: A Brief History." *Pacific Economic Papers* 112. Canberra: Australian National University.

Drysdale, Peter. 1988. *International Economic Pluralism: Economic Policy in East Asia and the Pacific.* New York: Columbia University Press; and Sydney: Allen & Unwin.

Drysdale, Peter, and Hugh Patrick. 1979. "An Asian-Pacific Regional Economic Organization: An Exploratory Concept Paper" (prepared for the US Congressional Research Service). Washington: US Government Printing Office, July.

Dunn, Lydia. 1983. *In the Kingdom of the Blind: A Report on Protectionism and the Asian-Pacific Region.* Special Report No. 3. London: Trade Policy Research Centre.

Findlay, Christopher, and Ross Garnaut, eds. 1987. *The Political Economy of Manufacturing Protection: Experiences of ASEAN and Australia.* Sydney: Allen & Unwin.

Finlayson, Jock, and Mark Zacher. 1981. "The GATT and the Regulation of Trade Barriers: Regional Dynamics and Functions." *International Organization*, 35, no. 4, Autumn.

Garnaut, Ross. 1981. "Australian Trade Policy and Western Pacific Economic Growth." *Economic Papers*, 65, June, 14–30.

Garnaut, Ross, and Kym Anderson. 1980. "ASEAN Export Specialization and the Evolution of Comparative Advantage in the Western Pacific Region." In Ross Garnaut, ed., *ASEAN in a Changing Pacific and World Economy.* Canberra: Australian National University Press.

Grossman, Gene M., and J. David Richardson. 1985. "Strategic Trade Policy: A Survey of Issues and Early Analysis." *Special Papers in International Economics* 15, Princeton University, April, 1–34.

Hathaway, Dale E. 1987. *Agriculture and the GATT: Rewriting the Rules.* POLICY ANALYSES IN INTERNATIONAL ECONOMICS 20. Washington: Institute for International Economics, September.

Hay, Keith A. J., and B. Andrei Sulzenko. 1982. "US Trade Policy and 'Reciprocity.'" *Journal of World Trade Law,* 16, November–December.

Hock, Lee Kiong. 1987. "Malaysia: The Structure and Causes of Manufacturing Sector Protection." In Christopher Findlay and Ross Garnaut, eds., *The Political Economy of Manufacturing Protection: Experiences of ASEAN and Australia.* Sydney: Allen & Unwin.

Hufbauer, Gary Clyde, and Howard F. Rosen. 1986. *Trade Policy for Troubled Industries*. POLICY ANALYSES IN INTERNATIONAL ECONOMICS 15. Washington: Institute for International Economics, March.

Itoh, Motoshige. 1988. "Organizational Transactions and Japanese-Style Business Relations." Presented at a public seminar at the Australia–Japan Research Center, Australian National University, Canberra, 5 September.

Johnson, Harry. 1976. *Trade Negotiations and the New International Monetary System*. Geneva: Graduate Institute of International Studies; and London: Trade Policy Research Centre.

Keating, Paul. 1988. *Economic Statement*. Canberra: Australian Government Publishing Service, May.

Keohane, Robert O. 1986. "Reciprocity in International Relations." *International Organization*, 40, no. 1, Winter, 1–27.

Keohane, Robert O., and Joseph Nye. 1977. *Power and Interdependence: World Politics in Transition*. Boston: Little, Brown.

Kojima, Kiyoshi. 1971. *Japan and a Pacific Free Trade Area*. London: Macmillan.

Kojima, Kiyoshi, and Hiroshi Kurimoto. 1966. "A Pacific Economic Community and Asian Developing Countries." *Hitotsubashi Journal of Economics*, 7, no. 1, June.

Krasner, Stephen D. 1986. "Trade Conflicts and Common Defense: The United States and Japan." *Political Science Quarterly*, 101, no. 5, 787–806.

Lawrence, Robert Z. 1987. "Imports in Japan: Closed Markets or Minds?" *Brookings Papers on Economic Activity* 2, 517–54.

Pangestu, Mari, and Boediono. 1987. "Indonesia: The Structure and Causes of Manufacturing Sector Protection." In Christopher Findlay and Ross Garnaut, eds., *The Political Economy of Manufacturing Protection: Experiences of ASEAN and Australia*. Sydney: Allen & Unwin.

Patrick, Hugh. 1987. "The Management of the United States–Japan Trade Relationship and Its Implications for Pacific Basin Economies" (mimeographed). Background paper for the Project on the Impact of Japan–US Economic Relations on Other Pacific Basin Nations, US National Committee for Pacific Economic Cooperation.

Saxonhouse, Gary P., and Robert M. Stern. 1988. "An Analytical Survey of Formal and Informal Barriers to International Trade and Investment in the United States, Canada and Japan." In Robert M. Stern, ed., *US–Canadian Trade and Investment Relations with Japan*. Chicago: University of Chicago Press.

Snape, Richard. 1984. "Australia's Relations with GATT." *Economic Record*, 60, no. 168, March.

Soesastro, Hadi. 1983. "Institutional Aspects of Pacific Economic Cooperation." In Hadi Soesastro and Sung-Joo Han, eds., *Pacific Economic Cooperation: The Next Phase*. Jakarta: Centre for Strategic and International Studies, 3–53.

Stoeckel, Andy, and Sandy Cuthbertson. 1987. *Successful Strategies for Australian Trade*. Canberra: Centre for International Economics.

Summers, Robert, and Alan Heston. 1984. "Improved International Comparison of Real Product and Its Composition: 1950–1980." *Review of Income and Wealth*, June.

Takeuchi, Kenji. 1988. "Does Japan Import Less Than It Should?" *Policy Planning and Research Working Paper* 63. Washington: World Bank, July.

Tan, Norma A. 1987. "The Philippines: The Structure and Causes of Manufacturing Sector Protection." In Christopher Findlay and Ross Garnaut, eds., *The Political Economy of Manufacturing Protection: Experiences of ASEAN and Australia*. Sydney: Allen & Unwin.

Wonnacott, R. J. 1984. "Aggressive US Reciprocity Evaluated with a New Analytical Approach to Trade Conflicts." Montreal: Institute for Research on Public Policy.

10

A Free Trade Agreement Between Mexico and the United States?

Ignacio Trigueros

Beginning in July 1985 the Mexican government implemented what eventually turned out to be a strong and rapid import liberalization program. The unfavorable prospects of the Mexican economy, derived from the weakness of the world oil market and the scarcity of foreign funds, that resulted from the debt crisis, induced the Mexican authorities to break with an old and embedded tradition of import substitution. The extraordinary economic performance of some Southeast Asian countries that followed export-led growth economic strategies may also have played an important role in that decision.

From the point of view of many observers of the Mexican economic scene, the import liberalization program, even if necessary to enhance economic growth and increase productivity in the long run, was inappropriately timed in view of existing commercial policy trends. An import liberalization program in the face of increased protectionism on the part of industrialized countries would result in large costs in terms of both uncertain access of Mexican products to foreign markets and a loss in the terms of trade that would be necessary to overcome trade barriers in the industrialized countries. It may have been preferable to postpone an ambitious import liberalization scheme and proceed instead by removing what may be termed the most flagrant vices of the past economic strategy, namely, import permits and excessive regulation.

However, even if protectionism on the part of the industrialized countries had been pervasive, given Mexico's unfavorable economic prospects, the postponement of the import liberalization program would certainly not have been the only option. One alternative would contemplate another set of

Ignacio Trigueros is a professor of economics at the Instituto Tecnologico Autonomo de Mexico.

actions (in the area of trade negotiations), implemented along with tariff reductions, that would help to overcome the protectionist barriers imposed by Mexico's trading partners.

A matter of concern in this respect is the increasingly widespread feeling about the failure of multilateral trade agreements (that is, the General Agreement on Tariffs and Trade) to create a favorable environment for enhanced and secure access for their members' products to each other's markets. Recent negotiations between the United States and Canada, and within the European Community (EC) toward increased regional economic integration are evidence of this concern. This evidence in turn raises the question of whether each participant in world trade, and in particular those countries that like Mexico are in the wake of a major inception into the world economy, should become a member of a large trading bloc, in order to obtain a favorable outcome from their trade policy.

This chapter addresses this issue from the perspective of a Mexico–US free trade agreement. Special emphasis is given throughout to the potential economic gains for Mexico of such an agreement. Rather than analyze in detail all the possible ramifications of a free trade area (FTA) encompassing Mexico and the United States, this chapter focuses on two basic questions:

☐ Given the rapid and strong import liberalization program implemented so far by Mexico, to what extent may additional reductions in trade barriers contribute to Mexico's overall economic strategy?

☐ What is the actual and potential incidence of protectionism and other commercial policy actions taken by the industrialized countries, and especially by the United States, on Mexican exports?

Considering that an FTA involves essentially a bilateral reduction in trade barriers, the answers to these questions are of crucial importance in assessing the economic implications of such an agreement.

The first section of this chapter presents an update of Mexico's foreign trade policy. The effects that the import liberalization program has had so far in the economy are analyzed, and those areas of the trade regime in which further reforms may be desirable are noted. The second section analyzes the specific role an FTA between Mexico and the United States may have in promoting a better trade policy from the Mexican point of view. This section discusses the potential trade diversion that such an agreement could involve, and assesses the actual and prospective threats posed by the commercial policy of industrialized countries on the performance of Mexican exports. The final section presents the conclusions of this analysis.

Mexico's Commercial Policy: Summary Description and Assessment

In assessing which type of commercial policy is appropriate for a country like Mexico, at least two factors deserve to be emphasized. The first has to do with the size of the economy. The Mexican economy is too small to support an efficient industrial sector under an autarkic scheme. Some specialization and foreign trade is therefore necessary to attain an efficient scale of production in many industries.

The second factor has to do with the outcome of the import substitution strategy followed by Mexico since the early 1950s. Perhaps the best way to summarize the effects of this strategy on the Mexican economy is to look at the figures on productivity gains among the different activities that comprise the industrial sector (Samaniego 1985). Those figures show that during the period 1974–81 productivity gains were absent or negative in 16 of 35 industries. For 22 of the same 35 industries, productivity gains were lower during the period 1977–81 than they were in the previous four years.

Even if several factors may in principle account for the low or negative advances in productivity in many industrial activities, there is no doubt that the limited exposure of the Mexican industrial sector to foreign competition played an important role in that respect. That policy was enforced through a regime of import permits, which were rarely granted when the imported good was produced domestically. Thus, the degree of protection conferred to domestic firms was absolute.

However, the effects of protectionism on resource allocation and productivity went far beyond those suggested by supply-and-demand analysis. The Mexican case illustrates that the import substitution regime provides fertile ground for the implementation of an increasing number of regulations that interfere with market activity. Those regulations also explain the failure of the Mexican industrial sector in recent years. However, without the protectionist scheme followed by Mexico, the tight regulation of industrial activities might never have materialized. In fact, in recent years, as a result of an import liberalization program to be described below, the Mexican authorities have been following a more cautious approach regarding both the implementation of additional regulations, and the way in which current regulatory schemes are applied.

In any case, the low productivity gains in the Mexican economy during the latter years of the import substitution regime illustrate how bad things could get as a result of protectionism. By the mid-1970s the Mexican economy had gone a little too far regarding import substitution. Nevertheless, economic growth and an increasing standard of living were temporarily possible, first as a result of the oil boom, and then as a result of the extraordinary amount of foreign borrowing contracted up to 1982. However, in the actual situation, with a low price for oil and with the absence of foreign funds that followed the debt crisis, a more open foreign trade strategy seems to be one of the few options for attaining a rapid and sustained resumption of economic growth in Mexico.

It would be wrong to assert that, because other countries had attained an extraordinary economic performance despite widespread restrictions on imports, the Mexican economy could succeed following a protectionist policy. The current situation of the Mexican economy is different from that of any of the economic miracles of the last 30 years, because none of those economies started with a fairly obsolete industrial sector. Different kinds of illness require different medicines, and for the Mexican economy import liberalization appears to be the right prescription.

In fact, previous discussions about a Mexico–US free trade agreement (for instance, Weintraub 1984) placed special emphasis on the convenience, from the Mexican point of view, of pursuing a more open foreign trade strategy, as the basic rationale for promoting a move toward regional economic integration. It was also argued that, despite the development gap between the two nations, a rather favorable pattern of specialization would emerge from the agreement. Freer trade between Mexico and the United States would not necessarily condemn Mexico to become a supplier of raw materials and simple manufactures. Instead, Mexico's comparative advantage in labor-intensive manufactures and its strong industrial infrastructure were considered a guarantee of both the survival of major portions of the industrial sector, in the face of a more open foreign trade strategy, and a successful outcome from an outward-looking economic policy.

Today, although the general conclusions of previous studies may still be valid, the discussion about the potential benefits of an FTA between Mexico and the United States should be framed in somewhat different terms, regarding at least two aspects:

□ From the Mexican point of view, the policy choice is no longer one between a practically closed economy and an economy opened to trade with a much more advanced partner;

□ Mexico's foreign trade structure has been drastically altered as a result of the debt crisis and the reduction in the world price of oil.

The first of these factors is important because, with a more open import regime already in place, the need to negotiate an FTA with the United States is perhaps less pressing. The second factor provides more solid ground for assessing the possible reaction of the Mexican economy to additional trade reforms.

Table 10.1   Recent reforms in commercial policy, Mexico, 1985–87

| | 1985 | | 1986 | | 1987 | |
	June	December	June	December	June	December
Coverage of import permits (%)[a]	92.2	47.1	46.9	39.8	35.8	25.4
Coverage of official prices (%)[a]	18.7	25.4	19.6	18.7	13.4	0.6
Average tariff rate (%)[b]	23.5	28.5	24.0	24.5	22.7	11.8

a. With respect to tradeable output.
b. Output weighted.

Table 10.1 points out clearly the dramatic trade reforms recently undertaken in Mexico. At first sight, Mexico's current import regime is not very much unlike that of many industrialized countries, in terms of both tariff rates and the presence of quantitative restrictions in some sectors of the economy.

In less than three years, the Mexican economy moved from an extremely restrictive import regime in which almost every item was subject to an import permit, granted only at the will of foreign trade officials and not at all in the case of some products, to a regime in which quantitative restrictions apply only to a few selected sectors of the economy—agriculture, oil and derivatives, motor vehicles, pharmaceutical products, footwear and electronic equipment—that comprise only 25 percent of the domestic output of tradeable goods. One observes a similar trend regarding the abolition of official prices, which had been used quite often as a protective device, fixed many times above their international counterparts and then used as a reference to determine ad valorem import taxes.

Finally, import tariffs have reached reasonably low levels, having been reduced from a 0 to 100 percent range at the beginning of the process to a 0 to 20 percent range as of December 1987. It may be noted that the pace of the import liberalization program surpassed that of the original government plan, according to which import tariffs would be in the 30 percent range at the end of 1988. Needless to say, considering the long protectionist tradition of the Mexican economy, the pace of the import liberalization program was well ahead of that expected by the business community before July 1985.

This fact is important because rapid import liberalization has led to an impasse in terms of additional reforms to the trade regime. Even though an impasse was likely, given the transition to a new administration in Mexico, there is not the perception that trade reform by itself will be a top priority in the economic policy agenda of the Salinas administration.

The effects of the import liberalization program on the evolution of the economy have been quite favorable so far. From 1985, the year that marks the implementation of the first strong reforms of the trade regime, to 1987, nonoil exports almost doubled and thereby helped to absorb the impact of decreased domestic demand that resulted mainly from the declining world oil prices. One should mention that none of those factors traditionally highlighted as the major evils of an import liberalization program, such as widespread closures of domestic firms and massive purchases of imported durable goods, have so far been observed in the Mexican economy.

It would be wrong, however, to attribute the extraordinary performance of Mexico's nonoil exports only to the import liberalization program. As mentioned above, there was a sharp reduction in domestic aggregate demand as a result of the negative (from the Mexican point of view) oil price shock of 1986. Thus, foreign markets turned into a shelter for products that could not clear the domestic market. Also, a large reduction in domestic real wages—during August 1988 the real wage rate for unskilled workers was 50 percent below its previous peak—provided a strong competitive edge for domestic firms.

In fact, it is not entirely clear at first sight whether Mexico's export behavior could be sustained once real wages recover to higher levels. However, even though the experience with import liberalization is relatively short, and therefore there are not enough data to give a clear-cut answer to this question, several factors point toward the sustainability of increased Mexican nonoil exports.

First, the extraordinary growth in Mexican exports of the last few years occurred under rather unfavorable conditions. Both the domestic infrastructure and the regulatory framework applying to Mexican firms, built within an import substitution regime, have created strong domestic distortions that interfere with foreign trade. However, there is now a strong movement on the part of the Mexican authorities toward removing these distortions and adapting Mexico's infrastructure to the new trade strategy. This movement will almost certainly be accelerated by the Salinas administration.

Second, the import liberalization program has allowed cost reductions by domestic firms that are far beyond those derived from a lower wage bill. The improved quality of inputs and lower costs from inventory management are only a few of the cost-saving devices induced by a more competitive environment in the market for intermediate products.

Third, a boom in capital goods imports, which grew by 74 percent during the first eight months of 1988 in the face of a rather flat level of domestic demand, is perhaps evidence of investment activity in those sectors oriented toward foreign markets, and therefore of a more permanent change in Mexico's export performance.

Finally, on the more practical side, the reaction of Mexican nonoil exports to two successive external shocks—the first one at the beginning of the debt crisis and the second one arising from the 1986 fall in the price of oil—was much more favorable in the latter period, when the reforms to the trade regime were already in motion. Thus, factors other than aggregate demand management, (that is, import liberalization) seem to have been important in explaining the growth of Mexican nonoil exports. Rough statistical estimates tend to confirm this assertion, as they point toward the presence of an independent and significant effect arising from the change in the import regime.[1]

Thus, the reduction in aggregate demand and the resulting fall in domestic real wages have been important elements in providing a competitive edge to domestic firms, which helped them to face increased foreign competition in the initial stages of trade liberalization. However, the fact that more fundamental changes are gradually taking place at the level of training and investment decisions by domestic economic agents, as well as in the institutional framework, points to the ability of Mexico's productive apparatus to compete internationally in a wide range of products on a long-term basis.[2]

The presumption of a favorable outcome from an import liberalization program, even if not entirely well-grounded, considering the short and scattered evidence one can reasonably use to assess its long-term implications, still raises the question about which areas of the economic policy spectrum are deemed suitable for further reform, in light of an overall economic strategy that demands a fast and sustainable resumption of economic growth.

I have mentioned the necessity of changes in domestic infrastructure and regulation, so that they become more congruent with an outward-looking economy. From what one can read from current economic policy trends, as well as from the demands of the business community, it is clear that these two areas will be given top priority in the policy agenda of the Salinas administration.

---

1. Multiple regression analysis involving nonoil export growth as the dependent variable and both current and lagged values of the real exchange rate (as a proxy for the level of aggregate demand) and the fraction of the domestic output of tradeable goods not subject to imports permits (as a proxy for the reforms to the trade regime) as independent variables show a strong and significant effect of the latter variable.

2. The fact that during 1987 more than one-third of Mexico's top 100 items exported to the United States were not exported in 1984 is revealing in this respect.

The import regime, even though much more open than the one that prevailed three years ago, is hardly exempt from problems. Two protectionist aspects of current trade policy deserve special attention: the lack of uniformity of import tariffs and the prevalence of import permits in some sectors of the economy.

Once an outward-looking economic strategy has been adopted, a nonuniform import tariff could make sense only as an intermediate step in the process of import liberalization. Those sectors that enjoyed the highest rate of protection during the import substitution period may need more time to adapt to an environment of freer trade. Therefore a more gradual process of tariff reduction for those sectors may be desirable. However, besides this short-term consideration, for a small country like Mexico there does not seem to be an economic rationale for a nonuniform import tariff, particularly when higher tariff rates are granted to those products closer to the stage of final demand (20 percent against a zero minimum tariff). As is well known, this type of protective scheme may give rise to levels of effective protection that are many times higher than the maximum tariff rate, a feature that may eventually become a threat to both the export expansion and productivity gains.

One notices a similar kind of problem regarding the prevalence of import permits. In addition, in three of the sectors in which import permits prevail— electronic equipment, motor vehicles, and pharmaceuticals—special industrial promotion programs have an extreme protectionist flavor. In fact, import permits were kept in place in order to prevent the interference of foreign competition with some elements of those promotion schemes. According to these programs, which are based on the ideas of "backward linkage" and "industrial multipliers," final goods industries are protected by quantitative restrictions, and at the same time they are required to incorporate a certain amount of domestic components in their production processes. Hence, the protection granted by import permits spills over to a wide range of activities linked to the sectors benefiting from industrial promotion programs. This of course makes information about the structure of protection based on the level of import tariffs somewhat misleading. Furthermore, giving shelter from foreign competition to sectors such as electronic equipment that have important effects on the productivity of other sectors of the economy and are subject to a rapid rate of technical change, is worrisome from every perspective.

Thus, despite the rapid and profound changes in Mexico's import regime, the commercial policy reforms are far from complete. However, given both the rapid pace of import liberalization and an overloaded economic policy agenda, which in many areas places traditional political support at stake, any new reforms to the trade regime are not likely to be undertaken

Table 10.2   Mexico's regional trade patterns[a]

	1981	1982	1983	1984	1985	1986	1987
United States	55.29	52.47	58.41	57.95	60.35	67.29	69.65
	(63.82)	(59.82)	(60.46)	(62.36)	(66.62)	(67.14)	(73.53)
Japan	5.97	6.84	6.78	7.66	7.73	6.42	5.58
	(4.99)	(5.68)	(3.90)	(4.43)	(5.38)	(6.25)	(7.07)
Other industrial	22.18	24.06	20.32	20.31	20.06	14.75	15.89
countries	(18.83)	(22.60)	(19.75)	(19.11)	(18.02)	(19.60)	(14.25)
Latin America	9.83	8.76	7.46	6.37	5.42	6.03	4.64
and Caribbean	(4.90)	(4.64)	(3.18)	(4.32)	(4.69)	(2.96)	(1.51)
Other developing	6.54	6.42	4.84	4.26	4.24	3.46	2.41
countries	(1.92)	(2.38)	(1.64)	(1.67)	(2.03)	(2.34)	(1.83)
Other[b]	0.19	1.45	2.19	3.44	2.19	2.05	1.83
	(5.54)	(4.88)	(11.07)	(8.10)	(3.27)	(1.71)	(1.31)

a. Percentage of Mexico's total exports. Figures in parentheses are percentage of Mexico's total imports.
b. Not elsewhere specified and nonmembers of the International Monetary Fund.

Source: International Monetary Fund. Direction of Trade Statistics, Yearbook 1988.

unilaterally. Whether the implementation of such reforms would be more likely within the framework of a trade agreement, depends largely on actual and potential trade restrictions facing Mexican products, an issue that we discuss in the next section.

Implications of a Mexico–US Free Trade Agreement for Mexico's Trade Policy

Mexico's regional trade specialization pattern is strongly biased toward the United States. During 1987, 70 percent of Mexican exports went to the United States, and that ratio has been increasing in recent years, despite both the depreciation of the dollar against other major currencies and the rapid growth and greater product diversification of Mexican exports (table 10.2). Mexican imports from the United States have behaved similarly. The high regional concentration of Mexico's foreign trade indicates little scope for trade diversion arising from an FTA between Mexico and the United States.

Another indicator in this respect is the fact that the US economy is fairly open, and even in those sectors such as textiles in which US trade policy has been more restrictive the magnitude of trade diversion should be of

Table 10.3 Nontariff barrier coverage on Mexican exports to selected industrialized countries, 1986
(percentages of 1984 nonoil exports)

Country/group	Strict NTBs	Quasi- tariff NTBs[a]	Total
United States	4.95	8.39	13.34
Japan	45.55	0.15	46.70
European Community	9.29	6.25	15.54

a. Includes countervailing duties, seasonal tariffs, supplementary tariffs, and specific taxes.

Source: Ten Kate (1988).

minor importance, considering that these sectors have also enjoyed a high degree of protection in Mexico.

Thus, for the Mexican case, further trade liberalization carried on unilaterally or only with respect to the United States is almost one and the same thing. However, as mentioned above, the possibility of further unilateral trade liberalization is now practically absent. Further trade liberalization within the framework of an FTA with the United States is in principle more likely, especially if such talks help clarify the actual and potential trade barriers facing Mexican products in the United States and in other industrial countries.

It is not easy to make a case for asphyxiating protectionism in Mexico's trading partners in a situation where its export revenue has been growing at annual rates above 20 percent for a period of more than two years. Even if one looks at the performance of exports of specific products such as textiles, iron and steel, and sugar, which are subject to fairly widespread trade barriers in industrialized countries, the situation is no less favorable. During 1987 the rates of growth of Mexican exports of these products were 79 percent, 42 percent, and 167 percent, respectively (Banco de Mexico 1988).

In fact, the figures on the coverage of nontariff barriers (NTBs) against Mexico's exports presented in table 10.3 are far from alarming, except perhaps in the case of Japan. In the case of the United States, which remains Mexico's main trading partner and has become increasingly so in spite of Mexico's major export drive, the incidence of NTBs on Mexican "potential" exports turns out to be particularly low. Moreover, in not a few cases the data refer to countervailing and antidumping duties (table 10.4), which do not necessarily mean increased protectionism.

Table 10.4 Nontariff barrier coverage of Mexican exports to the United States (percentages of 1984 nonoil exports)

	1981	1982	1983	1984	1985	1986
Strict NTBs	2.26	2.07	2.27	2.27	4.95	4.95
Voluntary restraints	—	—	—	—	2.62	2.62
Multi-Fiber Agreement	1.00	1.00	1.00	1.00	1.00	1.00
Health and safety regulations	0.98	0.98	0.98	0.98	0.98	0.98
Quota	0.30	0.30	0.40	0.40	1.00	1.00
Other	0.26	0.06	0.26	0.26	0.26	0.26
Quasi-tariff NTBs	4.47	4.47	7.62	7.99	8.39	8.39
Countervailing duties	0.11	0.27	1.41	1.77	2.21	2.21
Antidumping duties	0.80	0.80	0.80	0.80	0.80	0.80
Seasonal tariffs	2.98	2.98	2.98	2.98	2.98	2.98
Other	0.58	0.42	2.44	2.44	2.40	2.40

— = none in force.
Source: Ten Kate (1988).

However, the effects of NTBs on the export performance of some specific economic sectors have been at times dramatic. For instance, as a result of voluntary export restraints, US imports of iron and steel products from Mexico fell by 39 percent between 1984 and 1986 (Sales 1988). Moreover, as Mexico's export capacity expands, it is likely that a larger set of import restrictions will become binding,[3] and that new ones will be implemented.[4]

Even if world protectionism against Mexican products were not currently so pressing, considering the long-term character of foreign trade policy it is the current *trend* in world protectionism that matters. The figures in table 10.4 make clear the presence of an upward trend in protectionism facing Mexican products, at least in the US market. This trend is likely to continue and may even become steeper as a result of both a possible slowdown in the US economy, arising from the eventual adjustment of its fiscal deficit, and increased imports from Canada arising from the Canada–US FTA. The

---

3. For instance, although in previous years import quotas on Mexican textiles were rarely binding, during 1987 US imports of Mexican products belonging to 30 different categories under the US–Mexico bilateral agreement were almost suspended.

4. The fact that two-thirds of US countervailing duty investigations initiated against Mexican products involved products with a previous export increase of more than 50 percent illustrates the likelihood of this event.

reduction in trade barriers among the members of the EC may have a similar implication regarding protective measures facing Mexican products in that region.

Given Mexico's actual economic prospects, however, world protectionism is no reason to retreat from import liberalization. The negative impact that protectionism had in the past on the productivity of Mexico's industrial sector would imply a devastating effect on the economy, now that oil prices are low and the support provided by foreign borrowing is quite restricted. Nevertheless, world protectionism would result in a less successful import liberalization effort, regarding both terms-of-trade losses and a slower reaction in some sectors arising from an uncertain access of their products to foreign markets.

Therefore, considering the benefits on the Mexican side of both additional trade liberalization and a wider and more secure access of Mexican products in the US market, an FTA between Mexico and the United States would certainly improve Mexico's economic prospects. Moreover, trade concessions by the United States in some key products, such as textiles, iron and steel, automobiles and parts, and some agricultural products, may be an important political element for inducing further trade liberalization in Mexico.

Conclusions

This chapter has analyzed the basic economic implications of a free trade agreement between Mexico and the United States. Special attention has been placed on the potential economic gains, from the Mexican point of view, derived from such an agreement. In this respect the following factors should be emphasized.

Traditional gains from trade arguments suggest that greater benefits from import liberalization arise for economies whose economic structure fulfills two characteristics: strong differences between its trading partners, and flexibility in the resource allocation process. Fulfillment of the first of these conditions seems fairly obvious for the case of Mexico and the United States. The rapid response of Mexico's nonoil exports to the joint effect of the 1986 oil price slide and the import liberalization program points favorably to the fulfillment of the second. Moreover, the response of the Mexican economy to increased foreign competition in a wide range of products suggests a favorable outcome in terms of long-term productivity gains from a more open trade strategy. In any case, slow growth in the productivity of Mexico's industrial sector during the latter years of the import substitution regime points up the advantage of a more open trade strategy.

In this respect the rapid and profound changes implemented recently in Mexico's import regime are more than welcome. However, regarding commercial policy, the task is far from complete. The actual structure of protection still results in marked discriminatory treatment toward different sectors of the economy, and this may eventually preclude some of the advantages of trade liberalization mentioned above. Thus, the current economic strategy would be better grounded if additional trade reforms were implemented.

Further trade liberalization carried on within the framework of an FTA with the United States may have additional advantages in terms of providing an effective mechanism for overcoming trade barriers on Mexican exports. Even though world protectionism is not currently a matter of great concern from the point of view of Mexican exports, the recent extraordinary growth of Mexican nonoil exports as well as actual trends toward greater protectionism in industrial countries suggest that this problem will become more pressing in the future. Moreover, considering the pace of Mexico's import liberalization, as well as the fact that economic reforms lag in other areas, it is hard to imagine an immediate movement toward a freer trade regime without some concessions on the part of Mexico's main trading partner.

References

Banco de Mexico. 1987. *Indicadores del Sector Externo,* December.

International Monetary Fund. 1988. *Directions of Trade Statistics.* Washington: International Monetary Fund.

Sales, Carlos. 1988. *Proteccionismo Comercial de los Estados Unidos Hacia Mexico, 1980–1986* (dissertation). Mexico City: ITAM.

Samaniego, Ricardo. 1985. "The Evolution of Total Factor Productivity in the Manufacturing Sector in Mexico, 1972–1982." *Documentos de Investigacion.* Mexico City: El Colegio de Mexico.

Ten Kate, Adrian. 1988. "Mexico's Participation in the Uruguay Round, Issues Related to Non-tariff Barriers" (typewritten). Mexico City: January.

Weintraub, Sidney. 1984. *Free Trade Between Mexico and the United States?* Washington: Brookings Institution.

Comments

Joseph A. Greenwald

Much of the discussion of the free trade area (FTA) question revolves around broad principles or particular country issues. What I am going to do is use the US–Mexico case to walk through the options for trade liberalization on a bilateral basis following the conclusion of the US–Mexico Framework Agreement on Trade and Investment of November 1987. The options include formulas for bilateral negotiations that fall short of an FTA as well as more comprehensive agreements. They are not mutually exclusive. In some cases, more than one option could be pursued.

I believe this is not just an academic exercise. Professor Trigueros' paper indicates that trade liberalization has worked well for Mexico and that Mexico probably will look favorably on further steps forward. My hope is that our work on liberalization options not only will be useful in the US–Mexico context, but also will throw some light on the concrete problems that arise in connection with proposals for bilateral negotiations between countries at different levels of development.

Another reason for taking this broader approach of looking at all options rather than just an FTA (however defined) is that the real risk to the multilateral system is not from genuine FTAs that satisfy the requirements of GATT Article XXIV, but from dubious arrangements that fall short of a true FTA. The history of FTAs in the GATT era is checkered, to say the least. The EC–EFTA agreements and the EC arrangements with North African countries are good examples of the abuse of the FTA concept.

The first and simplest option, which is being followed now, is the process set in motion by the "Immediate Action Agenda" appended to the Bilateral Framework Agreement. This agenda calls for consultations on a number of product sectors—textiles, agricultural products, steel, and electronics—as well as functional areas such as investment, technology transfer, intellectual property, and services. To date, this has been primarily a problem-solving (in the cases of steel, textiles, and alcoholic beverages) and information-exchanging (in the case of electronics, investment, intellectual property, and services) operation.

It is difficult to tell at this early stage where these consultations might lead. Of course, product sector discussions have the potential to result in restrictive or managed arrangements, or sectoral liberalization deals.

The second option is the classic bilateral negotiation of trade concessions

Joseph A. Greenwald is former Assistant Secretary of State for Economic and Business Affairs.

to be applied on a most-favored-nation (MFN) basis. This liberalization of border measures could be done outside or within the context of GATT multilateral negotiations. The problem with this option is finding enough "principal supplier" items that would not result in unrequited third-party benefits.

The third liberalization option is sectoral negotiations. If such bilateral negotiations were directed to product sectors and "substantially all" trade was not covered, a GATT waiver or violation might be involved. However, GATT rules currently do not cover functional issues such as investment, services, and intellectual property. As such, there could be purely bilateral agreements on these functional issues without running into GATT problems. A hybrid variation might couple MFN tariff cuts with preferential, functional concessions.

The fourth liberalization option is preferential treatment (for example, duty-free treatment) of Mexican goods entering the United States. This option would require new US legislation, even if it were to be implemented under the Generalized System of Preferences program. It also would raise fundamental problems regarding consistency with the GATT.

The fifth option is a GATT-consistent FTA or comprehensive trade and investment agreement on the US–Canada model, possibly including a bilateral dispute settlement arrangement. This option could take the form of an interim agreement leading to the formation of an FTA as foreseen in GATT Article XXIV, paragraphs 5(b) and 7. To take account of the disparity in the level of economic development between the parties, the interim agreement could provide for a certain décalage or asymmetry in the plan and schedule the reduction and removal, within a reasonable period of time, of duties and other restrictive regulations of commerce on substantially all the trade between the constituent territories in products originating in such territories. In other words, the United States would move more rapidly than Mexico to implement trade reforms. In the initial stage, Mexico's contribution might be in the services, intellectual property, and investment areas, with a commitment to further liberalization.

The final suggestion is for a North American Free Trade Area, or NAFTA. In essence, this would involve Mexico joining the Canada–US Free Trade Area. It seems to me that simple Mexican adherence probably is not feasible in the near term. In any event, such a move would require substantial renegotiation of the Canada–US FTA. Whether it might be a step that follows the US–Mexico FTA option or a direct move to a NAFTA is pretty far in the future and will depend on the evolution of trade relations in North America.

Since the 1988 elections in the United States and Mexico, both sides have repeated their desire for further progress in trade liberalization. The new

Mexican Secretary of Commerce, Jaime Serra Puche, has talked about seeking bilateral sectoral accords as the first step toward a comprehensive agreement with the United States. However, for GATT reasons, and in light of the US experience with Canada, the sectoral approach may not prove fruitful. It is difficult to agree on the sectors to be included and even harder to negotiate a balanced package of concessions.

11

Multilateralism Versus Preferential Bilateralism: A European View

Paul Luyten

A number of distinguished personalities in this part of the world have hailed the Canada–US free trade agreement as one that maintains the momentum for trade liberalization; that boosts the GATT and the Uruguay Round; that could serve as a directional beacon offering guidance to a rudderless trading system; and that is pathbreaking in the areas of investment and services. Never before have I heard so many North Americans—indeed, hardly ever Europeans—speak and write so effusively, in lofty, almost sublime terms, about a preferential trading arrangement.

A prosaic appreciation more simply suggests that the Canada–US agreement neither strengthens the multilateral system nor erodes it. What it will do is enlarge the share of world trade that is conducted free of border obstacles. Whether the solutions in the agreement that cover unfair trade issues and dispute settlement and the subject matters of services and investment will eventually serve as a catalyst for the Uruguay Round in these areas remains to be seen.

Nevertheless, the euphoria brought about by this agreement seems now to have led some leading Americans to seize upon this newly discovered free trade area technique as a means to solve all kinds of trade problems, both those that find their source within the United States and those it encounters with several of its partners. Part of it all may well be the brandishing of this approach as a threat to exercise pressure on trading partners.

I shall try here to offer a view from Western Europe—tinted by European Commission glasses—but no longer speaking on behalf of the commission, which I left more than a year ago to lead a less agitated life.

Paul Luyten is an adviser to the European Service Industries Forum and was formerly a deputy director general of the European Commission in Brussels.

271

EC Preferential Trade Arrangements

Many who are familiar with the preferential trade policies of the European Community (EC) over the last 30 years may well be waiting with amused or even ironic curiosity to hear how an ex-representative of the EC copes with the subject of free trade areas. I shall try not to disappoint this healthy curiosity. To start, a very short flashback on that part of the EC's external relations history that deals with preferential trading arrangements may well be in order.

Some time after the successful ending of the Kennedy Round in 1967, during a GATT debate on discrimination in trade, a British minister, talking about the EC's sprawling network of preferential arrangements, said that it reminded him of the saying that Great Britain had built its empire "in a fit of absentmindedness."

During the life span of the GATT, the EC has been the major user of its Article XXIV provisions concerning customs unions and free trade areas. Indeed, it is itself the expression not simply of a customs union, but of an economic union, even if a still imperfect one. From the very outset, in 1958, going beyond the common market of the six, free trade was progressively generalized between the EC and the overseas countries and territories in Africa, then mostly dependencies of France, the Netherlands, Belgium, and Italy. These territories had, in accordance with special GATT provisions, traditionally enjoyed duty-free access to their metropolitan markets, on which all depended for their economic survival.

From 1961 on, starting with Greece and followed by Turkey and thereafter all the other countries bordering the Mediterranean, with the exception of Albania and Libya, the EC negotiated preferential agreements of various kinds as part of what came to be known as the EC's global Mediterranean policy. In the meantime, upon obtaining their independence, the previous colonies with one exception renewed their preferential links with the EC in the Yaoundé Convention, which later on became the Lomé Convention.

With the first enlargement of the EC in 1973, this overseas network was further extended to cover a number of African, Caribbean, and Pacific countries with links with the United Kingdom, and in Western Europe free trade agreements were concluded between the nine EC members and each of the remaining countries of the European Free Trade Association (EFTA), so that the free trade already achieved among the EFTA countries was preserved.

All this naturally raised criticism in the GATT. A number of critics, led by the United States, maintained that none of these arrangements met the essential test of GATT Article XXIV concerning the elimination of barriers to substantially all trade, particularly as regards agricultural products. The

EC, for its part, as well as the partners to the various arrangements, maintained on the other hand that all the GATT requirements had been fully met and that it was up to the GATT contracting parties, if they wished to do so, to reject the arrangements or to recommend modifications. The resulting standoff in the GATT contributed to a growing sense of dissatisfaction with the GATT system in a number of countries and unquestionably led to increased friction between the EC and the United States over trade policy.

Finally, in 1974, the EC reached an understanding with the United States on what was then called the "proliferation issue." Although never formalized and rather imprecise, the sense of the so-called Casey–Soames understanding was that the EC would geographically limit its preferential policy to countries bordering the Mediterranean and that it would no longer insist on reverse preferences from the African, Caribbean, and Pacific associates and from its less developed Mediterranean partners. What the EC considered it obtained in exchange was an armistice on the legal issue in the GATT and on the possible trade consequences of these preferences for the United States. This expectation was to be disappointed later on in the US–EC dispute over citrus products.

In accordance with the understanding, the agreements with almost all the developing partners accorded preferential status became one-way free entry into the EC (i.e., a kind of much improved Generalized System of Preferences [GSP]). The only exceptions were Malta, Cyprus, Israel, and Turkey; with these countries the intention was confirmed to implement full Article XXIV agreements in due course.

This brief summary of a lengthy and complicated history shows that the EC has been and remains a champion practitioner of preferential trade arrangements, and that this is something it ought to remember when it looks at the behavior others might wish to adopt.

Beyond Geographical Regionalism

How then does the EC see its own policies with respect to preferential bilateralism, and how does it look at a possible new American approach? The EC's point of departure, its axiom, is that Western Europe has a natural vocation to unify, if not politically at least economically. Preferential regional agreements in conformity with the GATT, bringing together contiguous customs territories, are likely to lead to single marketplaces with trade creation effects exceeding some inevitable trade diversion effects.

The second point is that the EC's other arrangements, the non-Western European ones, apply as between the EC and developing countries, with

Israel arguably an exception. Those pacts with overseas countries (i.e., the African, Caribbean, and Pacific countries in the Lomé Convention) are all one-sided, granting almost complete and unlimited access in a kind of enhanced GSP to the benefit of what are mostly least-advanced developing countries.

The third point is that all other arrangements at present remain within the geographic limits of the Mediterranean basin, in the immediate neighborhood of the EC—what the Romans used to call *mare nostrum*. Size apart, this coverage is geographically and technically not dissimilar from the one-way arrangement of the United States with the Caribbean.

While the GATT rules about customs unions and free trade areas are silent on the issue of geographical proximity, it is a striking fact that most of the reciprocal preferential trade arrangements that exist in the rest of the world—in Europe (Finland with Eastern Europe), in Latin America and the Caribbean, in Australasia, and in North America—can be considered as "geographically" regional. Outstanding exceptions are the US–Israel free trade area, the intra-Comecon arrangements that link Eastern Europe with Cuba, North Korea, and Outer Mongolia; and the so-called Generalized System of Trade Preferences among developing countries, which has been under negotiation for quite a while.

Set against all that, what is being contemplated now by some in the United States goes well beyond "geographical regionalism" in the narrow sense. Nor is it any longer about granting one-way preferential access to less advanced nations as in the Caribbean case. The novelty is preferential reciprocal bilateralism beyond any regional concept that would, in addition, go beyond tariffs, quantitative restrictions, and other border barriers into many other areas of commercial and economic policy such as fair trade rules, nontariff barriers, services, investment, and intellectual property.

I submit that such a crisscrossing of the world with bilateral deals could hardly help the American economy, let alone the trading system, and, what is even more important, that it would prevent the United States from ensuring its necessary continued leadership in world trading affairs.

Implications for the EC

An assessment of the possible impact on the EC of the conclusion of further free trade areas by the United States with countries such as Japan, Korea, Taiwan, the ASEAN countries, or Australia hinges on a multitude of assumptions about the partners to such pacts, on their content and particularly their subject matter, and on the length and modalities of transitional periods.

Before formulating any views on the consequences of such developments, one must recall that today, in the industrialized countries, thanks to the successes of the GATT over the last 40 years, tariffs and other classic border obstacles are by any historical standards very low for most goods, except the major temperate zone agricultural products. Thus the overall evolution of trade flows is currently much less influenced by the removal of the remaining such barriers than by other incomparably more potent factors such as movement of real exchange rates, the expansion or contraction of national economies, the flows of direct investments or disinvestments, or even massive export promotion campaigns.

The argument of a relatively minimal impact would apply to the US market and that of Japan, and for obvious reasons those of Hong Kong and Singapore as well, if we limit the analysis to the consequences of classic free trade areas, that is, trade pacts dealing strictly with tariffs, quantitative restrictions, and other formal border barriers to trade.

Exports of the EC to the United States that could be hit are relatively few: textiles and clothing, shoes, ceramics and porcelain, glassware, processed fish, and some other products where high tariffs still apply. Agricultural exports to the United States, because of their composition and the present obstacles that hamper trade, would not be significantly affected.

In other nontariff barrier areas, such as government procurement, technical standards, sanitary regulations, escape clause measures, and similar actions, the possibility of most-favored-nation (MFN) suppliers being hurt on the US market remains much more substantial, even if, with regard to fair trade rules, it looks hardly likely that a preferential treatment of any real substance would be offered by the United States to any of the putative partners. It was precisely fear of action by the United States in some of these areas that constituted a powerful inducement for the Canadians to strike a deal with their neighbor. Whatever assurances they obtained are not necessarily going to be offered to other possible free trade partners, however.

Japan's tariffs on manufactured products are on the whole low, and there are few import quotas or similar formal barriers to imports of industrial products at the border. Agricultural exports to Japan are hampered by high barriers and are thus minimal. Some already suffer from de facto discrimination in favor of the United States. However, a free trade area with the United States would end any hopes of ever improving the EC's presence in the Japanese market in many agricultural product areas. More importantly, it is unclear what a free trade area could achieve in terms of changes in informal barriers, imbedded in Japan's economic system and culture, such as the distribution system, the old boy network, the buy-Japan mentality, and restrictive business practices. Another unanswerable question is whether, if somehow lifted for the United States, those hidden obstacles could continue to operate as efficiently as before against other partners of Japan or, on the contrary, whether they would become the catalyst of their speedy disappearance.

Evidently, the preferential abolition in favor of the United States of the still formidable border obstacles maintained by Korea, Taiwan, and the ASEAN countries (other than Singapore and Brunei), as well as those of Australia, although to a decreasing extent, could hit EC exports hard. In 1987 these markets absorbed, respectively, 1.08, 1.01, 1.68, and 1.64 percent of total EC exports.

It would be even more hazardous to make a guess about the possible consequences of the exchange of preferential concessions between the United States and its various possible partners in fields such as services, intellectual property, and investment, not hitherto under GATT discipline, and where the wave of liberalization that reduced obstacles such as tariffs and eliminated quantitative restrictions has not yet applied. There the scope for discriminatory treatment against third parties could theoretically be large and the repercussions severe. An example of this is the preferential treatment Korea is bestowing on the United States in the field of patents. Because of its relatively limited scope, at least initially, the precedent set by the United States and Canada is reassuring, particularly in view of the fact that these two countries are much closer and more similar in cultures and traditions than any other pair of countries considered here. Over the longer term, reciprocal preferential liberalization probably would develop and could thus gradually damage interests of third parties such as the EC. The conclusion of such trade agreements would also have repercussions on the general trade policy behavior of the United States and its various possible partners and affect third parties.

Jean Royer, a Havana Conference delegate for France who later became the deputy of Eric Wyndham White, the GATT's first director general, used to claim that partners in free trade areas would normally be inclined to reduce customs duties vis-à-vis third parties in all cases where they did not protect local production and in fact only ensured a margin of preference for the industries of the partner. He claimed that in exchange for reciprocal concessions from third parties the free trade partner would more readily reduce such obstacles. If there is something to this argument, it is probably that a free trade area, and even a customs union as the recent experience of Spain and Portugal shows, enhances competitive pressures and thus leads to the elimination of certain activities, which in turn facilitates the removal of obstacles against third countries.

What is to be expected, however, is that once the United States through its free trade arrangements has obtained from its partners access for its own products and possibly services, third parties will no longer be in the position they were before, when the United States obtained access through bilateral pressures to claim identical treatment on the basis of the MFN rule of the GATT. Up to now, discrimination in favor of the United States, consequent upon its bullying and threats, often took the form of product selection, as for example in the Taiwan market, which was opened for cigarettes and wine and beer, but not for spirits, which is of small interest to US exporters.

It is hard to see what the rest of the developed world, including the EC, would be prepared to offer—indeed what it could offer—in terms of improved access to its own markets to obtain MFN liberalization from the United States' free trade partners. Markets are on the whole already wide open, and the substantial obstacles that remain, such as for major temperate zone agricultural products, textiles and clothing, and a few others, are the hard core—those that require tremendous political stamina to remove.

Thus, the immediate negative effects do not seem to be as important as the potential longer-term ones, with discrimination in the markets of the partners of the United States deepening with the progressive reduction of barriers and the widening of agreements to cover an expanding range of trade-related policies. The United States, a pathbreaking bulldozer opener of the relatively closed markets of several of these Asian partners, would no longer be there to help other GATT partners enjoy at least some of the benefits on the basis of the MFN rule. What one could expect, however, would be a further rise in tensions between the EC and those of the potential partners that maintain highly protective import policies (except vis-à-vis the United States) and that accumulate huge and rising trade surpluses overall and with the EC.

I will conclude this brief and inevitably highly tentative assessment of the repercussions on the EC of such a bilateral preferential policy of the United States with a prediction. Although not greatly affected by the immediate and direct impact of any such free trade areas that the United States might wish to conclude beyond its geographic region, the EC would consider such a move regrettable primarily because of its adverse effects on the quest for a balanced and strengthened multilateral trading order. A secondary concern would be the direct economic damage not so much on the US market, but rather on those of the rapidly growing and still little-accessible markets of several of the possible Asian partners.

Because of its size and its present and potential links with other nations of Europe and of the rest of the world, the "juggernaut," as the EC was called in the GATT some years ago, would be quite capable of taking care of itself. Likely consequences would be a reinforcement of the internal cohesion of the EC, a further broadening and deepening of its special links with many partners and associates, and the conclusion of further preferential agreements with those nations in the world that might turn to it for help and comfort.

Conclusion

Through their active participation in the Uruguay Round, both the United States and the EC demonstrate that their trade and related economic policies continue to focus on multilateralism. That is obviously the course to be preferred. Bilateral approaches in parallel to the main global thrust are welcome as long as they move nations toward a more open trading system without discrimination in the form of privileged access or import commitments.

Bilateral preferential formulas taking the form of geographically regional free trade areas or customs unions are acceptable, provided they conform to the GATT provisions and thus increase trade not only between the countries concerned, but with other partners as well. Arrangements that are not geographically regional should be avoided, as they are not likely to lead to single markets and thus to create trade, but will rather divert it. Such deals tend to disrupt the present trading order.

I would add that, if the multilateral negotiations in Geneva, now entering their third year, were to show that truly multilateral results cannot be achieved in the coming few years, I feel certain that not only the United States but also the EC, tired by the GATT's delays, will without formally disengaging from the multilateral system enter into trade pacts with groups of countries willing to do so. In their mildest form, they would consist of plurilateral agreements with like-minded partners in certain subject areas within or outside the present GATT purview. The benefits would be restricted to the participants, access to other GATT members would be open on the basis only of reciprocal commitments, and, as far as possible, standard GATT rights to equal treatment of outsiders would not be abridged by the new disciplines.

If other parties refuse to allow such arrangements to be administered in the GATT (like some of the Tokyo Round codes), then the OECD framework or an ad hoc formula will be sought. This process then would simply be the recognition of a new reality, namely, that the multilateral world requires more options—preferably inside the GATT, otherwise outside.

In an alternative, much more aggressive scenario the United States, exasperated by the GATT's morass, might choose the bilateral preferential course and set about crisscrossing the world with bilateral free trade areas and mutually beneficial ties beyond its regional sphere. Such a course would have a profound impact on the still basically multilateral trading order patiently built up over the last 40 years. In that event, I would predict, the EC would for its part also move further in that direction, not simply in response to requests from its partners as hitherto, but robustly as an initiator of such deals, with countries to the east and west in Europe and beyond. That would be tantamount to consciously and vigorously resuming what was until 1973 a drift into preferentialism throughout the Mediterranean, when the Casey–Soames understanding brought it to a halt and turned the African, Caribbean, and Pacific pact and the Maghreb and Mashrek country agreements into one-way free trade arrangements.

In an extreme version of this scenario, the two trading giants, polarizing parts of the world around them, would fragment the international economy to the detriment of all nations, small and large, and particularly those that depend on an open world economy to redress their present external imbalances. The EC, for its part, is big enough to find this approach viable, but I am convinced that it would not wish to carry the responsibility for unleashing such a turn of events.

For both the EC and the United States it would be far better to continue to focus energies on shaping an international cooperative approach to the management of trade and the world economy. It would be far preferable also to strengthen the GATT, not ignore it, and to clarify and broaden the application of its rules, so that they can be enforced more easily rather than resort to poker-like tactics and strategies that risk dividing the world and reducing the prospects for peace and prosperity for all.

12

The Effect of New Free Trade Areas on EFTA

Per Magnus Wijkman

This chapter considers what effects free trade agreements between the United States and countries around the Pacific Basin would have on the six members of the European Free Trade Association (EFTA): Austria, Finland, Iceland, Norway, Sweden, and Switzerland. Unlike most other European countries outside the European Community (EC), the EFTA countries are highly integrated into the international trading system that binds the market economies together. Consequently, any changes in the trade regimes prevailing among them could have an immediate and major impact. Two such impacts are discussed in this chapter: the impact on EFTA trade flows and the impact on the international trade system. Thereafter, likely policy responses by EFTA countries are discussed in a general way.

Some Characteristics of EFTA Countries

With their average population about 5 million, members of EFTA are rather typical small, open economies. Each EFTA country is trade dependent, with exports of goods amounting to about one-quarter of GDP, and imports to a couple of percentage points more. The EFTA countries' trade is concentrated in Western Europe (i.e., the 18 countries of the EC and EFTA), with about 70 percent of exports going there and 75 percent of imports originating there.

The EFTA countries are thus closely integrated through trade with other countries in Western Europe. This integration is not confined within each of the two groupings, EFTA and the EC, but applies between countries in

Per Magnus Wijkman is Director of the Economic Affairs Department, EFTA Secretariat, Geneva. The author is solely responsible for the views expressed, which do not necessarily represent the views of the EFTA Council or of the Member Governments.

different blocs as well. Individually, the EFTA member states are as integrated in the EC through trade as are the EC member states themselves. No sharp economic borderlines can be drawn separating the 18 countries of Western Europe; rather, these countries constitute a single economic space. In this space, the EFTA countries collectively are equivalent, as Paul Krugman has phrased it, to "another France—hardly a minor addition" (Krugman 1988, 13). As a group, they constitute the EC's largest trading partner, equivalent to the United States and Japan combined.

The EFTA countries are more dependent on the EC than the EC is on EFTA. First, the EC simply has more and larger members than EFTA. Second, the EC countries conduct a common external trade policy, whereas the EFTA countries do not. Each EFTA country tends to deal individually with the EC Commission.

Two important policy conclusions follow from these characteristics. First, trade dependency makes the EFTA countries strong supporters of free trade. There is widespread public awareness in these small, full-employment economies that a tariff on imports constitutes a tax on exports. The EFTA countries have been prepared to reduce their tariffs in exchange for market access globally and regionally. Their governments have participated actively in the GATT's negotiating rounds. As a result, the EFTA countries' most-favored-nation tariff rates on industrial goods are low, ranging from an average of 1.9 percent in Switzerland to an average of 5.7 percent in Austria. The EFTA average tariff of 3.0 percent on industrial goods is less than the EC average of 4.0 percent (see Herin 1986, table 1). The EFTA countries are among those industrial countries with the lowest industrial tariffs.

In addition, the EFTA countries have reduced barriers to trade regionally through trade arrangements in conformity with the GATT. Today, the 18 countries of EFTA and the EC, with a combined population of 350 million, constitute the largest free trade area (FTA) for industrial goods in the world. Tariffs and quotas on trade in industrial products were eliminated within Western Europe by 1984, but many nontariff measures remain.[1]

Second, the EFTA countries' smallness explains why they support a strong international trading system—one that is transparent, liberal, and nondiscriminatory and possesses an effective dispute settlement mechanism. They favor a trading system that allows trade to be determined by competitive power in the marketplace rather than by political power around the

---

1. Tariff reduction took place in two steps. The first was the elimination of tariffs and quantitative restrictions on industrial goods within the EC and EFTA blocs. The second step, after the United Kingdom and Denmark left EFTA for the EC in 1972, involved tariff elimination between the two blocs pursuant to identical free trade agreements between an enlarged community and each remaining EFTA member.

Table 12.1 Distribution of EFTA countries' exports of manufactures, 1987 (percentages)

Country	EC	US	Japan	ASEAN	Korea	Australia	Pacific	World
Austria	63.0	3.7	1.2	0.7	0.4	0.4	6.5	100.0
Finland	39.0	5.5	1.2	1.0	0.3	1.0	9.0	100.0
Iceland	52.8	10.3	7.2	0.0	0.0	0.0	17.5	100.0
Norway	47.2	7.2	1.7	1.9	0.7	0.9	12.3	100.0
Sweden	49.1	12.1	1.5	1.2	0.4	1.2	16.4	100.0
Switzerland	55.4	8.9	3.9	1.8	0.5	0.9	16.0	100.0
Total EFTA	52.3	8.3	2.2	1.3	0.4	0.9	13.2	100.0

Source: United Nations, *COMTRADE.* Manufactures consist of SITC 5-8. For statistical reasons, Taiwan is not included.

negotiating table. They have resisted the use of instruments of the "new protectionism" such as orderly marketing and voluntary restraint agreements and other gray area measures. These nontransparent, discriminatory, and bilaterally applied measures politicize trade. In the game of power politics, small countries stand to lose. They therefore prefer a system that applies the same rules of the game to big players as to small.

There is no conflict between participation in regional free trade in Europe and the EFTA countries' support for a strong multilateral, liberal international trading system. Both regional and multilateral reductions of tariffs and nontariff barriers are motivated by a desire for freer trade. Given the low external tariffs of the member countries, trade diversion due to regional free trade is limited.

The Impact on EFTA Trade of More FTAs

A preferential arrangement discriminates against outsiders by definition. Discrimination will be serious for an outsider if its major markets and its major competitors join in a preferential area with large preference margins. Such a combination of factors in an FTA makes trade diversion likely. How will free trade arrangements between the United States and countries in the Pacific Basin affect the EFTA countries? Table 12.1 indicates the overall importance of the United States and selected countries in the Pacific Basin as markets for the EFTA countries' exports of manufactures.[2] The select

---

2. Ninety percent of EFTA exports to the region consist of manufactures (Standard International Trade Classification [SITC] 5–8); hence we concentrate on these.

Pacific Basin countries together take 13 percent of EFTA countries' exports, which is almost as much as the EFTA countries' exports to each other. To minimize the importance of the Pacific Basin countries listed in the table would therefore be to minimize the value of EFTA cooperation itself. Iceland, Sweden, and Switzerland are more dependent on that region as an export market than the EFTA average. Austria and Finland are less dependent, since trade with Eastern Europe plays a more important role for them. The United States is the major market among these countries and accounts for three-quarters of EFTA exports to the region. The share of Japan and the Asian newly industrializing countries (NICs) is small but growing rapidly. Trade diversion on the US market therefore will be a primary concern for all EFTA countries if free trade agreements are concluded between the United States and East Asian countries.

The Pacific Basin also contains major competitors of the EFTA countries. The experience of Sweden is probably representative. The relative importance of major countries and country groups as competitors to Swedish manufactures on the North American and Western European markets is summarized in table 12.2. Since 1970, Japan, ASEAN, and the NICs have rapidly emerged as major competitors in this market. Together these countries account for 18 percent of the competition that Sweden faces in this market in 1984, and they surpass the United States and equal West Germany in importance. Their importance as competitors in the US market alone and in each others' markets is considerably greater. Hence, most EFTA countries will find that free trade agreements between the United States and East Asian countries will include major competitors.

In sum, trade agreements between the United States and countries in the Pacific Basin combine important and growing markets for EFTA exports with major and growing competitors of the EFTA countries. This creates a presumption that such agreements could have a nonnegligible impact on EFTA exports.

The importance of intra-trade, or trade within the proposed preferential trade arrangements, is a rough indicator of the scope for trade diversion. Of course, the extent of trade diversion is affected as well by the size of preferential margins and by elasticities of supply for members relative to nonmembers. While recognizing these factors in passing, I focus here on the current level of intra-trade in a proposed free trade area.

Table 12.3 presents the data for five posited FTAs. For each area, imports of manufactures from the world, from members of the same bloc (intra-trade), and from the EFTA countries are given.[3]

---

3. In the following I shall assume that the FTA being contemplated concerns only goods and not services. Whether it includes agricultural goods as well as industrial

Table 12.2   Relative importance of selected competitors to Sweden in Western Europe and North America
(percentages)[a]

Country/group	1970	1975	1981	1984
West Germany	21.1	20.7	19.3	18.2
United States	11.9	11.1	11.7	9.9
Japan	5.4	6.8	9.0	9.9
France	7.1	8.3	8.2	7.7
United Kingdom	10.6	8.3	7.3	6.4
Select EC	19.2	20.1	19.8	19.6
Select EFTA	8.4	8.0	8.0	7.6
Select OECD	6.2	5.2	5.1	6.5
Socialist countries	2.7	3.5	2.9	2.1
ASEAN, NICs	2.3	3.7	5.9	8.1
Other	5.1	4.2	3.0	4.2
Total	100.0	100.0	100.0	100.0

a. Data are given as percentage shares of each country's or group's exports in the imports (of manufactures, SITC 5-8) of the 15 major North American and Western European countries, weighted by these 15 countries' shares in Sweden's exports.

Select EC: Belgium, Denmark, Italy, Netherlands, and Spain.
Select EFTA: Austria, Finland, Norway, and Switzerland.
Select OECD: Australia, Canada, Iceland, New Zealand, and Portugal.
NICs: Brazil, Hong Kong, Mexico, South Korea, and Taiwan.

Source: Juth (1985).

The value of EFTA exports to each of the first four bilateral FTAs listed in table 12.3 is approximately $US 10.5 billion. It is considerably larger when all four of these FTAs are aggregated and multilateralized. It is considerably less when the United States is excluded. While it must be borne in mind that effects on specific firms, industries, and sectors can be quite different, table 12.3 suggests some aggregate effects.

Case 1

The threat for EFTA of trade diversion is smallest in the case of an FTA with Australia. Trade diversion is likely to be limited to the Australian

goods is not of primary concern for the EFTA countries. We therefore focus on manufactures. Equivalent statistics are given in the text for machinery and transport equipment (SITC 7) when appropriate.

Table 12.3 Imports of six hypothetical FTAs, 1985
(manufactures)

Free trade area	Area's imports from (million $US)			Share in total imports (%)	
	World	Area	EFTA	Area	EFTA
1. US + Australia	277,635.9	5,213.3	10,306.1	1.9	3.7
2. US + Korea	277,124.3	14,136.7	10,219.0	5.1	3.7
3. US + ASEAN[a]	298,582.7	20,320.2	10,771.5	6.8	3.6
4. US + Japan	295,248.6	84,452.2	11,134.4	28.6	3.8
5. US + all four	372,024.2	157,731.1	14,103.3	42.4	3.8
6. Excluding US	83,998.0	37,461.0	4,661.0	44.6	5.5

a. The six ASEAN countries' imports from each other are included in area imports. ASEAN is, however, far from being a single market.

Source: United Nations, *COMTRADE*, SITC 5-8.

market, as US exports to Australia could benefit from relatively high preference margins there. However, the Australian market has a low weight for EFTA countries (0.9 percent), although it may be important for individual firms. An FTA between the United States and Australia would have little intra-trade (2 percent).

Case 2

An FTA with the Republic of Korea would have an intra-trade ratio of 5 percent in manufactures. Trade flows between these two countries are larger than in the first alternative. While South Korea is less important for the EFTA countries as a market than in Australia, it is more important as a competitor. Thus, the EFTA countries would experience trade diversion in the important US market in addition to trade diversion in the Korean market, as the result of large preference margins in the latter.

Case 3

An FTA with the ASEAN countries would have an intra-trade ratio of 7 percent in manufactures (8 percent in machinery). The ASEAN is a larger market for the EFTA countries (1.3 percent) than is Korea. Trade diversion on the ASEAN market would be greater than in the preceding case, whereas trade diversion on the US market might be about the same. The ASEAN countries are unlikely to realize internal free trade in the near future.

Case 4

The fourth case is dramatically different. An FTA with Japan, while representing the same amount of imports as in the preceding case, would have 29 percent of intra-trade in manufactures (38 percent in machinery). The potential for trade diversion is large both on the Japanese market and on the US market. Although preference margins are not as large as in preceding cases, preferential abolition of quotas would have large equivalent effects.

Case 5

The bilateral FTAs considered in the four previous cases may be added together and multilateralized to include trade between each pair of participating countries. The total imports of manufactures into the preferential area rise by one-third, to $372 billion in 1985, representing about one-third of world trade. Of this, 42 percent is intra-trade (50 percent for machinery). This is hardly surprising, as the area includes the two largest industrial countries of the world. These countries trade intensively with each other; each is also a major trading partner for other countries in the region. In a number of participating countries, preference margins will be sufficiently large to divert trade. These countries took 13 percent of EFTA countries' imports in 1987.

The conclusion to be drawn from all of these cases depends on how informal nontariff barriers to trade are regulated in the bilateral agreements. Should the FTAs effectively prohibit the use of quantitative restrictions against participating countries, the EFTA countries could expect greater competition in markets where they are currently indirectly protected by various gray area measures (Hamilton 1988). Conversely, for many potential partners in an FTA with the United States, the major gain probably lies in obtaining secure and unrestricted market access rather than in eliminating low tariff rates.

The Systemic Impact of More FTAs

As strong supporters of a multilateral, liberal trading system based on rules rather than on power, the EFTA countries would have reason to be concerned about the realization of two of the Pacific Basin options discussed above because of their systemic effects as well.

Any single bilateral agreement other than a US–Japan agreement, which would have a systemic impact, would not by itself be cause for concern. Preferential arrangements have several negative impacts on the international trading system. As already stressed, they are inherently discriminatory and outsiders suffer from trade diversion. They increase the role of bargaining power in trade policy and lead to bloc building. They can reduce the momentum for global liberalization as insiders resist most-favored-nation tariff reductions in order to protect preferential margins.

Taken together, the four bilateral options in table 12.3 would pose an even more serious threat to the international trading system than a US–Japan agreement. Such an outcome would create a network of bilateral trading arrangements, with the United States as the hub country. The United States and each party to a bilateral agreement would provide each other with privileged access to their markets. (Designing and enforcing rules of origin could well prove a daunting task.) These access rights would be especially valuable in high-tariff economies. In each of these arrangements the United States would be the dominant party. The small, peripheral countries would become more dependent on the United States than they are today. The benefits that the United States could negotiate for itself would not be multilateralized to other parties to the agreements. Trade diversion could be significant in the US market, until now the largest and most open market in the world. Minimal trade creation would occur among the peripheral countries.

The net effect of this hub-and-spoke pattern of trade policy could well be to overpower the smaller countries in Asia. It is reminiscent of the club-and-poke policies applied in Central Europe in the 1930s. It would jeopardize US credibility as an adherent to the GATT system. It is not possible for the world's major trader to play the bilateral game and the multilateral game at the same time. They are two different games.

The fifth case, which multilateralizes all four previous FTAs, results in more trade creation within the region and unbalanced bargaining relationships. In theory, the smaller countries could form coalitions against the larger ones in order to protect their interests. However, this case would also mean that the international trading system would be sidestepped by the United States. Negotiations for trade liberalization would cease to occur in the GATT. Instead the GATT would become a "small claims court"—a forum for settlement of disputes between the smaller countries.

EFTA Country Reactions

A classic response by outsiders to an FTA is to attempt to erode members' preference margins through multilateral tariff negotiations.[4] However, this response is hardly an option for small countries. The Kennedy Round was partly inspired by a desire to reduce the preferential margins enjoyed by members of the European Community. It was successful because a major power, the United States, was an outsider and could bring considerable negotiating power to bear on the EC. After the disappointments of the GATT Ministerial in 1982, the United States employed the same strategy, but now as an insider. By entering preferential trade agreements the United States aimed not only to obtain preferential access to important markets but also to increase the pressure on outsiders to liberalize trade on a multilateral basis through a new round of GATT negotiations. However, this strategy is unlikely to work if the strongest of the liberal trading powers is a member of important preferential arrangements.

With Japan and the United States inside the same FTA, few major players would remain on the outside who are capable of effectively negotiating tariff reductions on a multilateral basis. This option is not feasible for the EFTA countries, although they certainly would support attempts by others. The natural candidate to take the lead is the EC, but the EC is preoccupied with enlargement and completing its internal market. Intra-trade accounts for a larger share of EC members' GDP (13 percent) than does external trade (9 percent), and this gives an indication of its priorities.

It is certainly not feasible for the EFTA countries to take the lead, although they would support attempts by others. A more likely response for small countries is to join in the bloc building. The emergence of a large regional trading bloc in the Pacific Basin, encompassing two of the largest and some of the fastest growing market economies, will help overcome any reluctance on the part of smaller countries to join existing trade blocs, or to form new ones.

In this respect, the EFTA countries have two options. One is to join the Pacific Basin countries in an industrial free trade area. This option should not be rejected out of hand, since the EFTA countries have proved their skill at managing this type of arrangement. Another option would be to

---

4. Since EFTA is not a customs union, any response would primarily be by the individual member governments. This section therefore considers only possible responses of a typical member country.

hasten the realization of a homogeneous European Economic Space, encompassing both the EC and EFTA. The EC's current attempts to complete its internal market have already inspired the EFTA countries to seek to match its moves, so that completion will not result in trade diversion within Western Europe. The urgency of this task is bound to increase, and, some might add, the resistance in the EFTA countries to participating in a "fortress Europe" may well weaken if citadels are constructed elsewhere. Thus, FTAs by the United States could trigger an avalanche of membership applications to the EC.

The end result of this process would be to divide the market economies into two blocs, Western Europe and the Pacific Basin, with the developing countries as powerless bystanders.

Continental Arrangements

From the EFTA countries' viewpoint, preferential trading arrangements in the Pacific Basin should not include the United States. The systemic impact would be too unfavorable.

Case 6 in table 12.3 presents a less threatening alternative: an FTA including only Japan, Korea, ASEAN, and Australia. Such a grouping would involve a much smaller share of world trade. The share of the group's imports that comes from within the group is 45 percent for manufactures (more for machinery). The share that comes from the EFTA countries also is larger than in the other cases. Thus, while the prospect of trade diversion is at least as large for the EFTA countries as when the United States is included, it affects a much smaller volume of trade. Such a grouping is likely to have positive effects on the trading system by increasing the bargaining power of small, liberal trading nations in international forums.

This conclusion does not imply that the United States should not engage in free trade agreements at all. It is well to bear in mind that the United States, as a federation of 50 states, is already a free trade area, the most comprehensive and efficient of them all and a model for others. The vision of a continental European market embodied in "1992" is, in fact, inspired by the US example. Europe sees itself as "catching up" with the United States, as attempting to create a playing field of equal size. The United States should not feel urged to pursue even larger intercontinental FTAs. The correct parallel action to 1992 for the United States is to increase economic integration on the North American continent. Table 12.4 gives the data for free trade agreements with Mexico and/or Canada. An FTA with Mexico would involve the same amount of intra-trade and EFTA trade as an FTA with ASEAN. Geographical proximity suggests that trade creation will be greater and trade diversion less.

Table 12.4 Imports of hypothetical FTAs involving the United States, Canada, and Mexico, 1985 (manufactures)

Free trade area	Area's imports from (million $US)			Shares in total imports (%)	
	World	Area	EFTA	Area	EFTA
US + Canada	320,156.8	92,478.1	10,509.4	28.9	3.3
US + Mexico	270,362.9	16,931.8	9,782.8	6.3	3.6
US + Canada + Mexico	322,513.9	110,080.4	10,850.2	33.1	3.3

Conclusions

From an EFTA perspective, major trading nations such as the United States should not enter into intercontinental free trade agreements. An FTA to which the United States is one party is not just any FTA. The United States is already a vast domestic market with strong internal competition under a single set of rules. It encompasses a large part of world trade. It has been the liberal hegemon of the postwar trading system. If it goes bilateral, the effect on the international trading system will be profound. The same applies to the EC, which is now an equivalent trading bloc.

The international trading system now lacks a liberal hegemon. This fact places extra demands not only on the United States but also on the EC and Japan to ensure the survival of an open multilateral trading system. The EFTA countries are bound to support their efforts.

Acknowledgments

The author is indebted to Emil Ems, Kare Halonen, and Thomas Wieser of the EFTA Secretariat for comments as well as to some members of national delegations.

References

Hamilton, Carl B. 1988. "Restrictiveness and International Transmission of the 'New' Protectionism." In Robert E. Baldwin et al., eds., *Issues in US–EC Trade Relations.* Chicago: University of Chicago Press.

Herin, Jan. 1986. "Rules of Origin and Differences between Tariff Levels in EFTA and in the EC." Occasional Paper no. 13. Geneva: EFTA Secretariat.

Juth, Per. 1985. "Konkurrensvikter för svensk export." Working Paper from the Research Secretariat, National Board of Trade, Stockholm, and unpublished update.

Krugman, Paul. 1988. "EFTA and 1992." Occasional Paper no. 23, Geneva: EFTA Secretariat, June.

13

Europe 1992 and Its Possible Implications for Nonmember Countries

Bela Balassa

A common market has been defined as combining a customs union with free factor movements, where a customs union involves free trade within the union together with common tariffs (Balassa 1961, 2). After noting the extent to which the European Community (EC) has conformed to this definition of a common market, this chapter considers the changes that the implementation of the Europe 1992 program is expected to bring about.

The chapter begins with a discussion of the freeing of all trade in goods within the EC, followed by an analysis of the freeing of trade in services and the freeing of factor movements. Finally, the possible impact of Europe 1992 on nonmember countries is considered.

The Movement of Goods

The EC has completed a customs union as defined in the GATT. Tariffs on intra-area trade were eliminated between 1 January 1958, and 1 July 1968; a common external tariff was established on 1 July 1968; and quantitative import restrictions on intra-area trade for goods produced in the Common Market countries were also abolished. Nevertheless, intra-area trade still encounters barriers. Border formalities are encountered in transporting goods from one country to another; monetary compensation applies to agricultural products; countries try to limit the transshipment of goods imported under quotas; government procurement tends to favor national sources; and technical barriers limit the shipment of goods across frontiers.

Bela Balassa is a Visiting Fellow at the Institute for International Economics, Professor of Political Economy at The Johns Hopkins University, and a consultant to the World Bank.

Border Formalities

Border formalities are maintained within the EC for the following reasons:[1]

☐ Differences in value-added tax rates and excise duties

☐ Monetary compensation on agricultural products

☐ Enforcement of bilateral trade quota regimes with third countries

☐ Differences in technical and public health standards

☐ Control of road transport licenses and compliance with national regulations

☐ Collection of statistical data.

These formalities impose an economic cost on the member countries. They include:

☐ Internal administrative costs borne by exporting and importing firms

☐ External costs incurred by exporting and importing firms in conjunction with customs clearance

☐ Costs to exporting and importing firms through delays imposed by customs procedures

☐ Costs to public authorities of maintaining customs posts and associated administrative services

☐ Opportunity costs associated with the loss of trade due to the maintenance of border formalities.

The internal and external costs of border formalities to firms were estimated on the basis of a firm survey (Commission of the European Communities 1988a, 48). The results showed that internal costs amounted to 5.9 billion ECU and external costs 1.6 billion ECU, for a total of 7.5 billion ECU.

The cost of frontier delays is indicated by the often-cited example that a 1,200-km truck trip takes 36 hours within the United Kingdom but 58 hours between London and Milan, excluding the time required for Channel crossing. The total cost of delays was estimated at 0.8 billion ECU, of which one-half may be absorbed by compulsory rest periods timed to coincide with delays at customs points.

---

1. The following discussion is largely based on Commission of the European Communities (1988a and b).

The budgetary cost of border formalities to the public authorities was estimated at 0.5 to 1.0 billion ECU. The lower figure represents the customs services' estimate and the higher figure an independent estimate. These figures include the staff costs of some 15,000 to 30,000 customs officials.

In total, the cost of border formalities is estimated to be between 8.4 and 9.3 billion ECU, corresponding to 1.7 to 1.9 percent of the value of intra-EC trade and 0.3 percent of community GDP. These figures do not include the opportunity cost of lost trade due to border formalities. The increase in trade resulting from the removal of these formalities was estimated at 1 percent by importers and 3.2 percent by exporters, reflecting a more sanguine view by the latter as to the possibilities for trade expansion.

Nor do the estimates include the cost of border formalities to individuals. On the other side of the coin, it has been suggested that the lack of border formalities may ease the tasks of drug dealers and terrorists in the member countries.

Implications of Differences in Value-Added Tax and Excise Duty Rates

As noted above, differences in national value-added tax (VAT) and excise duty rates provide a reason for maintaining border formalities among EC countries. The question arises, then, to what extent VAT and excise duty rates would need to be harmonized once these formalities are abolished.

Standard VAT rates vary from 12 percent (Luxembourg and Spain) to 25 percent (Ireland). Some countries apply increased rates, ranging between 25 percent (Belgium) and 38 percent (Italy), on selected commodities such as cars, jewelry, and electrical equipment. Also, some countries have reduced rates ranging from zero (United Kingdom) to 10 percent (Ireland) on some items. The range of reduced rates is the broadest in the United Kingdom, covering most foods, children's clothing, books and newspapers, water, fuel and power, and public transport and construction, totaling about 30 percent of consumer spending (Davis and Kay 1985). The EC Commission proposed to reduce the range of standard rates to between 14 and 20 percent, with a band of 4 to 9 percent applicable to a limited range of necessities. The Commission also proposed maintaining the destination principle on the VAT while changing its practical application, with exports subjected to the exporting country's VAT and an adjustment to the VAT of the importing country effected in the latter. This procedure would permit retaining different national VAT rates without the need for harmonization.

The only rationale for the harmonization of VAT rates lies in the desire to avoid cross-border purchases by individuals. For this purpose, however, it would suffice to set minimum tax rates. Since the costs of cross-border shopping are borne by the member country that chooses to set higher tax rates than its neighbors, there is no reason for the Commission to restrict its freedom to do so.[2] In this connection, state sales taxes vary from zero to 9 percent in the United States without an appreciable problem of cross-border purchases. In view of the high cost involved in cross-border shopping, one may also consider maintaining the reduced zero rate in the United Kingdom.

There is considerable variation in excise duties. In the case of cigarettes, specific duties vary from 0.01 ECU (Greece and Spain) to 1.52 ECU (Denmark) per pack, and ad valorem duties (inclusive of VAT) between 34 percent (United Kingdom) and 71 percent (France), with the total tax (including VAT) ranging from 0.12 ECU (Spain) to 2.76 ECU (Denmark) per pack for the most popular category of cigarettes. Excise duties on gasoline vary from 0.20 ECU (Luxembourg and Spain) to 0.53 ECU (Italy) per liter and on diesel oil from 0.03 ECU (Spain) to 0.29 ECU (Ireland) per liter. Finally, excise duties range from 0.14 ECU (Greece) to 10.50 ECU (Denmark) on a bottle of alcoholic spirits, from zero (Germany, Greece, Italy, Portugal, and Spain) to 2.79 ECU (Ireland) on a liter of wine, and from 0.03 ECU (France and Spain) to 1.13 ECU (Ireland) on a liter of beer.

The Commission proposed equalizing excise duties throughout the EC. The proposed rates are 0.38 ECU per pack (specific duty) and 52 to 54 percent (ad valorem, including VAT) for cigarettes; 0.34 ECU per liter of gasoline and 0.18 ECU per liter of diesel oil; and 3.81 ECU per liter of alcoholic spirits, 0.17 ECU per liter of wine, and 0.17 ECU per liter of beer (Lee et al. 1988, chapter 5).

The unification of excise duties would represent substantial changes in national rates that have been established on the basis of the conditions existing in each country. At the same time, one wonders if unification of rates is necessary. In the United States, no particular adverse effects have been observed, although excise rates vary enormously: from 2 to 29 cents on a pack of cigarettes, from 8 to 19 cents on a gallon of gasoline, and from $1.50 to $6.50 on a gallon of alcoholic beverages (Commission of the European Communities 1988b, 541).

Nevertheless, extensive transshipments of excisable goods should be avoided. It could be accomplished by identifying the country of final sale by a stamp or other distinguishing marking on packs of cigarettes, bottles of alcoholic beverages, and shipments of fuels.

At the same time, to the extent that countries wish to discourage their nationals from purchasing excisable goods in other countries, they can do

---

2. This point is made in Lee et al. (1988, 35).

so by lowering excise duty rates. In this way, pressure to reduce differences in excises would be exerted by the market rather than by harmonization imposed by legislative fiat.

Monetary Compensation Amounts on Intra-EC Agricultural Trade

Intra-EC trade in agricultural products has been liberalized, while EC agriculture is protected under the Common Agricultural Policy. At the same time, monetary compensation has been introduced periodically to ease the effects of changes in the value of member country currencies on the agriculture of individual countries. This means that farmers in a country with a revalued currency do not fully feel the impact of increased competition from the partner countries.

Monetary compensation amounts (MCAs) take the form of border taxes and subsidies that permit the maintaining of different prices for agricultural products within the EC. With the abolition of border formalities, MCAs will also disappear. At the same time, the resulting gains have not been estimated because there have been considerable variations in the amount of MCAs over time.

Third-Country Quotas

In cases where national quotas are applied on imports from nonmember countries, the transshipment of goods in intra-EC trade can be blocked by the EC Commission at the request of member countries. This can be enforced in the course of the application of border formalities.

Import quotas apply to textiles and clothing and to automobiles throughout the EC; individual member countries may also apply quotas on particular products, such as footwear and bicycles. The textiles and clothing quotas have been established in the course of the renegotiation of the Multi-fiber Arrangement that takes place at regular intervals.

A case of widely disparate import quotas involves Japanese automobiles. Italy admits only 11,000 cars annually from Japan; the French quota equals 3 percent of domestic sales; the quota is 10 percent of domestic sales on the United Kingdom; the other EC countries do not apply quotas.

The abolition of border formalities would not permit the maintenance of national quotas. Thus, EC-wide quotas will have to be established or import quotas abolished. The first alternative has been chosen for textiles and clothing and for automobiles. For other commodities, no decision has been reached as yet.

Public Procurement

Public procurement was not included in the Treaty of Rome establishing the European Common Market. In the 1970s, the Commission attempted to induce governments to purchase from other member countries. Its directives called for advertising in the *Official Journal of the European Communities* all public supply contracts worth more than 200,000 ECU and all public works contracts worth more than 5 million ECU.

The rules did not cover water, energy, transportation, telecommunications, or defense. But even in other sectors little cross-country procurement occurred. Thus, only 2 percent of public supply contracts and public works contracts have been awarded to firms from other member countries, out of total contractual procurement of 240 to 340 billion ECU, amounting to 7 to 10 percent of Community GDP and over one-half of intra-EC trade (Cecchini et al. 1988, 16).

A variety of factors explain the limited extent of interpenetration as far as public procurement is concerned. There has been abuse of the exceptions from normal tendering and award rules, illegal exclusion of bidders from other member countries, discrimination in scrutinizing bidders' technical capacity and financial standing, and discrimination in the awarding of contracts (Commission of the European Communities 1988a, 56). At the same time, in many countries purchasing is substantially decentralized, making transparency rules hard to enforce. Finally, bids have often been divided into smaller units to avoid exceeding the limits set for the publication of tenders.

The new regulations for Europe 1992 will tighten significantly the enforcement of the current rules and increase the transparency of public procurement. Also, companies will be provided with means of legal redress to avoid discrimination against them. At the same time, the rules will be extended to cover currently excluded markets in water, energy, transportation, and telecommunications.

It has been estimated that the direct effects of liberalizing procurement in the form of purchases from lower-cost sources would bring cost savings of 4.4 billion ECU. There is further said to be a competitive effect of 2.3 billion ECU, with increased competition from the partner countries reducing domestic prices and costs. Finally, gains from economies of scale would amount to 7.2 billion ECU (Commission of the European Communities 1988a, 57).

The total gain from these sources has been estimated at 13.9 billion ECU, or 0.5 percent of Community GDP (Commission of the European Communities 1988a, 57). In addition, the liberalization of defense procurement would bring further gains, estimated at 4.0 billion ECU.

Technical Barriers

Although according to customs union theory and GATT rules free trade is established once tariffs and quantitative import restrictions have been abolished, there may be technical barriers that interfere with free trade. These barriers include differences in industry standards, in legal regulations, and in testing and certification procedures.

Industry standards refer to product specifications that may differ from country to country. Legal regulations pertain to health, safety, and environmental protection and may also vary among countries. Finally, there may be differences in testing and certification requirements, often involving an additional certification procedure to that required in the country of origin.

Technical barriers involve a cost because of the need to adapt products to national standards and regulations and because of additional testing and certification requirements. They are thus similar in their effects to trade barriers in limiting the amount traded.

Differences in standards abound in the building materials industry, where the standard used in France differs from the standard employed in Germany, reducing trade in building materials. Different standards are also used in regard to telecommunications equipment, for example, limiting purchases by the national post and telecommunications companies from the partner countries.

Differences in regulations represent an important technical barrier in the case of foodstuffs. Member countries may restrict the use of a generic product name, such as pasta, to products manufactured according to a specific recipe. Also, there may be restrictions on the use of particular ingredients. Finally, packaging and labeling requirements may limit the sales of a product in a given country.

As far as regulations on automobiles are concerned, much harmonization has been achieved, but differences remain in regard to tires, weight and size, and windshields. There are also unique national requirements, such as side repeater headlights in Italy, reclining driver's seats in Germany, dim-dip lighting in the United Kingdom, and yellow headlight bulbs in France.

Certification rules play a particularly important role in the pharmaceutical industry. If a product is to be admitted to a particular national market it must first receive approval by the national registration authority, when criteria vary from country to country. Testing and certification procedures differ also with respect to electrical products and machinery.

Originally, the Common Market aimed at unifying standards, regulations, and certification requirements. While this approach has brought results in some cases, it could not be applied generally. An example is the harmonization process for foodstuffs drawn up in 1973, which listed far in excess of 50 directives to be put in place. By 1985 only 14 directives had been adopted.

In the White Paper from the EC Commission to the Council entitled "Completing the Internal Market" (28–29 June 1985), a new strategy was adopted, involving the mutual recognition of national standards and regulations. The basis for this approach lies in Article 30 of the Treaty of Rome, according to which "quantitative restrictions on imports and all measures having equivalent effect shall be prohibited between member states."

An antecedent of the new approach is found in the 1979 Cassis de Dijon case. The EC Court of Justice decided that Germany cannot keep out French cassis on the grounds that it does not qualify as liquor under German regulations as long as it meets the definition applied in France. Subsequently the court found that, despite the Bavarian requirement that beer contain no additives, the sale of foreign beers containing additives could not be prohibited. Finally, in the recent pasta case, the court overruled the decision of its Italian Advocate General and permitted the importation of pasta containing soft wheat into Italy.

The mutual recognition of national standards and regulations will be complemented by EC directives on the harmonization of health and safety requirements. Furthermore, in the case of high technology products, the development of European standards has been entrusted to private bodies, including the Comité Européen de la Normalisation (CEN) as well as sectoral organizations, such as Conférence Européenne des Postes et des Télécommunications for telecommunications.

The elimination of technical barriers promises considerable cost savings. According to one study, the savings would amount to 5.7 percent in the case of automobiles, equivalent to more than three-quarters of net profits achieved by the eight leading European car manufacturers in 1987.[3]

Trade in Services

Customs union theory deals exclusively with trade in goods. The Treaty of Rome also envisaged the liberalization of trade in services. However, only limited progress has been made in this regard, although trade in services has assumed considerable importance among the EC countries. Also, services have come to account for more than 50 percent of Community GDP.

The following discussion concerns road transportation, air transportation,

---

3. *Financial Times*, 18 May 1988, 2.

financial services, business services, and telecommunications services. In each case, existing barriers, proposals for their removal, and the possible effects of removal of the barrier are considered.

Road Transportation

Trucks carry about one-half of intra-EC surface transportation by bulk and substantially more in terms of value. Competition is distorted by the need for licenses to undertake cross-border trade. Bilateral permits negotiated between member countries for truck trips, measured in ton-kilometers, regulate much of this trade. Only about one-sixth of the trips are undertaken under EC-wide permits. At the same time, cabotage, involving transportation by out-of-state truckers within a member state, is prohibited.

The present permit system and the prohibition of cabotage are reflected in the cost of empty moves. This cost has been estimated at 1.2 billion ECU, of which 20 percent is said to be related to regulatory restrictions. There is also a black market in EC-wide permits, the cost of which has been estimated at 23 percent of a truck's normal annual costs. According to the EC Commission's estimate, road transport costs would decline by 5 percent in the event of the liberalization of restrictions (Commission of the European Communities 1988a, 97).

In June 1988, an agreement was reached to liberalize regulations on road transport. On 1 July 1988, the number of EC-wide permits was increased by 40 percent, with a further increase of this magnitude taking place a year later. By mid-1991 all national restrictions will be scrapped, and the only requirement will be an EC-wide truck driver's permit, as long as the enterprise is professionally sound. The prohibition of cabotage will also be eliminated.

Air Transportation

Airfares in the EC are substantially higher than in the United States, but profits are not, reflecting the fact that costs are considerably higher in Europe. Allowing for differences between American and European airlines in terms of the average length of the trip, the type of aircraft, fuel costs, and landing charges, European costs exceeded American costs in 1980 by 50 percent overall; by 12 percent for maintenance per capacity ton-mile; by 315 percent for ground and passenger service costs, and by 365 percent for administrative overheads.

These cost differences in part reflect inefficiency, in part higher staff costs in Europe. The five leading European airlines average 6.70 hours of flying time per day on narrow-bodied jets, compared with 8.33 hours for American airlines. Also, among the major European airlines, pilots earned 670 percent more than the average annual wage on Air France and 590 percent more on KLM and Alitalia, compared with 370 percent for American airlines; only British Airways pilots' earnings were lower (Pelkmans et al. 1988, 49).

The regulatory regime in effect has contributed importantly to the high costs of European airlines. This regime is based on bilateral agreements between individual countries. Rights by an EC carrier based in one country to offer services between two other member states (so-called fifth freedom rights) are effectively prohibited, with only one exception. Entry is restricted and price competition is limited, with revenues on city pair routes often pooled and split 50:50 between the two carriers.

Within the framework of the Europe 1992 program, in December 1987 the Council of Ministers agreed to an initial three-year package covering airfares, capacity control, and market access. There will be greater flexibility in lowering fares and in introducing new discount fares; in regard to bilateral capacity control, the initial 50:50 division will give way to a 45:55 range in the first two years and 40:60 in the third year; greater competition will be achieved by allowing a large number of airlines to operate, especially on dense traffic routes, and certain fifth freedom rights will be exercised by airlines within the EC (Commission of the European Communities 1988a, 97–8).

Financial Services

The financial services sector is of growing importance within the EC, accounting for 6.5 percent of GDP. Financial services include insurance, banking services, and investment services.

There has been freedom of establishment in insurance services throughout the EC, although national regulations differ to a considerable extent from country to country. However, restrictions apply to cross-border insurance. The existence of these restrictions has contributed to the observed large intercountry differences in insurance rates.

For standard services, the results of a survey show that term insurance rates vary from 150 ECU (United Kingdom) to 392 ECU (Italy), home insurance rates from 118 ECU (Belgium) to 266 ECU (United Kingdom), car insurance rates from 316 ECU (United Kingdom) to 942 ECU (Italy); commercial fire and theft insurance rates from 1,204 ECU (Luxembourg) to 4,896 ECU (Italy); and public liability cover rates from 714 ECU (Netherlands) to 1,852 ECU (France).[4]

---

4. Commission of the European Communities (1988b, 280). A list of the standard

To liberalize cross-border insurance, the EC Commission took four countries to the European Court of Justice for blocking such business. In a well-known case involving a German broker who had been fined for finding cheap industrial insurance for his clients in London, the court ruled in favor of the transborder selling of insurance; however, it limited this practice to customers that are big enough to form a view as to the soundness of the foreign insurance company, until this was made subject to EC rules.

In June 1988, cross-border insurance was liberalized for so-called "big risks"—nonlife insurance for companies with more than 500 employees or 25 million ECU turnover. The directive, adopted by the Council of Ministers, will go into effect in July 1990. The Commission is also preparing a proposal for the liberalization of car insurance and hopes to have this in force by 1992. It is preparing a draft directive for life insurance, but this raises difficulties because of differences in tax provisions governing the treatment of life insurance among the member countries.

Freedom of establishment for foreign banks exists throughout the EC. However, national banking regulations hinder cross-border banking activities. For example, the active solicitation of deposits on a cross-border basis is generally not permitted. Also, in some member states banks cannot engage in the securities business.

These limitations have contributed to differences in the costs of standard banking services among the member countries. Costs vary from 4,375 ECU (France) to 6,875 ECU (United Kingdom) for commercial loans, from 12 ECU (Belgium) to 46 ECU (Denmark) for consumer credit, from 37 ECU (France) to 99 ECU (Italy) for credit cards, from 290 ECU (United Kingdom) to 800 ECU (Spain) for mortgage loans, from 22 ECU (Netherlands) to 120 ECU (Spain) for foreign exchange drafts, from 5.0 ECU (Denmark, Luxembourg, and the United Kingdom) to 7.5 ECU (France) for traveler's checks, from nil (Belgium and the Netherlands) to 240 ECU (Italy) for current accounts, and from 425 ECU (Denmark) to 750 ECU (Spain) for letters of credit (Commission of the European Communities 1988b, 280).

In the Second Banking Co-ordination Directive, proposed in February 1988, the ECU Commission introduced the concept of a "single banking license." This will allow any bank that has been authorized by a member state to market its services in any other state without further authorization. Apart from banking, the freedom to offer financial services extends to the securities business.

The directive aims at establishing the freedom of financial services by the

---

financial products and services to which these rates and other prices quoted from this survey refer may be found in Commission of the European Communities (1988a, 89).

banks by 1992. In the meantime, agreement will need to be reached on harmonizing capital and solvency ratios, deposit guarantees, control rules, qualification of managers, and related issues.

While the single banking license is based on the principle that banks are regulated by their home countries, there are three exceptions to this rule: the conduct of monetary policies, the monitoring of the liquidity position of banks, and the regulation of the securities activities of banks. Furthermore, the European Court of Justice ruled in 1986 that host countries may limit the freedom of financial services on grounds of "general interest," in particular consumer protection.

Several directives have been adopted in regard to securities markets to coordinate investor protection, improve market transparency, and facilitate simultaneous listing on the stock exchanges of different member states. At the same time, there remain considerable differences in regard to the cost of securities services. For standard transactions, costs vary from 9 ECU (France) to 23 ECU (United Kingdom) on private equity transactions, from 21 ECU (Italy) to 180 ECU (Spain) on private gilt transactions, from 719 ECU (United Kingdom) to 3,453 ECU (Spain) on institutional equity transactions, and from 3,597 ECU (Luxembourg) to 21,583 ECU (Belgium) on international gilt transactions (Commission of the European Communities 1988b, 280).

The first step regarding securities transactions in the framework of the Europe 1992 program was the establishment of an EC-wide regime for the issue of unit trusts (mutual funds). The directive lays down broad rules governing the kinds of investments the unit trusts may make and the characteristics of their managers, leaving the determination of precise rules to the country where the fund is based. The host country controls only the methods of selling the funds to investors.

The EC Commission is in the process of drafting a directive concerning investment services, except for services provided by the banks that are covered by the directive cited earlier. The directive is based on home country control. Once a securities firm has been authorized by its home country regulators, it will be able to do business throughout the EC.

The draft directive further states that each country will designate a competent authority to supervise securities business. This authority will be responsible for monitoring the capital adequacy of the securities firm and the acceptability of its major shareholders, and firms will have to comply with host country rules on advertising and marketing. Each country will also draw up conduct of business rules on internal controls, segregation of client funds, compensation for bankruptcy or default, and conflicts of interest.

The liberalization of financial services would permit the reduction of their costs in the EC. It has been estimated that the cost of financial transactions would decline by an average of 10 percent, amounting to 20.6 billion ECU, or 0.7 percent of GDP in savings. There would be a gain of a similar magnitude in consumer surplus (Commission of the European Communities 1988a, 92).

Business Services

Business services represent about 5 percent of the EC's GDP. Sales of professional business services in 1986 were as follows: engineering and related services, 7.5 billion ECU; managerial consultancy, 3.5 billion ECU; advertising and public relations, 57 billion ECU; computing services, 13 billion ECU; research and development, 15 billion ECU; legal services, 13 billion ECU; and financial review (including accounting and audit services), 13 billion ECU (Commission of the European Communities 1988b, 251).

The importance of barriers to trade in professional business services varies. Barriers were reported to have been most significant for engineering and related services, where they pertained to national differences in technical standards, lack of recognition of professional qualifications, and restrictions on government procurement. At the other end of the spectrum, financial review services and managerial consultancy do not encounter barriers. The intermediate category includes advertising and public relations (satellite broadcasting barriers, national differences in advertising laws and allocation of media time, and recognition of qualifications), computing services (government and post and telecommunications procurement), research and development (government procurement), and legal services (licensing of professionals). It has been estimated that the freeing of trade in professional business services in the EC would reduce their cost by 3 percent (Commission of the European Communities 1988a, 95–6).

Telecommunications Services

Telecommunications services play an increasingly important role today. In the EC, sales amounted to 63 billion ECU in 1985, or about one-half of US sales. Telephone services accounted for 85 to 90 percent of the total, with 10 percent derived from data transmission and 5 percent from telex; the latter proportions are much higher in the United States and are expected to grow rapidly in the future in the EC. Even more rapid growth is expected in value-added networks (VANs), such as data banks, electronic mail, and electronic data interchange (Commission of the European Communities 1988a, 98–9).

The basic objectives of EC policy were set out in the Green Paper on the Development of the Common Market for Telecommunications Services and Equipment [COM (87) 290, June 1987]. The Green Paper accepted the role of the national telecommunications administrations to provide basic network infrastructure and basic telephone services (primarily voice telephone services). In turn, the unrestricted provision of so-called competitive telecommunications services, including in particular value-added services, was proposed.

The Commission subsequently made proposals in the telecommunications area in its communication entitled "Towards a Competitive Community-Wide Telecommunications Market in 1992. Implementing the Green Paper on the Development of the Common Market for Telecommunications Services and Equipment" [COM (88) 48, February 1988]. The communication called for the full opening of the terminal equipment market to competition by the end of 1989; the progressive opening of the telecommunications services market by the end of 1989, with some exceptions; and the full application of the general principle that telecommunications tariffs should follow overall cost trends by the end of 1991. The Commission further proposed the clear separation of regulatory and operational activities; the EC-wide definition of general requirements on providers of competitive services in the framework of open network provisions; the establishment of a European Telecommunications Standards Institute; the full mutual recognition of type approval to terminal equipment; the creation of transparency in the financial relations between member state governments and the national telecommunication administrations; the assurance of fair conditions of competition; and the independence of procurement decisions and the opening of public procurement.

The implementation of these provisions would bring important cost savings. It has been estimated that open competition for equipment procurement could lead to a reduction in tariff levels and thereby higher demand, permitting the exploitation of economies of scale, with annual cost savings of 0.75 billion ECU. Additional cost savings would be achieved in competitive services through a liberalized equipment certification program (0.5 to 0.7 billion ECU), the liberalization of VANs (0.3 to 0.4 billion ECU), and open network provisions (0.2 billion ECU). There would further be cost savings of 4 billion ECU from moving tariff structures nearer to costs (Commission of the European Communities 1988a, 100–1).

Factor Movements

A common market also involves the freeing of factor movements, and the Treaty of Rome contains several provisions to this effect. In the following, the freeing of factor movements is considered under two headings: capital movements and labor movements.

Capital Movements

Capital movements were liberalized under EC directives in 1960, 1962, and 1986 and under policies adopted in the individual member states. Capital movements are practically free in the United Kingdom, Germany, Denmark, Luxembourg, and the Netherlands; there remain a few restrictions in Belgium, France, and Italy, while restrictions continue to be in effect in Greece, Ireland, Portugal, and Spain. These restrictions pertain largely to short-term capital transactions and to the establishment of bank accounts abroad.

On 24 June 1988, the Council of Ministers published a directive for the implementation of Article 67 of the Treaty on the freeing of capital movements. According to Article 1 of the directive, "Member States shall abolish restrictions on movements of capital taking place between persons resident in Member States."

Under the directive, all domestic rules and administrative provisions that discriminate between residents and nonresidents in the performance of capital transactions will be eliminated. Also, transactions made for purposes of capital transfer will be implemented at the same exchange rate as current account transactions (this amounts to the abolition of dual exchange markets maintained in Belgium and Luxembourg).

The developed EC countries will liberalize capital movements by July 1990, except that Belgium and Luxembourg can maintain their dual exchange markets until 1992. Greece, Ireland, Portugal, and Spain can delay liberalization for two years, and Greece and Portugal may request an additional two years' extension.

Article 73 of the Treaty of Rome provides a safeguard clause for the liberalization of capital movements in the event of balance of payments difficulties. The June 1988 directive adds another safeguard clause, permitting the introduction of restrictions up to six months under authorization by the EC Commission, "where short-term capital movements of exceptional magnitude impose severe strains on foreign exchange markets and lead to serious disturbances in the conduct of a Member State's monetary and exchange rate policies . . ." (Article 3).

At French insistence, the provision was added that "the Commission shall submit to the Council, by 31 December 1988, proposals aimed at eliminating or reducing risks of distortion, tax evasion, and tax avoidance linked to the diversity of national systems for the taxation of savings and for controlling the application of these systems " (Article 6:5). In fact, such measures are desirable in view of differences in national taxation systems.

First of all, distortions in investment decisions may occur in response to differences in business taxation. Other things being equal, countries with lower tax rates will be favored in the establishment of new companies and, in particular, in decisions taken by companies in nonmember countries to invest in the EC.

Furthermore, investments in securities will be favored in countries that do not have withholding taxes. Such is the case for interest income in Denmark, Luxembourg, the Netherlands, and the United Kingdom and for dividends in France and Germany. Also, capital gains generally are not taxed in Belgium, Germany, Italy, Luxembourg, and the Netherlands. Finally, differences in income tax rates may contribute to the flow of capital.

While it has been suggested in EC circles that the liberalization of capital movements would contribute to stability in exchange rates, the opposite may be the case, because small differences in interest rates and speculation about currency values may trigger large movements of funds. Although the EC established a medium-term credit facility in June 1988, it may not suffice in the event of large movements of speculative funds.

Labor Movements

The movement of labor has been free within the EC. There remain, however, practical obstacles that discourage migration. The removal of these obstacles would involve the reinforcement of the right of residence (droit de séjour) in the event of unemployment or short-term work contracts, the full equality of treatment in public sector jobs, and the portability of social security benefits.

Agreement has recently been reached on the mutual recognition of educational diplomas. The Commission has also made proposals for the mutual recognition of vocational training. This will eventually culminate in the introduction of a European "vocational training card," serving as proof that the holder has been awarded a specific qualification.

The Commission originally sought directives harmonizing the qualifications needed for specific professions. This has in fact been done in regard to doctors, dentists, pharmacists, nurses, midwives, veterinarians, and architects.

In view of the slowness of the process, the Commission has forsaken this route, and it now aims at the mutual acceptance of professional qualifications. In fact, in June 1988 the EC trade and industry ministers agreed that the holders of professional qualifications should be able to work anywhere in the EC.

In conjunction with labor migration, reference may also be made to efforts toward harmonizing social conditions. The July 1987 Communication of the Commission set out a four-year program for safety, health, and hygiene in the workplace. This has led to various initiatives, including proposals for directives on the exposure of workers to certain carcinogenic agents, on the safety of machinery at the workplace, and on safety standards for machinery.

An earlier proposal for mandatory worker consultation in all large companies operating in the EC (the so-called Vredeling proposal of 1980) was withdrawn, but suggestions have again been made for the consultation of workers in company decisions. This remains a matter of controversy, however.

Implications for Nonmember Countries

Jacques Delors, the President of the EC Commission, emphasized that the Europe 1992 program should not lead to a "Fortress Europe." He is also reported to have said, however, that "the external aspect of the internal market will have to be strengthened if we don't want this internal market to be of primary benefit to foreign investors." [5]

It also appears that the member countries differ in their attitudes to external protection following the creation of a single European market. At the time of the French presidential election campaign, President Mitterrand took a position in favor of increased protection: "Let us contemplate as clearly as possible the dangers which menace us. If the large market is not better protected than the present Common Market, the 'extra-Europeans' will rush to the 320 million consumers which we are and which constitute the most important melting pot in the world."

Similar views have been voiced in the new Southern European member states. In turn, the Germans and the British have taken a position against increasing import barriers in the EC. The Benelux countries are also free traders, while Italy generally supports France.

This concluding part of the chapter considers the possible impact of the Europe 1992 program on nonmember countries. Some of the measures to be taken will automatically affect nonmembers; in other cases there are specific provisions concerning these countries.

In regard to the movement of goods, note has been taken of the proposed abolition of border formalities; the elimination of MCAs affecting agricultural products; the removal of national import quotas; the liberalization of

---

5. *Financial Times,* 27 June 1988, 2.

6. *Le Monde,* 8 April 1988.

government procurement; and the harmonization or mutual recognition of standards. All these measures will have implications for outsiders.

In view of British opposition, it is far from certain that border formalities will be abolished within the EC. But in any case the cost of these formalities will be reduced through simplification of the regulations. This is equivalent to reductions of tariffs on intra-area trade that have trade-diverting effects by favoring partner country producers over nonmember countries.

Similar considerations apply to the elimination of MCAs for agricultural products, which are equivalent to import tariffs and export subsidies on intra-EC trade. At the same time, the export subsidy aspect is of little practical importance, since MCAs aim to safeguard high-cost producers. Thus, MCAs basically amount to import tariffs, the abolition of which involves trade diversion.

The abolition of national quotas in the framework of the Multi-Fiber Arrangement presumably will mean the establishment of EC-wide quotas equal to the sum of national quotas. In this case, imports under the Multi-Fiber Arrangement will not be affected.

In the case of automobiles, there is pressure from France and Italy, which have the smallest import quotas on Japanese cars, to set the EC-wide quota at a low level.[7] At the same time, the Common Agricultural Policy does not augur well for the establishment of EC-wide quotas.

At first glance the liberalization of government procurement legislation would not appear to affect nonmember countries. However, to the extent that purchases have been made from these countries, there may be trade diversion, since under the Europe 1992 program member country producers would be favored over nonmember country producers.

The lack of harmonization and the absence of mutual recognition of standards presently hurt member country as well as nonmember country producers. Complying with the standards of the importing country involves a cost that would disappear as far as member country producers are concerned under the Europe 1992 program. This will, then, result in trade diversion, if national standards are accepted within the EC.

EC-wide standards would, however, benefit nonmember countries because they will have to comply with one set of standards only. On the other hand, nonmember producers will not be involved in their establishment. The

---

7. Thus, Raymond Levy, Chairman and Chief Executive Officer of Renault, called for the protection of the European car industry from Japanese imports following the creation of a single European market in 1992. Levy stated, "Europe must defend itself but if Europe does not take measures, I want France alone defending itself" (*Financial Times*, 29 September 1988).

standards thus can be expected to favor member country producers, representing another form of discrimination against nonmembers.

It appears, then, that in goods trade the completion of the internal market in the EC will give rise to trade diversion. Trade diversion, in turn, will give incentives to investment by nonmember countries in the Community. The trade creation resulting from the measures taken under the Europe 1992 program will provide similar incentives.

In the case of services, in particular financial services, the EC Commission has proposed the application of the principle of reciprocity that has been incorporated in directives on banking and investment services. Under this principle, nonmember countries could not establish in the EC unless they offer access on similar terms to EC firms in their own country, although existing establishments would continue to operate.

The application of the principle of reciprocity may cause difficulties for nonmember countries. For example, the EC is introducing universal banking, under which banks can engage in the entire range of investment services, which is not the case in the United States. The strict application of the principle of reciprocity may then lead to discrimination against US banks.

Discrimination could be avoided if national treatment is applied, as is the case under friendship, commerce, and navigation treaties. These treaties ensure that foreign firms are treated in the same way as are domestic firms.

Additional issues relate to telecommunications. In this field, the EC is establishing common standards. If these standards are not compatible with those used in the United States and Japan, discrimination against the firms of these countries will ensue. Also, the application of reciprocity provisions may amount to the introduction of "Buy European" preferences.

We have considered here trade diversion in goods and services that may result from the measures to be taken under the Europe 1992 program as well as the opportunities offered for foreign firms in the EC. Nonmember countries will further be affected by the acceleration of economic growth following the completion of the internal market of the EC.

According to an estimate made by the EC Commission, the measures taken under the Europe 1992 program would lead to a 4.5 percent increase in the GDP of the EC countries in the medium term. The gain may reach 7 percent if accompanying macroeconomic policies are applied in regard to government budgets and prices (Cecchini et al. 1988, 101–2).

Higher growth rates in the European Community during the adjustment period will benefit nonmember countries through increased imports. There may also be adverse effects, however, to the extent that productivity increases occur in sectors that compete with imports. Thus, the effects of the acceleration of economic growth in the EC on nonmember countries are ambiguous.

References

Balassa, Bela. 1961. *The Theory of Economic Integration.* Homewood, Ill.: Richard D. Irwin.

Cecchini, Paolo, et al. 1988. *The European Challenge 1992, The Benefits of a Single Market.* Aldershot, Hants, England: Wildwood House.

Commission of the European Communities. 1988a. "The Economics of 1992, an Assessment of the Potential Economic Effects of Completing the 'Internal Market of the European Community.' " *European Economy,* no. 35 (March).

Commission of the European Communities. 1988b. *Research on the "Cost of Non-Europe": Basic Findings.* Vol. 1. Basic Studies: Executive Summaries. Brussels: Commission of the European Communities.

Davis, E. M., and J. A. Kay. 1985. "Extending the VAT Base: Problems and Possibilities." *Fiscal Studies,* vol. 6, no. 1.

Lee, Catherine, Mark Pearson, and Stephen Smith. 1988. *Fiscal Harmonization: An Analysis of the European Commission's Proposals.* IFS Report Series no. 28. London: Institute for Fiscal Studies.

Pelkmans, Jacques, and L. Alan Winters, with Helen Wallace. 1988. *Europe's Domestic Market.* Chatham House Papers no. 43. London: Routledge.

Comments

André Sapir

The current mood in Washington in favor of setting up a constellation of free trade areas (FTAs) centered around the United States is based, *inter alia,* on a misconception about Europe 1992. It is important to distinguish between 1992 and bilateral arrangements such as the one proposed between the United States and Japan. The first is about economic integration, while the second is a mere FTA.

Since 1973 Europe has undergone a prolonged period of slow growth and high unemployment. Most observers point toward the same diagnosis of the European malaise: the existence of market rigidities responsible for the sluggish response of the European economies to the shocks of the 1970s and 1980s. The policy challenge of 1992 consists precisely in the implementation of structural changes designed to create the conditions for renewed growth of output and employment in Europe—1992 is a vast enterprise in deregulation aimed to invigorate Europe (Jacquemin and Sapir 1989).

Another purpose is to catch up with the United States and Japan in high-technology sectors (such as computers and telecommunications), which are viewed as vital for social welfare. To the extent that these sectors are subject to scale economies, the fragmentation of the European market by domestic protectionist measures has undermined the European industry.

The attempt to liberalize trade inside Europe is akin to a GATT round in several respects. First, it involves a sizable number of countries—the 12 member states of the European Community (EC)—negotiating on a plurilateral basis. Second, the 1992 program covers a broad range of issues, allowing for plenty of mutually beneficial trade-offs. Finally, it has a clear deadline: December 31, 1992. In addition to these GATT-type features, the European liberalization has a special dimension. It will be accompanied by redistribution mechanisms and other instruments designed to ensure that the required structural adjustment will leave everyone in Europe better off. Clearly the success of 1992 will depend to a large extent on the implementation of these transfer mechanisms.

Although the 1992 program was conceived for purely internal reasons, the importance of the EC in world trade is such that 1992 could have important implications for third countries. Much will depend on the commercial policy adopted by the EC.

If successful, the removal of barriers within the EC is likely to promote

---

André Sapir is Professor of Economics at the Free University of Brussels.

world trade and augment extra-Community imports via an income effect. Moreover, faster growth would reduce unemployment and, thereby, the demand for protectionism in Europe. Despite this positive note, some uncertainty remains about the future shape of Europe's commercial policy (Sapir 1989). At this stage, one can offer only general comments.

Although a central part of the Treaty of Rome creating the EC was the establishment of a common commercial policy, the Treaty did not in fact provide a definition of its scope. As a result, there has been a longstanding dispute over the division of powers between the EC and its member states. The completion of the European internal market will require an extension of the Community's jurisdiction on external trade in areas covered by the 1992 program. In other words, common attitudes will have to be adopted by the 12 EC member states toward third countries in such areas as safeguard clauses, technical barriers, government procurement, and services.

In all these areas GATT rules are either inadequate, incomplete, or nonexistent. The key question for third countries, therefore, concerns the kind of reciprocity the Community will demand from its trading partners in order to grant them the benefits of the fully liberalized internal market. Will it be bilateral reciprocity or multilateral reciprocity? In principle, the EC has opted in favor of multilateral negotiations in the Uruguay Round based on nondiscriminatory reciprocity, but it might be tempted by bilateral deals in some instances. In fact, if the past is any guide to the future, I would predict that Community partners will fall into one of two categories: preferred countries or nonpreferred countries.

In the past, the Community has increasingly transgressed the principle of nondiscrimination by constructing a complex hierarchical system of preferential arrangements with respect to the common external tariff. Since the late 1970s, this so-called "pyramid of privileges" comprised three layers. At the top are the countries granted duty-free access for all their manufactured exports: the 6 countries of the current European Free Trade Association, the 12 Mediterranean countries, and the 66 African, Caribbean, and Pacific states of the Lomé Convention. The middle layer includes all other developing countries, with the exception of Taiwan, which are beneficiaries of the EC's Generalized System of Preferences. At the bottom, a handful of industrial countries, including the United States and Japan, are subject to the full common external tariff.

The EC is likely to extend to countries at the top of the pyramid the same special treatment with regard to nontariff barriers as to tariffs. The real question is whether the Community will be tempted by bilateral reciprocity with countries in the middle layer (which includes the newly industrializing countries) or at the bottom of the pyramid. There are several reasons why the Community should resist that temptation. The main one is that to be successful after 1992 Europe needs an open trading system based on multilateral principles. This would ensure two requirements. On the one hand, an open attitude toward imports would provide the necessary discipline to discourage European producers from noncompetitive behavior. On the other hand, newly invigorated European firms will require open export markets in which to sell their output.

References

Jacquemin, Alexis, and André Sapir. 1989. "Introduction—1992: A Single but Imperfect Market." In Alexis Jacquemin and André Sapir, eds., *The European Internal Market—Trade and Competition*. Oxford: Oxford University Press.
Sapir, André. 1989. "Does 1992 Come Before or After 1990?" In R. Jones and Anne Krueger, eds., *The Political Economy of Trade Policy*. Oxford: Basil Blackwell.

14

The Canada–US Free Trade Agreement: Special Case or Wave of the Future?

Richard G. Lipsey and Murray G. Smith

The reelection of a majority Progressive Conservative government in November 1988, after an intense election campaign centering on the free trade issue, has confirmed Canada's acceptance of the Canada–US Free Trade Agreement. That agreement calls for a complete removal of tariffs on trade between the two countries over a 10-year period starting early in 1989, an ending of many nontariff barriers and a restricted use of others, right of establishment and national treatment for firms producing a range of traded services, removal of many trade irritants, and regularization of many practices with respect to each country's investment in the other. It also introduces two dispute settlement mechanisms: an innovative general mechanism to deal with disputes arising out of the application of the agreement itself; and a binding appeal mechanism for settling disputes arising from the application of each country's trade laws, which can also review changes in trade laws.

The existence of this new regional free trade agreement raises a series of questions about future trade policies for both Canada and the United States, which we address in this chapter, from the Canadian point of view. Although many of these are of particular concern to the two signatories, we try to emphasize those aspects that may offer lessons of wider applicability or may have global repercussions.

The first section of this chapter shows why free trade agreements appeal to trading countries such as Canada. We argue that the Canada–US agreement achieved goals for Canada (and the United States) that could not have been achieved through multilateral negotiations, and that it does not impose explicit, de jure, constraints on the commercial policies of either country

Richard G. Lipsey is a Senior Research Fellow at the C. D. Howe Institute in Toronto. Murray G. Smith is head of the International Economics Program of the Institute for Research on Public Policy in Ottawa.

toward third countries—although the possibility of implicit de facto inhibitions cannot be ruled out.

In the next section, we address the implications of alternative options for future bilateral trade agreements involving either or both partners. First, we examine the implications of possible third-country accession to the Canada–US agreement. Then we study the possibility that either country might go it alone with new FTAs, and how the other partner might react. Finally, we ask, if one of the two member countries negotiates one or more bilateral agreements with third countries, how will these relate to the existing agreement, and will amendments be required to that agreement?

In the final section, we consider the compatibility of the Canada–US Free Trade Agreement with the multilateral trading system, examine the implications for Canadian (and also US) participation in the Uruguay Round, and discuss the potential interaction between the negotiation of future bilateral FTAs and the evolution of the multilateral system.

Bilateral Gains and Implications for Trade Policies

What does the Canada–US agreement achieve for the two signatories, and what are the broader consequences? In this section, we argue two points. First, the agreement offers the two countries significant economic gains and the prospect of more stable bilateral economic relations that are almost certainly unattainable through the multilateral route. Second, the agreement does not put significant constraints on the commercial policies that either country can follow with respect to third countries.

Are Free Trade Agreements Redundant?

Opponents of regional agreements often dismiss them on the grounds that they can achieve nothing that cannot be achieved through multilateral negotiations. This view is expressed, for example, by Anne Krueger in her comments in this volume. It was also strongly advocated by the Canadian opponents to the Canada–US agreement.

There may be good reasons for opposing any new regional trade agreement. Effective opposition is not helped, however, by asserting that such agreements are valueless to their participants. Informed support for, or opposition to, such agreements requires an appreciation of the major benefits that they can bring to the contracting parties—particularly the smaller ones. For this reason, the Canadian case is worth studying.

Canadian supporters of the bilateral agreement argued that it and the current round of multilateral trade negotiations were integral parts of a two-pronged trade liberalization strategy. On the one hand, the Uruguay Round obviously offers Canada gains not available through the bilateral agreement. One example is trade liberalization with countries other than the United States. A second is the chance to address issues that are difficult to resolve bilaterally because of the importance of third-country subsidies and trade barriers. Trade in agricultural goods is a case in point. On the other hand, the bilateral negotiations offered gains that could not realistically be expected to be achieved through multilateral negotiations. The following paragraphs summarize some of the main points. (For further detail, see Lipsey and York 1988.)

First, the Canada–US agreement offers complete elimination of tariffs on all Canadian exports to the United States that meet the stipulated rules of origin. This covers nearly 80 percent of Canada's total exports, and provides a level of general tariff reduction not even contemplated in the Uruguay Round. The maximum tariff cut permitted under the US negotiating authority contained in the Omnibus Trade and Competitiveness Act of 1988 is 50 percent. Furthermore, the agreement encompasses tariff removal on a number of products, such as textiles, clothing, petrochemicals, and steel, that neither country would be willing to extend to all GATT members on a most-favored-nation (MFN) basis.

Second, a number of nontariff barriers (NTBs) are prohibited completely, and the use of others is restricted. Quantitative restrictions are eliminated, including provisions under the US meat import and atomic energy laws. The circumstances under which escape clause action against import surges is allowed are significantly restricted. The agreement makes it very difficult to use national defense as an excuse for restricting imports. Mutual recognition of the test data and efforts to promote harmonization of standards will curtail technical barriers to trade. These and the many other constraints on NTBs included in the agreement are difficult to achieve through multilateral negotiations.

Third, most commercial services are covered by the agreement. These are given rights of establishment and of national treatment in the partner's territory. In light of the interdependence of the service sectors of the two economies, these provisions are advantageous to both countries, create a more stable framework for private-sector decision makers, and could provide useful precedents for the GATT negotiations (see Schott and Smith 1988). Both countries felt that they could get further with liberalizing trade in services bilaterally than multilaterally, where the resistance of many less-developed countries (LDCs) has to be overcome.

Fourth, a number of specific trade disputes were settled, and the terms of settlement were written into the agreement. For example, a festering dispute over automotive trade and investment was resolved in a way that avoids a potential unfair-trade action (Wonnacott 1988). It would have been much more difficult to reach many of these settlements in negotiations conducted one issue at a time. Such piecemeal negotiations would have lacked the overall incentives both of not wanting to jeopardize the broader agreement and of being able to judge the package of concessions as a whole.

Fifth, agreement was reached on a more liberal and stable regime with respect to each country's investment in the other. A number of longstanding American complaints against Canadian practices governing foreign investment were also dealt with, although less was accomplished than the US negotiators had wished. The Canadian concessions, although mild by world standards, caused a political uproar in Canada. It would have been very difficult for a Canadian government to make them, had they not been embedded in a broader agreement that promised major economic advantages.

Sixth, some major shields were provided to Canada against increases in US protectionism. There are significant restrictions on the application of safeguard measures between the two partners. This eliminates the situation that has occurred in the past whereby a US safeguard measure aimed at third countries sideswiped Canada. Under the legislative watchdog function, Canada is exempt from any US trade-restricting law unless it is mentioned by name in the legislation, and any US legislation that does concern Canada must be discussed bilaterally before it is passed. It is inconceivable that the United States would extend to other countries this remarkable concession of allowing Canada to scrutinize US domestic legislation before it is passed by the Congress.

Seventh, the agreement institutes an innovative general dispute settlement mechanism (DSM). At the outset of any dispute, the complaining country can elect to use either the GATT or the bilateral mechanism. The bilateral mechanism is arguably superior to the GATT mechanism in a number of ways, not the least of which are the right to initiate a panel, and procedural deadlines establishing an orderly timetable. The parties may agree to an option of binding dispute settlement. Although some aspects of the agreement's DSM may be adopted by the GATT, the agreement offered at the time a substantial improvement over GATT procedures.

Finally, the agreement provides a unique mechanism for settling disputes arising out of the application of each country's domestic laws pertaining to countervailing and antidumping duties. This bilateral mechanism is an alternative to judicial review by the domestic courts. The fairness with which US (and Canadian) laws are applied by its own administrative agencies (e.g., the US Department of Commerce and the International Trade Commission) will be judged by a binational panel whose decisions are final and binding. Changes to trade laws are subject to review to determine their consistency with the agreement and with the GATT. These arrangements were only accepted by the United States at the last moment when the whole agreement seemed threatened. It is hard to believe that the US Congress would ever extend such a right to other countries.

Although other examples have gone unlisted, we hope that what has been said is sufficient to make our point: there is no way that many of the pathbreaking and powerful trade liberalizing measures included in the Canada–US Free Trade Agreement could have been obtained by Canada through any foreseeable round of multilateral negotiations. In some cases, the two signatories would have been unwilling—for political and/or economic reasons—to extend certain sections of the agreement to all GATT members; in other cases, other GATT countries would have been unwilling to accept some sections; in yet other cases, agreements reached on specific sections would have been unacceptable to one country or the other if judged individually instead of as part of an overall package.

Implications for Canadian Commercial Policies

Does the Canada–US agreement place constraints on the commercial policies of either partner with respect to third countries? It seems obvious to us that the agreement imposes no explicit legal constraints. After all, it is of the essence of a free trade agreement that either partner is at liberty to alter its trade barriers against third countries, either through multilateral GATT negotiations or through such plurilateral trade arrangements as further free trade agreements.

During the Canadian debate over the agreement, some opponents argued that the United States could use its "nullification and impairment" provisions to invoke the DSM against any reduction of Canadian trade barriers against third countries. This argument made a mockery of the concept of nullification and impairment as it has been developed in GATT jurisprudence. Neither country has a formal property right in the preferences, which are incidentally created by the removal of bilateral trade barriers by the Canada–US Free Trade Agreement. Each country simply has claims on maintaining the degree of access to the other market achieved through the free trade agreement.

A more subtle concern is that there may be de facto pressures that are implicit in the agreement, even if not included in it de jure. On the one hand, some worry that Canadian industries, presented with unlimited access to the vast US market, may diminish their concern for selling in other markets. Furthermore, they may become jealous of their preferential treatment in the US market—which will be reduced by every subsequent multilateral tariff cut. In the former case, a key pressure acting on the

Canadian government for active participation in the MTN negotiations could be reduced, whereas in the latter case Canadian producers will want the United States to preserve barriers imposed on third countries.

Similar Canadian pressures may resist further US bilateral free trade agreements. Canadian exporting interests are likely to be disappointed if they lose their preferential treatment vis-à-vis some third country because the United States concludes an agreement with that country. Had there been no Canada–US Free Trade Agreement, the Canadian firms would have been disadvantaged to an even greater extent by the US action; however, with the agreement in place, Canadian producers have an interest in resisting other such agreements involving the United States.

On the other hand, success in the US market may make Canadian firms better able (through reduced costs) and more willing (through increased self-confidence) to compete with firms in other countries. Furthermore, industries will seek to lower their input costs through negotiation of reductions in trade barriers imposed on inputs imported from third countries. As rationalization of production in the North American market proceeds, there is an incentive in the free trade area (FTA) for each of the partner countries to negotiate reciprocal reductions in tariffs on trade with third countries. Not only will the domestic industry become more competitive, but since some of the gains from protection occur to economic interests in the partner country, there is an incentive to offer reductions in the protective barrier in return for improved access to third-country markets. Thus, FTAs are likely to be more outward-looking than customs unions such as the European Community (Smith 1988).

The asymmetries in the Canadian and US economies appear to reinforce the outward-looking dynamic of FTAs. US negotiators can be expected to disregard Canadian pressure to maintain US trade barriers, while no Canadian negotiator or political leader could be seen to be responding to US interests.

Other Free Trade Areas

Now assume that, for whatever reason, other countries become interested in reaching free trade agreements with Canada and/or the United States. What are the implications of the various bilateral options?

Third Countries Might Accede to the Canada–US Agreement

Including other countries in the agreement poses some more or less technical problems, concerning such things as the phase-out period for third-country tariffs, and the rules of origin for the wider FTA. It also raises questions concerning those aspects of the agreement that were designed to respond to bilateral concerns. These are considered in the following paragraphs.

Energy—The provisions of the agreement's energy chapter are controversial on both sides of the border. Canadians worry about the prohibition of export taxes (which is customary in FTAs) and about the specific allocation rules governing supply cutbacks and rationing in time of government-declared shortages. Concern on the US side relates to the exemption of the energy sector from the provisions liberalizing investment and the lack of untrammelled access to Canadian energy resource development. The careful balancing of conflicting concerns over energy that characterizes the Canada–US agreement is unlikely to be appropriate for trade agreements with third countries such as Japan or Korea, which are heavy energy importers.

Auto Trade—The automotive provisions of the agreement give preferential treatment to Canadian and US auto manufacturers over foreign-owned firms located in the United States and Canada by grandfathering existing Auto Pact provisions; there are a few foreign firms whose existing preferential treatment is also grandfathered. The provisions also give protection to Canadian and US parts producers by increasing the restrictiveness of the rules of origin. Extending these provisions to the automobile industries of other countries that acceded to the Canada–US agreement would probably meet with determined resistance from Canadian and US car and parts manufacturers. Modifying them to meet the concerns of domestic firms while maintaining the principle of nondiscrimination against a new partner's industries would be fraught with difficulties.

Institutional Arrangements—The general DSMs in the agreement's Chapter 18 establish carefully delineated time limits and a preselected roster of panelists to adjudicate the process. Although this mechanism could be generalized to include third countries fairly readily, there would be a few administrative difficulties. For example, introduction of third (and fourth) country participants could create difficulties in choosing the roster of panelists and make it more difficult to conclude the process within the time limits desirable for this type of DSM. No doubt, however, these difficulties could be overcome.

It appears more difficult to generalize the mechanisms set up in Chapter 19 to review the application of trade laws. Although there are technical differences, Canadian and US trade laws are remarkably similar. It would be more difficult to apply the agreement's appeal mechanism for decisions involving antidumping and countervailing duties to third countries whose domestic trade laws and administrative procedures differed substantially from those of the United States and Canada. Each country might be reluctant to subject its internal decisions concerning the application of its own laws to binding decisions reached by a multinational panel—the degree of reluctance probably increases exponentially with the number of countries involved. Even with the best will in the world, it would be increasingly difficult to find an international roster of experts informed in each country's domestic trade laws as the number of participating countries increased.

The agreement's trade law review mechanism is in any case intended as an interim arrangement pending the outcome of negotiations on a new set of rules with respect to trade remedy laws. Introduction of a third country into this negotiation process could make reaching an agreement on the thorny issues involved even more difficult than it already will be. No one knows the outcome of the negotiations, but it will undoubtedly reflect a careful balancing of different national sensibilities. Furthermore, it would seem unlikely that a third country—with different sensibilities of its own and invoking different sensibilities on the part of Canadians and Americans—could easily be accommodated into the completed agreement for a new code covering unfair trade practices.

Services—Extension of the principle of national treatment and right of establishment to service industries in acceding countries should not pose serious problems. Indeed, either country can extend these provisions to third countries at its own discretion now, but the partner country is not obliged to extend such treatment. Furthermore, depending on the circumstances, Canada could receive the benefits if the United States removed restrictions on services trade with third countries because of the commitment to national treatment.

Serious problems would arise, however, because the agreement grandfathers existing derogations from both national treatment and the right of establishment. Although the grandfathered derogations differ in the two countries, a general consensus must have been developed that the two countries' overall packages of derogations were more or less equivalent. The universal grandfathering approach would be more difficult to apply to third countries whose laws violating national treatment were very different in kind and scope—and possibly also in transparency. If a new partner had much more restrictive laws than the United States and Canada, the universal grandfathering approach would lead to major complaints from North American service industries that they gained much less access to the new market than they conceded in their own. This happened with financial service industries under the present agreement, where different domestic restrictions meant that national treatment gave more opportunities to US firms operating in Canada than to Canadian firms operating in the United States. This problem would be more serious if a country whose laws were significantly more restrictive were brought in. To avoid the problem, difficult negotiations would be needed to lower the new partner's restrictions to the general levels existing in Canada and the United States. Alternatively, Canada and the United States could adjust their restrictions against the new partner to its levels.

Conclusion—Although the process of negotiating third-country accession would be difficult for all parties, such an accession would have several virtues, when compared with possible separate bilateral agreements between the third country and Canada on the one hand, and the United States on the other. First, accession to the agreement would ensure the two present contracting parties more balanced treatment with respect to the new partner. For example, would Canada be able to obtain the same terms in a separate bilateral FTA with Japan that the United States could obtain? Second, resolving some of the technical issues associated with accession, such as phasing in reductions in trade barriers and rules of origin among the three countries, would provide a more stable and orderly framework for private sector planning and investment decisions than if there were three separate bilateral agreements. Third, compared with a situation in which the United States made a separate agreement with a third country, accession to the agreement would avoid the problem of Canada finding itself less favored in the US market than the third country.

Either Country Could Negotiate Its Own FTAs With Third Countries

Either Canada or the United States might also wish to negotiate free trade agreements with other countries. Indeed there is already a proposal from New Zealand to link the Australian–New Zealand Closer Economic Relationship with Canada (Holmes et al. 1988). In the case of Australia and New Zealand, Canada might see few adjustment problems other than in sensitive agricultural sectors and might be attracted by the Pacific Rim linkage. (Canada would undoubtedly find an arrangement that excluded elements of the agricultural sector, and those instruments of agricultural policy permitted under GATT Article XI, easier to accept.) Classic Article XXIV reciprocal FTAs with South Korea, Mexico, and Thailand might offer greater economic efficiency gains, but the adjustment costs in the industrial sector would be correspondingly larger.

It is quite possible that the United States and Canada would come to different judgments about the balance of gains and losses in such FTAs. Interestingly, Canada may have a greater interest in an FTA with Japan than does the United States. Since tariff escalation creates more of a problem for Canada, with its heavy dependence on primary resource exports to Japan, Canada may gain relatively more from an FTA with Japan than would the United States. The high value of the yen might moderate some of the challenging Canadian adjustment problems in the industrial sector.

What Would Be the Relationship Among These Bilateral FTAs?

Some US officials have expressed interest in developing a net of FTAs as a pressure on GATT negotiations or as a substitute for them in the case that the Uruguay Round is judged a failure. Such FTAs might serve a broader purpose than merely exploiting the gains from trade. Canada, where protectionist pressures are strong, might choose to stay out of some or all of these new FTAs.

Whatever their motivation, the growth of a series of overlapping FTAs could cause serious problems. The resulting complicated web of overlapping FTAs could raise many technical problems with respect to such matters as rules of origin and the phasing in of tariff reductions. These difficulties might be reduced by creating a common bridging mechanism involving mutually agreed rules of origin for cumulation of trade involving multiple sourcing of products from countries that are partners to a series of bilateral trade agreements. This bridging mechanism could be an umbrella FTA that governed trade among the bilateral FTAs, which, in turn, would have much more specific and detailed architecture. The bridging mechanism could stop at common rules of origin, or it could go further to define a core of elements common to all the FTAs (e.g., free trade in all goods), leaving other details to vary among the FTAs.

The design of the rules of origin in the umbrella FTA and their relationship to the rules of origin in the existing Canada–US agreement raise some technical issues. Since the costs of compliance with any set of rules of origin are nontrivial, the rules of origin in the umbrella FTA could come to dominate the utilization of the Canada–US origin rules, particularly if the umbrella FTA has more restrictive criteria. For example, the EFTA–EC bilateral rules of origin have dominated the internal EFTA rules of origin.

Must the Existing Agreement Be Renegotiated If One Partner Enters Into an FTA With a Third Country?

Assume that the United States negotiates a new agreement, possibly with an Asian country. Problems could arise if the United States gave that country more favorable treatment than Canada receives under its agreement with the United States. This could not be an issue with tariffs, because no country can gain more than the complete elimination of tariffs that the Canada–US agreement provides. On certain nontariff measures, however, there are potential problems whenever there are derogations from national treatment. For example, the Asian country may get access to a share of the US procurement market that is larger than the small share that Canada obtains under its FTA with the United States. Alternatively, services not covered by the Canada–US agreement might be covered by the new FTA. For example, air transportation might be covered, whereas all transport industries are excluded from the Canada–US agreement.

The issue is more complicated with respect to derogations from national treatment for covered services (or investment issues). In the case of financial services, Canada is assured of national treatment with respect to future changes to the Glass–Steagall Act. The United States could, however, modify a specific derogation from national treatment for services or investment, which is grandfathered in the Canada–US agreement, in a way that only provided national treatment for a third country. Admittedly, the significance of such derogations from national treatment is limited, but the possibility that future US bilateral agreements may go further than the Canada–US agreement must be considered.

There are two basic ways to handle this issue. One anticipates it before it arises; the second reacts to it when it arises.

Unconditional MFN—One way to meet the problem before it arose would be to insert an unconditional MFN clause into the agreement (or enter into a separate understanding to this effect) now. This would specify that no other country could be given more favorable treatment by either the United States or Canada as a result of a bilateral agreement with a third country by either of these countries. If more favorable treatment were given, for example by the United States, equivalent treatment would automatically be extended to Canada as a result of the unconditional MFN treatment.

Now that the agreement has been concluded, it is extremely difficult to arouse the political will needed to change it in response to an anticipated rather than a present problem. Regrettably, unconditional MFN has gone out of fashion since the time of Cordell Hull. If either country seriously considers opening its own negotiations with a third country, however, the other partner should press vigorously for the addition of such a provision to the existing agreement.

Optional MFN—An alternative and possibly more feasible approach would be a separate understanding committing each side to an optional MFN principle involving possible extensions to the Canada–US agreement. Thus, for example, if the United States and Japan were to conclude a free trade agreement that involved a substantially larger share of procurement purchases under the coverage of the agreement than that covered under the Canada–US agreement, then Canada should have the opportunity to seek to renegotiate the Canada–US agreement to expand its coverage with respect to procurement, or should have the opportunity to opt into this element of the US–Japan arrangement by offering reciprocal coverage of procurement purchases. Of course, the United States should have an equivalent optional MFN opportunity if Canada negotiates a bilateral agreement with a third country.

Issues Requiring Renegotiation—There are at least two issues that might call for a reopening of the Canada–US agreement. First, a general case can be made that the rules of origin for duty-free treatment within an FTA should be made more liberal as the external tariffs of the parties are reduced either on an MFN basis or through negotiations of further regional FTAs. The purpose of rules of origin is to prevent deflections of trade that can arise due to disparities in the external trade barriers of the FTA partners. For example, the United States textile and apparel industries were concerned that the Canadian apparel industry would expand exports to the United States utilizing low-cost textiles from third countries and circumvent United States barriers to textile imports. To meet US industry concerns, the Canada–US agreement provides for elimination of tariffs for apparel produced from textiles manufactured in either country as well as a quota for apparel produced from third-country textiles. If, however, the United States were to conclude a free trade agreement with Korea, the restrictive rules of origin for textiles and apparel in the Canada–US agreement should be liberalized to allow more Canadian sourcing of textiles from third countries.

Second, the new bilateral FTA agreement might allow for a faster phased reduction of tariffs than the 10-year period (with exceptions for faster reductions) under the Canada–US agreement. The temporary distortions of competitive positions that would be implied by the different phase-in periods could be removed by renegotiating the Canada–US phase-ins.

Compatibility With the GATT and the Multilateral Trading System

In this final section we consider the compatibility of the agreement, and other FTAs that may follow in its footsteps, with the multilateral approach.

The Canada–US Agreement

Canadian Views

Is there any problem of compatibility between the agreement and the GATT? Canadian supporters of the bilateral negotiations saw no conflict between them and the Uruguay Round negotiations, although opponents asserted otherwise. Supporters argued, first, that there were sufficient negotiators and support staff to run both sets of negotiations during the period of their overlap, and that the bilateral negotiations would be completed prior to the critical latter part of the Uruguay Round negotiations. Second, they argued that the concerns addressed in the two sets of negotiations were sufficiently different that preoccupation with one would not deflect interest and effort from the other.

Once the agreement was reached, supporters argued that it was a step toward general trade liberalization rather than toward a fortress North America, as opponents charged it was. The agreement's supporters advanced several reasons for their position. First, rationalization on the basis of the large Canada–US market was an important step in helping Canadian industry to compete in other markets. Second, solving the major issues relating to trade with its most important trading partner would free Canadian negotiators to address issues with other countries during the Uruguay Round negotiations. Third, some of the more novel aspects of the agreement might provide guideposts for the Uruguay Round to follow.

The supporters' case seems to be widely accepted in Canada now that the Canadian debate is over. No conflict is now seen between the commitment of Canada and the United States to their bilateral agreement on the one hand, and their commitment to the current multilateral negotiations on the other.

International Perspectives

Formal Compatibility—Although the Canada–US Free Trade Agreement has yet to be examined by a GATT working party, the agreement appears to conform with the criteria of Article XXIV of the GATT. The Canada–US agreement does eliminate barriers on "substantially all trade," including agricultural trade except for those agricultural trade restrictions explicitly permitted under Article XI of the GATT (and thus permitted by Article XXIV). Once the 10-year implementation period is completed, all tariffs and many quantitative restrictions will be eliminated between the two partners. Furthermore, it would appear that in the Canada–US agreement "the duties and other regulations of commerce maintained in each of the constituent territories and applicable at the formation of such free trade area" in fact will "not be higher or more restrictive than the corresponding duties and other regulations of commerce existing in the same constituent territories prior to the formation of the free trade area" (GATT Article XXIV).

Consistency in Spirit—More to the point, the Canada–US agreement appears to conform not only with the letter of Article XXIV, but also with its original spirit. The architects of the GATT and the postwar multilateral trading system were not schizophrenic in drafting Article XXIV as an exemption from Article I (MFN). As Clair Wilcox, the principal American negotiator of the GATT, wrote:

Preferences have been opposed and customs unions favored, in principle, by the United States. This position may obviously be criticized as lacking in logical consistency. In preferential arrangements, discrimination against the outer world is partial; in customs unions, it is complete. But the distinction is nonetheless defensible. A customs union creates a wider trading area, removes obstacles to competition, makes possible a more economic allocation of resources, and thus operates to increase production and raise planes of living. A preferential system, on the other hand, obstructs economy in production, and restrains the growth of income and demand. It is set up for the purpose of conferring a privilege on producers within the system and imposing a handicap on external competitors. A customs union is conducive to the expansion of trade on the basis of multilateralism and non-discrimination; a preferential system is not (cited in Lowenfeld 1988).

Thus, the Canada–US Free Trade Agreement would seem to fall within the wide bounds of tolerance that have become accepted in the application of Article XXIV; indeed, the agreement appears consistent with the original spirit of Article XXIV based on the potential gains from trade creation.

A Consensus of Support—Supporters of multilateralism, while opposing a possible proliferation of regional FTAs, have shown little hostility to the Canada–US agreement. Their support presumably goes beyond asserting formal compliance of the agreement with the GATT. The absence of conflict in any wider sense between the Canada–US FTA and the Uruguay Round was attested to by strong comments made during 1988 by GATT supporters in other countries that rejection of the agreement by the Canadian electorate would be a setback to the multilateral negotiations.

There seems to be a strong, worldwide feeling that Canada and the United States are natural free trade partners. This feeling comes from the same people who often express concern over further FTAs, involving, say, the United States and some other Pacific Rim countries. A theorist should wonder what it is that distinguishes a Canada–US FTA, for example, from one between the United States and Japan. What makes one acceptable and the other objectionable to multilateralists?

Is it that Canada and the United States are neighbors? Geographic proximity has never been seen as a useful theoretical category or a significant economic factor. Wonnacott and Lutz, however, suggest in this volume that long-distance FTAs may create greater potential for trade diversion due to transport and communication costs. This, however, would be an empirical factor to be assessed on a case-by-case basis.

Is it that one country is large and the other small? There is no theoretical presumption that the balance of gains and losses—either for the member countries or the world as a whole—varies systematically with the ratio of the sizes of the member countries.

Is it that there are greater potential economies of scale in the Canada–US agreement? Certainly the substantial proportion of intraindustry trade between Canada and the United States supports this conjecture, which is borne out by some of the general-equilibrium analysis (Harris and Cox 1983).

Try as we may, however, we cannot find economic reasons for blessing the one FTA, while condemning its possible followers on a priori grounds about trade diversion or trade creation. We suspect the reasons stem partly from vague geopolitical sentiment and partly from political economy. From distant vantage points, Canadians and Canada often appear indistinguishable from Americans and the United States. "So if they are really the same," this geopolitical sentiment would say, "why not bless their union?" (It is precisely this kind of geopolitical sentiment that is at the root of many Canadians' concerns about the Canada–US agreement.)

More substantive political–economic considerations would work back from the general objective of preventing the breakup of the trading world into regional blocs with falling barriers within them and rising barriers between them. The Canada–US agreement is not seen as contributing to this development. This is partly because the economic size of the whole is only 10 percent more than the size of the larger single part, and partly because the two countries are perceived as drawn together by virtue of geography, language, history, ethnic backgrounds, and a host of other common features that go well beyond a desire to exploit their mutual gains from trade or commercial power. Perhaps the most important factor is that the Canada–US FTA avoids a fortress North America approach.

These rather casual thoughts do serve to suggest a need for some further theorizing on what type of FTAs are a threat to the multilateral system and what types are not, and why.

Is Big Necessarily Bad?—The attitudes of many observers to further bilateral FTAs by the United States may, as suggested above, reflect considerations of size. As Olivier Long observes:

Those who drafted the article (Article XXIV) certainly did not have in mind a structure of the size and importance of the European Economic Community (EEC), but rather arrangements between two or three countries, such as Benelux for instance. They did not envisage the conclusion by the EEC of preferential arrangements with developing countries with whom member countries of the EEC had been linked in the past by special relationships. Neither did they foresee that many developing countries would seek, through regional integration, the promotion of their economic development and that, in so doing, they would adopt the model of a customs union or free-trade area despite lacking the economic resources necessary fully to meet the strict criteria of Article XXIV. . . (Long 1985, 19).

On this view, the Canada–US agreement is acceptable because it does not greatly increase the size of the economy in the trade agreement over the economic size of the largest partner. The EC would, however, be unacceptable if it came up now, as would an FTA involving the United States and Japan or other countries of large economic size.

Other Free Trade Areas

The above comparisons have already taken us into the last topic of the relation between possible future FTAs and the multilateral trading system.

Multilateralism is Best—In our view the first-best result for the world's trading system is substantial liberalization of trade through the Uruguay Round of GATT negotiations combined with a solution to various problems such as intellectual property rights and a strengthening of the GATT institutional mechanisms, particularly in the area of dispute settlement. In this situation, the impetus for future bilateral FTAs involving either Canada or the United States would be greatly lessened. Even if such agreements were pursued, the preferences created by them would be smaller the greater the tariff reductions negotiated in the Uruguay Round.

Other Negotiations Should Not Precede the Completion of the GATT Round—More serious issues would arise if negotiations toward other bilateral FTAs involving the United States and/or Canada with third countries were to take place before the Uruguay Round is completed. Consideration of such negotiations might prove a useful prod to progress in the multilateral trade negotiations. Unless the multilateral negotiations slip beyond the formal deadline of 1990, however, bilateral negotiations of other FTAs would not be sufficiently advanced to influence the detailed outcome of the Uruguay Round. Such bilateral negotiations could also divert attention from the multilateral negotiations during their most critical phase.

If the Uruguay Round Fails—The final possibility arises if the Uruguay Round is judged to be a failure. The appeal of further bilateral FTAs would then be strengthened substantially. Canada, the United States, and the Pacific Rim countries would seriously reassess their trade options, giving serious consideration to further bilateral FTAs. It has long been recognized that such regional agreements need not be in conflict with the principles of the gains from trade liberalization, because they can be trade creating rather than trade diverting. One of the authors has argued previously that FTAs are much more likely to be compatible with the dynamic evolution of a multilateral trading system than is a customs union or a common market (Smith 1988). Nonetheless, the apparent failure of the Uruguay Round and the development of a series of bilateral FTAs, although it could be benign, would be much more likely to be the first stage of the breakup of the multilateral trading system into a series of trading blocs—a development that few economists would welcome.

Conclusion

Since more than 50 regional trading arrangements have been notified to the GATT under Article XXIV, and some, such as the formation and expansion of the European Community, have been larger (at least in terms of volume of trade), it may seem surprising to pose the question of whether the Canada–US agreement is a special case or the wave of the future.

Certainly there are special aspects of the Canada–US agreement that make accession by third countries somewhat difficult. Bilateral agreements with third countries by either the United States or Canada are feasible, but there are questions as to how they would relate to the existing Canada–US agreement, particularly since that agreement lacks an MFN obligation. Failing an amendment to the agreement inserting an MFN clause (which is unlikely), we propose that Canada and the United States negotiate an optional MFN commitment for derogations from national treatment. Under such an optional MFN arrangement, the partner could have the opportunity to negotiate expanded coverage under the Canada–US agreement, or to opt into a plurilateral arrangement involving the third country. Eventually a bridging mechanism or umbrella free trade agreement might well emerge to liberalize trade among these bilateral agreements.

The Canada–US agreement clearly conforms with GATT practice under Article XXIV and, indeed, appears consistent with the original spirit of the architects of the multilateral trading system such as Sir James Meade and Clair Wilcox. Although many outside observers support the Canada–US agreement on these grounds, many reservations are expressed about future bilateral FTAs negotiated by the United States.

The question of whether the Canada–US agreement is a special case is primarily a question about US trade policy. If the United States presses ahead with a series of bilateral FTAs, particularly with a large economy such as Japan, it will have far-reaching consequences for the global trading system. If Canada, however, concluded a free trade agreement with Australia–New Zealand or another Pacific Rim country, it would have minimal impact on the global system.

If substantial progress is achieved in the Uruguay Round in all the main negotiating areas, then the impetus for future bilateral free trade agreements will be reduced and any agreements that did emerge would be less corrosive to the system. If, however, the Uruguay Round fails, or is perceived to fail, then bilateral agreements could become a serious option for many countries.

References

Harris, Richard, and David Cox. 1983. *Trade, Industrial Policy and Canadian Manufacturing.* Toronto: Ontario Economic Council.

Holmes, Frank, Ralph Lattimore, and Anthony Hass. 1988. *Partners in the Pacific.* Wellington: New Zealand Trade Development Board.

Hudec, Robert. 1988. "Comments on Dispute Resolution Mechanisms," in Jeffrey J. Schott and Murray G. Smith, eds., *The Canada–United States Free Trade Agreement: The Global Impact.* Washington and Halifax: Institute for International Economics and Institute for Research on Public Policy.

Lipsey, Richard G., and Robert York. 1988. *Evaluating the Free Trade Deal*. Toronto: C. D. Howe Institute.

Long, Olivier. 1985. *Law and its Limitations in the GATT Multilateral Trade System*. Dordrecht: Martinus Nijhoff.

Lowenfeld, Andreas. 1988. "What GATT Says (Or Does Not Say)." In William Diebold, Jr., ed., *Bilateralism, Multilateralism and Canada in U.S. Trade Policy*. Cambridge, Mass.: Ballinger for the Council on Foreign Relations.

Schott, Jeffrey J., and Murray G. Smith, eds. 1988. *The Canada–United States Free Trade Agreement: The Global Impact*. Washington and Halifax: Institute for International Economics and Institute for Research on Public Policy.

Smith, Murray G. 1988. "What Is at Stake?" In William Diebold, Jr., ed., *Bilateralism, Multilateralism and Canada in U.S. Trade Policy*. Cambridge, Mass.: Ballinger for the Council on Foreign Relations.

Wonnacott, Paul. 1988. "The Auto Sector." In Jeffrey J. Schott and Murray G. Smith, eds., *The Canada–United States Free Trade Agreement: The Global Impact*. Washington and Halifax: Institute for International Economics and the Institute for Research on Public Policy.

15

The New Minilateralism and Developing Countries

Winston Fritsch

Over the past few years the United States has adopted a more aggressive bilateral stance in trade matters, progressively drifting away from the principles of multilateralism and most-favored-nation (MFN) treatment that have guided its trade policy since the mid-1930s.[1] The negotiations relating to temperate-zone agriculture, competition in global oligopolies and voluntary export restraints (VERs), and the new policy of reciprocity under the Generalized System of Preferences (GSP) are clear illustrations of this recent trend in US trade policy.

Another important aspect of this trend has been the proliferation of preferential trade agreements such as the Caribbean Basin Initiative (CBI) and the free trade area (FTA) with Israel, and, most recently, a far-reaching FTA with Canada. Whereas the Caribbean and Israel initiatives were clearly motivated by restricted geopolitical reasons,[2] the Canada–US FTA has broader motivations and, certainly, wider implications.

A pair of common perceptions helped give impetus to the Canada–US agreement. First, both countries were frustrated with certain inherent features of the multilateral trade liberalization process under the General Agreement on Tariffs and Trade (GATT), especially the free-rider and least-common-denominator or "convoy" problems (Wonnacott and Lutz, this volume). Second, there were advantages seen in escaping the constraints imposed on the scope, depth, and pace of the negotiations by the MFN clause and a multilaterally negotiated agenda (Whalley 1988, 175).

However, there were also important individual motives. From the view-

---

1. For a brief scholarly presentation of the history of the US position on these issues, see Diebold (1988). A good review of recent trends is to be found in Jackson (1987, 377–84).

2. For a discussion of the motives behind the US–Israel agreement, see Rosen (this volume).

Winston Fritsch is a professor of economics at the Catholic University of Rio de Janeiro.

point of Canada—which was, in fact, the *demandeur* of the agreement—the FTA was basically an isolated initiative justified by the overwhelming importance of the United States in Canadian trade. On the US side, however, it also reflected the broader trend toward bilateralism or "minilateralism" in American trade policy. Thus, it is not surprising that the political momentum generated by the very success of the FTA negotiations with Canada would prompt US government officials to revive the old notion that the enlargement of a US-centered FTA could provide an alternative—although admittedly a second-best and nonexclusive one—to the GATT liberalization process (Camps and Diebold 1983).

As former Secretary of the Treasury James A. Baker III, recently stated, "If possible, we hope . . . liberalization will occur in the Uruguay Round. If not, we might be willing to explore a 'market liberalization club' approach, through minilateral arrangements or a series of bilateral agreements. In this fashion, North America can build steady momentum for more open and efficient markets" (Baker 1988, 41). The US government has informally initiated follow-up contacts in this direction with several East Asian countries, including Japan (Baker 1988, 41).

This chapter discusses the consequences this recent trend in US trade policy may have for developing countries. The first section discusses the trade and welfare gains accruing to small countries that form an FTA with a larger partner and assesses whether comprehensive agreements covering a substantial portion of trade between the United States and individual developing countries are indeed likely to occur. The second section addresses the systemic consequences of the new US minilateral initiative from a developing country perspective. A third section summarizes the main conclusions.

Developing Country Gains From Free Trade With the United States

It is well known that bilateral or minilateral FTAs may not improve economic welfare in the participating countries. As Viner (1950) showed, formation of an FTA, besides allowing the substitution of cheaper imports from the preferential trade partner for the output of inefficient domestic producers (the trade creation effect), can also displace previously cheaper imports from sources outside the FTA (the trade diversion effect); the net welfare effect depends on whether the trade creation effects exceed the trade diversion effects. Economic analysis shows that the formation of preferential FTAs is almost always a second-best alternative compared with a nonpreferential, multilateral tariff cut, which results only in trade creation.[3]

---

3. Cooper and Massel (1965). The consideration of the existence of nontariff barriers

In practice, however, the economic incentives to the formation of a particular FTA depend on certain characteristics of the potential partners. Thus, assessing the prospects for more FTAs between the United States and developing countries is complicated by the great heterogeneity of the very large group of potential partners. Some basic insights can, nevertheless, be provided by bringing into the analysis some stylized facts concerning relative size, the commodity and country patterns of trade, and the height and structure of protection in a representative developing country and in the United States.

If one ignores terms-of-trade changes following integration stemming from differences in size, the net static welfare gains from the standpoint of a particular country forming an FTA with the United States are likely to be greater:

☐ the higher the level of protection in the United States (i.e., the more competitive the partner is with the United States), and the greater the importance of the United States as a market for the partner's exports; and

☐ the more efficient the United States is compared with third suppliers (this is very important, for, given that protection in developing countries is generally high, relative US inefficiency can be the source of significant trade diversion effects).

On the basis of this a priori reasoning, a set of rough rules can be devised to assess which developing countries are likely to be attracted to an FTA with the United States.[4] Countries likely to benefit should be those that export a reasonably large proportion of manufactures, on which protection is generally higher in the United States; that have the United States as an important market for their exports; and that derive a relatively large share of their imports from the United States, thus indicating that US producers are competitive relative to other suppliers.

Calculating the weight of the United States in the trade of each of a sample of developing exporters of manufactures provides a neat way of identifying

---

such as quantitative restrictions introduces some complications in the analysis, because the welfare impact of trade liberalization comes to depend on the size and country distribution of the scarcity rents generated by the restrictions. A discussion of the economics of FTAs is provided by Wonnacott and Lutz (this volume).

4. A strong but provisional caveat is made for ignoring complications stemming from differences in relative country sizes, the existence of selective nontariff barriers in the United States, and the domestic distributive effects of liberalization in highly protected developing countries, as well as other possible determinants of gains from integration, whose practical importance is discussed below.

Figure 15.1 US share in exports versus share of non-US suppliers in imports of 35 countries, 1985

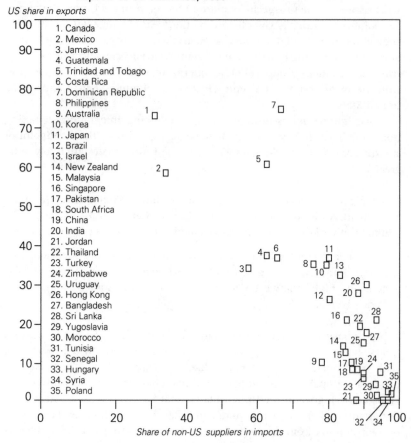

US share in exports

1. Canada	
2. Mexico	
3. Jamaica	
4. Guatemala	
5. Trinidad and Tobago	
6. Costa Rica	
7. Dominican Republic	
8. Philippines	
9. Australia	
10. Korea	
11. Japan	
12. Brazil	
13. Israel	
14. New Zealand	
15. Malaysia	
16. Singapore	
17. Pakistan	
18. South Africa	
19. China	
20. India	
21. Jordan	
22. Thailand	
23. Turkey	
24. Zimbabwe	
25. Uruguay	
26. Hong Kong	
27. Bangladesh	
28. Sri Lanka	
29. Yugoslavia	
30. Morocco	
31. Tunisia	
32. Senegal	
33. Hungary	
34. Syria	
35. Poland	

Share of non-US suppliers in imports

Source: International Monetary Fund, *Direction of Trade Statistics.*

likely gainers from commercial integration with the United States. Figure 15.1 is a scatter diagram which plots the share of the United States in the exports of each of a sample of 35 less-developed countries (LDCs) against the share of third (i.e., non-US) suppliers in the imports of each of the same countries. The sample includes all World Bank developing members with more than $500 million of exports and at least 20 percent of manufactures in total exports in 1985.[5] It can be seen that the list of developing countries

---

5. Australia, Canada, Japan, and New Zealand are also shown as references. The year 1985 was chosen as the latest for which data were available. Tests performed for

having both a reasonable degree of competitiveness and substantial trade with the United States is limited to a small group including Mexico and a few Caribbean countries.

The presumption that only a few developing countries are likely candidates for FTAs with the United States is reinforced by some basic facts about trade regimes in the United States and in the developing world, by considerations relating to the irrelevance of the American tariff relative to the recent sharp fluctuations in real effective exchange rates of the dollar, and, last but not least, by the implications of the huge difference in size between the United States and the representative LDC for adjustment costs in the latter.

Consider first the complications posed by some specific features of the American structure of protection to the incentives for developing countries to join an FTA. A first and fundamental problem is how the United States could further discriminate in favor of partners that are already entitled to some preferential margins by virtue of the US GSP, which grants duty-free treatment to eligible products, or by virtue of special and more comprehensive agreements in terms of product coverage under the CBI.[6] This could be done either by withdrawing the GSP offer from all nonparticipating LDCs, or by selectively enlarging it to the participating countries, increasing the number of eligible products so as to include products of export interest to them. However, the former alternative seems unthinkable in terms of US foreign policy, whereas the latter is bound to face great domestic political resistance, as GSP exclusion not infrequently reflects the opposition of US producers to duty-free treatment. In fact, enlargement of the US GSP to include import-sensitive products is unlikely even in the case of very small LDCs, as the experience of the CBI—which excludes, among other products, textiles, clothing, and shoes—clearly demonstrates. This difficulty would also apply to the abolition or reduction of VER quotas and insurance against arbitrary and protectionist antidumping actions. As these barriers are the greatest single source of bilateral trade conflicts between the United States and the larger, semi-industrialized developing countries, the prospect of their abolition could otherwise provide an important additional inducement for these countries to negotiate bilateral liberalization arrangements.

---

other years in the early 1980s show that the appreciation of the dollar does not significantly alter the general picture.

6. It is interesting to note that the threat of GSP graduation can also act as a negative incentive for a developing country to consider an FTA with the United States if such benefits are perceived as important determinants of its competitive edge. This seems indeed to have been the case in the US–Israel agreement as reported by Rosen (this volume).

A second consideration is that, in a world of wildly fluctuating real exchange rates between key currencies, and very low tariffs in the OECD countries, small economies that enjoy greater independence in their choice of exchange rate regimes may reap far greater positive trade effects by belonging to a depreciating currency area than by joining its issuing nation's customs area through an FTA.[7] Thus, as long as the current US external disequilibrium and recurrent pressures on the dollar persist, developing countries can look to pegging their exchange rates to the dollar as a unilateral way to benefit from trade diversion against nondollar area competitors in US markets without any of the reciprocal ties imposed by an FTA. This alternative has, of course, domestic macroeconomic consequences different from those involved in creating an FTA with the United States, but for countries whose currencies are traditionally tied to the dollar and are likely to remain so (such as, for instance, those of Latin America) this is an irrelevant consideration.

The crucial argument demonstrating both the limited gains developing countries are likely to derive from forming FTAs with the United States and the suboptimality of this policy alternative relates, however, to the size difference between the trading partners and the developing country's willingness to liberalize. From the standpoint of a small developing country, entering into an FTA with a large and open country such as the United States—if it were comprehensive in terms of product coverage as demanded by GATT Article XXIV—would be tantamount to trade liberalization.[8] If we also make the reasonable assumptions that large differences in resource endowments exist between the United States and the developing country and that there are high trade barriers in the latter, it is natural to conclude, according to orthodox theory, that free trade with the United States will lead to a large reallocation of resources in the small partner and, therefore, give it an opportunity to reap substantial static gains.

The political response to that opportunity in each case will, of course, depend on beliefs held by the relevant domestic actors in the developing country as to the benefits of trade liberalization and their assessment of the political costs of the sizable adjustment involved. The interesting point to

---

7. The proviso of independence in defining exchange rate policy is an important one. American pressure on some Asian superexporters to let their currencies appreciate against the dollar may, in fact, induce them to look favorably at preferential arrangements for access to the US market as a means of preserving competitiveness against third suppliers.

8. Given the huge difference in size between the United States and the representative LDC, when tariff barriers fall the latter's relative prices are likely to adjust fully to those of the United States, which are roughly equal to world prices in most cases.

note, however, is that, on the one hand, if they tend to favor the maintenance of a restrictive trade regime, the proposal of an FTA is by definition a nonstarter, whereas on the other hand, if they are willing to liberalize, they should in fact do so on an MFN basis to avoid the negative trade diversion effects of the formation of an FTA. This conclusion can be reached much on the lines of the arguments presented in Cooper and Massel's classic paper (1965) challenging the alleged second-best properties of a customs union.[9] Thus, under neither of these two possible assumptions as to the domestic propensity to liberalize is the formation of an FTA with the United States an optimum policy choice. In addition, fears of retaliation by third partners are obviously likely to loom large in the decision in those small countries that, besides imposing high trade barriers, do not derive an extremely high proportion of their imports from the United States. The vast majority of developing countries fall in this category.[10]

This analysis of the benefits and costs of adjustment to developing countries of forming an FTA with the United States leads to the conclusion that, because the economic incentives are likely to be small, the number of such agreements is bound to be very limited. Nevertheless, two objections could still be levied against such a conclusion.

The first is the usual point that the static benefits or losses identified in conventional analysis are low in relation to possible dynamic gains.[11] Among these, the most often quoted in the context of free trade between partners of widely differing size are the scale economies realizable by firms located in the smaller partner because of the increased size of the common market after integration occurs. It should be stressed, however, that for the great majority of developing countries such gains are purely notional. Not only do scale economies not usually prevail in a large number of labor intensive industries, but, more importantly, supply constraints and/or uncertainty as to the stability of the preferential arrangement are likely to more than

9. Although the first-best properties of unilateral tariff liberalization shown by Cooper and Massel have been strongly qualified in Wonnacott and Wonnacott (1981), it still holds true that, for highly protected countries, bilateral liberalization may entail heavy trade diversion effects and efficiency losses.

10. This last point could also be seen as a strong additional disincentive to the formation of an FTA with the United States for countries lying too far to the right in the diagram shown in figure 15.1.

11. The term is attributed to Balassa (1962) and usually implied to cover gains resulting from the impact of commercial integration on growth rates of participating countries through the operation of a large variety of rather unrelated effects on efficiency at the firm or industry level. For a review of these effects, see El-Agraa (1988, 26ff).

outweigh the positive effects of potential economies of scale, as the fiasco of the GSP as an instrument for industrialization abundantly shows.

The second and more substantial argument draws on effects stemming from the consideration of intraindustry trade and direct investment flows not captured by conventional theoretical analysis. If strong product differentiation and economies of scale exist at the firm level, the distributive losses arising from trade liberalization are likely to be dampened by positive consumption effects generated by the availability of a wider range of products the greater the existing degree of trade overlap, given trade partners' factor endowments (Krugman 1981). Although the net effect is likely to become negative the greater the difference in trade partners' factor endowments, this result seems to provide a strong rationale for attempts at integration on a single-industry basis or across a limited range of products.

Of course, agreements that do not cover "substantially all trade" between the contracting parties are not allowed under GATT Article XXIV. However, deals patterned on the US–Canada Auto Pact, a clear example of the kind of agreement referred to above, can be replicated in certain instances. Such restricted agreements may come about not only because, as suggested above, they seem more attractive to the representative developing country than comprehensive deals, but also because in the context of the present trend in US trade policy toward bilateralism and "aggressive reciprocity" (Cline 1982), they should look natural from the American standpoint, even if not entirely in conformity with Article XXIV.

This tendency toward integration within a limited range of products also seems to be reinforced, although not necessarily on a strict intraindustry basis, by the consequences of worldwide sourcing and the globalization of industrial activity within multinational firms. Examples of special provisions in US and host countries' trade laws to facilitate sectoral or vertical integration in processing abound, and their ad hoc amplification in the context of bilateral agreements, such as the so-called "super 807s" (free access beyond quotas for products manufactured with US materials) allowed in the CBI, has occurred. Indeed, there is evidence that the importance of intrafirm trade in FTAs is growing (Dunning 1982, 430). Thus, in predicting the reactions of small countries to the offer of an FTA with the United States, account should be taken of the perceived effects of free trade on their locational advantages as recipients of foreign direct investment flows.

These arguments clearly show that the complexity of the analysis increases sharply as the focus is narrowed to take into account existing institutional realities. This suggests that any organized discussion about the likely response of LDCs to the US drive toward the formation of FTAs should try to divide the large number of developing countries into relatively homogeneous groups according to certain key features. A first characteristic to be noted is that, given current trade patterns, the regions of greatest interest from the US perspective are the Pacific Rim and Latin America and the Caribbean. It would seem that for the 50-odd ACP (African, Caribbean, and Pacific) countries (with the exception of a few Caribbean countries) as well as the so-called Mediterranean countries, the possibilities of FTAs with the United States are sharply reduced by their traditional dependence on the EC preferential umbrella; for their part the specialized oil exporters have very little to gain from free trade under the present structure of protection in the United States. As the developing countries in the Pacific Basin are the object of detailed treatment in other chapters in this volume, it may be useful to focus here on the Latin American and Caribbean countries to illustrate some of the general points made above.

This large group of countries can be divided for analytical purposes into four main subgroups: (1) South America, (2) Mexico, (3) the CBI economies, and (4) the other small countries in Central America and the Caribbean, excluding Cuba and Nicaragua.

Although a reasonably heterogeneous group themselves, the South American countries have in common a smaller dependence on US markets and suppliers than do the other Western Hemisphere countries. The greater geographical diversification of South America's trade pattern can be seen in figure 15.2, where, except for oil-producing Ecuador and Venezuela, all the countries of the continent cluster in the lower right corner.

Together with the high level of protection usually prevailing in South America, its diversified trade pattern would seem to indicate, as suggested above, reduced incentives to free trade with the United States. Moreover, the bleak current prospects for capital inflows facing the larger semi-industrialized countries in the region, stemming from their high levels of foreign debt, mean that far-reaching liberalization attempts as implied by free trade with the United States are almost certain to backslide, thus creating severe problems of credibility from the US standpoint.

The case of Mexico, discussed in greater depth by Trigueros (this volume), has great similarities with that of the other semi-industrialized Latin American economies. Mexico's peculiarity stems from the fact that its trade flows are much more heavily oriented to the United States, as can be seen in figure 15.2. In this sense, the Mexican case provides a graphic illustration of the near equivalence of forming an FTA with the United States and full-fledged trade liberalization. The chances of a comprehensive Mexico–US free trade agreement depend, therefore, on the result of the inevitable political confrontation over the design of trade policy between those who favor the traditionally cautious stance regarding liberalization[12] and the

---

12. The following statement by Victor Urquidi (1986), the former president of the

apparently more liberal technocracy emerging within the ranks of the hegemonic Partido Revolucionário Institucional.

It is unlikely that something as radical as an FTA with the United States will be sought by the Mexican government in the foreseeable future. However, as in all indebted countries, the feasibility and, thus, the likelihood of any attempt at liberalization depends crucially on the availability of external financial resources, a variable entirely outside the Mexican authorities' control. In any event, the momentum provided by the current US drive toward North American economic integration, the crucial dependence of Mexican economic performance on export growth, and, last but not least, the strategic importance Mexico holds for the United States may be instrumental in helping to shape additional, sectorally limited forms of commercial as well as industrial integration, which could serve as a nucleus for more ambitious initiatives in the future.

Finally, the small Central American and Caribbean primary product exporters, with few exceptions, are heavily dependent on the US market (figure 15.2). The position of the CBI countries—among which the main suppliers of nonoil exports are the Dominican Republic, Costa Rica, Guatemala, Honduras, and El Salvador—is rather unique, and it is very unlikely that they could be enticed to give something for nothing and form an FTA with the United States before the Caribbean Basin Economic Recovery Act expires in 1996. In relation to group 4, an important change in the export outlook of a number of ACP countries in the Caribbean is likely to take place in 1992, with the end to the substantial benefits these countries now derive from export subsidies and guaranteed quotas in sugar and bananas granted by the EC.[13] As combined current exports of these two staples are 50 percent greater than manufactured exports from those countries, this may turn the management of US sugar quotas and guaranteed access to banana exports from these countries to the American market into an important element in bilateral trade negotiations (World Bank 1988, 18). Together with the generalization of some concessions now granted to the CBI countries in trade in manufactures, they could prove important bar-

---

International Economic Association, on the possible consequences of a comprehensive FTA among the three North American economies upon Mexican industry is representative of the view held by large sectors of Mexican opinion: "the mere notion that Mexico, from a weaker economic position than the other two, should open its tariff border would mean the rapid demise of most of Mexican manufacturing industry, before it even had a chance to start making inroads—if it could—into the US and Canadian markets."

13. I thank Paul Meo for drawing my attention to this point.

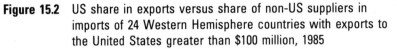

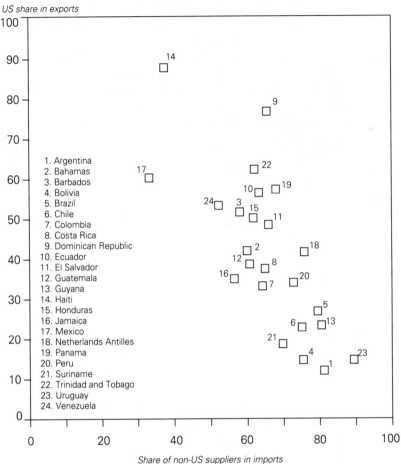

US share in exports

1. Argentina
2. Bahamas
3. Barbados
4. Bolivia
5. Brazil
6. Chile
7. Colombia
8. Costa Rica
9. Dominican Republic
10. Ecuador
11. El Salvador
12. Guatemala
13. Guyana
14. Haiti
15. Honduras
16. Jamaica
17. Mexico
18. Netherlands Antilles
19. Panama
20. Peru
21. Suriname
22. Trinidad and Tobago
23. Uruguay
24. Venezuela

Share of non-US suppliers in imports

Source: International Monetary Fund, *Direction of Trade Statistics.*

gaining chips in reciprocal liberalization deals if the United States were at all interested in investing in such negotiations with this large number of very small economies. The inevitable consequence, of course, would be the erosion of preferences now enjoyed by the CBI economies.

Systemic Effects of Minilateralism and the Developing Countries

Having discussed the potential attractiveness of an FTA with the United States by analyzing its direct impact on an individual developing partner, we must now consider the systemic consequences of the new US strategy from the developing country perspective.

A first point to note is that the negotiating procedures implicit in the sequential process of widening the group of free trading nations around the United States are fundamentally different from those of the GATT in terms of the incentives to negotiate: minilateral enlargement through FTAs avoids the free-rider problem (Cooper 1985). This has crucial implications for the developing countries, since joining the club implies de facto abandonment of their right to special and differentiated treatment in dealing with fellow members. It is this legal umbrella that provides perhaps the single most important incentive for the vast majority of developing countries to participate in the GATT.

A second aspect of general importance to developing countries is that it is very unlikely that agreements of the scope of the Canada–US FTA could be negotiated with any significant number of them. If they occur at all, they will most likely be restricted to noncomprehensive, sectorally selective agreements tailored to the characteristics of individual developing country partners.[14] In any case, the number of prospective developing partners will be small, both because the United States will have to offer selective treatment in nontariff barriers so as to make the agreements attractive, and because negotiating problems would increase exponentially with the number of countries involved. Of course, even a small number of such arrangements may prove to be a strong irritant in US economic relations with those countries being discriminated against, especially if the individual beneficiaries are relatively large developing countries. However, given that few FTAs are likely to be negotiated, they are unlikely to have significant systemic implications such as erosion of the MFN principle or weakening of the GATT as a relevant forum.

However, there are strong asymmetries in the global trade impact of the creation of a US FTA with large and small countries. Indeed, the analysis of systemic effects should take into account that the formation of FTAs between the United States and large third parties affects the prospective gains to be reaped by a particular developing country in forming FTAs with the members of the new free trading club. This change may be considerable in the event that the United States forms a free trade bloc with a third party

---

14. For a similar view, see Katz (1988, 178).

that is also an important trade partner of the developing country in question. Such a "domino effect" can be easily illustrated with the help of figures 15.1 and 15.2. The developing country would move substantially "north-westward" if a US–third party bloc is substituted for the United States as the developing country partner, thus indicating increased potential gains from joining the larger FTA.

This scenario is not merely hypothetical. It could well materialize in the event a US–Japan FTA is formed—such as an agreement recently hinted as a possible objective by high-level US government officials if the Uruguay Round falters.[15] In that case, the prospective gains of countries such as ASEAN members or Korea, which are also substantial trade partners of Japan, are likely to rise. In a situation in which high expectations regarding the benefits of the GSP have clearly given way to worries over long-run market access for manufactures in the United States among the relatively advanced developing economies of East Asia, the incentives to join a US–Japan FTA should become almost irresistible.

The formation of a discriminatory Pacific free trading club around a US–Japan FTA (which could eventually include Australia and New Zealand) could have a large impact on how different groups of developing countries fit into and behave toward the trading system. A crucial determinant of this impact will be the way in which the EC reacts to the weakening of multilateral discipline against discrimination implicit in such a scenario. One should keep in mind that from the creation of the present system and throughout the postwar era it was the United States that most consistently and actively (although not always successfully) opposed the atavistic attempts of former European colonial powers to rebuild their network of preferential ties.[16] In this sense, an active shift in US policy toward granting discriminatory preferences to a relatively large number of developing countries in the Pacific Rim (which could be enlarged to include Mexico and further to Central American and Caribbean countries) would represent a marked departure from America's traditional stance on a crucial aspect of multilateral trade policy, which may weaken the European restraint to discriminate.

This possibility has worrying implications for the positions of many developing countries in the system. In a situation in which trade policy in

---

15. Former US Treasury Secretary James Baker noted the possibility that the United States might explore follow-up agreements to the Canada–US FTA if the Uruguay Round falters. "Ambassador Yeutter has reported that there are voices in other nations—including Japan, South Korea, Taiwan and some of the nations of the ASEAN—that have indicated that they do not wish to be left behind" (Baker 1988, 41).

16. For a brief but enlightening analysis of these developments, see Murray (1977).

Europe may be under protectionist pressures stemming from a weakening dollar superimposed on high structural unemployment and adjustment to 1992, this could lead to mercantilist pressures for the widening of existing preferential margins in the EC, with particularly damaging consequences to the European exports of non-ACP and non-Mediterranean developing countries. In this still unlikely but notionally possible scenario, the larger South American and Asian countries not belonging to the ACP group, with their more diversified geographical trade patterns, could face the worst of both worlds, being discriminated against with respect to other LDCs in the two larger OECD free trade areas. If, on the other hand, current US initiatives in the Pacific materialize without bringing about these negative European spillovers, the result may be an increasing isolation from the longstanding G-77 coalition of those East Asians joining with the United States—a prospect which, especially for those primary commodity exporters in ASEAN, may entail some political costs.

A crucial systemic question from the developing country perspective is, therefore, what is going to result from the "Pacific Round" of minilateral trade negotiations in which the United States is presently engaged parallel to the GATT talks? Unfortunately, this question begs another old and still rather open question in the positive theory of economic integration, namely, the fact that some argument alien to conventional trade theory must be put in place to explain the occurrence of FTAs and, as Krauss (1972) nicely puts it, to falsify the proposition that "there is . . . precious little that a country cannot do for itself that it can do better with the aid of some other country." [17]

Conclusions

This chapter has discussed, from a developing country perspective, the implications of the new thrust in US trade policy toward the formation of bilateral or minilateral free trade arrangements. Both the existing incentives for small countries to form FTAs with a large trade partner as well as the systemic consequences of the new US initiative were analyzed.

As far as the inducements to developing countries are concerned, the high trade barriers generally prevailing in those countries pose a fundamental difficulty to forming comprehensive FTAs with the United States consistent with existing GATT rules. The basic problem is that, as the adjustment costs

---

17. Krauss (1972, 424). In his classic analysis of discriminatory arrangements Patterson argues that in the move toward integration in the 1960s, in all of the schemes except the EFTA, "it was repeatedly emphasized that the political aspects were as important, or much more important, than the economic" (Patterson 1965, 146).

of freeing trade with such a huge partner are equivalent to those of multilateral trade liberalization, those costs are likely to be high, and thus the formation of the FTA is likely to face strong domestic opposition. It can therefore be argued that the real policy issue is whether the country is willing to liberalize; if it is, there is no compelling economic reason to do so on a bilateral basis. Besides efficiency arguments, incentives to MFN liberalization also stem from the fact that the selective removal of high trade barriers in favor of the United States implies strong discrimination against third parties in the developing country market and a high probability of retaliation. This discrimination is bound to be felt especially by other OECD countries competitive with the United States, which, being substantial importers from LDCs, have strong powers of retaliation.

The number of comprehensive agreements covering a substantial portion of trade between the United States and individual developing countries is thus likely to be very small. There is, nevertheless, the possibility that the political momentum generated by the current US drive may lead to a number of sectorally restricted agreements exploiting cross-border industrial specialization and integration opportunities envisaged by US corporations especially in the countries in the Caribbean and Pacific basins.

As to the systemic issues raised by the US initiative, two points are of interest to developing countries. The first is that liberalization through minilateral free trade deals allows no free riding and thus implies the abandonment of the special and differentiated treatment granted them under the GATT. The second point is that, as the lack of incentives implies that the number of developing countries forming FTAs with the United States is likely to be small, no great erosion of the MFN principle or of the importance of the GATT should be expected.

The incentives for small countries to join an FTA would increase, however, with the formation of a US–Japan FTA, which, because of positive externalities associated with the direction of existing trade flows, would be an attractive free trade partner to some of the East Asian developing countries. The formation of a large and comprehensive trans-Pacific FTA may generate reactions in Europe, which would reinforce the drift toward strengthening large regional blocs, which in turn would hurt the trade positions of many diversified developing countries and have far-reaching negative consequences for the multilateral trading system. One cannot, therefore, underestimate the crucial systemic importance of the formation of a US–Japan FTA to world trade policy and, in particular, to developing countries. If these conjectures are correct, the current situation illustrates to perfection the dictum attributed to former Canadian Prime Minister Pierre Trudeau that the grass trembles not only when elephants fight, but also when they make love.

References

Baker, James, III. 1988. "The Geopolitical Implications of the US–Canada Trade Pact." *The International Economy*, January–February.

Balassa, Bela. 1962. *The Theory of Economic Integration*. London: Allen & Unwin.

Camps, Miriam, and William Diebold, Jr. 1983. *The New Multilateralism: Can the World Trading System Be Saved?* New York: Council on Foreign Relations.

Cline, William R. 1982. *"Reciprocity": A New Approach to World Trade Policy?* POLICY ANALYSES IN INTERNATIONAL ECONOMICS 2. Washington: Institute for International Economics, September.

Cooper, C. A., and B. F. Massell. 1965. "A New Look at Customs Union Theory." *Economic Journal*, 75, December.

Cooper, Richard N. 1985. "The Future of the International Trading System." In David W. Conklin and Thomas J. Courchene, eds., *Canadian Trade at a Crossroads: Options for New International Agreements*. Toronto: Ontario Economic Council.

Diebold, William, Jr. 1988. "The History and the Issues." In William Diebold, Jr., ed., *Bilateralism, Multilateralism and Canada in U.S. Trade Policy*. New York: Council on Foreign Relations.

Dunning, John H. 1982. "International Business in a Changing World Environment." *Banca Nazionale del Lavoro Quarterly Review*, December.

El-Agraa, Ali M. 1988. "The Theory of Economic Integration." In Ali M. El-Agraa, ed., *International Economic Integration*, 2nd ed. London: Macmillan.

Jackson, John H. 1987. "Multilateral and Bilateral Negotiating Approaches for the Conduct of U.S. Trade Policies." In R. M. Stern, ed., *U.S. Trade Policies in a Changing World Economy*. Cambridge, Mass.: MIT Press.

Katz, Julius L. 1988. "Comments." In Jeffrey J. Schott and Murray G. Smith, eds., *The Canada–United States Free Trade Agreement: The Global Impact*. Washington: Institute for International Economics, and Halifax: Institute for Research on Public Policy.

Krauss, Melvyn B. 1972. "Recent Developments in Customs Union Theory: An Interpretive Survey." *Journal of Economic Literature*, June.

Krugman, Paul. 1981. "Intra-Industry Specialization and the Gains from Trade." *Journal of Political Economy*, 89 (5).

Murray, Tracy. 1977. *Trade Preferences for Developing Countries*. London: Macmillan.

Patterson, Gardner. 1965. *Discrimination in International Trade: The Policy Issues, 1945–1965*. Princeton, N.J.: Princeton University Press.

Urquidi, Victor L. 1986. *Is a North American Free Trade Area Viable? The Mexican Perspective* (mimeo). Atlanta: The Carter Center (University of Georgia).

Viner, Jacob. 1950. *The Customs Union Issue*. New York: Carnegie Endowment for International Peace.

Whalley, John. 1988. "Comments." In Jeffrey J. Schott and Murray G. Smith, eds., *The Canada–United States Free Trade Agreement: The Global Impact*. Washington: Institute for International Economics, and Halifax: Institute for Research on Public Policy.

Wonnacott, Paul, and R. Wonnacott. 1981. "Is Unilateral Tariff Reduction Preferable to a Customs Union? The Curious Case of the Missing Foreign Tariffs." *American Economic Review*, 71 (4).

World Bank. 1988. *The Caribbean: Export Preferences and Performance*. Washington: World Bank.

16

Implications for the GATT and the World Trading System

Gardner Patterson

The General Agreement on Tariffs and Trade (GATT) was intended to be a set of rights and obligations whose major characteristics were commitments to negotiate reductions in trade barriers, to pursue unconditional most-favored-nation treatment, to provide national treatment once foreign goods cleared customs, and to set out rules minimizing discrimination in all trade controls. The GATT sought to provide reciprocity not only in the sense, as Diebold puts it, "that when a country takes on obligations it receives the advantages (and rights) that resulted from the obligations of others," but also in the sense that there should be "overall reciprocity" in the negotiated reduction of trade barriers, not country by country or sector by sector (Diebold 1988, 11). The system also established procedures for settling the disputes that inevitably arise under international agreements. This is all reasonably clear in the General Agreement itself, though it too has many ambiguities.

There is widespread agreement that the GATT served the world well for many years. But over the more than 40 years of its life the GATT has been subjected to any number of abuses by its members (contracting parties), and there have been sea changes in the composition and structure of international trade, in the number of members, and in their roles and relative importance. From the outset, the GATT has pursued what is often called a pragmatic approach, which meant solving or dealing with the problems before it as best it could at the time, even if this meant, as it often did, severely bending the rules.

Moreover, the world trading system includes not only what goes on under the aegis of the GATT, but also what goes on within the several existing regional trading systems, the trade policies of those nations that are not

---

Gardner Patterson is the former Deputy Director-General of the GATT.

GATT members, and the activities covered by the more than 200 sectoral-regional arrangements that fall outside the GATT—the voluntary export restraints (VERs), orderly marketing agreements (OMAs), and various government-supported "crisis cartels."

As a consequence, more is written today of the system's shortcomings than of its accomplishments (which have been considerable). The GATT is commonly characterized as "in disarray," or "moribund," or "irrelevant," or "outmoded," or maybe all of these things. In fact the GATT is very much alive, as anyone wandering around its headquarters at the Centre William Rappard in Geneva will attest. But the widely held perception in the United States, and especially in the Congress, that the system is simply not up to the task of helping the United States satisfactorily cope with its current and foreseen trade problems accounts for much of the current interest in turning to more free trade areas (FTAs).

Implications for the Structure, Quality, and Amount of World Trade

Because the sole concern of the GATT and the world trading system is with trade, the first question one must ask in assessing the implications of more FTAs is what their effect is likely to be on the volume and quality of international trade. Unfortunately, even if FTAs were "pure"—that is, if they removed all trade barriers on all products—absent very detailed information on the specific terms of any given FTA and the economic structure of the trading partners, the structure and pattern and heights of their border barriers, consumer preferences, possible retaliation by non-members, and so on, one can say very little about the overall trade effects of any given FTA, let alone a group of them. They will certainly increase trade between the partners. Some of this increase will be at the expense of producers in one of the partners to a given FTA and so will be clearly trade creating. But some will inevitably be at the expense of trade with third parties. Should this trade diversion lead to retaliation, third-party trade of the FTA members will in turn be further adversely affected. At the same time, if the FTAs operate to increase the GNP of their members, third-country exporters stand to benefit.

But one cannot expect an FTA to be "pure." Trade policy is determined by political as well as economic considerations and often by local and special interests rather than national and general ones. Always present is the concern expressed by the Deputy Secretary of the US Treasury before an August 1988 meeting at the Institute for International Economics in discussing the European Community's current drive toward creating a single integrated market in 1992 (McPherson 1988). Will the members of any new FTA seek to reduce the pressure of the increased competition from the trade-creating effects of the FTA from their FTA partner by limiting competition from the rest of the world? Would not the temptation in an FTA agreement be of the same sort as he saw for the European Community (EC): "to find a solution [to the problem of political pressures to ease the pain of adjustment] that meets the demand of the more protectionist policy interest"? That is, there is a strong tendency for FTA negotiators to seek out trade-diverting solutions because it is easier to obtain domestically needed support in each country for an FTA if any exporting problems fall on third countries rather than the area's own producers.

There is another major and serious potential problem for the structure and amount of world trade: the possibility of the United States entering into *several* FTAs. Assuming the United States and country A sign an FTA, were the United States then to enter into another FTA with country B, would this not likely result in serious erosion of the relative position of some of A's suppliers in the US market while the US producers would continue to enjoy undiminished preferences in A's market? [1] Such an event would seem certain to create considerable political frictions. Moreover, because the balance of benefits between country A and the United States would be upset, would it not threaten to unravel the first accord? Were an attempt made to avoid this by limiting the coverage of the second FTA to products not affected by earlier FTAs, would not the whole movement degenerate into a series of bilateral preferential arrangements for individual products? That would divert a great deal of production from more to less efficient sources and reduce the range of consumer choice. Such a development, together with the likely retaliation by other countries adversely affected, would make a shambles of the GATT system even as it exists and would almost certainly reduce the amount and the quality of world trade. It would be a clear move back toward what we experienced in the "happy thirties."

What is virtually certain is that any increase in the total amount and/or quality of trade resulting from the formation of several FTAs will be less than the increase if the same countries made the same reduction of trade barriers in the context of a multilateral, nondiscriminatory, barrier-reducing exercise. This leads to the question of the implications of a series of new FTAs for the Uruguay Round.

---

1. See Murray G. Smith, "What is at Stake," in Diebold (1988).

Implications for the Uruguay Round

It has often been argued by US officials that FTAs are an effective way of moving toward a wider, more liberal multilateral trading system. Secretary of State George Shultz, speaking at Princeton's Woodrow Wilson School in April 1985, stated, "From a global perspective, a splintering of the multilateral trading system into a multitude of bilateral arrangements would be a backward step. Bilateral free trade agreements, however, . . . need not have this result; they can stimulate trade and strengthen the multilateral system. Our hope . . . is that the example of greater liberalization—and the recognition that the United States can pursue another course—will motivate a larger group of nations to tackle the job of expanding trade on a global basis." [2]

This statement, repeated in substance many times by other US officials, offers an FTA both as a model for and a threat to the Uruguay Round. The Council of Economic Advisers in the 1985 *Economic Report of the President* seems to have added a third element when they stated, "Perhaps most importantly, however, the possibility of FTA negotiations offers the United States and others the option of using a free-trade instrument rather than protectionism as a lever against protectionist countries" (Council of Economic Advisers 1985, 126). Does this imply that FTAs are seen as an alternative to and/or a means for eliminating section 301 actions and the various gray area restrictions (VERs, OMAs, etc.) that have been such a prominent feature of US trade policy in the 1980s? If this were indeed to be a consequence of FTAs, it certainly would be a major plus for them.

It may well be that the *threat* to negotiate FTAs will stimulate others—fearing their discrimination and trade-diverting effects—to participate more seriously in the Uruguay Round. On the other hand, it is easy to imagine, as William Diebold has pointed out, that this threat could be interpreted as yet another signal that the United States is really abandoning multilateralism for bilateralism and thus stimulate other countries to negotiate whatever special deals they can with their trading partners.

It must also be recognized that, once an FTA has been signed, an important constituency has been created in each of the participants *against* any wider multilateral negotiations lest they prejudice, destroy, or weaken the preferential benefits exporters in each of the signatories expect to receive from the FTA. Such benefits, it needs recalling, often are the primary purpose of entering into the regional arrangement in the first place, although not all the provisions of an FTA involve the granting of preferences. Thus, once an FTA has been signed, powerful vested interests are created within an FTA

---

2. The Shultz quotation is cited by Murray G. Smith in Diebold (1988, 91).

against any multilateral action that could alter the hoped-for effects of the FTA.

Moreover, an FTA will create pressure for adjustment to the new competition resulting from any internal trade-creating effects, and one must wonder if this will serve to reduce the enthusiasm of the participants for vigorously pursuing the Uruguay Round, which could result in the need for still more adjustment. As we have noted, this appears to be a concern of the US government with the current plans for further consolidation of the EC.

To be sure, it can be argued that if those third countries discriminated against (or fear they will be discriminated against) by a completed FTA are economically and politically powerful enough, the fact of an FTA may spur them into action to force a major multilateral negotiation for a deep and broad reduction of barriers, thus reducing or eliminating the feared adverse effects on them of the regional arrangement. A case can be made that had it not been for the anticipated adverse effects on US exports following from the formation of the European Community, there would have been no Kennedy Round. But that case does not provide a plausible precedent. The situation we are looking at here finds the big and powerful—those who have the capacity to influence greatly the success of the Uruguay Round— the United States and Japan, as members, not outsiders, in the proposed regional arrangements. The other giant, the EC, has not yet indicated it would take the lead in defending the GATT against regional undertakings.

There is still another, and important, kind of problem here. It is amply clear now that the complexities of the Uruguay Round are so great that only extremely vigorous participation by the United States, as well as others, can make it succeed. If the movement toward more and more FTAs continues and reaches the dimensions covered by this conference, it would diminish not only the enthusiasm but also the administrative capacity of many countries, including the United States, to pursue multilateral negotiations vigorously. These negotiations require of the participants a huge amount of time, effort, and talent to collect data; determine national interest; set priorities both on what one wants and what one can give; develop useful concepts, especially in the whole area of services; set fallback positions, and so on. Much blood typically is spilled on the floor in each participating country before the domestic political and economic interests and conflicts are resolved and a national negotiating position is arrived at. All this may well be simply beyond the will and capacity of countries who are also negotiating FTAs and learning to live with them. It will certainly have a dampening effect on the participation of those who are not all that enthusiastic, or hopeful, about the new round in any case.

But is there not another aspect of the Uruguay Round that introduces an important offsetting consideration? This round is dealing with a great many new problems, particularly in the field of services, where there are few if any useful precedents on which to build. This means virtually everything has to be negotiated: definitions, coverage, exceptions, and procedures as well as the substantive rules, rights, and obligations. The difficulty of such tasks mounts rapidly as the number of people sitting around the table increases. Although procedures, not very satisfactory to be sure, have been developed to limit severely the number of people entitled to enter the negotiating room in the Uruguay Round, their number is still large and their interests are diverse. Is it therefore not reasonable to expect that a series of FTA negotiations, which can be expected to include something at least on services, can indeed serve as a model in the services area and so greatly facilitate that enterprise in the multilateral talks?

Jeffrey Schott, citing several specific examples in the Canada–US FTA, emphasizes the considerable benefit the multilateral negotiations should receive from the experience gained by the US and Canadian negotiators in both "the substance and tactics required to craft trade agreements in difficult new areas" (Schott and Smith 1988, 161). There obviously are important possibilities here. The trick is to achieve agreement in the FTA that is genuinely trade liberalizing and that can be accepted by others, or can be modified to meet the needs of others, without requiring a major renegotiation of terms of the agreement. That is not impossible, but if it requires modifications other than some differences in the kinds of services covered, it will not be easy. Moreover, there is the risk—even the probability—that the multilateral negotiations on these matters would be held up while a series of bilateral FTA talks goes on. Such a delay would seriously prejudice the multilateral enterprise.

A considerable momentum has gathered in the Uruguay Round. The complex infrastructure (negotiating groups, terms of reference, agenda, interim time schedule, etc.) for the undertaking is in place. Many thoughtful and imaginative proposals on some of the most knotty issues have been tabled and been subjected to initial examination. Some parameters of possible agreements in some areas are emerging. Where needed, legislative authority to pursue the task has been obtained. The difficult substantive problems are all ahead, but the process is moving. Nonetheless, for the reasons already outlined, and because of the additional facts that the round is not likely to go further than the United States is prepared to push it, and FTAs would meet some of the more pressing trade needs of the United States, it seems evident that the Uruguay Round will fall much further short of the objectives set out at Punta del Este than it would in the absence of more FTAs.

The question we should be asking today is this: does not the progress now being made in the multilateral talks, and the threat more FTAs would pose to its success, remove what US officials and others have repeatedly given as a major reason for pursuing the FTA approach?

Implications for the Trading System

What would be some of the more important consequences for the world trading system if the United States negotiated several more FTAs?

First, it would not lead members to invoke GATT Article XXXI and withdraw from the GATT. After 40 years and several rounds of trade negotiations, most members, and certainly the United States, have a lot of rights under the GATT that they value highly and would want to preserve. That these are treasured is evidenced by the large number of formal complaints about GATT violations and impairment and infringement of GATT rights that have been presented in Geneva in recent years.

A major worrisome implication of the spread of FTAs is that it will surely spawn a substantial increase in political frictions in the resulting system. This is so for several reasons. Preferences and discrimination are inherent in FTAs, and discrimination has proven to be a far more fertile source of resentment than higher but nondiscriminatory restraints on trade. A combination of the GATT and a series of FTAs will result in a complex, fragmented, overlapping set of subsystems that will be a source of misunderstanding, mistrust, and disputes as to which rules and rights and obligations are applicable: those the parties agreed to under the GATT or those in an FTA. Third parties can be expected to have their own views on this matter, which will certainly frequently differ from those of the FTA participants. Michael Aho recently cited another possible source of international friction when he wrote that US legislative action on a series of separate bilateral agreements ". . . opens up the possibility that trade will be used as a weapon of foreign policy against countries that don't follow US foreign policy initiatives. Some legislators pressed by special interests may seek to discriminate in the application of domestic law. All this would create serious frictions and tensions and raise trade policy from 'low level' to 'high level' foreign policy" (Aho 1988, 26).

The "management" of the international trading system is an uncertain, amorphous, and delicate thing. Its function and purpose are to foster mutually advantageous arrangements among the members of the system by, *inter alia,* periodically reducing barriers to commerce, increasing the transparency in trade, providing certainty and stability in trading conditions, expanding knowledge and information on trading partners' policies and activities, anticipating and dealing sooner rather than later with differences and disputes, and minimizing the frictions that are inherent in any complex system.

A case can be made that the GATT, in its untidy, pragmatic way, has done and is doing a lot here. Apart from the periodic rounds of trade negotiations, the GATT is a place where many working parties report on a host of topics of concern to its members; where dispute resolution panels' findings and recommendations are studied and debated; where the monthly GATT Council meetings encourage debate and discussion on almost any trade item a member wants to put on the agenda; where the many periodic reports on a wide range of trade and trade-related issues that members are required to make are examined; and where the facilities the institution offers for quiet discussion are in constant use. It is a place where studies requested of the Secretariat often put controversial issues in useful perspective. It is also a place where the good offices of the senior members of the Secretariat and officials of the contracting parties provide for confidential and extensive exchange of information, which serves to defuse many disputes before they reach a formal conflict stage. It is a place where a great deal of useful information is obtained by the members.

The point is that all this activity contributes in an important way to a well-functioning international trading system, not least because it permits third parties—especially the smaller countries—to be much better informed than they could otherwise be about what is going on and to better understand how and why the major countries conduct their trade affairs. Moreover, third countries big and small often have a stake in what is seen as primarily a bilateral matter. The way bilateral disputes are settled or resolved often impinges upon third parties. The present GATT system lets their voices be heard.

This extremely valuable "management" role seems likely to be weakened with the spread of FTAs. Many of the issues FTA partners would have put before the GATT would now go before whatever appropriate new bilateral body has been set up. Moreover, as noted earlier, the FTA partners are likely to find it more difficult than before to provide the human resources necessary for full and effective participation in GATT activities. In other words, the GATT will be pushed further down on the agenda, and the management and operation of the trading system will suffer.

Perhaps the greatest adverse impact on the world trading system would be that noted by John Whalley, who wrote that the Canada–US FTA went a long way toward endorsing, and possibly accelerating, the drift of the United States toward bilateral and away from multilateral trade negotiations (Schott and Smith 1988, 175). There can be little doubt that more FTAs will be seen as turning that drift into established policy and, as noted earlier, will stimulate others to negotiate whatever special deals they can with their trading partners. It takes no great leap of the imagination to foresee this resulting in a race between the United States, the EC, and perhaps Japan to form their own preferential trading blocs. The consequence of this would be frightening.

The Role of GATT Article XXIV

But will not their GATT obligations force those entering into FTAs to design their arrangements so that no serious damage is done to the GATT system? That, after all, is the purpose and intent of GATT Article XXIV.

It is indeed standard operating procedure for those favoring the FTA approach to pay homage to the GATT principles and objectives and to insist that their FTA will be "GATTable." But of all the GATT articles, this is one of the most abused, and those abuses are among the least noted. Unfortunately, therefore, those framing any new FTA need have little fear that they will be embarrassed by some GATT body finding them in violation of their international obligations and commitments and recommending that they abandon or alter what they are about to do.

The effective destruction of Article XXIV as a serious restraint on FTAs and custom unions began in earnest when the European Community was examined and subjected to very extensive debate under these provisions in 1957–58. No agreement was reached as to the legal question of whether the EC satisfied the requirements of Article XXIV. Apart from political considerations, which dictated a tolerant attitude on the part of some, including the United States, the participants in these discussions concluded that the EC was going to go forward as set out in the Treaty of Rome, and if it were formally found to be "illegal," the GATT as an institution would be mortally wounded. The CONTRACTING PARTIES therefore, in a dramatic example of the "pragmatic" approach that was to become its trademark, formally decided that ". . . it would be more fruitful if attention could be directed to specific and practical problems, leaving aside for the time being questions of law and debate about the compatibility of the Rome Treaty" with the General Agreement (GATT 1959, 70). Other contracting parties formally "reserved their GATT position," and the EC always has operated as if its lawfulness had been formally and officially recognized.

The European Free Trade Association (EFTA) shortly thereafter received similar treatment, the CONTRACTING PARTIES stating in 1960 simply that ". . . there remain some legal and practical issues which would not be fruitfully discussed further at this stage. Accordingly, the CONTRACTING PARTIES do not find it appropriate to make recommendations to the parties . . ." (GATT 1961, 20). The precedent was set, and the CONTRACT-

ING PARTIES have never, I believe, since then been able to reach conclusions as to whether any of the customs unions, FTAs, and similar regional agreements that have been submitted to the GATT are consistent with Article XXIV. Moreover, the CONTRACTING PARTIES have never made recommendations to the members of such agreements to modify them, despite the fact that many of these, including several arrangements among developing countries and several agreements between the EC and its associates, fall much further short of Article XXIV requirements than do the EC and EFTA.

This situation led the authors of the recent GATT-sponsored study, the so-called Leutwiler Report, to conclude, "The exceptions and ambiguities which have thus been permitted have seriously weakened the trade rules, and make it very difficult to resolve disputes to which Article XXIV is relevant. *They have set a dangerous precedent for further special deals, fragmentation of the trading system, and damage to the trade interest of nonparticipants*" (Leutwiler et al. 1985, 41, italics added). They went on to note that this situation had been ignored for far too long, that the possibilities of rectifying some of the past mistakes should be explored, and that further mistakes and abuses should be prevented. They argued that the GATT rules on customs unions and FTAs should be examined, redefined, and more strictly applied.

The Punta del Este Ministerial Declaration that set out the negotiating agenda for the Uruguay Round does not specifically mention this problem; however, Article XXIV is subsumed under the heading "GATT Articles": "Participants shall review existing GATT articles, provisions and disciplines as requested by interested contracting parties, and, as appropriate, undertake negotiations." As of the fall of 1988 discussions were under way on many possible amendments of the provisions, but the differences of views among the negotiators on virtually every aspect were so great, and the substantive problems involved so difficult, that early agreement was certainly not foreseen (GATT 1988a). Among the many difficult issues on which agreement would be needed, if Article XXIV were to be sufficiently "strengthened" to ensure that any new FTAs were free of the abuses of the past, would be an agreement on the detailed criteria as to what constitutes "substantially all the trade" of partners on which trade restrictions are eliminated; whether the FTA or customs union members should be required to apply common quotas to third countries; how to assess and interpret the requirement that the duties and other regulations of commerce "shall not on the whole be higher or more restrictive" than before; and what should be the relationship between Article XXIV and Part IV of the GATT establishing special treatment for developing countries. Beyond this there was the operating fact that for some important countries the practices and procedures under Article XXIV as they have developed seem just fine, and therefore there is great resistance to doing anything.

Gray Area Measures: An Even Greater Threat?

In my view, however, the most damage to the GATT system in recent years, and the most serious threat to its future, has not been the actions *up to now* of FTAs and customs unions. Rather it has been the frequent recourse by the United States and others to a variety of sectoral and regional arrangements—the so-called "gray area measures." [3] These include voluntary export restraints (commonly administered by the exporting country), voluntary restraint agreements (essentially intergovernmental VERs), orderly marketing arrangements (multilateral arrangements enforced by the importing country), and various forms of government-supported "crisis cartels." A recent GATT publication lists more than 200 of these, not counting the scores under the Multi-Fiber Arrangement (GATT 1988b). These are especially common in steel, autos, textiles, food, clothing, machine tools, footwear, and consumer electronics. The most frequent, but by no means only, users on the import side are the United States and the EC. Their object is to protect domestic producers by limiting the volume, and sometimes the prices, of selected imports.

These gray area measures clearly violate the basic principles of the GATT, namely, that import restrictions should be nondiscriminatory, transparent, not in the form of quantitative restrictions, and should contain provisions for their phased elimination. They are also often in direct contravention of GATT Articles I, X, XI, XIII, and XVII:1c. Furthermore, they are designed to circumvent the multilaterally agreed safeguard procedures of Article XIX.

They are also costly. For example, it has been estimated that the welfare cost of the quota restraint on cars exceeded $1,000 per import in 1983 and 1984 (Feenstra 1988, 133). The textile and apparel restrictions have been estimated to have cost each US household $238 per year in 1986 (Cline 1987, 15). Beyond this, they limit the range of consumer choice, spread the "economic rent" arising from restricted supplies in an arbitrary fashion, and encourage and foster the formation of cartels in exporting countries. Such industrial understandings would seem to be inherently expansive in their nature and operation—witness the history of restrictions on textiles and apparel. They constitute a clear trend toward global market sharing.

They are popular for all the wrong reasons. They cope with an immediate problem, with little attention typically given to their long-run effects. Their effect on prices and availability and choice to consumers generally is not known to the public. They often elude effective parliamentary and judicial control and surveillance. They are tailored to the needs of a particular industry as communicated to governments by industry lobbies. In addition,

---

3. See Petersmann (1988). This excellent analysis has been heavily drawn upon here.

they create a government bureaucracy often interested in their continuation and expansion.

Bringing these "safeguard" measures within the scope of a new and revised Article XIX is a central task of the Uruguay Round. The failure to do so will greatly weaken the already wounded and embattled GATT.

One should not underestimate the difficulty of the task. The present GATT safeguard rules were designed to deal with problems of individual products. The gray area measures are directed at problems of entire industries, often those with worldwide excess capacity. The job of the Uruguay Round negotiators is to define precisely when quantitative restrictions, as distinct from tariffs, can be used for protection. International surveillance should be provided and firm rules agreed on for limiting the duration of the restrictive measures and, most important, tying their use to commitments to adjustment measures designed to remove the need for them. Fortunately, the Uruguay Round negotiators are coming to grips with the problem. They are not, as in the past rounds, ignoring or avoiding it.

If, and I have the gravest doubts, a consequence of more FTAs would be less need to resort to or to maintain such protectionist measures all around the world, it would go some way toward moderating my gloomy conclusions.

Conclusions

For a believer in the virtues—and the feasibility if pursued vigorously by the United States—of an updated, broadened, and strengthened GATT-type nondiscriminatory, multilateral trading system, the implications of a spread of US-fostered FTAs are downright ominous. The major consequences seem likely to be an uncertain effect on the amount and composition of world trade but one clearly inferior in both respects to comparable multilateral reductions in trade barriers; a substantial diminution in the accomplishments of the Uruguay Round; a great increase in trade-created political frictions around the world; a weakening of the present fragile international mechanisms for "managing" the trading system; and other nations concluding that the United States has abandoned its crucial role as supporter of a multilateral system, leading them to emulate the United States and strike such bilateral deals as they can. In such a milieu, the possibility of the system degenerating into a few large preferential trading blocs is real.

Perhaps it needs saying that whatever the case may be against a proliferation of free trade agreements, it does not add up to an argument against all bilateral negotiations.[4] There are always a great many difficult and specific

---

4. For a wide-ranging and sympathetic discussion of the role of "differentiation and

trade problems that are bilateral in nature and must be handled by the two parties on a case-by-case basis. The results need not be preferential. And in a multilateral trade negotiation, it is often the case that on some specific issues only a few of the participants are much interested, or that no progress is possible until certain differences among a few are resolved or narrowed. There is, of course, under an efficient and viable trading system, an important constraint on such bilateral or small group negotiations: the solutions worked out must not be at the expense of third parties.

References

Aho, C. Michael. 1988. "Most Bilateral Pacts Carry a Penalty." *Wall Street Journal*, 18 March.

Camps, Miriam, and William Diebold, Jr. 1983. *The New Multilateralism*. New York: Council on Foreign Relations.

Cline, William R. 1987. *The Future of World Trade in Textiles and Apparel*. Washington: Institute for International Economics.

Council of Economic Advisers. 1985. *Economic Report of the President*. Washington: Government Printing Office.

Diebold, William, Jr. 1988. *Bilateralism, Multilateralism and Canada in US Trade Policy*. Cambridge, Mass.: Ballinger for Council on Foreign Relations.

Feenstra, Robert C. 1988. "Quality Change Under Trade Restraints in Japanese Autos." *Quarterly Journal of Economics*, February.

GATT. 1959. *Basic Instruments and Selected Documents*. Seventh Supplement. Geneva: GATT.

GATT. 1961. *Basic Instruments and Selected Documents*. Ninth Supplement. Geneva: GATT.

GATT. 1988a. *FOCUS*. no. 55, June–July.

GATT. 1988b. *Review of Developments in the Trading System*, August.

Leutwiler, Fritz, et al. 1985. *Trade Policies for a Better Future: Proposals for Action*. Geneva: GATT Independent Study Group.

McPherson, M. Peter. 1988. "The European Community's Internal Market Program: An American Perspective." US Treasury Department Press Release, 4 August.

Petersmann, Ernest-Ulrich. 1988. "Grey Area Trade Policy and the Rule of Law." *The World Economy*, March.

Schott, Jeffrey J., and Murray G. Smith, eds. 1988. *The Canada–United States Free Trade Agreement: The Global Impact*. Washington: Institute for International Economics, and Halifax: Institute for Research on Public Policy.

---

selective action" by writers who, like this one, "consider that multilateralism is an essential characteristic of a sound international trading system," see Camps and Diebold (1983, 49–56).

Comments

John Whalley

I found Gardner Patterson's chapter to be comprehensive, carefully argued, and well written. It evaluates the pros and cons of free trade areas (FTAs) in light of GATT arrangements and generally argues that FTAs are bad for the GATT system, since they represent an erosion of multilateral principles and disciplines. Rather than argue the merits of the case for and against FTAs, I will evaluate some of the pressures on the global trading system, recognizing that FTAs and GATT disciplines coexist, and asking where we may be headed and, in light of these pressures, what this suggests. These comments are therefore complementary to the arguments made in Patterson's chapter.

Some of the narrower questions that arise relate to the legal compatibility of FTAs with the GATT, and particularly the application of Article XXIV. Article XXIV disciplines are widely agreed to be relatively weak. Only a small proportion of the FTAs that have evolved in the postwar years, and have been notified to the GATT, have been found to be compatible with Article XXIV by the working parties established at the time. The typical working party report uses phrases such as "one contracting party noted that" or "concerns expressed by one of the contracting parties," and the reports are generally inconclusive with regard to GATT compatibility. One issue therefore is whether a tightening of this relatively loose discipline under Article XXIV would limit the spread of FTAs.

The broader issues concern the evolution of the GATT system itself, which I see as largely based on the most-favored-nation (MFN) principle, a process of multilateral negotiation, and an objective of achieving protection only through tariffs—that is, a strong commitment to transparency of trade measures. An important issue is whether this system and the way it is evolving is likely to generate more pressures for FTAs as countries seek bilateral negotiations rather than the multilateral process as a way of dealing with their trade problems.

Within the system there is substantial heterogeneity among the players. There are large countries such as the United States, the EC, and Japan; intermediate-sized developed countries such as those in the European Free Trade Association (EFTA), Canada, Australia, and New Zealand; larger developing countries such as Brazil, India, Mexico, and Korea; and a number

John Whalley is Professor of Economics at the University of Western Ontario.

of smaller developing countries, most of whom have preferential trade arrangements with the larger developed powers. These include the Lomé countries in Africa, the Caribbean, and the Pacific, and the countries of the Caribbean Basin Initiative.

Generally speaking, the large developed countries within the GATT system have liberalized their tariffs on manufactures, whereas the smaller countries have liberalized less. Until recently there has been little liberalization in the developing countries, and liberalization in the intermediate-sized developed countries has been less than in the large developed countries. Part of the reason for this difference is that these groups of countries have been able to free ride, receiving the benefits of MFN treatment without making reciprocal concessions. In turn, the large developed countries have found that over time the pressures to avoid major adjustment difficulties have led them to take actions that are inconsistent with the spirit, and in some cases the letter, of their GATT obligations.

The list of these problem areas is well known. It includes lax GATT discipline in agriculture, the evolution of restrictions in textiles from the 1960s to the present, the spread of voluntary restraint agreements and other gray-area measures, and the growth in the use of contingent protection measures in the last ten years or so. Many of the actions of the larger developed countries have been targeted at smaller countries; in addition, there have been bilateral disputes among the large developed countries.

Thus, within the system there are great frustrations with the multilateral process. The large countries are frustrated by the limited liberalization in the smaller countries. In turn, the small countries are frustrated by the inability, as they see it, of large countries to live up to their GATT obligations, and by their own limited ability to enforce GATT disciplines on these large countries. The result is a system that is inevitably in flux, and it is into this system that the question of FTAs has to be injected.

Because of the vast differences among the participants in the GATT system, when discussing FTAs one also has to recognize the substantial heterogeneity of bilateral interests in joint arrangements. If one looks at the possibilities for FTAs among the major players (for example, the United States and Japan), one senses that the bilateral disputes that have dominated these trade relationships in recent years would be little changed by the formalization of a free trade agreement. At the same time, others in the system would have major concerns that they would be excluded and could suffer as a result.

If one looks instead at possible FTAs between the large and intermediate developed countries, one finds that the latter typically have dominant trade patterns with one large trading region. This is clearly the case with Canada and EFTA, for instance, and less so for Australia and New Zealand. Moreover, the intermediate countries want to maintain the access they now have to the markets of the larger countries as much as they want improvements in this access. They also want to develop mechanisms for using multilateral disciplines to protect this access.

In FTAs between large developed and large developing countries, the interest of the former is in removing barriers in the latter to improve market access. On the other side, the main objective is to strengthen GATT disciplines to deal with what these countries repeatedly refer to as a backlog of derogations from the GATT. These objectives underlie the disputes that presently preoccupy the GATT, and are at the heart of the developed versus developing country trade dialogue in the Uruguay Round.

Finally, in FTAs between large developed countries and smaller developing countries the interests of both groups are fairly clear. The cost to large countries, in mercantilist terms, of preferential access for these smaller countries is small, whereas the smaller countries have little interest in the wider system because they are so small. This is the area where in the past we have seen major growth in preferences, and clearly both parties view them as desirable.

There are many other possible bilateral combinations. At the moment, for instance, negotiations are under way to develop a system of trade preferences among the developing countries. However, it is doubtful that such arrangements could lead to much concrete or meaningful trade liberalization among these countries, for a variety of reasons including the unbound nature of their trade restrictions, and the fact that any agreements would also have to deal with many other trade-restricting instruments used by these countries.

Also important is the mixture of economic and geopolitical interests behind each bilateral or plurilateral arrangement and the changing array of bilateral and multilateral arrangements in the system. Generally one would expect that, in pursuing their economic objective of improved access abroad, large countries would prefer to negotiate bilaterally rather than multilaterally. By negotiating individually with smaller countries, large countries have more leverage and are able to obtain better deals on access. By contrast, the multilateral system provides major benefits to small countries, both in providing them an insurance policy that prevents some from being picked off selectively by large countries, and in enabling them to free ride on MFN trade liberalization among the larger countries.

Despite these incentives, we have seen in the postwar years a strong commitment to the multilateral system on the part of the large developed countries, and a relatively passive stance on the part of the intermediate and small countries. One can attribute this outcome in part to wider geopolitical interests of the leadership powers, particularly the United States, in maintaining the system. For this reason the recent change in the balance between geopolitical and economic interests compared to the late 1940s might account in part for the current surge of interest in FTAs. This reflects both the rise of Japan and Europe, yielding a tripolar system rather than the unipolar system that characterized the 1940s, and the relative weakening of the wider political objective of a unified alliance of free-market economies, given the growing rapprochement with the eastern bloc powers.

This change may be a little overdrawn, but to the extent that one accepts it, it does indicate important changes in the interests of the players. It indicates a stronger interest in bilateral negotiations on the part of the large developed countries, and correspondingly more multilateral activism on the part of the smaller countries.

This is exactly what happened in Punta del Este during the launch of the Uruguay Round. The intermediate-sized developed countries and the small, market-oriented developing countries (sometimes referred to as the "de la Paix" group) significantly influenced the outcome of what effectively was an agenda-writing negotiation by their so-called "Swiss–Colombia" proposal. Obviously, this leverage was not exerted independently of the large powers and to a large degree was used in concert with them, but nonetheless the activism and influence were there.

At this stage in the system's evolution, what can we expect as far as FTAs are concerned? First, the recently negotiated FTAs are extremely heterogeneous in terms of their implications. I see the Canada–US trade agreement, for instance, as largely a tariff-cutting agreement with some innovative attempts in the dispute settlement area whose importance will only be revealed over time, but whose long-run importance may not be that great. There are a number of other chapters in the Canada–US agreement, many of which have little content or importance, although some represent significant discipline on domestic policies in Canada. However, the agreement does not represent a wholesale change from the existing multilateral disciplines that bilaterally constrain trade policies in these two countries. At present, about 80 percent of Canadian exports to the United States enter duty free. The largest tariffs Canada faces on remaining tariff-constrained trade are in the textile area. In this area the agreement has made little difference, since the changes involve a new tariff quota that gives Canada relatively little, if any, additional access.

In Europe, the potential significance of the 1992 exercise has likewise been overblown. The initial attempt will be to remove trade barriers and remaining border impediments among the EC member states. These arise in a number of areas, including the administration of the value-added tax on a destination basis, monetary compensation amounts in the Common Agricultural Policy, the presence of country quotas on textile products and automobiles, and complications regarding rules of origin. Every one of these issues is problematic, and it is not obvious that any of them can be resolved quickly.

The wider issues in the 1992 exercise, including regulations over transport (particularly airlines and road transportation), financial institutions, and procurement practices, are also complex and difficult matters involving the laws of individual member states. Again the prospects for rapid change seem to be far weaker than many have claimed. Nothing that is done by 1992 will change the existing multilateral disciplines that the EC has undertaken, and there is very little in the 1992 exercise that will produce changes in existing multilateral arrangements.

Another example of a recent FTA is the US–Israel agreement. Like the others, it includes new tariff cuts, but the impact in terms of substantial trade liberalization seems to be quite small. Although it is not an FTA, the US–Mexico pact signed in November 1987 includes a broad framework agreement, covering 13 sectors with a commitment to discussion at 90 days' notice by either party. Concrete agreements have resulted thus far in the areas of textiles, wine, beer, and others. As of now, the incremental liberalization produced by this process is once again small.

All of these agreements have to be seen in the context of existing GATT arrangements. These new bilateral arrangements deal very little with long-standing disputes over agriculture, textiles, voluntary export restraints and other gray-area measures, and contingent protection. One wonders whether there is much in these new trade arrangements that represents either major change in, or a threat to, the present multilateral system.

A further issue is how far one can go bilaterally when there has been resistance to trade liberalization multilaterally. Experience thus far with the recent flurry of attempts at bilateral trade liberalization indicates little new penetration of protectionist barriers that have been resistant to previous multilateral liberalization.

I would argue that bilateral and multilateral arrangements have coexisted within the multilateral system in the postwar years. After all, the GATT in part multilateralized bilateral agreements that the United States had nego-tiated with a series of other countries following passage of the Reciprocal Trade Agreements Act of 1934. Indeed, a large majority of GATT contracting parties are currently participants in free trade arrangements of some form. In the Canada–US case, there is a 1935 bilateral trade agreement, the 1941 Defense Procurement Sharing Agreement, and the 1965 Auto Pact, which in my opinion may be more significant for Canada–US trade patterns than the current FTA. Another example is the formation of the EC in 1958.

One scenario that has been widely touted in recent months may be labeled the "regional scenario." In this scenario, frustration with the multilateral system increases among the EC, United States, and Japan, each of which proceeds to pursue bilateral arrangements of various types with smaller countries. The latter, in turn, feel themselves threatened by this disintegrating multilateral system and seek some assurance of access to markets in one of the three larger markets. This produces a system of three trading blocs with all the smaller countries seeking some form of attachment to one or more of the blocs. Moves to an adversarial major bloc system could then follow, with elevated tensions among the three blocs.

Under a different scenario, however, which I will deliberately overdraw to make the argument, FTAs turn out to be much less substantive in terms of economic impact than their proponents might have thought, for the reasons discussed above. Some may not come to fruition and others (perhaps Europe 1992) may not go very far. What then develops within the GATT is increased activism on the part of the intermediate-sized and smaller countries that were influential at Punta del Este. These include the EFTA countries, Canada, Australia, New Zealand, and the larger developing countries. Their common fear in the early 1980s was that a rising protectionism would exclude them from large-country markets. For them the Uruguay Round is largely about strengthening GATT disciplines to forestall new protectionism as much as it is about reducing trade barriers.

To the extent that this scenario develops, countries outside the big three may act in a more activist way to influence the multilateral system instead of accepting the move to a bloc system. In effect, they may act cooperatively and try to strengthen multilateral disciplines as a way of guaranteeing their access instead of attaching themselves through FTAs to the larger blocs. This scenario relies heavily on the multilateral process rather than regional processes, and emphasizes that actions of smaller countries as well as larger ones may well determine the eventual spread of FTAs and the overall direction of the trading system.

Interestingly, there are several recent examples of how countries outside of the big three have been moving to act multilaterally in the ways suggested above. In the agricultural area, the Cairns Group was successful in achieving a prominent role for agriculture in the declaration that launched the Uruguay Round in September 1986. This group has continued to operate as a forum to develop common negotiating positions. In addition, various coalitional activities and joint proposals in such areas as natural resources and safeguards have emerged.

Indeed, the activities of countries outside of the big three have been prominent both before and during the recent midterm review in Montreal. The latest count from the round suggests that, of a total of 600 papers and proposals filed, approximately 200 have been filed by the Secretariat or by chairmen of working groups, and another 170 have been proposals from developing countries, some of which have involved joint proposals among them or joint proposals with developed countries.

As such, these countries have begun to take a series of actions to solidify and strengthen the multilateral system. Such activities are, however, not without their problems. It is difficult for smaller countries to exercise much leverage multilaterally. However, the three major powers and other developed countries have increasingly recognized that many of the intermediate-sized developing countries represent rapidly growing and important markets whose leverage is not insignificant.

The large number of countries involved, however, makes it difficult to form cohesive coalitions; their lack of cohesion, in turn, weakens the power of these countries. Increasingly, however, these countries look at the trading system as a vehicle for exercising their influence, and in some circumstances have been willing to consider retaliation, as in the case of Indonesia and China. Thus, it is not at all clear that all of these countries will meekly accept the evolution of the global trading system into a series of regional arrangements as one they inevitably have to follow. They have a stake in a strengthened multilateral system; their recent actions demonstrate their willingness and readiness to move more actively in these directions.

Related to all these considerations is the question of whether or not FTAs are good or bad. There has been much discussion of the classic Vinerian issues of trade creation and trade diversion. I would not suggest that this debate is in any way misplaced, since it captures the essence of the economic evaluation of the relative merits of these types of arrangements. However, we must also consider whether we are simply comparing alternative trade arrangements, or also comparing the merits of alternative routes to trade liberalization.

Here the question is whether or not FTAs accelerate or retard trade liberalization, and on that basis whether they are good or bad. I have always felt that there is substantial confusion in the literature both about the nature and the purpose of MFN. We are all accustomed to praising MFN as a central principle of the GATT system that emphasizes nondiscrimination and the efficiency costs that can arise when countries do not import from their lowest-cost suppliers. However, the MFN principle also has its cost as a barrier to negotiation. If countries can free ride under MFN status, they are less likely to participate in active trade negotiations. The MFN principle is important to smaller countries because of the insurance it provides them against discrimination; however, the pressures the larger countries have exerted on the smaller countries in the postwar years has been the only effective way to persuade them to liberalize. (I have heard US negotiators take this position in characterizing the success of US trade policy in the late

1970s and 1980s.) Thus, multilateral process and liberalization do not necessarily go together.

One can argue that bilateral activity, such as the formation of the EC, tends to accelerate multilateral trade negotiations by producing large trading blocs that have more power and therefore force other parties to the negotiating table. It is often argued that the success of the Dillon and Kennedy Rounds, and to some extent the Tokyo Round, reflects the forces generated multilaterally by the formation of the EC. Therefore, one can argue that in the long run the formation of regional blocs would accelerate trade liberalization.

On the other hand, as Patterson argues in his chapter, the formation of a tripolar system may well retard trade liberalization because the three large blocs will spend much of their negotiating effort on arrangements with smaller countries, rather than centrally confronting trade issues with the large trading parties.

In conclusion, I am left with a sense that the world never has been and never will be purely multilateral, bilateral, or plurilateral; that all countries, large and small, will play a role in how the trading system evolves in the future; that GATT disciplines are real constraints and will partly determine the form of any future attempts at FTAs; and that the indications of a major shift in the trading system are not yet strong enough to say that there has yet been a wholesale change from the multilateral system of the postwar years. Whether this surge of bilateral activity is good or bad should not be determined only on the basis of the comparison of trade-diversion effects. One also has to look at the momentum, or the lack of it, these arrangements impart to multilateral negotiations, and ultimately to the wider trade liberalization process.

Annex A

Preferential Trade Agreements Notified to the GATT

Annex A. Preferential trade agreements notified to the GATT

Agreement	Date signed	Action by GATT (CP decision or adoption of WP report)	Source
France–Italy			
Customs union interim agreement	September 13, 1947	March 20, 1948	GATT/CP/1
Customs union agreement	March 26, 1949		CP/17
South African–Southern Rhodesian Customs Union	December 6, 1948	May 18, 1949	GATT/CP.3/9 II/29, II/176
South African–Southern Rhodesian Customs Union (authorized continuation until the 10th session)	December 6, 1948	November 17, 1954	3s/47
Nicaragua and El Salvador	March 9, 1951	October 25, 1951	II/30
European Economic Community	March 25,1957	November 29, 1957	L/626 6s/70
European Economic Community (examination continued)	March 25, 1957	October–November 1958[a]	7s/71
European Atomic Energy Community	March 25, 1957	November 29, 1957	6s/109
Central American Free Trade Area (participation of Nicaragua)	June 10, 1958	November 13, 1956[b]	L/508 5s/29

Agreement			
European Free Trade Association	January 4, 1960	June 4, 1960[c] November 18, 1960[d]	9s/70 9s/20
Latin America Free Trade Area	February 18, 1960	November 18, 1960	9s/21 9s/87
European Free Trade Association—association with Finland	March 27, 1961	November 23, 1961	10s/24 10s/101
Central American Free Trade Area and Nicaraguan import duties	June 10, 1958	November 23, 1961	10s/48 10s/98
European Economic Community—association with Greece	July 9, 1961	November 15, 1962	11s/56 11s/149
European Economic Community—association agreements with African and Malagasy States and Overseas Countries and Territories	July 20, 1963 February 25, 1964	April 4, 1966	14s/22 14s/100
European Economic Community—association with Turkey	September 12, 1963	March 25, 1965	13s/59
Arab Common Market	August 13, 1964	April 6, 1966	14s/20 14s/94
Central African Economic and Customs Union	December 8, 1964	March 2, 1964[e]	12s/73
New Zealand–Australia Free Trade Agreement	August 31, 1965	April 5, 1966	14s/22 14s/115

Annex A. Preferential trade agreements notified to the GATT (Continued)

Agreement	Date signed	Action by GATT (CP decision or adoption of WP report)	Source
United Kingdom–Ireland Free Trade Area Agreement	December 14, 1965	April 5, 1966	14s/23 14s/122
Caribbean Free Trade Agreement	circa 1968[f]	November 9, 1971	18s/129
European Economic Community—associations with Tunisia and Morocco	March 28, 1969 March 31, 1969	September 29, 1970	18s/149
Accession of Iceland to EFTA and FINEFTA	December 4, 1969[g]	September 29, 1970	18s/174
European Economic Community—association with African and Malagasy States	July 29, 1969	December 2, 1970	18s/133
European Economic Community—association with Tanzania, Uganda, and Kenya	September 24, 1969	October 25, 1972	19s/97
European Economic Community—agreement with Israel	June 29, 1970	October 6, 1971	18s/158
European Economic Community—agreement with Spain	June 29, 1970	October 6, 1971	18s/166

European Economic Community—association with Non-European Countries and Territories	September 29, 1970	November 9, 1971	18s/143
European Economic Community—association with Malta	December 5, 1970	May 29, 1972	19s/90
European Economic Community—association with Turkey	July 27, 1971	October 25, 1972	19s/102
European Communities—agreements with Austria	July 22, 1972	October 19, 1973	20s/145
European Communities—agreements with Iceland	July 22, 1972	October 19, 1973	20s/158
European Communities—agreements with Portugal	July 22, 1972	October 19, 1973	20s/171
European Communities—agreements with Sweden	July 22, 1972	October 19, 1973	20s/183
European Communities—agreements with Switzerland and Liechtenstein	July 22, 1972	October 19, 1973	20s/196
European Economic Community—association with Cyprus	December 19, 1972	June 21, 1974	21s/94
European Economic Community—agreement with Egypt	December 18, 1972	July 19, 1974	21s/102

Annex A. Preferential trade agreements notified to the GATT (Continued)

Agreement	Date signed	Action by GATT (CP decision or adoption of WP report)	Source
European Economic Community—agreement with Lebanon	December 18, 1972	February 3, 1975	22s/43
European Communities—agreements with Norway	May 14, 1973	March 28, 1974	21s/83
European Communities—association with Turkey	June 30, 1973	October 21, 1974	21s/108
European Communities—agreements with Finland	October 5, 1973	October 21, 1974	21s/76
Agreement between Finland and Hungary	May 2, 1974	October 31, 1975	22s/47
Agreement between Finland and Hungary (continue examination)	May 2, 1974	May 23, 1977	24s/107
Agreement between Finland and Czechoslovakia	September 19, 1974	June 14, 1976	23s/67
Agreement between Finland and Czechoslovakia (continue examination)	September 19, 1974	November 6, 1979	26s/327
ACP–EEC Convention of Lomé	February 28, 1975	July 15, 1976	23s/46

European Economic Community—association with Greece	April 28, 1975	June 14, 1976	23s/64
European Communities—agreement with Israel	May 11, 1975	July 15, 1976	23s/55
Agreement between Finland and German Democratic Republic	March 4, 1975	March 2, 1977	24s/106
Caribbean Community and Common Market	July 4, 1973	March 2, 1977	24s/68
Australia–Papua New Guinea Trade and Commercial Relations Agreement	November 6, 1976	November 11, 1977	24s/63
Bangkok Agreement[h]	July 31, 1975	March 14, 1978	25s/6 25s/109
European Communities—agreement with Tunisia	April 25, 1976	November 11, 1977	24s/97
European Communities—agreement with Algeria	April 26, 1976	November 11, 1977	24s/80
European Communities—agreement with Morocco	April 27, 1976	November 11, 1977	24s/88
European Economic Community—agreement with Portugal	September 20, 1976	July 26, 1977	24s/73
European Economic Community—agreement with Egypt	January 18, 1977	May 17, 1978	25s/114

Annex A. Preferential trade agreements notified to the GATT (Continued)

Agreement	Date signed	Action by GATT (CP decision or adoption of WP report)	Source
European Economic Community—agreement with Syria	January 18, 1977	May 17, 1978	25s/123
European Economic Community—agreement with Jordan	January 18, 1977	May 17, 1978	25s/133
ASEAN Preferential Trading Arrangements	February 24, 1977	January 29, 1979	26s/224 26s/321
European Economic Community—agreement with Lebanon	May 3, 1977	May 17, 1978	25s/142
Agreement between Finland and Poland	September 29, 1976	March 26, 1980	27s/136
Accession of Greece to the European Communities	May 28, 1979	March 9, 1983	30s/168
Agreement between the EFTA countries and Spain	June 26, 1979	November 10, 1980	27s/127
ACP–EEC Second Convention of Lomé	October 31, 1979	March 31, 1982	29s/119
European Communities—agreement with Yugoslavia	February 25, 1980	October 6, 1981	28s/115
Australia–New Zealand Closer Economic Relations Trade Agreement	March 28, 1983	October 2, 1984	31s/170

Agreement			Source
Accession of Spain and Portugal to the European Communities	June 12, 1985	October 19–20, 1988	*Official Journal of the EC*, L302, Vol. 28, 15 November 1985; *GATT Focus*, #58, November/December 1988.
ACP–EEC Third Convention of Lomé	December 8, 1984	September 22, 1988[i]	*The Courier*, (ACP-EC), No. 89, January–February 1985; *GATT Focus*, #57, September/October 1988.
Free Trade Area Agreement between Israel and the United States	April 22, 1985	May 14, 1987	34s/58
Canada–United States Free Trade Agreement	January 2, 1988		United States–Canada Free Trade Agreement, House Document 100-216.

CP = CONTRACTING PARTIES; WP = Working Party; EFTA = European Free Trade Association; FINEFTA = Association of Finland with EFTA; ACP = Africa-Caribbean-Pacific.

a. CP "conclusions."
b. Action taken on draft of Multilateral Central American Free Trade and Economic Integration Treaty.
c. Adoption of WP report.
d. Conclusions adopted by the CP.
e. Action on provisions of Convention which preceded the treaty.
f. In operation.
g. EFTA Council approved.
h. First Agreement on Trade Negotiations Among Developing Member Countries of the Economic and Social Commission for Asia and the Pacific.
i. Council took note of Working Party report.

Sources: GATT, *Basic Instruments and Selected Documents*, various issues; Jackson 1969, 592–99; Viner 1950, 141–69.

Appendix

Conference Participants
Washington, 31 October–1 November 1988

C. Michael Aho
Council on Foreign Relations

David Apgar
Office of Senator Bradley

David Appia
Embassy of France

Mohamed Ariff
University of Malaya

Stuart Auerbach
Washington Post

Thomas Axworthy
Charles R. Bronfman Foundation

Bela Balassa
Institute for International Economics

Carol Balassa
Office of the US Trade Representative

Claude Barfield
American Enterprise Institute

William Barnds
Japan Economic Institute

Max Baucus
United States Senate

Thomas O. Bayard
Institute for International Economics

C. Fred Bergsten
Institute for International Economics

Thomas Bernes
Department of Finance, Canada

Charles Blum
International Advisory Services Group

Joshua Bolten
Senate Finance Committee Staff

Carlos Alberto Primo Braga
Johns Hopkins University

William E. Brock
William E. Brock and Associates

Anne Brunsdale
US International Trade Commission

Ronald A. Cass
US International Trade Commission

Hoon Chae
Korea Trade Center

Steve Charnovitz
Office of the Speaker of the House

Siow Yue Chia
National University of Singapore

Patrick Choate
TRW

William Culbert
Boeing

John J. Curtis
Multilateral Trade Negotiations Office,
  Canada

Roy Denman
Delegation of the European Communities

Dean DeRosa
International Monetary Fund

I.M. Destler
Institute for International Economics

Peter Drysdale
Australian National University

Duncan Dwelle
American Fair Trade Council

John Eby
Ford Motor

Alfred Eckes
US International Trade Commission

Takashi Eguchi
Japan Center for International Finance

Andrew Elek
Department of Foreign Affairs and Trade, Australia

Kimberly Ann Elliott
Institute for International Economics

Richard Feinberg
Overseas Development Council

Ava Feiner
Feiner Public Affairs Consulting

Geza Feketekuty
Office of the US Trade Representative

C. David Finch
Institute for International Economics

J. Michael Finger
World Bank

Brent Fogt
Office of Congressman Pease

Lawrence Fox
Falls Church, VA

Isaiah Frank
Johns Hopkins University

Winston Fritsch
Catholic University of Rio de Janeiro

Thomas Gallagher
Shearson Lehman Hutton

Ross Garnaut
Columbia University and the Australian National University

David Gossac
Office of Senator Matsunaga

Richard Gephardt
US House of Representatives

Joseph Greenwald
Attorney/Consultant

Carl Grenier
Ministry of International Affairs, Quebec

David Hall
IFT International Investment Corporation

Constance Hamilton
US International Trade Commission

Blair Hankey
Embassy of Canada

Todd Homan
German Marshall Fund of the United States

Gary Hufbauer
Georgetown University

Helen Hughes
Australian National University

Nurul Islam
International Food Policy Research Institute

Julius L. Katz
Government Research Corporation

William B. Kelly, Jr.
Washington, DC

Naheed Kirmani
International Monetary Fund

Nobuyori Kodaira
Ministry of International Trade and Industry, Japan

Anne O. Krueger
Duke University

Makoto Kuroda
Ministry of International Trade and Industry, Japan

Ruth Kurtz
Office of Senator Roth

Sam Laird
World Bank

Jean-Pierre Landau
Ministry of the Economy and Finance, France

Robert Z. Lawrence
Brookings Institution

Richard Lipsey
C. D. Howe Institute

Mark Lutz
International Monetary Fund

Paul Luyten
European Service Industries Forum, Belgium

Sunder Magun
Economic Council of Canada

Gregory Mastel
Office of Senator Baucus

Sandra Masur
Eastman Kodak

Cynthia McKaughan
Institute for International Economics

G. Mustafa Mohatarem
General Motors

Sandy Moroz
Department of External Affairs, Canada

Robert J. Morris
US Council for International Business

Walter S. Mossberg
Wall Street Journal

Tracy Murray
US International Trade Commission

Henry Nau
George Washington University

William Niskanen
Cato Institute

Stephen Nordlinger
Baltimore Sun

Jack Norman
AP - Dow Jones Economic Report

Sylvia Ostry
Department of External Affairs, Canada

Yung Chul Park
Harvard University and Korea
   University

Steve Parker
Congressional Budget Office

Eliza Patterson
US International Trade Commission

Gardner Patterson
Washington, DC

Joseph Pelzman
George Washington University

Ernest H. Preeg
Center for Strategic and International
   Studies

David D. Preston
Department of External Affairs, Ottawa

Clyde Prestowitz
Carnegie Endowment for International
   Peace

Alfred Reifman
Congressional Research Service

William Reinsch
Office of Senator Heinz

J. David Richardson
University of Wisconsin-Madison

David Rohr
US International Trade Commission

Howard Rosen
Bank of Israel

Andrew Samet
Office of Senator Moynihan

Leonard Santos
Verner, Liipfert, Bernhard, McPherson
   & Hand

Andre Sapir
University of Brussels

Gary Saxonhouse
University of Michigan

Gregory Schoepfle
Department of Labor

Jeffrey J. Schott
Institute for International Economics

Susan Schwab
Office of Senator Danforth

Nancy Schwartz
Office of Management and Budget

Daniel Sharp
Xerox

Joanna Shelton
House Ways and Means Committee

Won-Shik Shin
Embassy of Korea

Michael B. Smith
Office of the US Trade Representative

Murray G. Smith
Institute for Research on Public Policy

Thomas Smith
Yamaichi Research Institute

Richard H. Snape
World Bank

Bruce Stokes
National Journal

John W. Suomela
US International Trade Commission

Joanne Thornton
The Washington Forum

Masakazu Toyoda
Ministry of International Trade and Industry, Japan

Thomas Trebat
Ford Foundation

Philip Trezise
Brookings Institution

S. C. Tsiang
Chung-Hua Institution for Economic Research, Taiwan

Ignacio Trigueros
Instituto Tecnologico Autonomo de Mexico

Brian Turner
AFL-CIO

Peter Uimonen
Institute for International Economics

Gustavo Vega
El Colegio de Mexico

J.H. Warren
Advisor to the Government of Quebec

Leonard Weiss
Arlington, VA

John Whalley
University of Western Ontario

Per Magnus Wijkman
European Free Trade Association

John Williamson
Institute for International Economics

Martin Wolf
Financial Times

Paul Wonnacott
University of Maryland

Nancy Worth
International Monetary Fund

R. T. Yang
Coordination Council for North American Affairs of Taiwan

Jung Ho Yoo
Korea Development Institute